Every

COVENANT

AND PROMISE

in the Bible

Every
COVENANT
AND PROMISE
in the Bible

LARRY RICHARDS

Illustrated by
Paul Richards

THOMAS NELSON PUBLISHERS
Nashville

Published in Nashville, Tennessee, by Thomas Nelson, Inc.

Library of Congress Cataloging-in-Publication Data

Richards, Larry, 1931–
    Every covenant and promise in the Bible / Larry Richards:
illustrated by Paul Richards.
        p.   cm.
    Includes indexes.
    ISBN 0-7852-1266-3. — ISBN 0-7852-1379-1 (pbk.)
    1. Covenants—Biblical teaching.   2. God—Promises—Biblical
teaching.   I. Title.
BS680.C67R45   1998
231.7′6—dc21   98-12176
                                                         CIP

Printed in the United States of America

                        1 2 3 4 5 6 7 8—02 01 00 99 98

CONTENTS

See Expository and Scripture Indexes for Complete Topical and Scripture Listings

PART ONE:
GOD'S AMAZING COVENANTS

❖

INTRODUCTION

There are times when every person wonders about his or her relationship with God. Karen's doubts emerged after a painful divorce, followed immediately by the loss of her job. She had felt close to God and sure of His love. But then her husband left, and the hospital she had worked for as a grief counselor was purchased by a giant health care organization that required a degree she didn't have. She felt so abandoned. Could she really count on God, or not?

For Stacey, it was the auto accident that left her in a wheelchair at age 17. How could she trust God if He let such a terrible thing happen to her? No, she hadn't been wearing a seat belt. And no, she knew the boy she was with had a reputation for reckless driving. But

❖

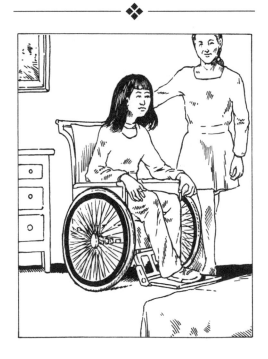

God shouldn't have let the terrible accident happen. Could she ever really trust a God who would let her become a cripple?

There are times in all our lives when events make us question our relationship with God. Even more, they make us question God Himself. What kind of God is He? Can we really, truly *trust* Him?

For everyone who has ever wondered, for everyone who has ever doubted, God's Word has a wonderful answer. We *can* trust God. He is a God who commits Himself fully to us. He is a God who makes us wonderful promises, and who keeps them!

But God's commitment to us and His wonderful promises do not guarantee a life without stress or pain. If we're to maintain our trust in God when troubles come, we need to know just what His commitments to us are, and which of His wonderful promises you and I can claim and count on today. That's why this book is more than a Bible resource, which answers questions you may have about specific verses. It's also a personal resource, which you can turn to in times of doubt and uncertainty, to find your faith restored as you meditate on the trustworthiness of our wonderful God.

CHAPTER 1

COMMITMENTS TO COUNT ON:

GOD'S COVENANT PROMISES

Genesis 12; Exodus 20; 2 Samuel 7; Jeremiah 31

Our understanding of the Bible and of God's purposes rests on special commitments God has made throughout sacred history. These special commitments are promises—but more. Promises can be conditional. "If you make my breakfast, I'll take you out to supper every Friday." Promises can be temporary. "I promise not to drink coffee before noon for the next six weeks." God's special commitments are not conditional and—with one exception—are not temporary.

Scripture applies a special name to these special commitments: They are called "covenants."

WHAT DOES THE WORD *COVENANT* MEAN?

The Hebrew word translated "covenant," *b*ᵉ*rit,* occurs 272 times in the Old Testament. The Greek word, *diatheke,* is used 33 times in the New Testament. *B*ᵉ*rit* was a familiar word in Old Testament times. In general, it meant a "binding agreement" or "contract."

When two people involved in a business deal worked out its terms, they wrote them into a *b*ᵉ*rit* (contract). When two nations wanted to define the relationship between them, or agree to defend each other, they wrote the terms of their agreement into a *b*ᵉ*rit* (treaty). When a ruler wanted to spell out his responsibilities to his subjects, and his subjects' responsibilities to him, he produced a *b*ᵉ*rit* (a national constitution). Even an informal pledge of friendship, like that made by David and Jonathan to each other (1 Sam. 18:3), is called a *b*ᵉ*rit* in the Bible. Marriage too is called a *b*ᵉ*rit,* because marriage involves the commitment of two people to each other (Mal. 2:14).

So the concept of covenant was both familiar and important in the ancient world. And the word *covenant* was used whenever people wanted to spell out the nature of a wide variety of relationships.

WHY DID GOD MAKE COVENANTS WITH PEOPLE?   *(Hebrews 6:13–19)*

In one passage, the book of Hebrews looks back on God's covenant with Abraham and explains why God chose to call this special commitment a "covenant." The passage says,

When God made a promise to Abraham, because He could swear by no one greater, He swore by

Marriage is a kind of contract.

Himself, saying, *"Surely blessing I will bless you, and multiplying I will multiply you."* And so, after he had patiently endured, he obtained the promise. For men indeed swear by the greater, and an oath for confirmation is for them an end of all dispute. Thus God, determining to show more abundantly to the heirs of promise the immutability of His counsel, confirmed it by an oath, that by two immutable things, in which it is impossible for God to lie, we might have strong consolation, who have fled for refuge to lay hold of the hope set before us. This hope we have as an anchor of the soul, both sure and steadfast (Heb. 6:13–19).

The writer of Hebrews tells us that when God made certain special commitments, He chose the familiar language of covenant, so that those to whom the promises were given might have an anchor for the soul. God made His special commitments legally binding to remove every doubt and fear.

Several words and phrases in this passage help us understand just how significant "covenant" is when it is applied to a divine commitment.

"God made a promise" (Hebrews 6:13). God's covenants are promises. The issues covered in biblical covenants are firm commitments made by the Lord.

"He swore by Himself" (Hebrews 6:13). God's covenants are promises that have been made legally binding by the taking of an oath (Heb. 6:16). In court a person about to give testi-

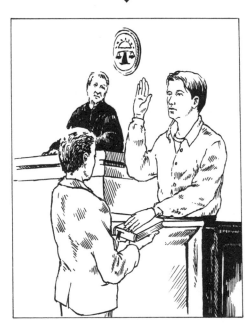

God confirmed His covenant by an oath (Heb. 6:17).

mony is asked, "Do you swear to tell the truth, the whole truth, and nothing but the truth?" Whenever the Bible mentions God's covenants, we're dealing with something God has confirmed with a binding oath, and has sworn "This is the truth, the whole truth, and nothing but the truth!"

"Determined to show the immutability" (*Hebrews 6:17*). God didn't need to put His special commitments in covenant form. God keeps His Word. But He chose to use the covenant form for mankind's sake, to make sure that we understood that God will never, ever change His mind about what each covenant declares. The covenants contain statements of God's fixed purposes: they tell us what He surely will do.

"An anchor of the soul" (*Hebrews 6:19*). God's covenant commitments are so secure that we can anchor ourselves to them. In the ancient world, large stones served as anchors for ocean-going vessels. When strong winds blew up, these stones were often dragged across sandy bottoms, and many ships were lost because of this. It's no wonder most mariners along the Mediterranean Sea preferred to find some cove where they could pull their little ships up on the beach.

But the writer of Hebrews tells us that we can anchor our very selves to God's covenant commitments. However fierce the storms of life, this anchor will never drag and threaten us with shipwreck. We will be safe, with our hope fixed for time and eternity in the covenant promises of God.

WHAT IS SPECIAL ABOUT GOD'S COVENANTS?

Two things are very special about God's covenants. The first is that they are unilateral and thus unconditional. And the second is that most of them are eschatological.

God's covenants are unconditional. If we check out most uses of *b*^e*rit* in the ancient world, and even those uses of *b*^e*rit* in the Bible when that word is used to describe relation-

ships between persons, we find something interesting. Most of these covenants are bilateral and conditional.

A business contract is executed by two parties. If one party fails to deliver contracted goods, the other party doesn't have to pay. Treaties are made between nations, and both parties are signatories. If one country breaks the treaty, the other is not bound by its provisions. If you're a ruler and your people rebel, you set aside your constitutional obligations and put down the rebellion. Even in marriage, if your spouse deserts you and refuses to live with you, you have grounds for divorce. In all these cases, the *b*^e*rit* is bilateral. Both parties to an agreement make promises. If one breaks his or her promise, the other is released from his or her obligations.

But a striking feature of biblical covenants is that they are *unilateral*. God is the only party who makes commitments under the covenants. And, *God does not make His commitments conditional on anything that people might do!*

This means that even when God's people fall short, or sin, or even temporarily abandon Him, God cannot and will not go back on His promises! The biblical covenants state what God surely will do—no matter what we human beings do.

It's no wonder then that the writer of Hebrews says we have an anchor for the soul. If receiving the blessings promised to us in God's covenants depended on us—on our faith, our obedience, or anything else we might do—we would be in trouble indeed. How wonderful then that God's covenant commitments— these special promises He has made and confirmed with an oath—do not depend on us. God has committed Himself to do what the covenants state, no matter what!

God's covenants are eschatological. This simply means that God's covenants describe what He will accomplish *at history's end.* The ultimate fulfillment of God's covenant always lies ahead.

At first this seems troubling. How can God's covenant commitments be an anchor for *our* souls if they're not for us right now?

A BᴱRIT (TREATY) BETWEEN EGYPT AND HATTI 1280 B.C.

After an indecisive battle at Kadesh [in Syria], Ramses II and Hattusilis III executed a treaty [bᵉrit] that kept the peace between the southern and northern powers for some 50 years. The following terms taken from the treaty illustrate this type of two-party covenant executed between nations.

Hattusilis agrees to this treaty with Ramses, creating peace and an eternal alliance between us. We are brothers and are at peace with each other forever.

I, Hattusilis, came to the throne of Hatti, when Myuwatallis died. Therefore, I agree to this treaty with Ramses, creating peace and an alliance between us. The state of peace and alliance between our lands is now better than in former times.

I, Ramses, agree to peace and an alliance. The successors of The Great King of Hatti will be allies with the successors of the Ramses. The relationship between Egypt and Hatti shall be like our relationship—one of peace and an eternal alliance. There will never again be war between us.

. . .

If a foreign army invades the lands of Ramses, and he sends a message to The Great King of Hatti, saying: "Come and help me against this enemy," The Great King of Hatti shall come and fight against the enemies of Egypt, his ally. If the Great King of Hatti does not wish to come personally, he may send infantry and chariots to fight against the enemy of Egypt, his ally.

Likewise, if Ramses is trying to put down an armed revolt, The Great King of

Hatti shall help him until all the rebels have been executed.

If a foreign army attacks The Great King of Hatti, Ramses shall come and fight against the enemy of Hatti, his ally. If Ramses does not wish to come personally, he may send infantry and chariots, as well as word to this effect, to Hatti. If the officials of The Great King of Hatti break their oaths of loyalty to him, Ramses . . . etc.

Compare the language of this two-party treaty-covenant with the language of God's covenant to Abraham (Gen. 12:1–3, 7). The uniqueness of this unilateral biblical covenant becomes clear.

Actually, while God's covenant commitments are to find their ultimate fulfillment in the future (they are eschatological), they have always had an impact on the believer's present (they are also experiential). As we examine each covenant, we'll see just how their ultimate fulfillment is achieved, and we'll also learn how we can experience the benefits promised in the covenant right now. But before we look at this in detail, there is an analogy that may help.

Suppose a grandparent left you $100 million in a trust, all of which is to be given to you when you reach age 50. If you are 25, you might feel frustrated. You have $100 million, but you have to wait 25 years to get it!

But suppose the trust is written so that while you don't get the $100 million until you reach age 50, every year you do receive the interest the trust monies earn? At just 5 percent interest, you'll have $5,000,000 a year to spend right now! You would be rich right now, even though you have to wait for the full $100 million.

God's covenant promises are like this. When Jesus returns, everything God has promised will become ours. But right now, as we trust Jesus and live close to Him, God pours out on us many of the blessings promised for history's end. We're rich right now, as we draw the interest on the covenant promises, experiencing God's blessings in our daily lives.

How exciting it will be as we look at God's great covenant commitments to discover just what benefits we can experience, and how to claim them today!

WHAT ARE GOD'S COVENANTS?

The Bible doesn't apply the word *covenant* to every promise made by God. This doesn't mean that God won't keep His other promises. It does mean that the commitments made by God in the form of covenants are *foundational*.

They are foundational, in that the covenant promises of God spell out for us His basic plans and purposes for history and for us. We'll look at each covenant in detail soon. But for now, we want to identify some of the basic purposes of God spelled out in covenant form.

The Noahic Covenant (Genesis 9). After the great worldwide flood described in Genesis, God promised never again to destroy the world by water. We can be sure that the earth and our race will remain until history reaches God's intended end.

The Abrahamic Covenant (Genesis 12). God made a number of promises to Abraham. God would be Abraham's God. The Lord would bless Abraham, and make his name great. God would bless those who blessed Abraham and curse those who cursed him. God would make Abraham a blessing to all peoples. And of course, God would give the land of Canaan to Abraham's ancestors as a permanent possession.

God's great commitments to Abraham included the promise that "in you all the families of the earth shall be blessed" (Gen. 12:3). And how the world has been blessed through Abraham along the way. Abraham was the ancestor of the Jewish people, and it has been through the Jews that God gave the world His written Word. And it was through the Jews and as a Jew that the Son of God entered our world, to live and to die for our sins.

A rainbow represents God's covenant with Noah.

the interest" on blessings promised in the Abrahamic Covenant for history's end.

God's second covenant commitment was that He would punish His people when they were unfaithful and disobedient. Instead of blessings, unfaithful generations would have all sorts of troubles until they returned to the Lord.

Each of these commitments was unilateral. Each stated in clear, unmistakable terms what God would do.

The Davidic Covenant. This is the name given to a special commitment God made to King David. God told David that there would always be a descendant of his qualified to take Israel's throne, and that one day a descendant of David would rule an everlasting kingdom (2 Sam. 7).

This is an especially precious covenant commitment to us, because the descendant of David whom God had in mind as ruler of the

❖

The Mosaic Covenant (Exodus 19; 20). Another name for this covenant is the "law covenant," a name which brings to mind the Ten Commandments. But the Mosaic Covenant was more than the Ten Commandments: it was a pattern for living that set down principles of morality, established sacrifices for sins, taught ways of worship, defined procedures for civil and criminal law, set up institutions for the care of the poor, and in general established a distinct way of life for God's Old Testament people. This covenant and the lifestyle it described was specifically given to Israel (Ex. 3:27), and is developed in the Old Testament books of Exodus, Leviticus, Numbers, and Deuteronomy.

When God gave His law to Israel the Lord also made two special covenant commitments to the Jewish people. God's first commitment was that He would bless them when they were faithful to Him and lived by His law. Thus faithfulness to God and His Word became the way any generation of Israelites could "draw

God made His covenant with Moses on Mount Sinai.

God promised David, "Your throne shall be established forever."

everlasting kingdom was Jesus Christ! Today Jesus rules as King in the hearts of those who trust Him as Savior and Lord. And one day, at history's end, Jesus will be acknowledged by all to be the ruler not only of this world but of the universe itself, and His kingdom will be forever.

The New Covenant. The Old Testament prophet Jeremiah promised that one day God would replace the "old" covenant He had made with Israel with a better covenant. The old covenant that God promised to replace was the Mosaic, or Law Covenant.

When Jeremiah compared the Old Covenant and the New Covenant, it was clear why replacement was in God's plan. The Old Covenant showed people what they ought to do, but it did not change their hearts so that they would want to live God's way. The Old Covenant had sacrifices that covered sins, but the New Covenant provided for a sacrifice that would take sins away and provide eternal forgiveness.

Perhaps the most important teaching in the Bible about the New Covenant is that it was put in force when Jesus died. God made His great New Covenant commitment to us on the cross.

Jesus' death and resurrection marked the beginning of the age of the New Covenant. When Jesus comes again, we will receive the complete inner transformation that the New Covenant promises. In this sense the New Covenant, like the Abrahamic and Davidic Covenants, is eschatological. It tells us what will surely happen at history's end. But like those other covenants, it is also experiential.

Through faith in Jesus, we can experience the New Covenant promise of full and complete forgiveness of our sins. By trusting Jesus daily and staying close to Him, we can experience the gradual transformation of our hearts and motivations. God the Holy Spirit is at work in us even now to make us more and more like Jesus.

WHAT'S SO SPECIAL ABOUT THE COVENANTS?

We've already seen several things that are special about the covenant commitments that God has made. Covenant commitments are unilateral, and they tell us what God will do. Covenant commitments find their complete fulfillment at history's end, but believers can experience the blessings that the covenants promise here and now. These commitments have been given to us in covenant form as an anchor for our souls. God wants us to be sure of His commitment to us, and to be positive that He will do what He has said.

But there's one other thing that's most special about the biblical covenants. Each of the major eschatological covenants is about Jesus Christ.

Jesus is the one who fulfills God's promise to Abraham to bless all people of the earth through him.

Jesus is the one who fulfills God's promise to David of a King who will rule forever.

The Cross marked the beginning of the New Covenant.

Jesus is the one whose death and resurrection marked the beginning of the New Covenant age, and whose coming again will see us transformed and blessed forever.

The covenant commitments that God has made throughout history are all about Jesus Christ. As we study them, we learn about Him. And our trust in God's love grows and grows.

LIFE-SAVING COVENANTS:

GOD'S PROMISES TO NOAH

Genesis 6—9

The first occurrence of the word *covenant* in the Bible is found in Genesis 6:18. God spoke with a man named Noah, and said "I will establish My covenant with you; and you shall go into the ark."

God told Noah that He intended to destroy human civilization with a great Flood. He also instructed Noah to build a great floating vessel, an ark. In the coming disaster, human and animal life would be wiped out. But God made the first of two wonderful commitments to Noah.

THE COVENANT OF DELIVERANCE

We can call God's first covenant commitment to Noah the covenant of deliverance.

But I will establish My covenant with you; and you shall go into the ark; you, your sons, your wife, and your sons' wives with you. And of every living thing of all flesh you shall bring two of every sort into the ark, to keep them alive with you (Gen. 6:18, 19).

Although the earth would be scoured clean and "all flesh in which there is the breath of life" would die, Noah and his family, along with pairs of animals needed to repopulate the earth, would be carried safely through the waters of judgment.

An examination of sacred history's first use of "covenant" reveals elements which help us understand all the covenants God has made with human beings.

THE CONTEXT OF THE NOAHIC PROMISE (Genesis 6:1–6)

In Genesis 6 we're suddenly confronted with a terrible specter. Sin has totally corrupted human society. "The LORD saw that the wickedness of man was great in the earth, and that every intent of the thoughts of his heart was only evil continually" (Gen. 6:5). The seed of sin planted in the Fall (Gen. 3) has come to full flower. Man's wickedness is the backdrop against which all God's covenant promises are made.

Man's Fall (Genesis 3:1–24). Genesis 3 tells the familiar story of the sin of Adam and Eve. God created the first pair sinless, and at first they enjoyed a close and loving relationship with the Creator. Placed in a beautiful park-like setting, Eden, Adam and Eve had been given only one instruction by the Lord. The first pair was not to eat the fruit of a certain tree in the garden.

There was a reason why God had planted that tree. Adam and Eve were created in God's image. So the Lord designed the place where they lived to provide opportunities to exercise every capacity He had given them. The forbidden tree was placed in Eden not as a trap but as a gift. It enabled Adam and Eve to be like God as moral beings rather than merely creatures of instinct. The tragedy is that Eve and Adam made the wrong choice. They disobeyed God, and as a result they lost their innocence. Their very natures were also warped and twisted.

God had warned Adam, "The day that you eat of [the forbidden tree] you shall surely die" (Gen. 2:17). In the language of Scripture, they did die that day—spiritually. Ephesians describes "spiritual death" when it portrays human beings as "dead in trespasses and sins, in which you once walked according to the

course of this world, according to the prince of the power of the air, the spirit who now works in the sons of disobedience, among whom also we all once conducted ourselves in the lusts of our flesh, fulfilling the desires of the flesh and of the mind, and were by nature children of wrath, just as the others" (Eph. 2:1–3).

Genesis points us back to Adam and Eve, reminding us that the crime, cruelty, violence, and abuse that we see in society today has its root in a tragic flaw in human nature itself—a flaw that the Bible calls sin—and spiritual death.

Evidence of the Fall (Genesis 4). God had warned Adam that the day he ate the fruit of the forbidden tree, he would die. While the processes that lead to biological death were initiated then, Adam and Eve died spiritually that very day. Innocence was lost forever, and the moral corruption which gained a foothold in human personality was transmitted by Adam and Eve to all their descendants.

The clearest evidence of this reality is seen in Genesis 4, which recounts the murder of one of Adam and Eve's sons, Abel, by his brother, Cain. Jealousy and anger now churned within the human heart, leading to fratricide. Genesis 4 gives us another example to show that human beings died spiritually. It tells the story of Lamech, who broke God's pattern for marriage by taking two wives, and who justified the murder of a young man by complaining that he had "wounded me" (Gen. 4:23). The seeds of sin had been planted deep in the human personality, and their fruit was bitter indeed.

A corrupt civilization (Genesis 6). Genesis 5 contains a lengthy genealogy which has two functions. First, it traces the family line of Noah, whose story begins in Genesis 6. Second, the genealogy tells us that many centuries passed between the time of the creation and Noah's day. The human race multiplied and multiplied again, establishing a widespread civilization. Yet that civilization was corrupt, reflecting the basic flaw in human na-

The first humans chose to disobey God.

Sin in the second generation: Cain murdered Abel.

ture. God's own evaluation of pre-flood society is that it was "wicked," and "every intent of the thoughts of his [mankind's] heart was only evil continually" (Gen. 6:5).

Finally, conditions on earth so grieved God that He determined, "I will destroy man whom I have created from the face of the earth, both man and beast, creeping thing and birds of the air, for I am sorry that I have made them" (Gen. 6:7).

It is against this background of human sin and divine judgment that Scripture introduces the first covenant made by God with any human being. In spite of the total corruption of humankind, the Lord said to Noah, "I will establish my covenant with you" (Gen. 6:18).

Listening to the divine evaluation of human society, we can understand why God, who is a moral judge, felt compelled to purge the earth. "The earth also was corrupt before God, and the earth was filled with violence. So God looked upon the earth, and indeed it was

corrupt; for all flesh had corrupted their way on the earth" (Gen. 6:11, 12). Yet in spite of this, God told Noah, "I will establish my covenant with you" (Gen. 6:18).

So the first thing to understand about the biblical covenants is that they are expressions of God's grace, given against a background of sin and judgment.

God must and will judge sin. But at the same time, God's covenant promises reveal a grace alternative.

PRINCIPLES UNDERLYING THE COVENANT OF DELIVERANCE

The principle of grace (Genesis 6:8). Genesis describes the background of sin and judgment against which the covenant with Noah was made, and then states, "But Noah found grace in the eyes of the LORD" (Gen. 6:8).

The expression *to find* is a figure of speech which means "to receive" or "to obtain." The same language is used in other biblical passages.

- Isaac "found" (received) a hundredfold increase at harvest time (Gen. 26:12).
- Mary "found favor with" (received grace from) God (Luke 1:30).
- Jesus entered heaven "having found" (obtained) eternal redemption for us.

The idiom, then, does not draw attention to Noah, as if he deserved or merited grace. "Finding grace" draws attention to the God who is gracious.

To understand what is being taught here, we need to look not to what the text tells us about Noah in the next verse, but to the meaning of the Hebrew word translated "grace." That word is *hen,* or *hanan,* and here the *Expository Dictionary of Bible Words* (Zondervan) is helpful. Grace, or favor, is "the compassionate response of one who is able to help another person in need." This source continues,

The Book of Psalms best illustrates the theological use of this Hebrew term. Ps. 51:1 expresses David's appeal to God for forgiveness: "Have mercy on me [*hanan*, 'grace'], O God, according to your unfailing love; according to your great compassion blot out my transgressions." The appeal is uttered out of a sense of helplessness. It turns away from self and looks to God as a loving and compassionate person. God's own nature is the basis on which help is expected. As David says, "Turn to me and have mercy [*hanan*, 'grace'] on me, as you always do to those who love your name" (Ps. 119:137) (*Expository Dictionary of Bible Words*, Zondervan, p. 317).

Noah obtained grace, not because of who he was or what he did, but because of who God is. For God is loving and compassionate and as the psalm affirms, showing grace is something He always does to those who love His name.

The principle of faith (Genesis 6:9, 22). Genesis makes two statements that seem contradictory. In Genesis 6:12, the Bible says that "all flesh had corrupted their way on the earth." Certainly the word *all* includes Noah and his family. No person is unaffected by sin within, nor is anyone unaffected by the sins of the society in which he or she lives.

Yet Noah is still described as "a just man, perfect in his generations" and as a man who "walked with God" (Gen. 6:9). It's important to understand that when the Old Testament identifies an individual as "righteous" or "blameless" [i.e., "perfect among his generations"] it is not suggesting that this person is sinless. The *Expository Dictionary of Bible Words* says, "The blameless OT believer accepted God's way and sought to live by it" (p. 128). This is what Genesis tells us about Noah. He was a man who, unlike the others in his world, was sensitive to the Lord. Noah tried his best to walk with Him.

The New Testament describes Noah's sensitivity to God as faith. Hebrews 11:7 says that "by faith Noah, being divinely warned of things not yet seen, moved with godly fear, prepared an ark for the saving of his household, by which he condemned the world and became heir of the righteousness which is according to faith." Noah was not sinless. He needed grace. But Noah was open to the Lord and receptive to the covenant which God

promised to establish with him. When God gave Noah the blueprint of the ark and announced His purpose, Noah demonstrated his faith. "According to all that God commanded him, so he did" (Gen. 6:22).

A principle of divine intent (Genesis 6:18). In Genesis 6, we see two clear statements of God's intent. God said, "The earth is filled with violence . . . and behold, I will destroy them with the earth" (Gen. 6:13). God intended then just as He intends now to judge sin.

The other statement of God's intent focuses on covenant relationship. God also said, "I will establish my covenant with you" (Gen. 6:18). God intended then and He intends now to establish a covenant relationship with people of faith.

These two "I will" statements express the two most significant options facing any human being today. The story of the Genesis Flood reminds us that God *will* judge sin. Yet our gracious and loving God is also eager to establish His covenant with people of faith. To all who respond to His word as Noah did, His promise of deliverance stands.

These three principles—grace, faith, and divine intent—govern this first expression of a covenant commitment by God.

THE NOAHIC COVENANT OF DELIVERANCE FORESHADOWS SALVATION BY CHRIST

The apostle Peter looked back on Noah's experience and found there an image of the salvation enjoyed by Christians. Peter spoke of Christ's suffering once for sins with the result that He brought us to God. Peter then added,

Being put to death in the flesh but made alive by the Spirit, by whom also He went and preached to the spirits in prison, who formerly were disobedient, when once the Divine longsuffering waited in the days of Noah, while the ark was being prepared, in which a few, that is, eight souls, were saved through water. There is also an antitype which now saves us; baptism (not the removal of the filth of the flesh, but the answer of a good conscience toward God), through the resurrection of Jesus Christ (1 Pet. 3:18–21).

While this passage has been frequently misunderstood, Peter's analogy becomes clear when we remember that he was drawing parallels between Noah's experience and that of the Christian.

The spirits in prison (1 Peter 1:19). Some have taken this as a reference to Christ preaching to spirits of the dead during the hours between His own death and resurrection. But Peter was speaking of the fact that Christ, through the Holy Spirit's ministry in Noah, preached a gospel to the disobedient people of Noah's day (1 Pet. 1:20). While the ark was being prepared, Noah warned those who scoffed at his giant boat being built on dry land. They failed to respond as Noah had, with faith, and so they perished. Their spirits are even now imprisoned, awaiting final judgment.

In which a few . . . were saved (1 Peter 3:20). In Noah's time, God ordained the construction of an ark. In that ark Noah and his family, just eight people, were carried safely through the waters of the great Flood. Peter draws a parallel between the waters, which stand for divine judgment, and the final judgment awaiting those who do not know Christ. For Christ is God's ark for our own time—the only vessel in which we will be safe.

"There is also an antitype . . . which saves us, baptism" (1 Peter 3:21). Some have mistakenly linked Peter's reference to baptism with the "water" in this passage. But "in the days of Noah," water was the medium of judgment, not the means of deliverance. The solution comes when we remember that "baptism" refers to a special work of the Holy Spirit as well as to immersion or sprinkling by water. First Corinthians 12:13 says that "by one Spirit we were all baptized into one body." When we trust Jesus as Savior, the Holy Spirit bonds us to Him, organically linking us not only to the Lord but also to all other believers.

No wonder then that Peter guards against our mistaking his point by saying that the baptism he refers to is "not the removal of the filth of the flesh" (1 Pet. 3:21). Peter is not speaking of the washing of water baptism, but of that work of the Spirit by which we are linked to Jesus.

But how does our link with Jesus save us? Peter says it is "through the resurrection of Jesus Christ." United to Jesus by the Holy Spirit's work, we die with Christ and are also raised with Him. The apostle Paul explained it this way: "Therefore we were buried with Him through baptism into death, that just as Christ was raised from the dead by the glory of the Father, even so we also should walk in newness of life" (Rom. 6:4).

Peter's analogy explained. With this background, we can now see the parallels between the experience of Noah and the experience of the Christian.

- Noah lived just prior to impending divine judgment. So do we.
- Noah heard a message of grace that promised deliverance. So do we.
- Noah responded to the message of grace with faith and entered the ark. We respond to the message of grace with faith and enter into a saving relationship with Jesus.
- Noah was carried safely through the waters of judgment in the ark. Linked with Jesus, we too are carried beyond judgment in Him.

There is one additional point in Peter's analogy. Peter notes that since we are united with Jesus, we should no longer "live the rest of [our] time in the flesh for the lusts of men, but for the will of God" (1 Pet. 4:2). When the floodwaters receded, Noah was deposited in a fresh new world, to live a new life free from the pressure to sin that existed in pre-flood society. In Christ we too have been deposited in a new world—a world where Jesus reigns in our hearts, and we are freed from domination by the "lusts of men." As Christians now, we are able to choose instead "the will of God."

In Christ a new and glorious world opens before us. And we are to live in the new world, rejecting the old world and its ways.

The ark offered the only salvation from God's judgment in Noah's day.

Our first experience with a covenant in Scripture, then, introduces us to wonderful and amazing truths. God judges sin and sinners, yet chooses to be gracious. He shares the good news of His firm intent to deliver human beings, and those who respond with faith are doubly blessed. They are delivered from the judgment that looms so darkly over lost men and women. And they are carried in Christ to a new, fresh world in which they can break old patterns and live the rest of their time in the flesh, doing the will of God.

And, according to Romans 12:2, the will of God is "good and acceptable and perfect" indeed.

THE COVENANT OF PRESERVATION

The first reference to covenant in the Bible is to what we have called the "covenant of deliverance" which God made with Noah. God announced His gracious intent to provide a means for Noah and his family to escape coming judgment.

After the floodwaters receded from the earth, God instituted another covenant. This second covenant is commonly referred to as "the Noahic Covenant." This second covenant was made not only with Noah, but with his descendants and indeed with all living creatures on earth.

Then God spoke to Noah and to his sons with him, saying:

"And as for Me, behold, I establish My covenant with you and with your descendants after you; and with every living creature that is with you; the birds, the cattle, and every beast of the earth with you, of all that go out of the ark, every beast of the earth."

"Thus I establish My covenant with you: Never again shall all flesh be cut off by the waters of the flood; never again shall there be a flood to destroy the earth."

And God said, "This is the sign of the covenant which I make between Me and you, and every living creature that is with you, for perpetual generations: I set My rainbow in the cloud, and it shall be for the sign of the covenant between Me and the earth" (Gen. 9:8–13).

THE CONTEXT OF THE COVENANT OF PRESERVATION

The Genesis Flood had scoured human civilization from the face of the earth, and with it animal life as well. The devastating judgment that God announced came as soon as the ark was finished, supplies were gathered, and the animals were assembled.

We can imagine the relief of Noah and his family members when, over a year after entering the ark, they stepped out on solid ground. We can also imagine the fear that mingled with their joy as they thanked God for their deliverance. God had revealed Himself to be a God of judgment, whose patience with sin does have limits. How long might it be before God would again act against the human race? Sin's grip on humankind had not been loosed by the judgment. Sinful humans would certainly fear in the future when storms raged and rains began to fall.

Against this background, God made a new commitment not just to Noah but to all human and animal life, "for perpetual generations" (Gen. 9:12). Never again would a "flood . . . destroy the earth" (Gen. 9:11).

PRINCIPLES EXPRESSED IN GENESIS' STATEMENT OF THE COVENANT OF PRESERVATION

As we look at Genesis 8 and 9, we note several important principles.

The principle of God's sovereign intent (Genesis 8:21–23). These verses tell us that God "said in His heart":

"I will never again curse the ground for man's sake . . . nor will I again destroy every living thing as I have done. While the earth remains,
   Seedtime and harvest,
   Cold and heat,

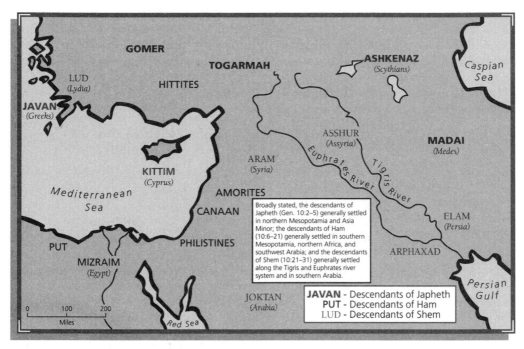

The Descendants of Noah

Within the map:

GOMER

TOGARMAH

ASHKENAZ
(Scythians)

Caspian Sea

LUD
(Lydia)

HITTITES

JAVAN
(Greeks)

ASSHUR
(Assyria)

MADAI
(Medes)

ARAM
(Syria)

Euphrates River

Tigris River

KITTIM
(Cyprus)

Mediterranean Sea

AMORITES

CANAAN

Broadly stated, the descendants of Japheth (Gen. 10:2–5) generally settled in northern Mesopotamia and Asia Minor; the descendants of Ham (10:6–21) generally settled in southern Mesopotamia, northern Africa, and southwest Arabia; and the descendants of Shem (10:21–31) generally settled along the Tigris and Euphrates river system and in southern Arabia.

ELAM
(Persia)

PUT

PHILISTINES

MIZRAIM
(Egypt)

ARPHAXAD

Persian Gulf

0 100 200
Miles

Red Sea

JOKTAN
(Arabia)

JAVAN - Descendants of Japheth
PUT - Descendants of Ham
LUD - Descendants of Shem

Winter and summer,
And day and night
Shall not cease"
    (Gen. 8:21, 22)

What is significant here is that the covenant promises God gave Noah and his family *originated as an intent in God's heart*. God determined in His own heart what He would do before He expressed His intent in the form of a covenant promise.

God's promise was freely made. It was in no way dependent on what Noah or any of his descendants might do or not do in the future.

The principle of God's sovereign control (Genesis 9:11). God said to Noah, "Never again shall all flesh be cut off by the waters of the flood; never again shall there be a flood to destroy the earth."

The principle established here is important. God is sovereign, and His will governs the future. God is no captive of what occurs as history unfolds. God is the author of what unfolds, in the sense that He retains control over

events so that whatever happens contributes to the accomplishment of His purposes.

Only a sovereign God could state with certainty that "while the earth remains," season would follow season (Gen. 8:23). Only a sovereign God could promise that no massive disruption like that caused by the Flood would occur again.

This early Genesis indication of God's control over future events is central to our understanding of all His covenant promises. God can make promises about what will happen because His sovereign control of the future is such that even the free choices of human beings, made without divine coercion, contribute to the accomplishment of what He has planned.

The principle of God's sovereign grace (Genesis 9:13–17). After announcing the covenant promise, God also said, "I set My rainbow in the cloud, and it shall be for the sign of the covenant between Me and the earth" (v. 13).

The Jewish sage Ramban noted that any visible object which serves as a reminder of an agreement (covenant) is called a "sign." Thus in Genesis 21:30 seven ewe lambs and in Genesis 31:52 a heap of stones are identified as "signs" of agreements between persons.

As a sign, the rainbow was a grace gift, a constant reminder that God had promised not to destroy the world by water ever again.

But why does God say, "The rainbow shall be in the cloud, and I will look on it to remember the everlasting covenant between God and every living creature" (Gen. 9:16)? Surely God could not forget His promise.

The answer is that in Scripture "to remember" is an idiomatic expression meaning "to act in accord with what is remembered." The rainbow was not needed to remind God of His commitment; it was a gracious gift reassuring Noah and his descendants that the onset of even the heaviest of rains posed no threat to the earth. God had made His covenant promise, and God would never go back on His word.

The principle of God's sovereign freedom (Genesis 8:22; 9:11). It is important to note that God's covenant of preservation does not limit His freedom to judge sin.

God freely committed Himself never again to "destroy every living thing" by water. "While the earth remains," no catastrophic judgment will disrupt the regularity of the seasons. Yet Peter looked back on the Flood and saw in it unmistakable evidence that God most certainly will judge our world. Peter said of those who scoff at the idea of coming divine judgment, "This they willfully forget: that by the word of God the heavens were of old, and the earth standing out of water and in the water, by which the world that then existed perished, being flooded with water" (2 Pet. 3:5, 6). The Flood serves as a precedent and as a warning: God most surely will judge sinful humankind.

In fact, Peter tells us that in history's final moment the heavens and the earth which are now preserved by the covenant promise of God "are reserved for fire until the day of judgment and perdition of ungodly men" (2 Pet. 3:7).

God's promise not to disrupt the regular patterns of the seasons in no way limits His freedom to judge individuals, to judge nations, or ultimately to burn up our earth, melting its elements in fervent heat (2 Pet. 3:10).

WHAT WE LEARN ABOUT "COVENANT" FROM GENESIS 6, 8, AND 9

The first occurrence of the word *covenant* in the Bible is in Genesis 6:18. The word occurs next in Genesis 9, where it is repeated several times. As a general rule, first occurrences of any important biblical term are especially significant. It's important to ask, then, what principles are established by the use of *b^erit* in the Noah story.

Covenants express God's intent. Covenants are "I will" statements expressing in unmistakable terms what God intends to do. The covenant of preservation made with Noah demonstrates God's ability to do what He intends. The covenant of preservation made with Noah and all living creatures shows us that God has plans which extend to history's end.

Covenants are instruments of God's grace. Covenant promises are made against the backdrop of human frailty and need. God has compassion on us in spite of the fact that we human beings are sinners. He extends His grace to us through unilateral promises to save, preserve, and bless. Noah was a recipient of God's grace, and was saved from death. Noah's descendants still receive grace in the form of God's preservation of our planetary home.

Covenants invite a faith response. Our appropriate response to God's covenant promises is to gladly welcome them, to trust the God who makes the promise, and to show faith by acting on His word. Noah built the ark as an act of faith, and was preserved when the flood waters came.

Covenants imply God's sovereignty. Only a sovereign God, capable of knowing and shaping the future, can make the kind of promises expressed in biblical covenants. As in the Noahic Covenant of preservation, God is able to guarantee future events "while the earth remains!" Only a sovereign being whose control of events is certain can make and keep such promises.

Covenants foreshadow the work of Jesus Christ. The covenant promises God makes express *what* He will do, but they do not tell us *how* He will do it. The apostle Peter shows us how Noah's experience parallels and foreshadows the believer's experience in Christ. As we explore the other key covenants of Scripture, we will see that each foreshadows the ministry of Jesus, and is fulfilled in and by Him.

CHAPTER 3

COMMITMENT TO A MAN OF FAITH:

THE COVENANT WITH ABRAHAM

Genesis 12; 15; 17

"**F**or better, for worse; for richer, for poorer; in sickness, and in health—till death do us part."

These familiar words of the traditional marriage ceremony express a commitment which two people make to each other. All too often that commitment is broken as the glow of first love fades in the harsher light of constant exposure to each other's weaknesses.

But imagine that God had made this kind of commitment to a human being. Suppose that His commitment was unconditional: that no matter what, He would remain faithful to His promise.

As we look further into the Bible book of Genesis, we discover that God did just that!

ABRAM/ABRAHAM

Following the Flood described in Genesis 6—9, the earth was gradually repopulated by Noah's descendants. Genesis 10 describes the settlement of different areas of the ancient world by various groups and peoples. Genesis 11 describes the origin of ethnic and language groups, and then provides a genealogy tracing the family of Abram (later known as Abraham) back to Noah's son, Shem.

Like other biblical genealogies, this list of ancestors is selective. It identifies key individuals but does not name *all* ancestors. While we can't guess how many years elapsed between Noah and Abraham, they should be measured in thousands rather than hundreds.

What is most important, however, is that by the time of Abraham, human civilization was again corrupt. Documents from the ancient Near East make it very clear that morally and spiritually humanity had abandoned the knowledge of God and His ways. As Joshua 24:2 reminds us, "Your fathers, including Terah, the father of Abraham and the father of Nahor, dwelt on the other side of the River in old times; and they served other gods."

In Noah's time, such wickedness had led to the judgment of the great Flood. That Flood established for all time the fact that God is a moral judge who *will* punish sin. But with Abraham God introduced a new and gracious approach to dealing with humankind. That ap-

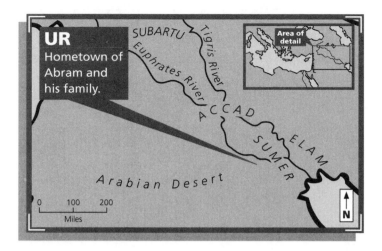

proach is summed up in Joshua 24:3: "Then I took your father Abraham from the other side of the River, led him throughout all the land of Canaan, and multiplied his descendants."

God chose Abram and initiated a long-range plan that would for all eternity establish the Lord as a God of love, who cares deeply for human beings in spite of our sinfulness. That plan is introduced in the covenant promises God made to Abram. And the rest of the Bible is the story of how that plan was carried out.

ABRAM THE MAN

We know little about Abram except that he was born in Ur of the Chaldees, an impor-

tant city-state where many pagan deities were worshiped. We know from Acts 7:2 that God spoke to Abram as an adult while he lived in Ur. We know that Abram journeyed to Haran, where his father and brother settled, and that after a time Abram continued his journey to Canaan. We know that Abram was well-to-do and traveled with flocks and herds and servants, as well as with his wife and his nephew Lot. We also know that, unlike Noah, Abram's call included no personal commendation by God.

The text of Scripture never indicates that when God spoke to Abram, he was "a just man, perfect in his generations" or that he "walked with God" (Gen. 6:9). In fact, from the stories of Abram told in Genesis, we know that he was a seriously flawed individual. Told by God to get out of his country and to leave his family and his father's house, Abram left Ur. But he took his father along. Even after his father died in Haran, Abram took his nephew Lot to Canaan with him.

There is other evidence that we are to understand Abram as a sinner. On a visit to Egypt, and again later in Canaan, Abram urged his wife to lie about their relationship out of fear that he might be killed by someone who wanted her. No wonder God had to accept Abram's faith for righteousness (Gen. 15:6). Abram, the idolater, was not an especially righteous man!

Abram's wealth was in his flocks and herds.

MERIT OR GRACE

As we look at the Abrahamic Covenant, we need to remember the principles defined earlier in our study of the Noahic Covenant. As "Noah found grace in the eyes of the LORD" (Gen. 6:8), so the Abrahamic Covenant was a grace gift from the Lord.

This vital truth was corrupted in the Judaism of the first century B.C., and in modern Judaism as well. The apocryphal book of Jubilees credits Abram with great piety before the Lord spoke to him. It says,

And the lad began understanding the straying of the land, that everyone went astray after graven images and after pollution. . . . And he separated from his father so that he might not worship the idols with him. And he began to pray to the Creator of

all so that he might save him from the straying of the sons of men (Jubilees 11:16, 17).

The same idea—that it was Abram's merit which led God to make His wonderful covenant promises—is reflected in a Sabbath devotional of Rabbi Shlomo Riskin, written for the November 7, 1992, *Jerusalem Post*. Rabbi Riskin related a famous tale told in Jewish Midrash intended to show that Abram "became worthy of divine trust and blessing." The story goes like this:

A famous tale relates how Abram, the son of a man who trafficked in idols, one day smashed those idols and then planted a stick in the arms of the largest one. When his astonished father, Terah, demanded an explanation, innocent Abram pointed to the idol holding the plank, as if that inanimate god were the culprit. He thus ridiculed idolatry by demonstrating that not even idol makers believed in their product.

Terah's shop was not some fly-by-night affair in temporary quarters, located near the busiest section in town, but rather a thriving center for idolatrous arts—more like the luminescent chambers of any large museum, with spotlights and acres of space to dramatize the repose of the idols. And Abram's action was not a mere childish prank, but a revolutionary stroke which changed the way humanity perceived reality for all subsequent generations.

While we can appreciate the imaginative telling of this story which, unlike the biblical account, has no roots in history or tradition, it's clear that both Jubilees and Jewish Midrash explain God's covenant promises by referring to Abram's supposed merits rather than to God's grace.

Yet it is there, in God's heart and character, that the explanation for His covenant promises lie. In saying that "there is none righteous, no, not one," (Ps. 14:1–3; cf. Rom. 3:10), the Old Testament and New Testament agree. We cannot look for an explanation for God's gracious acts in any supposed human goodness—not even in the supposed goodness of Abram, a true hero of the faith. No, we must look for the explanation of God's gracious acts in His compassionate heart.

Abram, like you and me, was a sinner who, apart from God's initiative, would have continued in the idolatrous path established by his forefathers. But God did choose to act. As Nehemiah 9:7 states, "You are the LORD God, Who chose Abram, and brought him out of Ur of the Chaldeans."

God initiated.

God chose.

And Abram responded with faith.

ABRAM'S FAITH RESPONSE
(Genesis 15:6; Romans 4)

The Abrahamic Covenant is stated three times in Genesis. Genesis 12 lists the series of promises that constitute the covenant. Abram responded with a *demonstration* of faith. As commanded, Abram left Ur to set out for Canaan.

When God restated several of the original covenant promises in Genesis 15, the Bible says of Abram that "he believed the LORD, and He accounted it to him [credited it to him] for righteousness" (Gen. 15:6).

The apostle Paul developed the significance of this verse in Romans 4. He argued that the key to personal relationship with God is not works—what we do—but faith. Personal relationship with God "is of faith," Paul wrote, "that it might be according to grace, so that the promise might be sure to all the seed" (Rom. 4:16). Paul concluded his thoughts by reminding us that faith was credited to Abraham for a righteousness which, despite rabbinic fictions, he did not possess. And, Paul indicated, this wonderful revelation of a righteousness that comes through faith in the gracious promises of God was not "written for his sake alone that it was imputed to him, but also for us. It [righteousness] shall be imputed to us who believe in Him who raised up Jesus our Lord from the dead, who was delivered up because of our offenses, and was raised because of our justification" (Rom. 4:23–25).

Abram, then, was a man like the rest of us, flawed by sin and without any merit to recommend him to God. Yet, God in His grace made a series of promises to Abram, and sealed them in that binding agreement known in the ancient world as a *bᵉrit*, or covenant. Those promises were freely and sovereignly given and, as we will see, mark out a wonderful future not only for Abram's physical descendants but also for all who respond with faith in the one in whom the covenant promises will be fulfilled.

THE CONTENT OF THE ABRAHAMIC COVENANT *(Genesis 12:1–3, 7)*

The basic content of the Abrahamic Covenant is spelled out in Genesis 12:1–3, 7, where God stated His intent to bless Abram and his descendants.

Now the LORD had said to Abram:
"Get out of your country,

From your family
And from your father's house,
To a land that I will show you.
I will make you a great nation;
I will bless you
And make your name great;
And you shall be a blessing.
I will bless those who bless you,
And I will curse him who curses
        you;
And in you all the families of the
        earth shall be blessed" (Gen.
        12:1–3).

Later God appeared to Abram and added this clause. "To your descendants I will give this land" (Gen. 12:7).

GOD CALLED ABRAM
(Genesis 12:1)

The first verse of Genesis 12 contains God's call to Abram, then living in Ur (Acts 7:2). Abram was to separate from his old associations and move to a land which God would show him.

Get out . . . to a land (Genesis 12:1). The Hebrew text adds the reflexive pronoun to the command "you get out," so that the text should read "go yourself." Commentators see two possible emphases.

Go by yourself. God may be saying, "Go by yourself" out of your country, from your family and your father's house. In this case, it's clear that while Abram obeyed God's command to leave, he did not go by himself. He went with his family, and even brought his nephew Lot to Canaan after his father Terah died in Haran.

Go for your own benefit. The great Jewish scholar Rashi understands the phrase "go yourself" to mean "go *for* yourself," that is, for your own benefit, for your own good. In commanding Abram to leave Ur, God was speaking graciously, with the intent of blessing Abram.

Each of these two interpretations reminds us that grace underlies the giving of all covenant promises. God's purposes, as expressed in the Abrahamic Covenant, has Abram's best interests at heart and, indeed, the best interests of all humanity.

From your country . . . family . . . father's house (Genesis 12:1). This call to abandon everything to follow the Lord moves from less to more difficult. It is hard to leave a society in which a person has grown up. It is harder to leave the extended family and that circle of relations who have helped us define who we are. It is hardest of all to leave our father's house, where relationships are closest and love deepest.

We see this reflected in Abram's story. First he left Ur, but took his family with him. Even after his father died in Haran, Abram took a nephew with him to Canaan. Perhaps this gradual severing of the ties that bound Abram to his former life served God's purposes as well as a sudden departure would have. In any case, God graciously accepted the gradual process. But it was not until after Abram and his nephew had separated (Gen. 13) that God formally confirmed the promises given Abram (Gen. 15).

To a land that I will show you (Genesis 12:1). God set the direction for Abram's move but did not state a destination. It is this, along with the call to leave all that was familiar behind, which reminds us that from the beginning, Abram's response to God's revelation was marked by faith. Abram trusted God enough to leave behind all that was familiar to set out for a life he could not imagine, to live in a place he had never visited (cf. Heb. 11:8–10).

It was faith that enabled Abram to claim the promises. But it was grace that moved God to make the promises in the first place.

GOD CONVEYS HIS INTENT TO ABRAM   *(Genesis 12:2, 3, 7)*

God's intent is expressed in a series of "I will" statements. As in other promise covenants, God's "I will" statements mark unconditional commitments. They express *what*

To keep peace between their herdsmen, Abram and Lot eventually went their separate ways.

God will do, without defining *how* He will accomplish what He has promised. We can see seven distinct statements of God's intent in Genesis 12:2, 3, 7.

(1) *"I will make you a great nation" (Genesis 1:2).* When Abram left Ur, he and his wife had no children. Yet God's promise to make Abram a great nation clearly required that the patriarch have children in the future, and that he have many descendants.

Even more is implied in the choice of the word for "nation," *goy*. This word is applied throughout Scripture to pagan nations, while Abram's descendants are typically identified as a *people* (`am). The use of the word *goy* in this verse implied that one day Abram's descendants would be more than an ethnic group: they would be a nation among the nations, with their own government and territory.

(2) *"I will bless you" (Genesis 1:2).* No specific content is implied here, although Jewish commentators tend to apply Proverbs 10:22, "the blessing of the LORD makes one rich," and take the phrase to mean that Abram was promised wealth.

Gorden Wenham, in his commentary on Genesis 1—15, (Word) notes that the root *b-r-*

a ("bless") occurs 88 times in Genesis, compared to 310 times in the rest of the Old Testament.

God's blessing is manifested most obviously in human prosperity and well-being: long life, wealth, peace, good harvests, and children are the items that figure most often in lists of blessing such as Genesis 24:35–36, Leviticus 26:4–13, and Deuteronomy 28:3–15. What modern secular man calls "luck" or "success," the OT calls blessing (p. 275).

Throughout his life Abram was to be blessed by God. Even when his actions did not merit it, God would show favor to Abram, even as God shows His favor to you and me today.

(3) *And make your name great (Genesis 12:2).* Several inscriptions from early second-millennium Mesopotamia show the concern of ancient kings in a "great" name. Man's life on earth is short, and for many in the ancient as well as the modern world, being remembered seemed to offer at least a semblance of immortality.

How fascinating that those kings who set their hearts on conquering other peoples and building great monuments have long been forgotten, while Abram, who spent a quiet no-madic life living in tents, has been honored for more than four thousand years!

(4) **"You shall be a blessing"** *(Genesis 12:2).* This is one of the most significant promises made to Abram. He was not only to be blessed. He was to become a conduit through which God's blessing might flow to others. Again, this statement of God's intent does not specify *how* Abram was to be a bless-ing. The *how* would become known only as the centuries flowed and God's plan unfolded more and more. But while Abram could not imagine how he would be a blessing to others, it was clear that God intended blessing to flow through Abram to others yet unborn.

(5) **"I will bless those who bless you, and I will curse him who curses you"** *(Genesis 12:3).* These two phrases are in the form of a poetic doublet, and they should be under-stood as a single statement of intent. When it comes to Abram, the normal operations of cause and effect in human relationships are set aside. God Himself will personally intervene, to provide those who support Abram with blessings, and to repay those who trouble Abram with troubles.

(6) **"And in you all the families of the earth shall be blessed"** *(Genesis 12:3).* The word translated "family" here indicates a ma-jor group between a tribe and a single house-hold. It is often translated "clan." We note that the passage does not say every individual on earth will be blessed in Abraham, but that members of every major group will be blessed.

It is interesting that the Jewish sages tended to take the Niphal form of "bless" here as a reflexive pronoun, and read it, "All the families of the earth shall *bless themselves* by you." Rashi took this to mean that people everywhere will one day say "be like Abra-ham" when expressing best wishes to others. But Rambam and others noted that if taken in the passive, to mean that Abram will become the source of blessing for all humanity, the verse fits a doctrine emphasized later in the prophets.

Truly all humankind has been blessed in Abram, and in what God has done through the patriarch and his descendants, the Jewish people.

(7) **"To your descendants I will give this land"** *(Genesis 12:7).* This seventh promise, or statement of God's intent, is separated from the first six. It is not only separated in the text. It was separated in Abram's experience.

The first six promises were given to Abram in Ur (Acts 7:2). It was only after Abram had left and actually traveled to Canaan that this seventh promise was made to him. There is good reason for the delay. God had told Abram to leave everything and every-one and travel to a land the Lord would show him. Only when Abram had arrived in the land, and seen it, could God say "I will give *this land.*"

To have meaning for Abram, "show" had to precede "give."

As we trace this specific promise through the Scriptures, we will see just how important it is. For now, however, it's enough to note two things. The land of Canaan could not be in-herited by Lot, for it was promised to Abram's descendants. And the land could not be pos-sessed by Abram then, for God said the land would be given to Abram's descendants. This promise was to be fulfilled in the future, not in Abram's present.

Abram, his son, and his grandson did live in the land of God's gift. In this sense, it be-came theirs too (see Gen. 13:17). But Hebrews 11:8–10 makes it very clear that Abram's true inheritance was much more than the land which God gave to his descendants. These verses remind us that "by faith he [Abram] dwelt in the land of promise as in a foreign country, dwelling in tents with Isaac and Ja-cob, the heirs with him of the same promise; for he waited for the city which has founda-tions, whose builder and maker is God."

Whatever God intended ultimately for Abram, it was far more than he could imagine from God's statement of these covenant promises. What God intended ultimately for Abram and for us became clear only as the centuries passed, and as Scripture revealed *how* God would keep the wonderful promises He had made.

GOD MAKES A FORMAL COVENANT WITH ABRAM   *(Genesis 15:1–21)*

Abram now lived in the land of Canaan. For some ten years Abram and his wife Sarai, with their flocks and servants, had wandered as nomads in the land God promised Abram's descendants were to inherit (Gen. 16:3). But Abram was now 85 and Sarai 75, and they were childless.

When God appeared to Abram again, promising to be his shield and "exceedingly great reward" (Gen. 15:1), Abram was frustrated. He asked, "LORD, what will you give me, seeing I go childless, and the heir of my house is Eliezer of Damascus?" (Gen. 15:2).

In essence Abram was saying, "LORD, what meaning does any reward You give me have, as long as I have no children?"

This challenge led to the formal restatement of two promises recorded in Genesis 12. Significantly, the two promises related to Abram's childless state: the promise of descendants and the promise that Abram's descendants would inherit the land of Canaan.

"So shall your descendants be" (Genesis 15:4, 5). Abram's concern over his childless state was understandable. God responded to that concern by promising, "One who will come from your own body shall be your heir" (Gen. 15:4). If this were not enough, God brought Abram outside his tent and told him to look to the heavens and count the stars, "if you are able to number them."

Even though only about three thousand stars are visible to the naked eye from any hemisphere, the stars are in fact beyond our ability to count. "So," God promised Abram, "shall your descendants be."

Abram would have a son, and in time he would have so many descendants that it would be impossible for a human being to number them.

THE IMPORTANCE OF SONS IN THE ANCIENT WORLD

Anyone who has wanted children but was unable to have them can sympathize with Abram and Sarai in their old age. But in the world of Abram, there were even greater pressures to have sons. The Story of Aqhat tells of a banquet Danil provided for the gods in an effort to move them to give him a son. In the story, the god Ba'al adds his appeal to that of Danil, and in the process suggests a number of practical and religious reasons why having a son was so important in the ancient world.

> Put a son in his palace.
> A son . . .
> To erect a stele for his ancestral gods,
>   To build a family shrine in the sanctuary.
> A son . . .
> To free Danil's spirit from death,
>   To guard his footsteps from the earth to underworld.
> A son—Aqhat . . .
> To enslave those who revolt against Danil,
>   To drive away those who invade his father's land.
> A son strong enough . . .
> To take Danil's hand,
>   —when he is drunk.
> To put Danil's arm over his shoulder,
>   —when he is full of wine.
> A son . . .
> To eat a funeral meal in the temple of Ba'al,
>   To offer sacrifice in the house of El.
> To patch Danil's roof when it leaks,
>   To wash Danil's clothes when they are dirty.

For Abram, of course, the motivation was even stronger. Abram needed a son if God's promises to him were to be fulfilled and if God's purposes through Abram were to be achieved. No wonder Abram asked, "What does reward matter as long as I am childless?" (cf. Gen. 15:2).

God promised a childless Abram more descendants than all the stars he could count.

"He believed in the LORD, and He accounted it to him for righteousness" (Genesis 12:6). This pivotal verse, discussed above, makes two statements.

He believed God. The *Theological Dictionary of the Old Testament* points out that the Hebrew word here means that "he relied on, gave credence to a message or considered it to be true, trusted in someone" (1:308). It is not that Abram had a general but hazy trust in God. What the passage asserts is that Abram relied on God's specific word, and considered what God said to be trustworthy and true. Abram truly believed that his descendants would be innumerable.

He accounted it to him for righteousness. The Hebrew word for "accounted" is used here in a legal sense. God counted Abram's faith as righteousness. Or, God credited faith to Abram's account as righteousness. This pivotal Old Testament verse tells us that God accepts faith in

His promise in place of a righteousness which neither Abram nor you and I possess!

This too is a grace gift from God. God did not have to accept faith in His promises and declare those who believe righteous. Yet this is exactly what the Lord did for Abram—and exactly what He does for us when we hear the promise of forgiveness of sins in Jesus, and by faith accept Him as our Savior.

"How shall I know that I will inherit it?" (Genesis 15:8). Abram believed God's promise. It would be wrong to take his question as an expression of doubt, as some do. Yet when God announced that "I am the LORD, who brought you out of Ur of the Chaldeans, to give you this land to inherit it" (Gen. 15:7), Abram did say, "How shall I know?"

A survey of Jewish and Christian commentators on this verse shows considerable confusion. Some Jewish sages suggest that the verse means "by what merit will I know my descendants will inherit the land," and answer that it is by the merit of the sacrifices described in the chapter. Other sages take the verse to mean, "How will I be able to show the nations that I and my descendants truly have title to Canaan?"

Christian commentators note that requests for a confirming sign occur elsewhere in Scripture, and that such signs are given in response to faith, not to unbelief (cf. Judg. 6:36–40; 2 Kin. 20:8–11).

However, the critical issue here is an apparent conflict between "Abram believed" and his question, "How shall I know?" The best answer is that the statement "Abram believed" describes Abram's *subjective* state. Abram's innermost self responded to God's promise, and he trusted God implicitly. He believed God.

In contrast, Abram's request was for *objective* confirmation: "How shall I know?"

Certainly God was not offended by Abram's request, because the Lord immediately provided objective confirmation. He did so by telling Abram to prepare animals for a *solemn covenant-making ceremony.*

We saw in chapter 1 that a covenant, a *b^erit,* was a legally binding, formal contract or agreement. God was now preparing to enter into just this kind of objective agreement with Abram, formally binding Himself to do what He had promised. This formal covenant, as recorded in tradition and later in Scripture, has provided the foundation of Israel's conviction that God truly did give Israel the promised land.

"He cut them in two" (Genesis 15:9, 10). Abram prepared for the covenant-making ceremony by dividing animals in two and placing the pieces side by side, leaving a path between the pieces. Much evidence exists in ancient Near Eastern texts that animals were slaughtered in treaty contract ceremonies. Some of the texts indicate that the two parties to a treaty walked between the parts of the freshly killed animals. Whatever the symbolism of this act, there is no doubt that this was one of the most binding of ancient *b^erits,* which some have called a "covenant of blood."

"A deep sleep fell upon Abram" (Genesis 15:12). That evening, after the animals were prepared for the treaty ceremony, Abram slept and had a vision. God told Abram that his descendants would become slaves in the land of Egypt, but that after 400 years God would judge Egypt and Abram's descendants would return to Canaan. The coming centuries would witness God's faithfulness to His promises to Abram.

"A burning torch that passed between those pieces" (Genesis 15:17). Normally both parties to this kind of covenant sealed the agreement by passing between the pieces of the animals. But in this case the Lord alone, represented by the fiery symbols, bound Himself in the covenant ceremony. Abram, who slept, was free of any obligation. God unilaterally bound Himself to keep the promises He had made: "To your descendants I have given this land."

The description in Genesis 15 of God executing a formal covenant with Abraham fo-cuses our attention on two of the seven promises recorded in Genesis 12. God had stated His intention to bless Abram, to make him a great nation, to give him a great name, and to bless all peoples through him. And God had stated that He would make Abram a great nation and establish that nation in the land of Canaan. Now these last two promises—the promise of multiplied descendants and the promise of Canaan as a homeland—are given formal expression in a binding, unilateral covenant that God made with His servant Abram.

GOD CONFIRMS HIS COVENANT WITH ABRAM *(Genesis 17:1–8, 19)*

It was fourteen years after God executed the formal covenant with Abram described in Genesis 15 that the Lord appeared to him again. In the interim, Abram had a son by his wife's servant, Hagar. This was a common practice in Abram's world. A childless wife might give her slave to her husband as a surrogate. Any child born to the slave was considered to be the child of the wife.

But when God appeared to Abram when he was 99 years old, the Lord announced that Abram would have a son by his wife, Sarai (Gen. 17:16). The descendants promised to Abram would be hers as well as his.

In this third statement of the Abrahamic covenant, the Lord again emphasized descendants and the land. And God expanded one of the "I will" statements of Genesis 12.

"I will multiply you exceedingly" (Genesis 17:2). Earlier God had promised to make Abram a great nation (Gen. 12:2). When the covenant was given formal expression, God told Abram his descendants would be innumerable. Now God further expanded this promise, saying, "I will multiply you exceedingly" and adding, "You shall be a father of many nations" (Gen. 17:4). Not just one nation would trace its origin to Abram; many would.

God further emphasized, "I will make you exceedingly fruitful; and I will make nations of you, and kings shall come from you" (Gen. 17:6).

"Your name shall be Abraham" (Genesis 17:5). At this point God changed Abram's name to Abraham. The name *Abram* means "exalted father." That meaning is intensified by the change in name, which also implies a change in status. *Abram* was to be the father of a (one) nation (Gen. 12:2). With his name universalized, *Abraham* would be the father of many nations! Multiplied peoples in addition to Israel would look back to Abraham as their fountainhead.

"I will establish My covenant" (Genesis 17:7). This confirmation of the covenant "between Me and you and your descendants after you" is now further explained.

"An everlasting covenant." The descendants of Abraham would inherit the promises made to him. But, as history and Scripture demonstrate, any given generation could benefit from the promises only by exercising and demonstrating a faith like that of Abraham.

"To be God to you and your descendants after you." Earlier God had said to Abram, "I will bless you." Now the Lord further explained the promise of blessing. God would bless Abraham and his descendants by being God to them.

While God's blessings do encompass what we call prosperity or success, there is no doubt that in Scripture all these hinge on personal relationship with God. It was because God was Israel's God that Abraham's physical descendants could be blessed. And it is only because God is our God through faith in Christ that every spiritual blessing (Eph. 1:3) is available today to us, who by faith have become Abraham's spiritual descendants (see Rom. 4:16).

"I give to you and your descendants after you the land" (Genesis 17:8). Once again, God confirmed His gift of the land of Canaan to Abraham and his descendants as "an everlasting possession." And again God stated, "And I will be their God."

Taken together, the original statement of God's intent (Gen. 12), the covenant execution (Gen. 15), and the covenant confirmation (Gen. 17) express what God intends to do in human history. These promises gave no details about how God intended to carry out His intent and fulfill His promises. Nevertheless they do identify certain vital elements of God's plan.

Through Abraham and his descendants, God planned from the beginning to bless all humankind. And through Abraham's descendants, He has done just that. Through the people springing from Abraham, Isaac, and Jacob, humanity has been given God's written Word. And from this people came His Son, Jesus Christ, our Savior.

THE OUTWORKING OF THE COVENANT

In chapter 1 we noted that the major biblical covenants are eschatological in character. They point to history's end for their ultimate fulfillment. Yet in many ways benefits promised in God's covenants have already been experienced by Old and New Testament believers. It's important, then, to note how the promises God made to Abraham have worked out in history.

"I will make you a great nation" (Genesis 12:2). This promise implies the "many descendants" promised in Genesis 15 and 17. But the word *nation* (*goy*) implies more than an ethnic identity. Abraham's descendants are to have a national identity, with their own territory and government.

The covenant promise first given to Abraham was transmitted to Abraham's son Isaac (Gen. 17:21) and then to his son Jacob (Israel) (Gen. 28:13), and then on to the tribes which sprang from Jacob's sons. Some 500 years after Abraham, the Lord identified the Israelites, whom Moses led out of Egypt, as the descendants of Abraham, Isaac, and Jacob and heirs to the land promised the patriarchs.

While the Israelites, the Jewish people, are the descendants of Abraham, Isaac, and Ja-

A Summary of the Abrahamic Covenant

Gen. 12	Gen 15	Gen 17
Make Abram great nation	Descendants uncountable	Multiply exceedingly Make many nations Many kings from
Bless Abram		Be God to Abraham Be God to descendants

Make Abram's name great
Abram to be a blessing
Bless, curse those who
    bless, curse Abram
All clans to be blessed
    in Abram		

Give land to Abram's descendants	Abram to inherit the land Land's extent defined	Descendants to have Canaan as everlasting inheritance

cob, they have not always been a nation. In fact, it was not until the time of David, around 1000 B.C., a millennium after Abraham's day, that the Israelites were united and established as a nation. The kingdom of Israel, which was established by David, lasted only through the reign of his son, Solomon. In 930 B.C., the united kingdom was divided into two independent nations, Israel in the north, and Judah in the south.

The nation of Israel lasted only until 722 B.C., when it was overrun by Assyria and the Jewish population was deported and resettled in the East. The nation of Judah survived to 586 B.C., when it was overrun by Babylon, and its population was also deported and resettled outside Canaan.

In spite of the fact that a small group of Jews returned to Jerusalem and resettled part of the Holy Land, no Jewish state was established in Canaan [Palestine] until 1948, when the modern state of Israel was formed. Between 586 B.C. and A.D. 1948, no Jewish nation existed anywhere in the world.

Does this mean that God broke the ancient covenant promises that He gave to Abraham and his descendants? As we'll see when we look at the Mosaic Covenant, not at all! Under Mosaic Law, God was obligated to bless given generations of Israelites only when they obeyed His commandments and worshiped Him alone. Israel was legally expelled from the land for repeatedly turning from God to idola-

try, and for their failure to live the holy life laid out in the Law. But even in the darkest of times, the Old Testament prophets looked forward confidently to a future in which God's promises would be fulfilled.

Isaiah, writing during the time when the Northern Kingdom was overrun by the Assyrians, envisioned a coming day when a deliverer would be born of David's line:

Of the increase of His government
    and peace
There will be no end.
Upon the throne of David and
    over His kingdom,
To order it and establish it with
    judgment and justice
From that time forward, even
    Forever (Isa. 9:7).

According to Isaiah, Israel would again be a nation, and a descendant of David would govern it.

This same conviction was expressed by Jeremiah, who lived through the Babylonian conquest of Judah (cf. Jer. 33:15, 16). Ezekiel, a contemporary of Jeremiah, gave one of the Old Testament's most impressive predictions of national restoration. Ezekiel was given a vision of a valley filled with dry bones, which he reported in chapter 37. Ezekiel was told to prophesy, and he saw the scattered bones come together, saw flesh cover them, and saw God's spirit restore them to life. Ezekiel was

In the valley of dry bones, Ezekiel found hope for Israel's future.

❖

then told that the bones represented the whole house of Israel, scattered among the nations. God would cause the people to come back to the land of Israel, even though they were spiritually dead. There God would next cover the bones with flesh. Then, at last, God would put His spirit in them "and you shall live, and I will place you in your own land" (Ezek. 37:14). Furthermore, God said through Ezekiel, "Surely I will take the children of Israel from among the nations, wherever they have gone, and will gather them from every side and bring them into their own land, and I will make them one nation in the land" (Ezek. 37:21, 22).

The Old Testament, then, does not suggest that God has reneged on the covenant promise that Abraham's descendants would become a nation. According to the Old Testament prophets who lived through and after the fall of the last Jewish kingdom, the promise of nationhood would surely be kept one day—a day that is still future in our time, a day that will dawn as history draws to a close.

"I will bless you" (Genesis 12:2). The promise was made to Abram, and it was kept. Abram was blessed with riches. He was blessed with victory when forced to fight to recover his nephew Lot from a hostile raiding force (Gen. 14:1–16). When Abram lied about his relationship with his wife, and she was taken into a harem in Egypt (Gen. 12:10–20), God not only guarded Sarai from a sexual encounter; He also protected Abram from punishment by the pharaoh. At the end of Abraham's life, as Genesis 24:1 states, "The LORD had blessed Abraham in all things." This covenant promise was kept indeed.

But Genesis 17:7 expanded and perhaps explained the concept of blessing. There God said He would "be God to you and your descendants." In this verse, God offered Himself to Abraham's descendants. The personal relationship with God that Abraham enjoyed, and the blessings that flow from that relationship, were to be accessible to Israel. The psalmist picked up this thought and expressed it in Psalm 33:12. He said, "Blessed is the nation whose God is the LORD, The people He has chosen as His own inheritance." And the psalmist went on to explain,

> Behold, the eye of the LORD is on
>   those who fear Him,
> On those who hope in His mercy,
> To deliver their soul from death,
> And to keep them alive in famine
>   (Ps. 33:18, 19)

The promise to be God to Israel is often repeated in the Old Testament. As God said in the time of Solomon, "I will dwell among the children of Israel, and will not forsake My people Israel" (1 Kings 6:13; cf. 1 Sam. 13:22; 2 Sam. 7:24; Ezek. 37:27).

There is also an eschatological aspect to this promise of blessing. Ezekiel looked ahead to the day when a descendant of David would shepherd God's people in their own land, and quoted the Lord, who said, "I will make them and the places all around My hill a blessing; and I will cause showers to come down in their season; there will be showers of blessing. . . . Thus they shall know that I, the LORD their God, am with them, and they, the house of Israel, are My people" (Ezek. 34:26, 30).

God's promise to bless, by being God for them, was a promise that any generation or individual could claim. God kept His word and has been God for Israel throughout history. Yet so often God's Old Testament people failed to claim Him as their own.

Psalm 33 reminds us that relationships are reciprocal. We can offer ourselves to another person, but only when that person responds to our offer will an actual relationship exist. Thus, while the Lord then and now was God for Israel, many generations of the Old Testament failed to respond to Him as Abraham had.

Today God has shown Himself in Christ to be God for all people. And God still waits outside the heart's door, eager to enter our lives and bless us.

How do we respond to God's willingness to be God for us in our own time? We should respond as Abraham did, and as the psalmist described it:

> Our soul waits for the LORD;
> He is our help and our shield.
> For our hearts shall rejoice in Him,
> Because we have trusted in His
>   holy name.
> Let your mercy, O LORD, be upon us,
> Just as we hope in You (Ps. 33:
>   20–22).

"And make your name great" (Genesis 12:2). This is the third covenant promise expressed in Genesis 12. God committed Himself to make Abraham's name "great." The reference here is to lasting honor and fame, a goal fixed on by many who desperately seek to find some significance to their lives beyond the few short years we have here on earth.

Shelley's poem, "Ozymandias," captured both the passion for greatness of ancient conquerors and the futility of that passion.

> I met a traveller from an antique land,
> Who said, "Two vast and trunkless legs of stone
> Stand in the desert. . . . Near them, on the sand,
> Half sunk a shattered visage lies, whose frown
> And wrinkled lip, and sneer of cold command,
> Tell that its sculptor well those passions read
> Which yet survive, stamped on these lifeless things,
> The hand that mocked them, and the heart that
>   fed;
> And on the pedestal, these words appear:
> 'My name is Ozymandias, King of Kings,
> Look upon my Works, ye Mighty, and despair!'
> Nothing beside remains. Round the decay
> Of that colossal wreck, boundless and bare
> The lone and level sands stretch far away."

Ozymandias has been long forgotten. Yet the name of Abraham—who built no empire and erected no statues, who lived a quiet, nomadic life but who responded with faith when God spoke to him—truly has become great.

Today Abraham is looked upon as the source of both the Arab and Jewish peoples. Abraham is respected as the fountainhead by three of the world's great religions: Islam, Judaism, and Christianity. Abraham is rightly considered a great man, not only famous but also significant, by hundreds of millions today, some four thousand years after he lived and died. What's more, not a single generation in all that span of time has lacked those who have honored Abraham as a truly great man.

God kept His covenant promise to Abraham, far more fully and completely than Abraham could ever have imagined. Even as God is "able to do exceedingly abundantly above all that we ask or think, according to the power that works in us" (Eph. 3:20).

"And you shall be a blessing" (Genesis 12:2). This is the fourth statement of God's intent found in the original statement of His covenant promises to Abraham.

While it appears to duplicate a similar promise in Genesis 12:3, the emphasis here is on Abraham himself. He is not simply the conduit through which blessing will flow to others. He is the fountainhead, the spring from which the waters of blessing will flow.

Thus, the emphasis here is on the role of Abraham in history rather than on the blessings which ultimately will come through his descendants. Certainly Abraham's role in history is unique. In choosing Abram, God set in motion a plan to redeem humanity through the descendants of one man. In this sense, Abraham is himself a blessing to all.

"I will bless those who bless you, and I will curse him who curses you" (Genesis 12:3). This promise functioned in Abram's day and has also worked itself out in the history of the Jewish people. When pharaoh took Abram's wife into his harem, even though unwittingly, God "plagued Pharaoh and his house with great plagues" (Gen. 12:17). Later, after the Israelites had been enslaved in Egypt, God punished that land with devastating judgments (Ex. 8—11).

The Old Testament correlates the rise and fall of mighty empires with their treatment of the Jewish people. God called Assyria to discipline His people (Isa. 10:5), yet the arrogant Assyrians went too far. So Isaiah quoted God as saying, "I will punish the fruit of the arrogant heart of the king of Assyria," (Isa. 10:12). In God's own time, Assyria fell to the Babylonians, whose rise to power was sudden and unexpected.

Isaiah also predicted the rise of Persia. A hundred years before that empire emerged, Isaiah even named the Persian ruler, Cyrus. Isaiah makes it clear that God replaced the Babylonian Empire with the Persian Empire so Cyrus could free God's people by permitting them to return to the land from which they had been torn by the Babylonians.

Says of Cyrus, "He is My shepherd,
And he shall perform all My
     pleasure,
Saying to Jerusalem, "You shall be
     built,"
And to the temple, "Your foundation
     shall
     be laid" (Isa. 44:28).

The cursing and the blessing of peoples who curse and bless Abraham's descendants may be delayed. But God does intervene to see to it that this promise to Abraham is kept.

Many see this principle at work even in the Christian era. Spain once rivaled England as a great power. Then a systematic persecution of the Jewish people and "conversions," Jews who had publicly converted to Catholicism, was carried out by the Spanish Inquisition. Within a century, Spain had been reduced to a third-class power.

More recently Nazi Germany initiated the Holocaust. Hitler's "thousand-year Reich" was crushed within a decade.

There are, of course, "natural" explanations for the rise and fall of nations. And yet believers are well aware that God often works through the flow of cause and effect to accomplish His purposes. And to keep His word.

"In you all the families of the earth shall be blessed" (Genesis 12:3). The earlier promise that Abraham would be a blessing draws attention to his role as the spring from which streams of blessing would flow. This promise looks ahead to the blessings themselves.

It was impossible for Abraham to guess what we know now about the blessings God intended to provide through him and his offspring. All that we know of God's plans and purposes, all that we know of His love and grace, has come to us in the Scriptures written by Abraham's descendants. Even more significantly, Jesus Christ in His human nature is a descendant of Abraham. And through Jesus all humankind is offered a salvation that can be claimed through a faith like that of Abraham. How wonderful these blessings are!

Yet what is stunning is that even greater blessing lies ahead. One day Jesus will return to earth, to take His place as King of kings. Then we will be raised from the dead, to reign with Jesus. One day this universe itself will flare out of existence and God will create a new heaven and earth. The last taint of sin will be removed, and we will enjoy a fellowship with God and others that we cannot begin to imagine.

Yes, all the families of the earth do trace God's blessings back to Abraham. And each individual who responds to God's promises as Abraham did, with faith, will be blessed endlessly.

"To your descendants I will give this land" (Genesis 12:7). As we've seen, this promise, first expressed in Genesis 12:7, is emphasized in both Genesis 15 and Genesis 17. In fact, the promises of descendants and their inheritance of the land of Canaan are closely linked throughout the Old Testament. These promises are repeated again and again.

Strikingly, the Israelites have never occupied the promised land to the full extent of God's land grant.

The entire land granted to Abraham's descendants has never been occupied, either by the ancient Israelites or the modern Jewish people. But the land commitment made in the Abrahamic covenant is repeated again and again throughout the Old Testament.

That covenant and the land grant were confirmed to Abraham's son Isaac (Gen. 26:3) and to his grandson Jacob (Gen. 28:13). Moses frequently mentioned the land in the first five books of the Old Testament. God told Moses that the Israelites in Egypt were the inheritors of the Abrahamic Covenant, saying, "I have also established My covenant with them, to give them the land of Canaan, the land of their pilgrimage, in which they [the patriarchs] were strangers" (Ex. 6:4).

At the end of Moses' life, as Israel stood poised on the edge of the Promised Land, God showed Moses Canaan from across the Jordan River, saying, "This is the land of which I swore to give Abraham, Isaac, and Jacob, saying, 'I will give it to your descendants' " (Deut. 34:4).

Under Moses' successor, Joshua, the Israelites defeated the Canaanites and did settle in the promised territory. Yet their occupation was partial at best. Then, some 450 years after Joshua's day, David unified the Israelites and extended the territory they had occupied some tenfold. For the first time a Hebrew nation was established in the Promised Land!

It would seem that the promise given to Abraham of a nation in Canaan for his descendants had at last been fulfilled. But even the united kingdom of David and Solomon failed to occupy all the land granted by God. And after Solomon's death, that kingdom was divided.

Through the next centuries, the fortunes of the two Hebrew kingdoms waxed and waned as rulers and their people turned to or away from God. For most of this time, the territory occupied by Judah and Israel fell far short of the land granted to Abraham's descendants.

It is fascinating, then, to see the ancient covenant promise that Abraham's descendants would possess the land repeated frequently in the writings of the prophets. After the fall of Israel to Assyria, Isaiah wrote, "The LORD will have mercy on Jacob, and will still chose Israel, and settle them in their own land" (Isa. 14:1).

Jeremiah and Ezekiel, who lived during the last days of Judah and witnessed the destruction of the last Hebrew kingdom, also referred to God's covenant promises as a basis for hope. God said through Jeremiah, "In those [future] days the house of Judah shall walk with the house of Israel, and they shall come together out of the land of the north to the land that I have given as an inheritance to your fathers" (Jer. 3:18; cf. also Jer. 30:3; 31:16; 32:37, 41; 33:7). Through Ezekiel God promised, "For I will take you from among the nations, gather you out of all countries, and bring you to your own land. . . . Then you shall dwell in the land that I gave to your fathers; you shall be My people, and I will be your God" (Ezek. 36:24, 28; cf. also Ezek. 37:25).

This covenant promise of Israel's occupation of the Promised Land, repeated again and again by the Old Testament prophets, has yet to be fulfilled.

In significant ways, then, the fulfillment of the ancient Abrahamic Covenant promises has been and is being worked out in history. Yet, the promises stated in this covenant provide the barest of outlines of the purposes God intends. The full extent of God's commitment, and His plan for achieving His purposes, have become clearer and clearer as the ages unfold. God also provides additional details concerning His plans in two other promise covenants—the Davidic Covenant and the New Covenant. As we study these covenants, God's good purposes for us and the world will become clear.

In particular, these covenants will unveil the central role of Jesus Christ in fulfilling all the covenant promises of God. All the promises of our Lord find their focus and fulfillment in Him.

THE SIGN OF THE COVENANT: CIRCUMCISION

God's covenant promises were given freely and unilaterally. While ultimately all find blessing in the promises given to Abraham, the promises were actually made to Abraham and his descendants. This leads to an important question. How are the "descendants" of Abraham to be identified?

Physical descent is not enough (Romans 9:6, 7). In Romans 9, Paul developed an important thought. He pondered the fact that while Jewish believers composed the earliest Christian church, not all Jews in his time accepted Jesus as the promised Messiah. Yet God had made His covenant commitments to Abraham and his descendants.

Paul explained rejection of the gospel by most Jews by pointing out that "they are not all Israel who are of Israel, nor are they all children because they are the seed of Abraham; but, 'In Isaac your seed shall be called' " (Rom. 9:6, 7). Paul's point is simple. Being a "descendant" of Abraham involves more than physical descent! Ishamael was Abraham's son, and thus Ishmael's descendants, the Arab peoples, are physical descendants of Abraham. But God did not give the covenant promises to Ishmael. The covenant promises made to Abraham were passed to Isaac, not Ishmael. Physical descent was never enough to qualify

a person as a "descendant" and thus an inheritor of the covenant promises.

Earlier in Romans, Paul noted another vital truth. Abraham's faith was accepted by God in place of the righteousness he did not have. God declared Abraham righteous "by faith." Paul argued from this that Abraham is the *spiritual father* of all who believe in God as he did, whether they are Jews or Gentiles biologically (Rom. 4:11)!

It follows that, throughout Old Testament history, only those Israelites who had a faith in God that was like Abraham's faith were his true descendants!

This insight helps us understand the tragic history of ancient Israel as recorded in the Old Testament. How can we explain the readiness of so many generations to abandon the Lord and turn aside to idolatry? How can we explain the fact that the Israelites were so often victimized by many powerful foreign enemies, in spite of God's covenant promises to them? Many generations failed to find God's blessing because, while they were Abraham's biological descendants, they were not Abraham's spiritual descendants. They were Jews. But they were unbelieving Jews.

Circumcision as a sign of covenant-faith (Genesis 17:9–14). Just before the birth of Isaac, when God reconfirmed the covenant promises He had given to Abraham earlier, the Lord added an unusual stipulation.

As for you, you shall keep My covenant, you and your descendants after you throughout their generations. . . . Every male child among you shall be circumcised . . . and it shall be a sign of the covenant between Me and you. . . . And the uncircumcised male child, who is not circumcised in the flesh of his foreskin, that person shall be cut off from his people; he has broken My covenant (Gen. 17:9–11, 14).

The "sign" of circumcision. There are three kinds of signs (`ot) in the OT. The first is a miraculous proof sign, which is given to convince the observer of something (cf. Ex. 7:3–5). The second is an acted-out prophecy, designed to resemble the situation a prophet describes (see Ezek. 4:3). The third kind of sign is mnemonic, designed to serve as a reminder. In our exploration of the Noahic covenants, we saw that the rainbow served as such a sign. God promised to look on the rainbow and remember [that is, to act on or keep] His promise never again to destroy the world by water.

Circumcision, as a "sign of the [Abrahamic] covenant," falls into this third category. It is a mnemonic sign: a reminder. But unlike the rainbow, circumcision is not a reminder to God of His promise. Circumcision is a reminder to Israel that they are God's covenant people.

The significance of circumcision. When Paul reminds us in Romans that not every biological descendant of Abraham is a spiritual descendant of Abraham, he also provides a clue to the significance of circumcision.

Circumcision as a sign of the Abrahamic covenant was so important that an uncircumcised Israelite, even though a descendant of Abraham, Isaac, and Jacob, had no claim to covenant relationship with God. He was cut off: from his people, from Abraham, and from God. At a bare minimum, an Israelite had to have enough trust in God to heed His word about circumcision if he and his offspring were to be counted among the covenant people.

Circumcision was significant as an indication that an individual believed in the God who had spoken to Abraham and made the covenant promises. It provided a way in which each generation could express faith by claiming its own participation in the promises God made to Abraham.

What is more, circumcision stamped in the very flesh of every male a reminder of God Himself. Those who failed to keep God's covenant by ignoring circumcision displayed a lack of faith in the God of the covenant, and it was the lack of a faith like Abraham's which cut them off from God's blessings.

Circumcision thus was a reminder to every Israelite that biological descent from Abraham was not enough to establish a personal relationship with Abraham's God. To have a vital relationship with Abraham's God, one must have a faith like Abraham's

In this way, this Old Testament sign supported and reinforced the truth Paul developed in Romans. Ultimately, relationship with God is based on faith.

WHAT WE HAVE LEARNED ABOUT THE ABRAHAMIC COVENANT

Earlier we saw that a "covenant" is a legally binding instrument by which promises were made in the ancient world. God made such a commitment to Noah and to all living things when He promised never again to destroy life on earth by water.

Centuries and possibly millenniums later, God chose one man, Abraham, and entered into a covenant with him and with his descendants. This covenant provides a key to understanding the Bible, for it reveals the purposes of God that the Scripture traces through history. Specifically, what we have learned about the Abrahamic Covenant is:

The Abrahamic Covenant expresses God's intent. The series of "I will" statements made to Abraham states what God intends to do, from Abraham's lifetime on into the future.

God stated He would create a nation from Abraham's descendants. This He did in the past, but according to the prophets, the complete fulfillment of this promise still lies ahead.

God stated He would bless Abraham. This God did during Abraham's lifetime by being God to the patriarch. God later extended this promise to be God to Abraham's descendants as well.

God stated He would make Abraham's name great. This God has done, as Abraham has been revered by millions through all of the years that have passed since Abraham died.

God stated Abraham would be a blessing. God fulfilled this promise, in that Abraham is the spring from which multiplied blessings have flowed.

God stated that He would bless those who blessed Abraham and curse those who cursed him. God kept this promise to Abraham during his lifetime, and extended it to cover Abraham's descendants. We can see this principle at work in Old Testament and modern times.

God stated that in Abraham all the families of the earth would be blessed. This promise has been fulfilled and is being fulfilled today. Yet, complete fulfillment of the promises lies ahead.

God stated that He would give the land of Canaan to Abraham's descendants. This promise was partially fulfilled in Israel's history during the kingdom period. Yet, the prophets foresaw a complete fulfillment of this promise in what is yet future.

The Abrahamic Covenant, then, gives an extensive preview of what God intends to do. But just how He will accomplish His purposes, and just what wonders each statement of intent involves, has unfolded gradually as God added revelation upon revelation through His word.

Jesus was the culmination of the covenants.

THE ABRAHAMIC COVENANT IS A COVENANT OF GRACE

God chose Abraham in spite of the fact that he was an idolator, and freely made promises to him. There was no merit in Abraham that caused God to act as He did. God's relationship with Abraham was rooted in, and is an expression of, pure grace.

THE ABRAHAMIC COVENANT INVITED A FAITH RESPONSE

Abraham responded to God's promises with faith. He displayed faith by leaving his homeland at God's direction. And Abraham believed God's promise of innumerable descendants, in spite of the fact that he was old and his wife Sarai had ceased menstruating (cf. Rom. 4:19).

The covenant also invited a continuing faith response from Abraham's descendants. This response is symbolized in circumcision,

which functioned as a sign of the covenant. Through circumcision, each new generation of Israelites was reminded that biological descent from Abraham was not enough. A faith response to God was essential if a person was to live in covenant relationship with the Lord.

THE ABRAHAMIC COVENANT IMPLIES GOD'S SOVEREIGNTY

The promises given in the Abrahamic Covenant would be worked out over the span of thousands of years. Only a God whose power is unlimited, and whose control of future events is sure, could make and keep the promises the Lord made to Abraham.

THE ABRAHAMIC COVENANT FORESHADOWS THE WORK OF CHRIST

While the means by which God intended to keep the promises made to Abraham remained a mystery in Abraham's day, we know today that these promises find their focus and fulfillment in Jesus Christ. He is the promised seed of Abraham; He is the one whose coming made it possible for God to bless all the families of the world.

As we go on in our look at the covenants, each of which adds additional information about how God's purposes are to be achieved, we will understand much more clearly how all the covenants *anticipate* Christ.

CHAPTER 4

A LAW TO LIVE BY:

THE MOSAIC COVENANT

Exodus 19—24; Deuteronomy

Every family needs rules. In a healthy family, the rules are designed to provide a structure within which children can grow to maturity. Without rules—without structure during the growing years—maturity can be slow in coming.

So it was with biblical Israel. God had chosen Abraham's descendants to be His covenant people, but more than 400 years had passed since God made His promises to Abraham. It was time for the Lord to provide the rules, the structure, that Israel would need to mature in their faith and in their relationship to Him.

God's call of Moses and His intervention on the Israelite's behalf was in harmony with a clause in the Abrahamic Covenant which promised the land of Canaan to Abraham's descendants. As God told Moses, "I have also established My covenant with them, to give them the land of Canaan." And so God promised "I will bring you into the land which I swore to give to Abraham, Isaac, and Jacob, and I will give it to you as a heritage" (Ex. 6:4, 8).

The story of Israel's Exodus from Egypt is among the most familiar in the Bible. Moses led about two million people out of Egypt and into the Sinai Peninsula. God showed His continuing presence with the Israelites, opening the Red Sea for them, providing them with manna to eat, and guiding them by a visible cloudy-fiery pillar.

That pillar led the Israelites to Mt. Sinai and there, in one of the most significant events recorded in the Old Testament, God through Moses gave His people a law to live by. That law is referred to in several ways in the Bible. It is called the Mosaic Covenant, the Old Covenant, the Law of Moses, and frequently just "the Law."

While the law given Israel by God was a *b*ᵉ*rit*, or covenant, it differs significantly from the Abrahamic and later biblical covenants. These others were unilateral covenants of promise, in which God bound Himself to do what He promised, regardless of what recipients of the promises might do. In contrast, the Mosaic or Law Covenant is a bilateral agreement, which specifies the obligations of both parties to the covenant.

Moses received the Law on Mount Sinai.

THE CONTENT OF THE MOSAIC OR LAW COVENANT

When the Israelites arrived at Mt. Sinai, Moses was called to the mount and given a law for God's Old Testament people. While many think of the law simply as the Ten Commandments, much more than a moral code was included in biblical law. The Law of Moses had rules for deciding civil and criminal cases. The Law of Moses ordained a priesthood for Israel, and set out a sacrificial system. The Law of Moses defined "clean" and "unclean" foods, which could and could not be eaten by Israelites. The Law of Moses regulated marriage and family life, military operations, worship and religious holidays, borrowing and lending, farming, the care of the poor,

relationships with aliens, hygiene, men's and women's clothing, the treatment of infectious skin diseases, and many other matters. All the major events of a person's life, from birth to marriage to child-rearing to old age and death, were dealt with in Moses' Law.

Jewish tradition says that there are not just Ten Commandments in Moses' Law: the Old Testament contains 613 commandments that the Israelites were to observe!

Perhaps the best way to sum up Mosaic Law is to say that it gave complete instructions to Israel on how they were to live in fellowship with God and one another. No wonder Moses' words to the Israelites recorded in Deuteronomy 4 celebrated the Law as a gracious gift.

MOUNT SINAI
Where God gave
Moses the Law.

Surely I have taught you statutes and judgments, just as the LORD my God commanded me, that you should act according to them in the land which you go to possess. Therefore be careful to observe them; for this is your wisdom and your understanding in the sight of the peoples who will hear all these statutes, and say, "Surely this great nation is a wise and understanding people." For what great nation is there that has God so near to it, as the LORD our God is to us, for whatever reason we may call upon Him? And what great nation is there that has such statutes and righteous judgments as are in all this law which I set before you this day? (Deut. 4:5–8).

In this passage Moses stated a truth reflected in Romans. Whatever one may say about Old Testament Law, it "is holy, and the commandments holy and just and good" (Rom. 7:12).

THE HISTORIC FUNCTION OF MOSAIC LAW

We noted earlier that both the Noahic and the Abrahamic covenants state what God intends to do in the future. There are no ifs, ands, or buts.

God committed himself to Noah and all living creatures. As long as earth remains, season will follow season and no cataclysm will wipe out all life (Gen. 8:21, 22).

God committed himself to Abraham and his descendants. God would plant a Hebrew nation in Canaan, bless those who blessed and

curse those who cursed His people, and through Abraham bless all the families on earth (Gen. 12:2, 3).

Each of these covenants was in essence a statement of God's intent—a promise which God was committed to keep.

In contrast, the Law Covenant is not a statement of God's intent. The Law Covenant is not a promise. In making the Law Covenant, God called on Israel to *agree to live by His rules.* And Israel did agree! Yet in that agreement, by which the people gave their consent to be governed by God's Word, God did spell out what He would do when Israel was obedient to His commands. And God did spell out what He would do when Israel was disobedient to His Word.

We can perhaps look at these statements of consequence as promises, for they do tell just how God would react to the choices made by His people.

How then is the Law Covenant related to the promises stated in the Abrahamic Covenant? Simply, the Law provided a way for any Israelite generation to experience that covenant's blessings.

In an earlier chapter I suggested an analogy. A person has been promised $100 million to be given to her at age 50. At age 25, she can only look ahead with some frustration. The $100 million is hers. But it does her no good here and now.

But what if the bequest to the $100 million included a way for her to draw out the interest on the principal each year? What if she could draw the interest only if she continued to live in the family home at least nine months of the year?

This analogy helps us understand the historic function of Mosaic Law and its relationship to the Abrahamic Covenant. God's promise to Abraham and his descendants will be completely fulfilled at history's end. Yet, each generation of Israelites could access the promised blessings in their own day—if they were loyal to God and lived by His Law!

The historic function of Moses' Law, then, was to provide a way for each generation of

Abraham's descendants to know blessing in their own time.

THE COVENANT STRUCTURE OF MOSAIC LAW

The covenants of promise, such as the Abrahamic Covenant, did not quite fit the normal pattern of covenants in the ancient world. The covenants of promise are unilateral covenants: they state what God intends to do, no matter what. In giving these statements formal expression as covenants, God bound Himself alone. The promise covenants are one-party agreements, not two-party agreements.

The Law Covenant is a very typical covenant that does fit the pattern of Middle Eastern covenants.

THE COVENANT STRUCTURE OF EXODUS 19—24

When we come to the Law or Mosaic Covenant, we find that there is a clear parallel between its statement in Scripture and another two-party agreement well known in the ancient world. The first statement of the Law Covenant in Scripture, in Exodus 19—24, follows the pattern established by the Hittite suzerainty treaty. This type of covenant was executed between a superior and an inferior. The superior, possibly a ruler or a dominant nation, stated the conditions of the relationship, and the inferior agreed.

Each of the elements of this kind of treaty are found in the Exodus passage. These elements are:

In the Exodus passage, God identified Himself as "the LORD your God, who brought you out of the land of Egypt" (Ex. 20:2). God then presented Ten Commandments which Israel is to obey, and illustrated their application by specific cases (Ex. 20:2—23:19). The Lord then stated the consequences of covenant keeping and breaking, by stating what He would do in each case (Ex. 23:20–33). The Israelites responded by accepting the covenant with its stipulations and conditions: "All the words which the LORD has said we will do," (Ex. 24:3).

The covenant was then formally executed, as animals were sacrificed and their blood was sprinkled on the altar and the people (Ex. 24:5–8).

THE COVENANT STRUCTURE OF DEUTERONOMY

The Law Covenant included more than the Ten Commandments listed in Exodus 20. Elements of the Law, and thus of the Law covenant, are found in four of the five books of Moses.

In fact, the entire book of Deuteronomy is written as a covenant. The historical prologue is contained in Deuteronomy 1:6—3:29. Basic stipulations are given in 5:1—11:32, followed by detailed stipulations in Deuteronomy 12:1—26:19. Blessings for keeping the stipulations are listed in 28:1–14, and the consequences of breaking the covenant are spelled out in 28:15–68. Deuteronomy 29:1—30:10 reviews the entire treaty between God and Israel.

THE CONSEQUENCES OF KEEPING AND BREAKING THE LAW COVENANT

The consequences of obedience and disobedience spelled out in Deuteronomy 28 are

Preamble	The superior is identified and his titles are given.	Ex. 20:1a
Prologue	The deeds of the superior on behalf of the subordinate are recounted.	Ex. 20:1b
Stipulations	The principles on which the relationship is to be based are stated.	Ex. 20:2–17
		Ex. 21:1—23:19
Consequences	Blessings and curses associated with keeping, breaking the covenant are specified.	Ex. 23:20–33
Oath	The subordinate gives an oath accepting the covenant and its provisions.	Ex. 24:1–8

significant. Here we sense echoes of the promise covenants, for God states in clear and unmistakable terms what He will do *for* those who keep the Law, and *to* those who break it.

Because of these provisions, we can perhaps call the Mosaic Covenant a unilateral covenant, for it does contain statements of what God intends to do and most surely will do.

Blessings for obedience (Deuteronomy 28: 1–14).

The blessings God promised for keeping His law are available to any generation of Israelites. "All these blessings" God promised, "shall come upon you and overtake you, because you obey the voice of the LORD your God" (Deut. 28:2). Moses went on, "And the LORD will grant you plenty of goods, in the fruit of your body, in the increase of your livestock, and in the produce of your ground, in the land of which the LORD swore to your fathers to give you. The LORD will open to you His good treasure, the heavens, to give the rain to your land in its season, and to bless all the work of your hand" (Deut. 28:11, 12).

Curses for disobedience (Deuteronomy 28: 15–68).

The list of consequences for failure to obey God's law is much longer than the list of blessings for obedience. To those generations which turn away from the Lord and His way of life, "The LORD will send on you cursing, confusion, and rebuke in all that you set your hand to do, until you are destroyed and until you perish quickly, because of the wickedness of your doings in which you have forsaken Me" (Deut. 28:20).

Among the list of disasters ordained for continuing rejection of God and His ways, Deuteronomy promises that God "will scatter you among all peoples, from one end of the earth to the other." The text adds, "Among those nations you shall find no rest, nor shall the sole of your foot have a resting place, but there the LORD will give you a trembling heart, failing eyes, and anguish of soul. Your life shall hang in doubt before you; you shall fear day and night, and have no assurance of life" (Deut. 28:64–66). How tragically Israel of the Old Testament and modern Jewry has seen this prediction fulfilled.

"The LORD will grant you plenty . . . in the produce of your ground."

Choosing actions, not consequences. The list of blessings and curses spelled out in the Mosaic Covenant brings us face to face with one of life's realities. Today as in biblical times we choose our actions. But we cannot choose our consequences. Yet, the contemporary fiction that human beings can make sinful moral and spiritual choices without experiencing painful consequences seems to be embedded in our culture. TV and movies depict promiscuity for pleasure as a natural and normal way of life. But in real life, those who follow the example set in the media learn too late the pain that follows—if not in unwanted pregnancy or disease, certainly in personal corruption, guilt, and broken relationships.

We can choose our actions.

But we cannot choose our consequences.

Consequences flow from all actions, and those who develop a habit of wrong choices rush assuredly toward personal disaster.

The lesson taught in the Mosaic Covenant's delineation of blessings and curses is a gracious one. God warned Israel of the consequences of disobedience in order that His people might choose wisely. Even the terrible consequences which came upon disobedient Israel were gracious in intent. For God intends such consequences to turn hearts away from sin and back to Him.

The tragedies experienced by Old Testament generations that turned their back on God are evidence of His love—gracious urgings to return to the One who is the source of all blessing.

THE RELATIONSHIP OF THE LAW COVENANT TO THE ABRAHAMIC COVENANT

The role of the Law Covenant and its relationship to the Abrahamic Covenant have often been misunderstood. Yet as we explore the Bible several things become clear. The Law Covenant did not replace the Abrahamic Covenant. The Law Covenant was never a way of salvation. And the Law Covenant had a limited and specific function in the Old Testament.

THE LAW COVENANT DID NOT REPLACE OR ANNUL THE ABRAHAMIC COVENANT

Writing in Galatians, the apostle Paul declared, "The law, which was four hundred and thirty years later, cannot annul the covenant that was confirmed before by God in Christ, that it should make the promise of no effect" (Gal. 3:17). God had told Abraham what He intended to do, and had even stated His promises in legally binding covenant form. The introduction of the Law had absolutely no effect on the promises made to Abraham. Those promises continue to stand.

It is important to remember that the Abrahamic Covenant, like other promise covenants, is *eschatological.* This means that complete fulfillment of the promises to Abraham awaits God's action at history's end. During the Old Testament era, many generations of Israelites abandoned God and His ways. In the time of the prophet Elijah, King Ahab and Queen Jezebel of Israel even attempted to stamp out the worship of Yahweh and to make Baal the northern Hebrew kingdom's official deity. They almost succeeded! At one point, Elijah felt so isolated that he was encouraged when the Lord reported that out of the hundreds of thousands in Israel, there were yet "seven thousand . . . whose knees have not bowed to Baal" (1 Kings 19:18). In the whole nation, nearly everyone had apostatized!

Again and again, the Old Testament reports of periods when God's people turned away from Him to worship idols, abandoning the precepts in God's Law. Did the unfaithfulness of these generations annul the promises given to Abraham? Not at all. Throughout the Old Testament era, God stood behind His promises, no matter what God's chosen people did.

The Mosaic Law, then, has no effect at all on the covenants of promise. God's promises to Abraham were never annulled or even threatened by the apostasy of different generations of Israelites.

THE LAW DID NOT PROVIDE
A WAY OF SALVATION

In Galatians, Paul points out another important truth about the Law. It is not a faith kind of thing. "But that no one is justified by the law in the sight of God is evident," Paul writes, "for *'the just shall live by faith.'* Yet the law is not of faith, but *'the man who does them shall live by them'* " (Gal. 3:11, 12).

Law is a works kind of thing. And, as Abraham's own experience with God demonstrated, God accepts our faith in place of a righteousness which no human being possesses. The Law, then, cannot be a way of salvation, since salvation is by faith and not by works.

THE MOSAIC LAW HAD A LIMITED AND SPECIFIC FUNCTION IN OLD TESTAMENT TIMES

Commentators have noticed a fascinating fact about the statement of the Ten Commandments in Exodus. Each is expressed in the second person singular: "you." The use of the singular pronoun is best understood as a way of speaking to all Israel collectively. It focuses on the way in which a *group of people* is to act and think, as if the group were one person.

While it is obvious that individuals were responsible to keep God's Law, the use of the singular here is significant. The Mosaic Covenant was made with Israel *collectively,* and not simply with individual Israelites. Thus, the blessings and curses defined in the Mosaic Covenant were *collective* blessings and curses. They were based on how the people *as a whole* responded to the Lord in any given generation.

We can see why this must be. Among the curses to be experienced by generations which abandoned the Lord were famines and foreign invasions. These were national, not individual, disasters. Even a godly person must suffer when the rains fail and crops dry up in the fields. Even a godly individual must suffer when a foreign nation invades his homeland, looting and killing and taking captives. Thus, the fate of a godly individual may be determined by the ungodly neighbors among whom he lives.

God, in giving the Mosaic Covenant, fully understood this reality. And the language of the Ten Commandments tells us that God made the Law Covenant with the people of Israel, the whole community or nation—not with individuals! The blessing or His curses as defined in the Law are national blessings and curses, not blessings or curses to fall on individuals.

This is not to say that the Lord made no distinction between the godly and the sinful person in times of national crisis. Yet we must understand that the Law Covenant was a covenant between God and the whole community of Israel, not between God and individual members in the community.

This explains the distinctive function of the Law Covenant as it relates to the Abrahamic Covenant. When a given *generation of Israelites* was faithful, God blessed. When a generation of Israelites turned their back on the Lord, God disciplined His people to turn the nation back to Him.

The limited and specific function of the Law in relation to the Abrahamic covenant, then, was to determine when a given generation should be blessed by God, and when a specific generation should be punished. The nation's experience of the blessings promised to Abraham's descendants was determined by how a generation of descendants related to God *nationally.*

THE RELATIONSHIP OF MOSAIC LAW TO THE INDIVIDUAL OT BELIEVER

The Mosaic or Law Covenant was made with corporate Israel. The blessings and curses that were decreed for keeping or breaking the law were national rather than individual. Today, living in a culture that emphasizes the individual and individual responsibility, we tend to miss this fact. Yet when we scan Deuteronomy 28, it is clear that national rather than individual consequences are intended.

The fact that the Mosaic Covenant is between God and corporate Israel does not imply that Moses' Law was not for individuals. But how did Moses' Law impact believing Israelites—those who were descendants of Abraham both biologically and spiritually?

THE TRUE BELIEVER DELIGHTED IN GOD'S LAW   (Psalm 119)

The covenant which God made with the community incorporated a Law which was the possession, and the obligation, of individual members of that community. For the true believer, the Law was welcomed as a loving word from God. The Law marked out a path that was not only right but good. The individual who lived by the Law found it a guide to a harmonious relationship with God and his or her neighbors. It is no wonder, then, that in his great psalm celebrating God's Law, David expressed utter delight in meditating on and keeping God's Law.

> How can a young man cleanse his
>   way?
> By taking heed according to Your
>   word.
> With my whole heart I have
>   sought You;
> Oh let me not wander from Your
>   commandments!
> Your word I have hidden in my
>   heart,
> That I might not sin against You (Ps.
>   119:9–11).

> Give me understanding, and I
>   shall keep Your law;
> Indeed, I shall observe it with my
>   whole heart.
> Make me walk in the path of Your
>   commandments,
> For I delight in it (Ps. 119:34, 35).

And

> Oh, how I love Your law!
> It is my meditation all the day.
> You, through Your
>   commandments, make me
>   wiser than my enemies;
> For they are ever with me.
> I have more understanding than
>   all my teachers,
> For Your testimonies are my
>   meditation.
> I understand more than the
>   ancients,
> Because I keep Your precepts.
> I have restrained my feet from
>   every evil way,
> That I may keep Your word.
> I have not departed from Your
>   judgments,
> For you Yourself have taught me.
> How sweet are Your words to my
>   taste,
> Sweeter than honey to my
>   mouth!
> Through Your precepts I get
>   understanding;
> Therefore I hate every false way
>   (Ps. 119:97–104).

GOD BLESSED THE TRUE BELIEVER WHO HONORED HIM AND HIS LAW
(Psalm 32; Ezekiel 18)

While the Law Covenant itself was made with the community of Israel, and the blessings and curses defined in that covenant were national, the Old Testament believer who lived by the Law could and did expect to be blessed. God would surely honor the person who honored Him.

This truth is expressed in another psalm of David, in which he celebrates the guidance God gives, and claims the blessing awaiting the person who walks in God's way.

> I will instruct you and teach you
>   in the way you should go;
> I will guide you with My eye.
>   . . .

"Your law . . . is my meditation all the day."

Many sorrows shall be to the
    wicked;
But he who trusts in the LORD,
    mercy shall surround him.
Be glad in the LORD and rejoice,
    you righteous;
And shout for joy, all you upright
    in heart! (Ps. 32:8, 10).

A striking example of the implication of
individuals keeping or breaking God's Law is
found in Ezekiel 18. There the prophet responded to those who heard his message of
the imminent destruction of Jerusalem, and
shrugged. Why should they change their
ways? If God has decided to judge the community because of the sins of the preceding
generations (Ezek. 18:2), what can an individual do about that?

The Lord decisively rejected this argument, and decreed that "the soul who sins
shall die" (Ezek. 18:4). God is not speaking

spiritually or of eternal judgment. This verse is
about biological death, and of the coming fall
of Jerusalem. When the Babylonians invade
and raze the city, God will distinguish between individuals. The person who has
"walked in My statutes and kept My judgments faithfully—he is just; he shall surely
live!" (Ezek. 18:9). God will guard the life of
the individual who has kept God's Law, in
spite of the corporate sin of Israel which has
brought judgment on the nation. On the other
hand, the person who has violated the law,
"He shall surely die!" (Ezek. 18:13).

Thus, while the Mosaic Covenant was between God and the whole community of Israel, individuals who faithfully kept God's law
could expect Him to guard them, even when
punishment was decreed for the nation as a
whole.

The Mosaic Law, then, had direct application to individual Israelites. The true believer,
who approached relationship with God as
Abraham had—with faith—found God's Law
a delight and was eager to follow its precepts.
And the true believer who responded in this
way to God's Word could and did expect to be
blessed by the Lord.

THE RELATIONSHIP OF JESUS
TO THE MOSAIC LAW

Jesus Christ was born a Jew, and He lived
as a Jew during His life on earth. In fact,
Christ alone of all human beings perfectly
kept God's Law. Hebrews 4:15 reminds us that
as a true human being, Jesus was "in all points
tempted as we are, yet without sin."

While Jesus lived a perfect life under the
Law, His teaching about the Law challenged
the understanding of its purpose held by the
people of His day. The by-faith nature of relationship with God displayed by Abraham was
ignored, and the religion of the day was
rooted in the belief that salvation came
through biological descent from Abraham plus
merit earned by keeping Moses' Law.

Jesus challenged this understanding of
Moses' Law, and put its function in clear perspective.

JESUS EXPLAINED THE TRUE MEANING OF MOSES' LAW
(Matthew 5:17–48)

In Matthew 5, a section of the Sermon on the Mount, Jesus spoke plainly about Moses' Law and His own role in relation to the Law.

"Not to destroy" (Matthew 5:17). Jesus' teachings seemed radical to His contemporaries. It was natural that they would feel threatened by the young prophet from Nazareth, whose fame was spreading rapidly (Matt. 4:24). In this passage, Jesus made it plain that He posed no threat to the Law.

Assuredly, I say to you, till heaven and earth pass away, one jot or one tittle will by no means pass from the law till all is fulfilled. Whoever therefore breaks one of the least of these commandments, and teaches men so, shall be called least in the kingdom of heaven; but whoever does and teaches them, he shall be called great in the kingdom of heaven. (Matt. 5:18, 19)

"But to fulfill" (Matthew 5:17). Rather than setting out to destroy the Law (a term frequently used of the entire works of Moses, and of the Old Testament as a whole, as well as of the commandments imbedded in them), Jesus came to "fulfill" the Law.

Western commentators have discussed how Jesus fulfilled the Law. Some have taken this statement to mean that Jesus kept the Law perfectly. Others have suggested it means that Christ fulfilled the prophecies the Old Testament contains. But Jesus' listeners understood exactly what Christ meant. For it was the desire of every sage and rabbi to "fulfill" the Law,

Jesus' Sermon on the Mount

in the sense of explaining its true and complete meaning.

What Jesus announced was that rather than being a threat to the Old Testament revelation, and specifically to the commandments it contained, He had come to explain the real, true, and underlying meaning of the words that God had given Moses so long ago.

With this introduction, and with Jesus' clearly stated confidence in the Old Testament as the authoritative Word of God (Matt. 5:18–19), Jesus was ready to unveil the Law's true import.

"Righteousness [that] exceeds the righteousness of the scribes and Pharisees" (Matthew 5:20).

This third preliminary statement of Jesus must have stunned His listeners. The scribes and Pharisees were highly respected in Judaism. The scribes were the trained group who spent their lives studying Old Testament Law and its interpretation by earlier sages. The Pharisees were members of a small group who had a reputation for keeping God's commandments down to the last detail, as those details were spelled out by the sages. In first-century Judaism, the scribes and Pharisees were viewed with awe by the general population, who agreed that if anyone had a chance at heaven, these people did.

To hear Jesus declare that to enter the kingdom of heaven a person's righteousness must exceed the righteousness of the scribes and Pharisees was stunning indeed.

The problem, of course, lay in the fact that the righteousness of the scribe and Pharisee was a works-based righteousness. Scribe and Pharisee alike assumed that the merit of being Abraham's descendants, plus merit earned by keeping God's Law, was the basis for acceptance by God. What Jesus said next challenged the underlying assumptions of first-century Judaism!

"You have heard ... but I say to you" (Matthew 5:21–48).

The rest of this extended section is composed of illustrations drawn from the Law. First Jesus quoted from the Law.

Then Jesus gave His own "but-I-say-unto-you" exposition of the commandment's true import.

The Law says, "You shall not murder." But Jesus says, "Whoever is angry with his brother without a cause" is in danger of the judgment (Matt. 5:21, 22).

The Law says, "You shall not commit adultery." But Jesus says that "whoever looks at a woman to lust after her has already committed adultery with her in his heart."

The series of statements continues in this vein.

What Jesus did here was to shift the Law's focus from behavior to motive, from actions to the heart. When God gave the Law through Moses, that Law regulated behavior. But Jesus tells us that what God was really concerned with was the human heart.

The Law said "Do not murder," but in so saying, it should be clear to us that the anger which moves a person to harm another is just as sinful as the act itself. The root, not just the fruit, is sinful.

The Law said, "Do not commit adultery," but in so saying, it should be clear that the lust that gives rise to adultery is just as sinful as the act itself. The root, not just the fruit, is sinful.

The righteousness that is required for membership in God's kingdom exceeds the righteousness of the scribes and Pharisees, because in their focus on behavior they ignored or denied the stirrings of sin in their hearts, and assumed that they were righteous. They convinced themselves that they pleased God because they observed the Law outwardly, never realizing that the commandments they tried so carefully to keep had already condemned them!

In shifting our attention from the external behavior defined in God's Law to the source of that behavior within the human heart, Jesus stripped the scribes and Pharisees of the basis for their claim of spiritual superiority. They kept the Law outwardly, but within they were as sinful as every other human being.

In this reinterpretation of the Law, Jesus laid a foundation for our need of His redeem-

THE MEKHILTA OF RABBI ISHMAEL

The Jewish rabbis assumed that righteousness came from keeping the Law. This commentary on the Law [Torah] goes even further. It indicates that the very possession of the Law by Israel proved that Israel *was* righteous in God's sight! Here Rabbi Ishmael envisions the response of other peoples to an approach by God offering them the Torah. All refuse it. All except "righteous" Israel.

8. A. Therefore the nations of the world were approached, so as not to give them an excuse to say, "If we had been approached, we should have accepted responsibility [to keep Torah]."
   B. Lo, they were approached but did not accept responsibility for them, as it is said, "The LORD came from Sinai" (Deut. 33:2).
9. A. The Lord came from Sinai (Deut. 33:2):
   B. When the Omnipresent appeared to give the Torah to Israel, it was not to Israel alone that He revealed Himself but to every nation.
   C. First of all He came to the children of the wicked Esau. He said to them, "Will you accept the Torah?"
   D. They said to Him, "What is written in it?"
   E. He said to them, "'You shall not murder'" (Ex. 20:13).
   F. They said to Him, "The very being of 'those men' and of their father is to murder, for it is said, 'But the hands are the hands of Esau,' (Gen. 27:22). 'By your sword you shall live'" (Gen. 27:40).
   G. So he went to the children of Ammon and Moab and said to them, "Will you accept the Torah?"
   H. They said to Him, "What is written in it?"
   I. He said to them, "'You shall not commit adultery'" (Ex. 20:14).
   J. They said to Him, "All of us are the children of fornication, for it is said, 'Thus both the daughters of Lot were with child by their father'" (Gen. 19:36).
   K. So He went to the children of Ishmael and said to them, "Will you accept the Torah?"
   L. They said to Him, "What is written in it?"
   M. He said to them, "'You shall not steal'" (Ex. 20:15).
   N. They said to Him, "This is the blessing that was stated for our father: 'He shall be a wild man' (Gen. 16:12). 'For indeed I was stolen away from the land of the Hebrews.'" (Gen. 40:15).
   O. But when He came to the Israelites: "From His right hand came a fiery law for them" (Deut. 33:2).
   P. They all opened their mouths and said, "All that the LORD has said we will do, and be obedient" (Ex. 24:7).
   Q. "He stood and measured the earth; He looked and startled the nations" (Hab. 3:6).

ing work. If God judges not only our actions but the thoughts and motives of our hearts, we must be changed *within*. And while law can regulate behavior, law can never transform the human heart.

JESUS REINTRODUCED THE GOOD NEWS OF A FAITH-RELATIONSHIP WITH GOD

The apostle John wrote that "the law was given through Moses, but grace and truth came through Jesus Christ" (John 1:17). Matthew in his Gospel declared that "all the prophets and the law prophesied until John" (Matt. 11:13), and in Luke 16:16 Jesus added to this comment. "The law and the prophets were until John. Since that time the kingdom of God has been preached."

It is clear from these few verses that with Jesus something new and different from the Law of Moses was introduced. The Old Testament and its Law were placed in fresh perspective and, as we will see in chapter 5 when we look at the New Covenant, Jesus reintroduced the basic reality that served as the foundation of Abraham's relationship with God and the covenant given to him. Salvation, including a vital personal relationship with the Lord, is possible only through faith in the promises of our God.

THE RELATIONSHIP OF THE CHRISTIAN TO MOSES' LAW

One of the most surprising things in the New Testament is its apparent negative attitude toward the Law of Moses. First Corinthians 15:56 says, "The sting of death is sin, and the strength of sin is the law." Galatians 3:12 says, "The law is not of faith," and Galatians 3:13 adds, "Christ has redeemed us from the curse of the law." In Romans 6:14 Paul is even so bold as to write, "Sin shall not have dominion over you, for you are not under law but under grace."

How can something which the true believer in Old Testament times found such a delight seem to the writers of the New Testament to be a curse from which we are freed by Jesus?

THE THREE FUNCTIONS OF LAW

Christian theologians have identified three functions of the Law of Moses, and especially of the Ten Commandments as its moral foundation.

Law reveals God's character. This is the first function of the Law, and it is a beautiful one. As we look at the standards that God established in the Law, we discover so many wonderful things about Him. The Law reveals God's character.

Does God say, "You shall not murder?" This is because to God every human being is precious, and every life has incomparable value. What a contrast is drawn in this law between our God, who cares for people, and the pagan deities of Old Testament times, who had no compassion for their worshipers.

Does God say, "You shall not commit adultery?" This is because God is loyal to His commitments and He values loyalty in others. Our unfaithfulness hurts Him, because He is utterly faithful to those whom He loves. His commandments thus reveal God Himself as a loyal and trustworthy being.

The Law then became a window through which we can see our God.

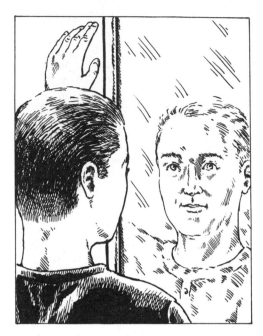

The Law shows us ourselves as we really are.

Law reveals sin. New Testament writers emphasize this aspect of the Law's ministry. In Romans 3:19, 20, Paul wrote, "We know that whatever the law says, it says to those who are under the law, that every mouth may be stopped, and all the world may become guilty before God. Therefore by the deeds of the law no flesh will be justified in His sight, for by the law is the knowledge of sin."

If the first function of the Law is to be a window through which we can catch glimpses of God, the second function of the Law is to be a mirror in which we can see ourselves clearly. When we honestly measure ourselves by God's standards, we see how far short we fall. And we turn away from works to find a new and different way to God.

Thus, Paul in writing to Timothy says, "We know that the law is good if one uses it lawfully, knowing this: that the law is not made for a righteous person, but for the lawless and insubordinate, for the ungodly and for sinners, for the unholy and profane, for murderers of fathers and murderers of mothers, for manslayers, for fornicators, for sodomites [homosexuals], for kidnappers, for liars, for perjurers" (1 Tim. 1:8–10). We use the law lawfully when we use it to show sin to be sin. We understand this use of God's Word when we realize that the Law was given to sinners to show them they are sinners, not to make sinners good.

To lead the believer into a holy life. This is what theologians call the third function of Law. It is this supposed function toward which the New Testament is so negative.

The passages quoted at the beginning of this section link being under the law with sin, not with holiness. Romans teaches that believers died to the Law with Christ (Rom. 7:1–4), and so are released from the Law—so that we can serve God in the new way of the Spirit (Rom. 7:6). Thus, Christ is the end of the Law for us (Rom. 10:4). Even the Jerusalem church came early to realize that the Law of Moses was a yoke that "neither our fathers nor we were able to bear" (Acts 15:10), and that Gentile Christians should not be asked to assume.

What these passages point out is that the Law, as an external standard, has no power to transform the inner person. Law can cry "do" and "do not." But Law cannot create a desire to love and to obey God.

As a tool to lead human beings into a holy life, then, the Law failed. And God in Christ has introduced a new and better way for people to be made truly good. For this reason, we are to turn away from the Law and law-keeping as a path to practical righteousness. We are to find a faith-pathway to living truly righteous lives.

THE LAW AND RIGHTEOUS LIVING TODAY

It frightens many believers if we say with Scripture that the Christian is not under the Law. Too many have visions of believers running amuck. If we don't *have to* keep God's Law, they assume that we won't.

But to say that the Christian today is not responsible to keep God's Law in no way implies that God doesn't expect us to live righteous lives. Romans 8:3 reminds us that Jesus died and condemned sin "that the righteous requirements of the law might be fulfilled in us, who walk not according to the flesh but according to the Spirit."

No, the point of the Christian's release from the obligation to keep the Law is simply that *trying to keep the Law will not work!* No one who tries to live up to God's Law will ever lead a truly righteous life. The secret of living a holy life is to respond not to the Law but to the Holy Spirit, who motivates us to love God and who enables us to obey Him.

God's Law is wonderful—as a window through which to see God's character.

God's Law is effective—as a mirror in which to see ourselves measured against His standards.

But trying to keep God's law is not the way Christians experience transformation within or become God's holy and righteous people. The secret of inner transformation is revealed not in the Mosaic Covenant, but in the New Covenant, under which Christians now live.

WHAT WE HAVE LEARNED ABOUT THE MOSAIC COVENANT

The Mosaic Covenant was executed at Mt. Sinai, between God and the Israelites as a people. Unlike the covenants of promise, this covenant follows a pattern long established in the ancient Middle East.

THE MOSAIC COVENANT DEFINED WHAT GOD EXPECTED FROM THE ISRAELITES

The Law Covenant was a two-party suzerainty covenant, like that used to define the relationship between superiors and inferiors. In this covenant, God is the acknowledged superior, and the Israelites are His subjects. As in all such covenants, the superior's expectations are spelled out, along with the consequences of obedience and of rebellion by the subjects.

THE MOSAIC COVENANT DEFINES MORE THAN MORAL CONDUCT

While we tend to think of the Mosaic Law as the Ten Commandments, it was far more. The Law defined how Israel was to worship God, established a priesthood and sacrificial system, identified social responsibilities, set up institutions to protect the poor, specified what could and could not be eaten, and in general governed the way of life of the Israelites.

THE MOSAIC COVENANT DID NOT REPLACE THE ABRAHAMIC COVENANT

The Abrahamic Covenant was a unilateral covenant in which God stated what He intended to do in the form of promises given to Abraham and his descendants. The promises in that covenant are to be completely fulfilled at history's end. The Mosaic Covenant is a bilateral covenant, in which the people of Israel as a community agree to obey God's commandments. Under this covenant, God commits Himself to bless Israel when the nation/community is obedient to Him, and to punish Israel when the nation/community is disobedient. By keeping God's Law, any generation of Israelites had access in their own time to the blessings guaranteed to Abraham's descendants at history's end.

THE MOSAIC COVENANT AND THE INDIVIDUAL ISRAELITE

The Mosaic Covenant was made between God and the whole people of Israel, rather than between God and individuals. However, individual Israelites who loved and trusted God took delight in following God's laws, and also were blessed by Him. Even so, individuals suffered when the nation sinned and God brought famine or sent foreign enemies against the land.

THE MOSAIC COVENANT AND JESUS CHRIST

Jesus lived as a Jew under the Mosaic Law, and He obeyed the Law perfectly. But Jesus challenged the view of the Law held by the religious leaders of His day. The religious leaders saw keeping the Law as a way of earning merit with God. Jesus pointed out that ultimately the Law is not about behavior, but about the human heart. To be acceptable to God, a person must be transformed within, so that his or her heart and motives are totally pure. Such a transformation cannot come through Moses' Law.

THE CHRISTIAN AND THE MOSAIC LAW

Christians are called by God to live righteous and holy lives. Such a life will surely be in accord with the moral standards revealed in the Mosaic Covenant. However, Christians are not under the Law. Our relationship with God does not depend on what we do, but it is rooted in God's forgiveness and His grace.

Rather than demanding that we try to keep the Law, God invites us to rely on the Holy Spirit to change our hearts and lead us in God's ways. The Christian who lives by the Spirit will live a holy life, with both motives and behavior purified by God.

Today we can read God's Law, and see God's holy character revealed. We can read God's Law, and by measuring ourselves against God's standards see areas in our life we need to ask God to transform. But Christians cannot expect that, by trying to keep the Law, we will either earn God's favor or grow spiritually. Instead, we seek to love God more and be responsive to the Holy Spirit as He speaks through God's Word, and within our hearts.

CHAPTER 5

PROMISE OF A COMING KING:

THE DAVIDIC COVENANT
2 Samuel 7; 1 Chronicles 17

The first generation of Israelites to live under the Mosaic Law was rebellious. All but two adults who had heard and seen God thundering from Mt. Sinai died in the wilderness during the next 38 years! But their sons and daughters trusted and obeyed God, and it was the second generation that successfully fought its way into Canaan.

The first two generations to live under God's Law illustrated its impact on the Hebrew people. Law brought a curse to the disobedient generation, blessing to the obedient.

The history of Israel in Canaan over the next several hundred years was marked by similar cycles of experience. The book of Judges recorded seven cycles of apostasy and repentance. Again and again, the Israelites turned away from God to idolatry, and were then dominated by foreign enemies until they repented and prayed to God for help. In response, God raised up a judge, a political/religious chieftain, who led the Israelites to victory over their enemy. The people remained faithful to God during the judge's lifetime, but after his or her death the tragic cycle was repeated again.

Keeping God's Law did bring national blessing. And turning away from the Lord and His Law brought Israel national disaster.

But history is more than an endless cycle of repeated experience. History has a goal and purpose: a goal expressed in wonderful covenant promises which God gave to Abraham. God chose Abraham and his descendants not only to be blessed, but to be a blessing to all. As sacred history moved on toward its intended end, more and more of *how* God intended to bless Israel and the world was unveiled.

At last, the time of the judges came to an end. In two generations the Israelites made the transition from a loose confederation of Hebrew tribes to a monarchy. Under its second and greatest king, David, Israel became the dominant power in the Middle East!

It was at this point that God, through a covenant made with King David, revealed more of His plan.

THE CONTEXT OF THE DAVIDIC COVENANT

David came to the throne of Israel about 1000 B.C. A true genius as well as a deeply spiritual man, David united the tribes of Israel and expanded the territory they controlled some tenfold. He established Jerusalem as the political and religious capital of the nation, redesigned the worship system that had originally been set for wilderness travel, and personally contributed many of the praise songs used in public worship. David trained and organized a powerful military machine and structured a centralized government for the nation.

When David grew old, his greatest desire was to build a temple to honor God, the source of his success and of Israel's resurgence. But through the prophet Nathan, God refused to let David build a temple. That privilege was to be reserved for Solomon, David's son. Instead, God told David that He would build David a house. The "house" that God would build David was his family line. David would never lack a descendant qualified by birth to sit on Israel's throne.

The line of David would eventually culminate in a ruler who would establish and govern a kingdom that would never end!

The original covenant promises to David are stated in 2 Samuel 7 and 1 Chronicles 17. God spoke to David and said:

I took you from the sheepfold; from following the sheep, to be ruler over My people, over Israel. And I have been with you wherever you have gone, and have cut off all your enemies from before you, and have made you a great name, like the name of the great men who are on the earth. Moreover I will appoint a place for My people Israel, and will plant them, that they may dwell in a place of their own and move no more; nor shall the sons of wickedness oppress them anymore, as previously, since the time that I commanded judges to be over My people Israel, and have caused you to rest from all your enemies. Also the LORD tells you that He will make you a house.

When your days are fulfilled and you rest with your fathers, I will set up your seed after you, who will come from your body, and I will establish his kingdom. He shall build a house for My name and I will establish the throne of his kingdom forever. I will be his Father, and he shall be My son.

If he commits iniquity, I will chasten him with the rod of men and with the blows of the sons of men. But My mercy shall not depart from him, as I took it from Saul, whom I removed from before you.

And your house and your kingdom shall be established forever before you. Your throne shall be established forever (2 Sam. 7:8–16).

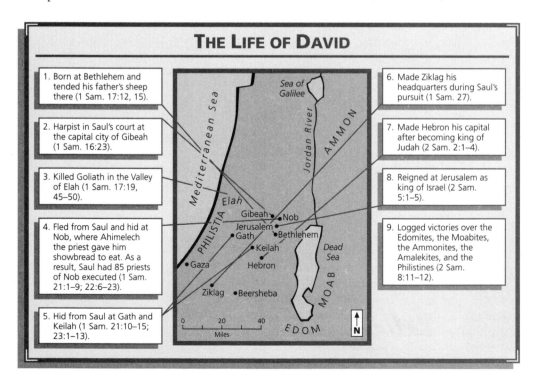

THE LIFE OF DAVID

1. Born at Bethlehem and tended his father's sheep there (1 Sam. 17:12, 15).

2. Harpist in Saul's court at the capital city of Gibeah (1 Sam. 16:23).

3. Killed Goliath in the Valley of Elah (1 Sam. 17:19, 45–50).

4. Fled from Saul and hid at Nob, where Ahimelech the priest gave him showbread to eat. As a result, Saul had 85 priests of Nob executed (1 Sam. 21:1–9; 22:6–23).

5. Hid from Saul at Gath and Keilah (1 Sam. 21:10–15; 23:1–13).

6. Made Ziklag his headquarters during Saul's pursuit (1 Sam. 27).

7. Made Hebron his capital after becoming king of Judah (2 Sam. 2:1–4).

8. Reigned at Jerusalem as king of Israel (2 Sam. 5:1–5).

9. Logged victories over the Edomites, the Moabites, the Ammonites, the Amalekites, and the Philistines (2 Sam. 8:11–12).

Mediterranean Sea · Sea of Galilee · Jordan River · AMMON · Elah · Gibeah · Nob · Jerusalem · Gath · Bethlehem · PHILISTIA · Keilah · Dead Sea · Gaza · Hebron · MOAB · Ziklag · Beersheba · EDOM

0   20   40
Miles

N

Scripture gives the status of a covenant, a legally binding agreement, to the promises incorporated in these verses. Psalm 89:3 quotes the Lord as saying, "I have made a covenant with My chosen, I have sworn to My servant David."

Also God's words to David follow the "I will" pattern set in the Abraham covenant, and this too marks them off as a covenant. Psalm 132:11 reminds the reader, "The LORD has sworn in truth to David; He will not turn from it: 'I will set upon your throne the fruit of your body.'"

While we are to understand God's statement of His intentions to David as a covenant, the passage does not make perfectly clear what God's promises imply. There are, in fact, three aspects to the covenant promise (1) There is an immediate aspect, fulfilled in the ascension of David's son, Solomon. (2) There is an intermediate aspect, fulfilled in the fact that throughout its history, Judah was ruled by descendants of David. And (3) there is an es-

chatological aspect, fulfilled in David's descendant, Jesus Christ.

IMMEDIATE AND INTERMEDIATE FULFILLMENT OF GOD'S PROMISE TO DAVID

One of the promises God made to David began to be fulfilled within a few years. "I will set up your seed after you, who will come from your body, and I will establish his kingdom. He shall build a house for My name" (2 Sam. 7:12).

This immediate aspect of the Davidic covenant was fulfilled even before David's death. David saw his son Solomon become king of Israel in 970 B.C. Solomon immediately set out to build the temple that David had designed, and for which David had set aside materials and a vast fortune. The temple was completed in seven years, and dedicated by Solomon. For the next 33 years, Solomon ruled a peaceful kingdom, safe from foreign enemies. God had established Solomon's kingdom.

Yet in Solomon's old age Solomon's pagan wives drew him into idolatry. Upon Solomon's death, the kingdom David had forged separated into two factions. While the south, Judah, was ruled by David's descendants, the north, Israel, was ruled by a series of non-Davidic and short-lived dynasties.

Solomon's failings, and the failings of other rulers of Judah over the next few centuries, were dealt with by God under conditions established in the Mosaic Covenant and restated in the Davidic Covenant. "If he [the descendant-king] commits iniquity, I will chasten him with the rod of men and with the blows of the sons of men. But My mercy shall not depart from him, as I took it from Saul, whom I removed from before you. And your house and your kingdom shall be established forever" (2 Sam. 7:14–16).

God kept this promise. After Solomon's apostasy, the Lord announced, "I will not take the whole kingdom out of his hand, because I have made him ruler all the days of his life for the sake of My servant David, whom I chose because he kept My commandments and My

David, a man after God's own heart

statutes. . . . And to his son I will give one tribe, that My servant David may always have a lamp before Me in Jerusalem, the city which I have chosen for Myself, to put My name there" (1 Kings 11:34, 36).

Later still, Solomon's grandson became king in Judah. Even though his heart was not loyal to God, "nevertheless for David's sake the LORD his God gave him a lamp in Jerusalem, by setting up his son after him and by establishing Jerusalem" (1 Kin. 15:4).

The immediate and intermediate aspects of the covenant promise made to David guaranteed that a descendant of David would rule in Jerusalem as long as the kingdom of Judah survived. And Judah survived for almost 350 years before being crushed by the Babylonians. Its population was deported from the land God had promised to Abraham's descendants.

THE ESCHATOLOGICAL FULFILLMENT OF GOD'S COVENANT WITH DAVID

God had told Abraham that his descendants would inherit the land of Canaan, and had precisely set the land's boundaries. In making His promise to David, the Lord restated this aspect of the Abrahamic Covenant. "I will appoint a place for My people Israel, and will plant them, that they may dwell in a place of their own and move no more" (2 Sam. 7:10).

As noted earlier, the promise to Abraham implied that his descendants would become a nation; they would have a state and not simply exist as an ethnic group. That thought is also expressed in the Davidic Covenant, but with a new revelation. Israel would possess the promised land, and a descendant of David would rule it! God said, "I will establish his kingdom. . . . I will establish the throne of his kingdom forever" (2 Sam. 7:12, 13).

God's summary statement of the eschatological aspect of the Davidic Covenant is "your house and your kingdom shall be established forever before you. Your throne shall be established forever" (2 Sam. 7:16).

It is this "forever" dimension of the promise to David that raises questions. What does the promise imply? Surely the years from David to Judah's fall do not constitute "forever." And when the nation no longer existed,

Three centuries after David, his people were carried away as captives to Babylon.

surely David's "throne" no longer existed either.

The best place to seek an answer is in the writings of the prophets, who were given visions of the future. They spoke often of the king who would come from David's line.

ISAIAH'S PROPHECIES CONCERNING DAVID'S ROYAL DESCENDANT

The book of Isaiah has been called the "Gospel of the Old Testament." It is filled with references to God's promised Messiah. Although Isaiah announced that severe judgments loomed because of Israel's sins, the prophet also spoke glowingly of a Savior whom God would send to deliver His people. Many passages in Isaiah identified that Savior as the descendant promised in the Davidic Covenant.

Isaiah 9:6, 7: He is to be God the Son. When we looked at the Abrahamic Covenant, we noted that it is essentially an eschatological covenant. It announces what God will accomplish by history's end. When God's plans and purposes are at last fulfilled, Abraham's descendants will possess the land. When God's plans and purposes have been fulfilled, every human family will be blessed.

As Isaiah explored this promised future he fit the promises made to David into the prophetic pattern. His message was that God would fulfill the Abrahamic promises through the agency of a person destined to be Israel's promised Davidic king! Isaiah 9 is one of the most significant of these prophecies.

> For unto us a Child is born,
> Unto us a Son is given;
> And the government will be upon
>   His shoulder.
> And His name will be called
> Wonderful, Counselor, Mighty
>   God,
> Everlasting Father, Prince of
>   Peace.
> Of the increase of His government

> and peace
> There will be no end,
> Upon the throne of David and
>   over His kingdom,
> To order it and establish it with
>   judgment and justice
> From that time forward, even
>   forever.
> The zeal of the LORD of hosts will
>   perform this (Isa. 9:6, 7).

What does Isaiah say here about this king who is to come from David's line and sit on David's throne?

He is a Son, although born a child (Isaiah 9:6). Hebrew poetry typically repeats thoughts in couplets. Yet there is something unique here. The coming ruler will be born a child. But at the same time, He is a gift—the Son of the Giver! These words might have meant little in Isaiah's time. But today we recognize Jesus Christ in this couplet. Born as an infant in Bethlehem, Jesus was nevertheless the eternal Son of God, given to take away the sins of the world. And Isaiah declared that the government—all rule and authority—would one day rest on His shoulders.

His name (Isaiah 9:6). Isaiah gave the promised Son a series of titles which reflect His deity. Among them the title "Everlasting Father" should be read, "the Father [source] of Eternity." Before the worlds were, the Son existed as the mighty God and He is the source of all that is.

"Upon the throne of David and over His kingdom" (Isaiah 9:7). It is this verse that provides the stunning information that the Son of God, born among us as a human being, is to be the promised Davidic king. Because this descendant of David is God the Son, His kingdom will be without end, existing "forever."

Isaiah 11: David's descendant will bless all. In chapter 11 of his prophecy, Isaiah identified the promised Davidic king as a "Rod from the stem of Jesse" (Isa. 11:1, 2). Jesse was David's father, and "rod" or "branch" becomes a title

Isaiah foresaw the birth of Jesus, God's Son.

used here and elsewhere of the promised Davidic king.

The chapter describes this king's righteous rule (Isa. 11:3–5), and the peace He will bring to nature itself (Isa. 11:6–9). The chapter includes an image of the blessing that His appearance will bring to Gentiles as well as Jews.

> And in that day there shall be a
>   Root of Jesse,
> Who shall stand as a banner to
>   the people;
> For the Gentiles shall seek Him,
> And His resting place shall be
>   glorious.
> It shall come to pass in that day
> That the LORD shall set His hand
>   again the second time
> To recover the remnant of His
>   people who are left (Isa. 11:10,
>   11).

The descendant promised to David is the key to the fulfillment of God's promise to Abraham

to bless all the families of the earth through him (Gen. 12:3).

Again and again in this great book the prophet shares visions of a future in which the covenant promises made to Abraham are kept through the agency of the Anointed One—the Messiah whose coming means the blessing of Israel and all humankind.

JEREMIAH'S PROPHECIES CONCERNING DAVID'S DESCENDANT

When Jeremiah wrote, Babylonian armies were about to destroy Jerusalem and raze the great temple which Solomon built. With that event, the nation of Judah would no longer exist. The Jews would remain a people—but a people without homeland or national identity.

Yet in these dark days, Jeremiah had a word of hope to offer God's people. One day God would keep His promise to David and raise up a ruler from his line. In that ruler's day, the ancient promises made to Abraham would finally be fulfilled.

Jeremiah 23:5–8. David's descendant would fulfill the ancient promises to Abraham. The promises that Jeremiah recorded clearly linked the coming Messianic King and God's promises to Abraham.

> "Behold, the days are coming,"
>   says the LORD,
> "That I will raise to David a Branch
>   of righteousness;
> A King shall reign and prosper,
> And execute judgment and
>   righteousness in the earth.
> In His days Judah will be saved,
> And Israel will dwell safely;
> Now this is His name by which
>   He will be called:
>   THE LORD OUR
>   RIGHTEOUSNESS.

"Therefore, behold, the days are coming," says the LORD, "that they shall no longer say, 'As the LORD lives who brought up the children of Israel from the land of Egypt,' but 'As the LORD lives who brought up and led the descendants of the house of

Israel from the north country and from all the countries where I had driven them.' And they shall dwell in their own land" (Jer. 23:5–8).

The prophecy predicted the coming exile of the Jewish people from their land. But it also stated that one day God would bring them back from "all the countries where I had driven them," to reestablish His people as a nation.

Jeremiah 30:3, 8, 9: David's descendant will rule a restored Israel. Jeremiah's message of hope continued to link a return of God's people to their land with the rule of a restored nation ruled by David's descendant.

"Behold the days are coming," says the LORD, "that I will bring back from captivity My people Israel and Judah," says the LORD. "And I will cause them to return to the land that I gave to their fathers, and they shall possess it. . . . Foreigners shall no more enslave them, but they shall serve the LORD their God, and David their king, whom I will raise up for them" (Jer. 30:3, 8, 9).

How certain is it that God will keep the covenant promise He made to David? Jeremiah answered with a "thus says the LORD." God says:

"If you can break My covenant with the day and My covenant with the night, so that there will not be day and night in their season, then My covenant may also be broken with David My servant, so that he shall not have a son to reign on his throne" (Jer. 33:20, 21).

This verse helps us understand an important aspect of the Davidic Covenant. As long as there was a nation Judah, one of David's descendants did sit on its throne. When the nation no longer existed, David would still have a descendant *qualified to take the throne when the nation was restored!* Jeremiah 33:17 stated it even more clearly: "David shall never lack a man to sit on the throne of the house of Israel."

EZEKIEL'S PROPHECIES CONCERNING DAVID'S DESCENDANT

The Babylonians made Judah a vassal state in 605 B.C., taking a number of captives to Babylon. Ezekiel was one of these captives. Later Judah rebelled against the Babylonians, and was finally destroyed in 586 B.C. Between 593 B.C. and 586 B.C. Ezekiel, like Jeremiah back in Judah, warned of the coming destruction of Judah and its capital city. Jerusalem was destroyed, and its people were sent into exile.

Then, after a dozen years of silence, Ezekiel began to prophesy again. This time his message was one of hope. Ezekiel announced that God intended to restore His people to their land and to establish a glorious kingdom ruled by the Messiah, a descendant of David!

Ezekiel 34:23, 24: David was to shepherd [rule] God's people. Through Ezekiel God announced,

I will establish one shepherd over them, and he shall feed them; My servant David. He shall feed them and be their shepherd. And I, the LORD, will be their God, and My servant David a prince among them; I, the LORD, have spoken (Ezek. 34:23, 24).

It would be easy to assume from this prophecy that God intended a resurrected David to rule. However, the language is idiomatic. It speaks of the promised descendant of David, a person whom Isaiah called the "Prince of Peace" (Isa. 9:6).

Ezekiel 37:22–27: The Abrahamic Covenant would be fulfilled when David's descendant ruled. One of the most striking of these prophecies linked several key elements of the Abrahamic Covenant to the coming reign of David's descendant.

I will make them one nation in the land, on the mountains of Israel; and one king shall be king over them all; they shall no longer be two nations, nor shall they ever be divided into two kingdoms again.

They shall not defile themselves anymore with their idols, nor with their detestable things, nor with any of their transgressions; but I will deliver them from all their dwelling places in which they have sinned, and will cleanse them. Then they shall be My people, and I will be their God. David My servant shall be king over them, and they shall all have one shepherd; they shall also walk in My judgments and observe My statutes, and do them.

Then they shall dwell in the land that I have given to Jacob My servant, where your fathers dwelt; and they shall dwell there, they, their children, and their children's children, forever; and My servant David shall be their prince forever.

Moreover I will make a covenant of peace with them, and it shall be an everlasting covenant with them; I will establish them and multiply them, and I will set My sanctuary in their midst forevermore. My tabernacle also shall be with them; indeed I will be their God, and they shall be My people (Ezek. 37:22–27).

What features of the Abrahamic Covenant would be fulfilled when David's descendant ruled as King? The chart below shows.

When the promised descendant of David finally ruled, all the promises made to Abraham would at last be fulfilled.

OTHER PROPHECIES ABOUT DAVID'S DESCENDANT

Isaiah, Jeremiah, and Ezekiel are known as "major prophets." The name comes from the length of their books. Each of them pictured a future in which God's promises to Israel would be fulfilled through the appearance of the descendant promised to David—a person who would rule a restored Jewish nation, according to God's promise.

The same theme appears in the writings of the "minor prophets," whose shorter books are also found in the Old Testament. They also spoke with confidence of the future promised by God, and they linked that future with the promised Davidic king.

Hosea foresaw a return to God (Hosea 3:4, 5). In a striking passage which pictured Israel without ruler or temple, Hosea predicted a return of Israel to the Lord. He wrote, "For the children of Israel shall abide many days without king or prince, without sacrifice or sacred pillar, without ephod or teraphim. Afterward the children of Israel shall return and seek the LORD their God and David their king. They shall fear the LORD and His goodness in the latter days" (Hos. 3:4–5).

Amos looked forward to future blessings (Amos 9:11, 13–15). Amos was called to warn the Northern Kingdom, Israel, of impending judgment. Yet as his prophecy came to a close, Amos like the other prophets looked ahead and foresaw a time of blessing, associated with a the rise of the "tabernacle [house, dynasty] of David."

> "On that day I will raise up
> The tabernacle of David, which
>   has fallen down,
> And repair its damages;
> I will raise up its ruins.
> And rebuild it as in the days of
>   old;
>   . . .
> "Behold, the days are coming,"
>   says the LORD,
> "when the plowman shall overtake
>   the reaper,
> And the treader of grapes him
>   who sows seed;
> The mountains shall drip with
>   sweet wine,
> And all the hills shall flow with
>   it.
> I will bring back the captives of
>   My people Israel;
> They shall build the waste cities
>   and inhabit them;
> They shall plant vineyards and
>   drink wine from them;

Abrahamic Covenant (Gen. 12:2–3, 7)	Ezekiel's prophecy of Messiah's rule (Ezek. 37)
Make you a great nation	Be one nation, with one king (v. 22). David will rule over you (v. 24).
I will bless you	Shall be My people, I will be their God (v. 23). David will rule forever (v. 25). Everlasting peace (v. 26).
All families on earth to be blessed	The nations to know that the LORD is God (v. 23).
To your descendants I will give this land.	Will dwell in the land God gave the fathers (v 25)

They shall also make gardens and
    eat fruit from them.
I will plant them in their land,
And no longer shall they be pulled
    up
From the land I have given them,"
Says the LORD your God (Amos 9:11,
    13–15).

There are many other prophecies like these woven throughout the writings of the Old Testament prophets. Here we have looked at only a few, and only predictions which specifically linked a Davidic king to the future blessings for Israel.

It is clear that the prophecies quoted have not yet been fulfilled. Even though the promised descendant of David has come, He has not yet established His rule here on earth.

Nor does He rule a redeemed Israel in the Holy Land.

THE BIBLE IDENTIFIED JESUS AS THE PROMISED DAVIDIC KING

The Gospels presented Jesus Christ as the descendant who fulfilled God's promise of a ruler to come from David's line. In biblical times this ruler was known as the Messiah.

The word *Messiah* is Hebrew for "anointed one." It reflects the Old Testament practice of pouring olive oil on the head of a person being ordained to a royal or priestly ministry. In the Greek language, the word for "anointed one" is "Christ." Thus, every time we refer to Jesus as "Jesus Christ," we are actually saying "Jesus the Messiah," or "Jesus, the promised descendant of David."

❖

Rebuilding the temple was a key part of the restoration promised by the prophets.

The identity of Jesus as the one who fulfilled God's promise to David of a descendant who would rule on his throne "forever" is critical to our understanding of Jesus and His mission.

JESUS' GENEALOGY ESTABLISHED HIS QUALIFICATIONS AS DAVIDIC KING

The Jewish people kept careful records of their family line. Pure descent was particularly important in the case of priests and Levites. It was also vital in the case of David's descendants, for God had promised that there would always be a descendant of David qualified to occupy Israel's throne.

So Matthew began his Gospel with the words, "The book of the genealogy of Jesus Christ, the Son of David, the Son of Abraham" (Matt. 1:1). He then traced Christ's line back to David and Abraham through Joseph, Mary's husband. As the legal son of Joseph, through whom the official Davidic line ran, Jesus was thus eligible to take David's throne.

But the Gospel of Luke also has a genealogy, which also traced the ancestry of Mary back to David. Through Mary, Jesus was the biological descendant of David. In both senses, biologically and legally, Jesus was qualified by birth to ascend David's throne.

JESUS' MIRACLES ESTABLISHED HIS IDENTITY AS THE PROMISED MESSIAH

While the Old Testament records a number of miracles, certain kinds of miracles that Jesus performed were without precedent in earlier ages. The majority of the miraculous signs Jesus performed involved healing. Jesus made the lame walk and the blind see. Jesus cast out demons, opened the ears of the deaf, and restored withered limbs.

What is striking about these miracles is that these specific wonders are linked in Bible prophecy with the appearance of the Messiah and the coming of the messianic age. Isaiah wrote that when God comes to save His people,

Then the eyes of the blind shall
   be opened,
And the ears of the deaf shall be
   unstopped.
Then the lame shall leap like a
   deer,
And the tongue of the dumb sing
   (Isa. 35:5, 6).

This line of prophecy was clearly linked to the appearance of the Messiah. When John the Baptist became discouraged after a long imprisonment, he sent disciples to ask Jesus if He truly were the Christ. Jesus had a simple response. He told John's disciples to tell the Baptist what they had heard and seen: "The blind see and the lame walk; the lepers are cleansed and the deaf hear; the dead are raised up and the poor have the gospel preached to them" (John 11:5).

The miracles Jesus performed were proof that He was the promised descendant of David, destined to restore Israel and sit on David's throne.

———————— ❖ ————————

Healing was one mark of the Messiah.

It is no wonder, then, that many who came to Jesus for healing cried out to Him, "Son of David, have mercy on us!" (Matt. 9:27). Those in need knew that the hope of Israel had arrived at last!

OTHER SCRIPTURES SUPPORT JESUS' IDENTIFICATION AS THE PROMISED MESSIAH

A number of scriptural references are cited by the writers of the Gospels and Acts to support the identification of Jesus as the Christ, the promised descendant of David.

How was Jesus David's son? (Matthew 22:42–45). In a challenge repeated in Mark and Luke, Jesus asked the religious leaders whose son the Messiah was to be. They answered, "The son [descendant] of David." Jesus then quoted Psalm 110:1 in which David referred to the Messiah as "my Lord." In the biblical world, a descendant was always considered to be inferior to his ancestor. But in this psalm, David called the Christ "Lord." How then, Jesus asked, "is He his Son?"

The question stunned His listeners, for they had no answer. Yet, there is an answer. David's descendant through Mary was also God the Son, incarnate as a human being. Thus, the very words of David about the one destined to fulfill the promise God made to him showed that the Messiah must be God Himself!

An angel announced Jesus' identity to Mary (Luke 1:31–33). Before Jesus was conceived, the angel Gabriel told Mary what would occur. He clearly identified Jesus not only as the Son of God, but also as the promised Messiah who would inherit David's throne and fulfill the covenant promises. The angel revealed,

You will conceive in your womb and bring forth a Son, and shall call His name Jesus. He will be great, and will be called the Son of the Highest; and the Lord God will give Him the throne of His father [ancestor] David. And He will reign over the house of Jacob forever, and of His kingdom there will be no end (Luke 1:31–33).

Jesus' resurrection showed He was the Messiah of the Old Testament (Acts 2:23–35). The resurrection of Jesus was a keystone of apostolic preaching. In Peter's first sermon in Acts, the apostle argued that the resurrection is proof that Jesus is the promised Messiah. Peter quoted Psalm 16 in which David said, "You will [not] allow Your Holy One to see corruption" (Acts 2:27). Peter pointed out that David is still in his tomb, so the passage cannot apply to him. Instead David, "knowing that God had sworn with an oath to him that of the fruit of his body, according to the flesh, He would raise up the Christ to sit on his throne" (v. 30), looked ahead and predicted Messiah's resurrection.

The resurrection of Jesus, then, to which all the disciples gave witness, showed conclusively that He was the Messiah of the Old Testament. As resurrected Lord, Jesus lives forever. Only He can fulfill the promise of an endless rule for David's seed.

JESUS WILL COME AGAIN TO RULE

After His resurrection, Jesus did not establish the kind of kingdom envisioned in the Old Testament. But history did not come to a close with Jesus' death and resurrection. Some 2,000 years have passed since the events recorded in the New Testment took place. An appropriate question, then, is, What happened to the covenant promises made to Abraham and David?

The best answer is not to assume that the covenant promises given to Abraham and David were symbolic, and have been fulfilled "spiritually" in the blessings Christians now enjoy. The Old Testament prophecies are far too specific for that. The best answer is to link the ultimate fulfillment of the covenant promises to Christ's return and the end of history.

Jesus promised to return (Matthew 24). This chapter of Matthew is eschatological. It describes events which will take place at history's end. The Gospels speak of a time of terrible tribulation here on earth. Jesus speaks of His own return to earth in great power. Matthew wrote, "They will see the Son of Man coming on the clouds of heaven with power and great glory. And He will send His angels with a great sound of a trumpet, and they will gather together His elect from the four winds, from one end of heaven to the other" (Matt. 24:30–31).

Revelation 19 describes Jesus' return in power to rule. This chapter of the book of Revelation depicts Jesus' return and His victory over God's enemies. Jesus is called KING OF KINGS and LORD OF LORDS (Rev. 19:16).

When Christ returns, He will not appear as suffering Savior but as King of kings. He will take the throne not only of Israel but of the whole world.

The early Christians expected the promises to David to be fulfilled at Jesus' return. Today many Christians have concluded that the ancient covenant promises given to Israel were set aside by Jesus, and that the commitments given to Abraham and his descendants have been fulfilled symbolically in the church.

This view was not held in the early church. The early Christians expected the covenant promises made to Israel to be fulfilled when Jesus returns. About A.D. 150 Justin Martyr wrote, "I and as many as are orthodox Christians, do acknowledge that there shall be a resurrection of the body, and a residence of a thousand years in Jerusalem, adorned and enlarged, as the prophets Ezekiel, Isaiah, and others do unanimously attest" (*Ante-Nicene Fathers,* Vol. I, p. 239). Martyr expected God to fulfill literally the promises of a Davidic kingdom that we have reviewed in this chapter.

Similarly, Irenaeus, a great missionary as well as a church father (died A.D. 202), wrote:

The Lord shall come from heaven in clouds, in the glory of the Father . . . bringing for the righteous the times of the kingdom, that is, the rest, the hallowed seventh day; and restoring to Abraham the promised inheritance; in which the kingdom the Lord declared that "many coming from the east and the west should sit down with Abraham, Isaac, and Jacob" (*Ante-Nicene Fathers,* Vol. 1, p. 560).

The early church fathers integrated the teaching of Revelation with Old Testament prophecy and with Jesus' own statements about the future found in Matthew 24 and Mark 13. Before the world came to an end, the church fathers expected Jesus to return and to institute the age of blessing spoken of in the Old Testament.

WHAT WE HAVE LEARNED FROM THE DAVIDIC COVENANT

God promised David that his descendants would occupy the throne of Israel perpetually. As we trace this covenant promise through the Old and New Testaments, we begin to realize that in making this covenant God has begun to reveal *how* He will fulfill the covenant made a thousand years before to Abraham.

THE DAVIDIC COVENANT HAD AN IMMEDIATE APPLICATION

David was told that his son Solomon would succeed him on the throne.

THE DAVIDIC COVENANT HAD AN INTERMEDIATE APPLICATION

As the histories of the united and divided Hebrew kingdoms are traced, we see that there was always a descendant of David on the throne of Judah.

THE DAVIDIC COVENANT HAD AN ESCHATOLOGICAL APPLICATION

As we move into the prophets, we begin to see an additional dimension of the Davidic Covenant. David is always to have a descendant qualified to sit on his throne—until the promise to David is fulfilled in a ruler who will establish an endless kingdom.

In addition, the Old Testament prophets linked the coming ruler, called the Messiah, or Anointed One, with specific promises made to Abraham. David's descendant will rule over a restored Hebrew kingdom, reestablished on the land promised to Abraham. God will bless His people then by being their God. And the Davidic King will be a banner to which even the Gentiles rally. So all families on earth will be blessed through Him.

JESUS CHRIST IS THE PROPHESIED DAVIDIC KING

The Gospels clearly identify Jesus as the Messiah promised in the Old Testament. Jesus was from David's line, biologically through His mother Mary and legally through His stepfather Joseph. Jesus' miracles were associated in prophecy with the coming messianic age. The angel who announced His birth predicted He would take the throne of His ancestor David. And Jesus' resurrection fulfilled prophecies made by David that his descendant and Lord would be raised from the dead.

The New Testament predicts a return of Jesus before the world ends. And it is as history draws to its close that the promises given Abraham are to be fulfilled by Jesus as God's agent and as David's great Son.

When we turn to the next great covenant—the New Covenant—we find even more wonderful truths about Jesus' role in carrying out God's eternal plan.

CHAPTER 6

THE BEST YET TO COME:

THE PROMISE OF A NEW COVENANT

Jeremiah 31—33; Hebrews 8—10

The fall of Judah and Jerusalem in 586 B.C. was a devastating blow to the Israelites. The one sure foundation of their lives had been God's covenant with Abraham and its promise of their homeland. Suddenly the citizens of Judah were torn from that land, even as their brothers in Israel had been sent into exile in 722 B.C. Was Israel still the chosen people? Had God finally rejected Abraham's descendants?

The Exile should have come as no surprise. In Deuteronomy 28, God had spelled out the consequences of repeated violation of the Law given on Sinai. Under the Law Covenant, the Lord was committed to bless those generations of Israelites that were faithful to Him. During the centuries that Judah had existed as a nation, national revivals had taken place under rulers like Hezekiah and Josiah. And those revivals, marked by renewed dedication to God and recommitment to keeping His Law, had in fact led to national blessing.

But the Law Covenant also committed God to punish the nation for apostasy. Rulers of Judah had often been disloyal to the Lord,

as the nation turned to idolatry and injustice. In particular, the 55-year reign of Manasseh (697–642 B.C.) had set the nation on a downward course which, despite a brief revival under Josiah, was continued by succeeding rulers.

God had stated in the Mosaic Covenant that such apostasy would lead to exile from the promised land. When the Babylonians launched their final invasion of Judah in 586 B.C., God's warning of the Law's ultimate national punishment was fulfilled.

> And it shall be, that just as the LORD rejoiced over you to do you good and multiply you, so the LORD will rejoice over you to destroy you and bring you to nothing; and you shall be plucked from off the land which you go to possess. Then the LORD will scatter you among all peoples, from one end of the earth to the other, and there you shall serve other gods, which neither you nor your fathers have known; wood and stone. And among those nations you shall find no rest, nor shall the sole of your foot have a resting place, but there the LORD will give you a trembling heart, failing eyes, and anguish of soul (Deut. 28:63–65).

The Law, which God had given to godly generations to enable them to experience the blessings promised to Abraham at history's end, had become a curse. Judah's disloyalty had led the Lord to cleanse the promised land of His sinning people.

Later a small group of Jews would return to their homeland. Yet from 586 B.C. to A.D. 1948, no truly independent Jewish state would exist on the land God had promised to Abraham. Even today, there are more Jews scattered among the nations than dwell in Israel.

Just before the Babylonian armies swept into Judah for the last time, the prophet Jeremiah delivered a message of hope to those about to be torn from their homeland.

Jeremiah lived and prophesied during the last 40 years of Judah's existence. He predicted the destruction of Jerusalem and urged his people to surrender to the Babylonians, and thus save many lives. His messages from God were ignored in his own day. But imbedded among the warnings of disaster were words of encouragement for future generations. "I know the thoughts that I think toward you," God told His people through Jeremiah.

Through Jeremiah, God told of a New Covenant.

"Thoughts of peace and not of evil, to give you a future and a hope" (Jer. 29:11).

God promised that a day would dawn when

you will seek Me and find Me, when you search for Me with all your heart. I will be found by you, says the LORD, and I will bring you back from your captivity; I will gather you from all the nations and from all the places where I have driven you, says the LORD, and I will bring you to the place from which I cause you to be carried away captive (Jer. 29:13, 14).

The Israelites' expulsion from Canaan did not mean that God had gone back on His covenant promise to Abraham. One day God would restore His people to their land, and keep every promise He had made.

But Jeremiah had an even more exciting message to share. Through Jeremiah, God revealed more about *how* He would keep His promises to Abraham. God would replace the Mosaic Covenant with a "New Covenant."

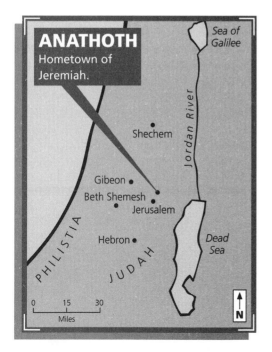

ANATHOTH
Hometown of Jeremiah.

Sea of Galilee

Jordan River

Shechem

Gibeon
Beth Shemesh
Jerusalem

Hebron

Dead Sea

PHILISTIA

JUDAH

0　15　30
Miles

N

THE NEW COVENANT PREDICTED BY JEREMIAH

When reading Jeremiah's words, it's important to remember that the prophet was *predicting* a New Covenant. God did not actually bring that covenant to fulfillment in Jeremiah's time.

The promise of a New Covenant is found in Jeremiah 31, as part of a longer promise concerning the future. God promised those about to go into exile that He would continue to be God for the families of Israel (Jer. 31:1). What is more, God would bring both Judah and Israel back to the promised land (Jer. 31:3–26)! Jeremiah's good news for Judah is that they "shall come back from the land of the enemy. There is hope in your future, says the LORD" (Jer. 31:17).

This promise of a return, expressed unequivocally in Jeremiah 31:27, 28, was to take place when God kept a New Covenant which He had yet to make with His people. That covenant is described in Jeremiah 31:31–34,

Behold, the days are coming, says the LORD, when I will make a new covenant with the house of Israel, and with the house of Judah—not according to the covenant that I made with their fathers in the day that I took them by the hand to lead them out of the land of Egypt, My covenant which they broke, though I was a husband to them, says the LORD.

But this is the covenant that I will make with the house of Israel after those days, says the LORD: I will put My law in their minds, and write it on their hearts; and I will be their God, and they shall be My people.

No more shall every man teach his neighbor, and every man his brother, saying, "Know the LORD," for they all shall know Me, from the least of them to the greatest of them, says the LORD. For I will forgive their iniquity, and their sin I will remember no more (Jer. 31:31–34).

These few verses found in Jeremiah are among the most significant in Scripture. We can outline the key elements of this revelation as follows.

"The days are coming" (Jeremiah 31:31). The promise given through Jeremiah was not the New Covenant itself. Instead, Jeremiah described a covenant that God would make in the future.

"I will make" (Jeremiah 31:31). The maker of this covenant is the Lord. God Himself, the guarantor of the Noahic and Abrahamic covenants, will guarantee the New Covenant as well. As God has faithfully distributed the appropriate blessings and curses due Israel under the Law Covenant, so God will faithfully keep the promises incorporated in the New Covenant.

"A New Covenant" (Jeremiah 31:31). This is the name of the covenant that Jeremiah promised God would make one day. The name echoes through the New Testament, for that covenant was implemented by Christ on the cross (see Matt. 26:26–28; Luke 22:19, 20; Rom. 11:27; 1 Cor. 11:23–25; Heb. 8:6–13; 10:14–18).

The parties to the covenant (Jeremiah 31:31). Jeremiah stated specifically that the New Covenant was to be made "with the house of Israel and with the house of Judah." Like the Abrahamic and Mosaic covenants, the New Covenant was made with the descendants of Abraham. Paul celebrated this role of the Jewish people as covenant bearers in Romans 9:4–5. There he wrote of "the Israelites, to whom pertain the adoption, the glory, the covenants, the giving of the law, the service of God, and the promises; of whom are the fathers and from whom, according to the flesh, Christ came, who is over all, the eternally blessed God."

It has always been God's intention to bless the entire human family through the covenants He made with Abraham and his descendants.

The covenant contrasted (Jeremiah 31:32). The New Covenant was specifically said to be "not like" the covenant God made when He led Israel out of Egypt. It is clear that Jeremiah was speaking of the Mosaic, or Law Covenant. In fact, that covenant was severely criticized here and in Galatians.

Because blessing under the Mosaic Covenant depended on Israel's obedience, blessing could not be guaranteed by God. Indeed, Jeremiah reminded the Israelites that they broke that covenant (Jer. 31:32), even though God "was a husband to them" (i.e., met His commitment to be loyal to them and supplied all their needs).

There was nothing wrong with the standards expressed in the Mosaic Law. The problem lay in human nature. Law was an objective, external expression of God's will. But Law could not provide the spiritual life so essential to true heart-response to God (Gal. 3:21).

The fact that the Covenant was "new" implied that the Law would be replaced. One day God's people would relate to Him in a new and living way.

The heart of the New Covenant (Jeremiah 31:33, 34).

The heart of the New Covenant was God's promise to transform. Rather than etching His Law in stone tablets, God said, "I will put My law in their minds, and write it on their hearts." With this inner transformation, Israel would come into a relationship with the Lord in which "I will be their God, and they shall be My people" in a new way. Indeed, Jeremiah said, "They all shall know Me." The key to this new relationship with the Lord will be the forgiveness of sins: "For I will forgive their iniquity, and their sin I will remember no more."

Under the Mosaic Law, the blood of sacrificial animals effected "atonement." The Hebrew word *kapar* means "to cover." Sins that had been atoned for were thus covered over, but they still remained. Yet, in the Old Testament God also spoke of forgiveness. This Hebrew word *nasa'* means "to lift up" or "take away." When the New Covenant was executed, it would become clear just how God would remove sins that under the Law could only be covered over.

The immutability of the New Covenant (Jeremiah 31:35–37).

After promising to make a New Covenant with Abraham's descendants in the future, God reaffirmed His earlier commitments to Abraham's descendants. The present exile did not mean the Lord had cancelled the covenants or abandoned Israel.

> "If heaven above can be measured,
> And the foundations of the earth
>   searched out beneath,
> I will also cast off all the seed of
>   Israel
> For all that they have done, says
>   the LORD" (Jer. 31:37).

The link to the Abrahamic Covenant (Jeremiah 31:1–30, 38–40).

While the New Covenant will replace the Mosaic Covenant, it does not alter the Abrahamic Covenant. God had promised Abraham to bless him and his descendants. He had promised that in Abraham all the families of the earth would be blessed. The New Covenant promises of forgiveness, intimate relationship with God, and inner transformation define *how* God intends to fulfill those promises.

It is also important to note that through Jeremiah God also reaffirmed His commitment to keep the promise to Abraham that his descendants would inherit Canaan and that a Jewish nation would be established there. This is stated in the strongest terms.

"It shall come to pass, that as I have watched over them to pluck up, to break down, to throw down, to destroy, and to afflict, so I will watch over them to build and to plant, says the LORD" (Jer. 31:28).

And:

"Behold, the days are coming, says the LORD, that the city shall be built for the LORD" (Jer. 31:38).

The link between the Abrahamic Covenant and the New Covenant is also seen in Ezekiel, a contemporary of Jeremiah.

Thus says the Lord GOD: "I will gather you from the peoples, assemble you from the countries where you have been scattered, and I will give you the land of Israel. . . . Then I will give them one heart, and I will put a new spirit within them, and take the stony heart out of their flesh, and give them a heart of flesh, that they may walk in My statutes and keep My judgments and do them; and they shall be My people, and I will be their God" (Ezek. 11:17, 19, 20; see also Ezek. 36:24–28).

The Lord gave His guarantee (Jeremiah 31:31–40). In these verses the words "says the LORD" occur eight times. God was fully committed to accomplish what He promised to do when the New Covenant is fulfilled and Israel has turned back to Him.

THE NEW COVENANT WAS EXECUTED BY JESUS

Through Jeremiah, God promised that He would make a New Covenant with His people one day. Over 600 years passed before God kept that promise.

In the interim, the Jewish people were scattered throughout the Mediterranean world. A total of 42,360 Jews returned to Judah in 538 B.C. to rebuild the Jerusalem temple, and much smaller groups returned in 458 B.C. under Ezra and in 444 B.C. under Nehemiah. But still Judah existed only as a tiny district in a minor province of the Persian Empire.

In 143 B.C. a struggle which was both a civil war and war of liberation from the Seleucid Empire brought the Jews a form of independence. But during this period a family of priests, the Hasmoneans, governed. No national state under a king was ever established. Then, in 34 B.C. the Jewish people and lands were incorporated into the mighty Roman Empire. By the first century A.D., only a few hundred thousand Jews lived in their homeland. By contrast, it has been estimated that some 10 percent of the population of the Roman Empire was Jewish, settled in cities throughout Roman lands. Over a million Jews lived in Alexandria, Egypt, alone!

Clearly, God's promise of restoration to the promised land had not yet been fulfilled. Just as clearly, no New Covenant between God and His people had yet been executed.

JESUS ANNOUNCED THE NEW COVENANT

During His years of public ministry, through public announcement and miracle, Jesus presented Himself to Israel as the promised Messiah. The response of God's people was marked by hesitancy and hostility.

While a small group responded to Jesus and followed Him, the nation as a whole concluded that Christ was nothing more than a great prophet (cf. Matt. 16:13, 14). The leaders, however, decided that Jesus was a threat to the established faith and their own position, so they determined to bring Him down. As the hostility of the leaders became more open, Jesus began to teach His followers that He must be put to death by His enemies.

This teaching shocked His disciples (cf. Matt. 16:21, 22). They could not imagine that God would permit this to happen to one whom they recognized as the promised Messiah and Son of God. Not until the night before His crucifixion did Jesus explain the meaning of what was about to happen.

The Gospels of Matthew, Mark, and Luke reported Jesus' words to His most intimate followers.

"For this is My blood of the new covenant, which is shed for many for the remission of sins" (Matt. 26:28).

And He said to them, "This is My blood of the new covenant, which is shed for many" (Mark 14:24).

Likewise He also took the cup after supper, saying, "This cup is the new covenant in My blood, which is shed for you" (Luke 22:20).

In these words to His disciples, Jesus told them for the first time the true significance of the Cross.

The Cross marked the making of the promised New Covenant. Jeremiah had promised that God would one day make a new covenant with the house of Israel. Jesus announced that he was about to fulfill that promise. The New Covenant would be established the next day, sealed in Jesus' blood.

The Cross was the sacrifice that sealed the New Covenant. Sacrifice was the means by which the Noahic, the Abrahamic, and the Mosaic covenants were established as legally binding instruments. The New Covenant was

At the Last Supper, Jesus connected the Cross and the New Covenant.

to be established by a sacrifice as well. But the blood that formally instituted the New Covenant would not be that of a sacrificial animal. It would be the blood of God's own Son.

The sacrifice on Calvary served as the basis of the forgiveness promised under the New Covenant. The Old Testament constantly linked forgiveness to sacrifice. God said of the Old Testament sacrificial system, "The life of the flesh is in the blood, and I have given it to you upon the altar to make atonement for your souls; for it is the blood that makes atonement for the soul" (Lev. 17:11).

The blood of sacrificial animals had covered sins committed under the old agreement. The blood of God's Son would pay for sins in full. Jesus' blood would satisfy the demands of justice and provide a basis for once-for-all forgiveness.

So it was by the death of Jesus on Calvary that God executed the promised New Covenant. The New Covenant promises that were made there have yet to be fulfilled. But even today, all who believe in Jesus can experience the promised blessings of God's New Covenant.

THE NEW COVENANT IN THE NEW TESTAMENT

The book of Hebrews develops the significance of the institution of the New Covenant. The writer, a Jew, set out to demonstrate to other Jews that relating to God through Jesus was far superior to trying to relate to God through the Law.

To show the superiority of Jesus, the writer contrasted the New and Mosaic covenants, as seen in the chart below.

What, specifically, does the writer of Hebrews say about the New Covenant?

The promise of a New Covenant implied fault in the Mosaic Covenant (Hebrews 8:8). The writer points out that "if that first covenant had been faultless, then no place would have been sought for a second" (Heb. 8:7). The very fact that God through Jeremiah promised "I will make a new covenant" and specified "not according to the covenant that I made with their fathers in the day when I took them . . . out of the land of Egypt," proves the Old Covenant was flawed.

The writer of Hebrews goes on to pinpoint the problem. Israel broke the Old Covenant. But God says of the New Covenant "I will put My laws in their mind and write them on their hearts . . . for all shall know me" and "their sins and their lawless deeds I will remember no more" (Heb. 8:10–12).

The New Covenant does not depend on human beings or their actions. The New Covenant is a covenant of promise, whose "I will" statements describe what God Himself will surely do!

Israel and Judah violated the Old Covenant and were punished for their sins. Under God's New Covenant, He will give His people a heart that is fully in tune with His own, so that His character, once expressed in stone, will be expressed in the lives of believers.

Jesus' blood "made" the New Covenant (Hebrews 9:14, 15). The text leaves no doubt. It was Jesus' blood, His life offered in place of our own, which cleanses dead works and enables us to serve God. "For this reason, He is the Mediator of the new covenant, by means of death, for the redemption of the transgressions under the first covenant, that those who are called may receive the promise of eternal inheritance" (Heb. 9:15).

The Mosaic Law defined sin. Failure to keep that law makes one guilty, and demonstrates the fact that all are sinners.

Jesus died to pay the penalty for our sins.

When we respond in faith to Him, we "receive the promise of eternal inheritance."

THE NEW COVENANT AS AN ESCHATOLOGICAL COVENANT

We've noted before that God's covenant promises look ahead to history's end. This is true of the New Covenant as well as the Abraham and Davidic covenants. But how does the New Covenant relate to them?

The eschatological covenants and corporate Israel. We noted earlier that God's covenants treat Abraham's descendants as a group rather than as individuals. We also saw that the promises tell what God will do for Abraham's descendants at history's end.

Under these covenants, God will at last plant the Jewish people in Canaan, where they will live under the Messiah, a ruler to emerge

Issue	Mosaic Covenant	New Covenant
Mediator	Angels	God's Son, who is superior to angels
Agent	Moses, a faithful servant in God's house	Jesus, heir and owner of God's house
Priesthood	Aaron's sons, ordained by God	Jesus, ordained God
Priesthood	Held by mortal men	Exercised by one who lives forever
Service	In a material sanctuary	In heaven itself
Quality	Faulty, to be replaced	Perfect, providing absolute forgiveness
Access	Did not provide worshiper access to God	Provides free access to God
Sacrifices	Repeated, thus inadequate	Offered once, adequate
Sacrifices	Blood of bulls and goats, which cannot take away sins	Blood of Jesus, wins full remission of sins

from David's family line. The New Covenant adds to this picture images of a forgiven, converted, and holy people who do God's will and live in intimate personal relationship with Him.

The New Testament reveals an unexpected aspect of God's plan. Before He could rule, the Messiah, Jesus Christ, had to die and in His death make possible the inner transformation promised in the New Covenant. The New Testament also predicts Jesus' return. When Christ comes back, all the covenant promises of God will be fulfilled in Him.

It is important to understand that God never promised that the land granted to Abraham would be possessed by every generation of Jews. In fact, for most of the past 2,500 years, no Jewish nation has existed in Palestine. This fact in no way indicates that God has been unfaithful to His people. Rather, it indicates that His Old Testament people have not been faithful to Him!

Before the Israelites were brought into the land given to Abraham, they were given the Mosic or Law Covenant. In that covenant, God made them an "along-the-way" promise. If a given generation was loyal to the Lord and kept His Law, God promised to bless that generation and let them enjoy some of the blessings promised in the Abrahamic Covenant. And God did just that. But the Lord also stated that if a given generation was not loyal to the Lord and if it broke His commandments, that generation would be punished with natural disasters, diseases, and foreign invasions. Ultimately, if generations remained disloyal, God would uproot His people from the promised land and send them into exile. This has also happened, and for most of their history the Jewish people have lived in exile.

The New Covenant, like the Abrahamic and the Davidic covenants, is essentially an eschatological covenant. It reveals more of the purposes God intends to achieve by history's end. When history reaches its intended culmination, God's own people will be forgiven and renewed. Sin itself will be banished, and God's Law will be written on the hearts of men and women who know and love Him. Jesus

Christ, who secured our salvation on Calvary, will rule as David's greater Son.

It is no wonder then that the first preaching of the apostles linked Christ's death and a national conversion with the fulfillment of the Old Testament's covenant promises. Speaking in Jerusalem, Peter declared,

Repent therefore and be converted, that your sins may be blotted out, so that times of refreshing may come from the presence of the Lord, and that He may send Jesus Christ, who was preached to you before, whom heaven must receive until the times of restoration of all things, which God has spoken by the mouth of all His holy prophets since the world began (Acts 3:19–21).

No national conversion took place at that time. Yet the apostle Paul warned Gentile believers not to be ignorant of the fact that national Israel had been set aside, "until the fullness of the Gentiles has come in" (Rom. 11:25). Then, Paul said, "All Israel will be saved, as it is written,

The Deliverer will come out of Zion,
And He will turn away ungodliness

Peter's first sermon linked Jesus and the covenants.

from Jacob;
For this is My Covenant with them,
When I take away their sins (Rom.
11:25–27).

The covenant promises recorded in the Old
Testament will yet be kept, for Paul reminds
us, "The gifts and the calling of God are irrevocable" (Rom. 11:29).

**The eschatological covenants and the believ-
ing individual.** While God's covenant promises were made with the Hebrew people as a
whole, and will be kept with national Israel,
the covenants have always had great implications for the individual.

Individual blessing. While the experience of individuals was always linked with the fate of
the nation, God did make a distinction between the believer who loved and obeyed
Him and the rebellious or indifferent. Thus,
Psalm 84 celebrates the fact that

Blessed is the man whose strength is
in You,
Whose heart is set on pilgrimage
(Ps. 84:5).

And Psalm 1 contrasts the consequences of a
person's decision to follow or abandon the
Lord.

Blessed is the man
Who walks not in the counsel of the
ungodly,
Nor stands in the path of sinners,
Nor sits in the seat of the scornful;
But his delight is in the law of the
LORD,
And in His law he mediates day and
night.
He shall be like a tree
Planted by the rivers of water,
That brings forth its fruit in its
season,
Whose leaf also will not wither;
And whatsoever he does shall
prosper.

The ungodly are not so,
But are like the chaff which the wind
drives away.
Therefore the ungodly shall not
stand in the judgment,
Nor sinners in the congregation of
the righteous.

For the LORD knows the way of the
righteous,
But the way of the ungodly shall
perish (Ps. 1:1–6).

While the Abrahamic and Mosaic covenants had both been made with the nation,
the individual who lived by God's Law could
expect to be blessed.

Personal salvation. While the covenants were
made with corporate Israel, salvation was always an individual matter. Abraham believed
God's promise, and it was "accounted to *him*
as righteousness" (Gen. 15:6). It was the same
for individual Israelites. The person who
heard God's promise and responded with faith
was credited with righteousness. As Paul argued in Romans, a "true" Israelite was not just
a biological descendant of Abraham, but one
who had Abraham's kind of faith. Salvation
was never a matter of keeping God's Law.

The Psalms especially reflect the true believer's sense of personal relationship with the
Lord. They also reflect the true believers' realization that this relationship is not rooted in
their own merits, but in God's grace to sinners. David, after his involvement with
Bathsheba and the conspiracy which led to the
death of her husband, cried out to the Lord.

Have mercy upon me, O God,
According to Your lovingkindness;
According to the multitude of
Your tender mercies,
Blot out my transgressions.
Wash me thoroughly from my
iniquity,
And cleanse me from my sin.

For I acknowledge my
transgressions,

And my sin is always before me.
Against You, You only, have I sinned,
And done this evil in Your sight
    (Ps. 51:1–4).

In Old Testament times, as in our own, individuals who turned to God as David did, trusting Him to forgive and cleanse, found a personal salvation which is like that found today by those who come to Jesus through the gospel's good news.

Resurrection. In a sense, the blessings promised the nation Israel at history's end pale in comparison with the blessings intended for individual believers. While the Old Testament does not emphasize resurrection, it does teach it. Old Testament saints, like New Testament believers, will be raised from the dead.

One authority pointed out:

The OT emphasizes the blessings of living on earth in obedient, intimate relationship with the Lord. In most cases, the "salvation" spoken of in the OT is deliverance from some present enemy or trouble. Yet it would be a mistake to conclude that the OT is a stranger to the doctrine of resurrection, or that OT saints enjoyed no such hope. In fact, saints who "died in faith" did look forward to a better country, to a city God would one day found (Heb. 11:8–16).

Many OT references may allude to the possibility of resurrection (cf. Gen. 5:22–24; Deut. 32:39; 2 Kings 2:11, 12). Other statements, whose meaning may not be perfectly clear, still make sense only in the context of a belief in resurrection (cf. Job 19:25–27; Ps. 16:9–11).

When we reach the prophets, we see this belief expressed clearly and confidently. One day death will be defeated (Isa. 25:8), and "your dead will live" as their bodies rise when "the earth gives birth to her dead" (Isa. 26:19). Daniel is very explicit. Those who "sleep in the dust of the earth will awake: some to everlasting life, others to shame and everlasting contempt" (Dan. 12:2).

When reading the OT, with its emphasis on God's blessings in this life, and with its majestic prophetic view of a cleansed and purified earth, it is good to remember that God does not forget the trusting individual. The saints of old will join us, sharing with us in the resurrection won for us all by Christ Jesus (*Richards' Complete Bible Handbook,* Word, p. 299).

It is in the resurrection that the full benefits of the New Covenant will be known. Then, God's law will be in our hearts and we will be fully like Him at last (1 John 3:2).

The promises stated in the New Covenant will be ultimately fulfilled not only in the conversion of corporate Israel, but also in the resurrection and ultimate transformation of believers at history's end.

THE NEW COVENANT AS AN EXPERIENTIAL COVENANT

In the chapter on the Mosaic Covenant, we saw that the Law functioned as a doorkeeper. Any generation which obeyed the Law was given access to many of the blessings guaranteed to Abraham's descendants at history's end. There we used the analogy of a person for whom $100 million was placed in trust, to be given to her at age 50. Though promised wealth in 25 years, such a person might live in poverty in the meantime!

Continuing the analogy, we supposed that there might be some way for her to get the interest on the $100 million now. If that could be done, she would live extremely well now, and the vast fortune would still be hers at age 50!

What the Law did for corporate Israel was to provide access to the "interest" on the covenant promises God made to Abraham. If the nation was loyal to the Lord and kept His Law, God would be with them and bless them, and they would prosper in the promised land.

In a similar way, individuals had access to blessing. Persons who trusted the Lord and sought to obey Him could expect personal blessing in this life, and not simply in the resurrection to come at history's end. The eschatological covenant had an experiential aspect. Promised future blessings could be experienced now.

The nature of the New Covenant blessings (Jeremiah 31; Hebrews 8). Looking back at the original statement of the New Covenant and at its review in Hebrews, we realize that the blessings promised in the New Covenant are spiritual.

The Abrahamic and Davidic Covenants emphasized prosperity of the nation in Canaan. The New Covenant emphasized personal relationship with God and spiritual renewal.

God's Laws in mind and heart (Hebrews 8:10). God intends to transform us from within. The first function of the Law is to reveal the character of God. By saying He will write His Law in our minds and hearts, God promises true inner transformation.

The Bible says that in the resurrection we will be like Jesus (1 John 3:2). This is the eschatological hope that the New Covenant offers. But the Bible also says that even now "we are being transformed into the same image from glory to glory, just as by the Spirit of the Lord" (2 Cor. 3:18). This is one experiential promise that is ours now under the New Covenant. We no longer have to be bound by the passions of our sin nature. God the Holy Spirit is at work within our hearts, to free us from sin's grip and to make us more and more like Jesus.

Direct access to God (Hebrews 8:10). Another New Covenant promise is that "I will be their God, and they shall be My people." Revelation promises that the resurrected believer "shall see His face" (Rev. 22:4). We will live in and enjoy the very presence of God. This is the eschatological hope expressed in the New Covenant.

But the Bible also invites us to "come boldly to the throne of grace, that we may obtain mercy and find grace to help in time of need" at this very moment (Heb. 4:16)! Right now we have immediate access to the Lord. We can come to Him in prayer, whether for mercy (forgiveness) or grace to help (strength). This is another New Covenant blessing that we can experience today.

Knowing God personally (Hebrews 8:11). In the Hebrew language, "know" is a rich concept. It moves us beyond intellectual knowledge to

Believers have direct, immediate access to God.

personal experience. It moves us from acquaintance to intimacy. In promising that "all shall know Me," God's New Covenant points us beyond knowing *about* God to a wonderful personal relationship *with* Him. This also is an eschatological hope.

Writing in Colossians, Paul reminds us that we can know God intimately and personally today. As we learn more about His will as revealed in Scripture and let our steps be guided by Him, we are promised fruitful lives. We will also grow to know God better (Col. 1:9–11).

Coming to know God is another of the New Covenant promises which we appropriate today. We can experience God, not as a distant deity, but as a friend who is deeply involved in our daily lives.

No remembrance of sins and lawless deeds (Hebrews 8:12). Under the New Covenant, the community of Israel is promised future forgiveness of sins. In saying that He will no longer "remember" sins and lawless deeds, God is making a significant statement. In the idiom of the Old Testament, to "remember" something is to act in accordance with it.

This New Covenant promise looks forward to a time when sins are paid for and gone and the demands of justice are met. In that time, God will treat His people graciously, for the guilt of their sins will be removed.

How wonderful that right now "we have redemption through His [Christ's] blood, the forgiveness of sins" (Col. 1:14). When Jesus instituted the New Covenant on the Cross, He paid for all our sins—past, present, and future. God now is free to treat *us* graciously and with mercy—not as our sins deserve.

And, because God is at work in our lives, writing His Law on our hearts, we who have experienced forgiveness are motivated to live lives that are pleasing to Him.

New Covenant blessings are spiritual in nature. And these blessings are available to us in Jesus today.

Establishing a New Covenant relationship with God. Jeremiah wrote that God would one day make a New Covenant "with the house of Israel." The New Covenant, like the Davidic Covenant, is a further development of the covenant that God made with Abraham and his descendants.

Who was the gospel for? One of the promises imbedded in the Abrahamic Covenant was that all families on earth would be blessed in Abraham. In making the Abrahamic Covenant and the New Covenant, God had more than the Jewish people in mind! God was thinking of everyone.

When the early church was first formed, it was composed of Jewish believers. Within a few years, many Gentiles had also responded to the gospel. When Cornelius, the first Gentile to become a Christian, was saved, the Jewish believers "glorified God, saying, 'Then God has also granted to the Gentiles repentance to life' " (Acts 11:18).

Through the missionary work of the apostle Paul, the Gentile church exploded. A council was held in Jerusalem because of this rapid growth. After listening to the report of the missionaries about what God was doing among non-Jews, James summed up a conclusion that had been inescapable since Simon Peter had reported the conversion of Cornelius.

Men and brethren, listen to me: Simon has declared how God at the first visited the Gentiles to take out of them a people for His name. And with this the words of the prophets agree, just as it is written:

> After this, I will return
> And will rebuild the tabernacle of
> David, which has fallen down;
> I will rebuild its ruins,
> And I will set it up;
> So that the rest of mankind may
> seek the Lord,
> Even all the Gentiles who are
> called by My name,
> Says the Lord who does all these
> things (Acts 15:13–17).

It was clear to the early church that the good news of Jesus, along with access to the New Covenant blessings, was given to Gentiles as well as to Jews. This development was in full harmony with the Old Testament's teachings.

The gospel was for all.

How was a New Covenant relationship with God established? The answer to this question was evident from the beginning. As Abraham responded to God's promise with faith, we are to respond to the gospel's promise of personal salvation.

While on earth, Jesus told Nicodemus, "God so loved the world that He gave His only begotten Son, that whoever believes in Him should not perish, but have everlasting life" (John 3:16). This simple message was preached by the apostles after Jesus' resurrection. "To Him all the prophets witness that, through His name, whoever believes in Him will receive remission of sins" (Acts 10:43).

This message is still preached today. It is by faith in Jesus that we establish a New Covenant relationship with God. By faith, all the spiritual blessings described in that covenant are poured out on us.

Experiencing New Covenant blessings today. In Old Testament times, keeping God's Law was the way that a generation of Israelites or an individual believer gained access to covenant blessings. But the problem with the Law was that failure to keep it not only cut a generation off from blessing; failure to keep the Law brought God's curse!

Because human beings are by nature sinners, being under the Law was inevitably a curse to His Old Testament people. This is one reason why Paul wrote in Romans 6:14 that "sin shall not have dominion over you, for you are not under law but under grace." Human failure meant that sin ruled, for its power brought judgment after judgment upon Israel.

So while the Law did in theory provide access to blessings promised in the Abrahamic Covenant, in practice the Law was much more likely to bring punishment and pain.

In saying that we are no longer under the Law but under grace, Romans reflects the fact that the Mosaic Covenant of Law has been replaced by the New Covenant. The question then is, How do we gain access to the blessings promised in the New Covenant, if not by trying to keep God's Law?

The answer is not given in a single passage but in a series of images found in different New Testament books.

Abide in Jesus (John 15:1–5). Jesus pictured Himself as a grapevine, and described believers as branches. Power for a godly life and the ability to bear spiritual fruit flows through the vine to its branches. Thus the key to spiritual vitality is to abide in Jesus—a phrase which means "stay close to Him." We stay close to Jesus by putting His teachings into daily practice. As we do, the Lord strengthens us and enables us to do His will.

Know, reckon, yield (Romans 8:4–13). In Romans 6, Paul pointed out that believers have been united to Jesus. We "died" in His death, and we were "raised" with Him in His resurrection. Thus, Jesus provides us with His own resurrection power, which enables us to live a new kind of life. We are to *know* what has happened to us through our union with Jesus, to *reckon* (count on) the power He provides, and to *yield* ourselves to the Lord, making each choice out of a desire to do His will.

Walk in the Spirit (Galatians 5:16). Galatians 5 contrasts "fruit" of the sin nature (adultery, un-

Jesus explained God's salvation plan to Nicodemus.

cleanness, hatred, jealousies, etc.) with "fruit" produced in the believer's life by the Holy Spirit (love, joy, peace, etc.). The imagery suggests a struggle between competing desires. We are pulled in one direction by desires rooted in the sin nature. We are pulled in another direction by desires prompted by the Holy Spirit.

To "walk in the Spirit" means to respond to the Spirit rather than to sin's urgings.

While there are other similar images in Scripture, these three highlight a central truth. The Christian experiences the blessings of the New Covenant *by nurturing a deeper personal relationship with Jesus.* It is not by trying to keep an external law that we find blessing, but by growing to love God more and more, and responding to Him as a person.

St. Augustine taught, "Love God and do as you please." The person who is truly in love with God will want to do what pleases Him. And when we want to do what pleases God, the Holy Spirit enables us to succeed! As we walk close to the Lord, the New Covenant's blessings are poured out on us in our own day.

LOOKING BACK:

The Covenants in Review

When we began our look at the biblical covenants, I suggested several reasons why understanding them is important for Christians. Let's briefly review those reasons, and see how what we've learned can help us.

THE BIBLICAL COVENANTS HELP US KNOW GOD BETTER

The God who reveals Himself in His covenant promises is truly a wonderful God. He is a God who is fully aware of human flaws and frailty, and He cares about humankind. He is a God who was moved by love to choose to help us, and to reveal His intentions in the form of covenant promises. He is a God of grace, who has set out to bless us not because we deserve it, but because He cares. The God of the covenants is a God who is utterly trustworthy. He is a sovereign God with the power to accomplish all He has promised. He is a God who wants us to understand how completely He is committed to keeping His promises. And He is a God who has shown Himself willing to accept our faith in His promises in place of a righteousness that we human beings simply do not have.

What a wonderful God is revealed to us in the biblical covenants.

THE BIBLICAL COVENANTS PROVIDE A ROAD MAP TO THE OLD TESTAMENT

The Old Testament perplexes many Christians. Why tell the stories of Abraham and the patriarchs? What is so special about the Jewish people? What purpose is there in speaking of kings who ruled a tiny land thousands of years ago? What is the meaning of the words of the prophets? Why don't we just start with Jesus and the New Testament and forget the Old Testament except for a few of its favorite tales?

When we understand the biblical covenants, everything falls into place. We realize that God chose Abraham and his descendants to become a channel of blessing for all humankind. We see the Old Testament stories as stops along the way to the blessings which God intends to bestow on all humankind. We see in the stories of judges and kings the outworking of God's eagerness to bless along with His willingness to discipline. And in comparing the goals set in covenants with Bible history and with the predictions of the prophets, we see the direction in which history is moving. This helps us gain a sense of what God may do next.

The son of David proclaimed by the crowds was also the Son of God.

THE BIBLICAL COVENANTS ARE A KEY TO INTERPRETING THE OLD TESTAMENT

When we understand God's covenant promises, we gain fresh insight into the significance of Old Testament people and events. We grasp the lesson taught in the fall of Jericho's walls followed by the defeat at Ai. We sense the foundation of the faith that supported Jeremiah's forty-year prophetic ministry in the face of ridicule and rejection. When we turn to the prophets, words that seemed obscure become clear as we link a prophet's vision to God's promises to Abraham or David.

Again and again, we see the covenant promises emerge as central themes of prophecy as well as history. The rise and fall of ancient empires is seen in a new light when understood in their relationship to the blessing or cursing of God's people. And at every turn the sacred history reflects another facet of a covenant promise that God made to Abraham and his descendants. We see more clearly the role of the Old Testament, and we begin to understand why Old Testament Law does not apply today, even though we are called to holiness, just as

Israel was. The covenants are a lens through which the meaning of the Old Testament comes into clear focus for modern believers.

THE BIBLICAL COVENANTS ENRICH OUR APPRECIATION OF JESUS CHRIST

When we understand the biblical covenants, we gain a fresh appreciation for Jesus. In the Old Testament, we discover aspects of His role we may have overlooked in reading the New. In the Old Testament, Jesus—the promised Davidic King—becomes the focal point of history. He is both the suffering Savior and the triumphant King.

Isaiah, who portrayed Jesus' sacrificial death in chapter 53, also provides sharp images of the Savior's triumphant rule throughout his book. In Jesus, the world is set right. In Him, the sin that has tormented humankind is done away with, and the earth itself is reshaped and nature pacified. Through Jesus, individuals as well as the nations of the world will be restored to harmony with God and one another. In Jesus, all the promises of God find their Amen.

THE BIBLICAL COVENANTS PROVIDE PERSPECTIVE ON MANY BIBLE PROMISES

As we read the Bible, we come across many wonderful promises that are made by God. Can we claim these promises as our own? Are they for us?

Understanding the biblical covenants, we will immediately recognize many promises as expressions rooted in what God has stated He intends to do for Israel, or through the Messiah. Some are conditional and depend on His Old Testament people being loyal to Him and His Law. Recognizing such promises will help us immensely as we sort through all of God's promises and wonder, "Is this promise for me? Can I claim it today?"

Promises that have a direct link to the covenants and which were made to God's Old Testament peoples often have some application to us as well. But we as modern believers should not assume that every biblical promise was meant for today.

As we move on to the next section of this book, we will learn many things. We will discover wonderful promises that we can count on as we grow in our own relationship with the Lord. And we will not be disappointed—if we understand the promises correctly and claim only those that are meant for us.

Understanding Bible covenants and God's covenant promises does make a difference to us today. It may seem tedious to study them as carefully as we have done in this first section. But when we understand the covenants thoroughly, the Bible becomes a more exciting and meaningful book.

PART TWO:
GOD'S WONDERFUL PROMISES

In the first part of this book, we looked at Bible covenants. These covenants state what God has said He most surely will do. They are divine commitments, expressed in what was considered to be legally binding form in Bible times.

These covenants are actually promises—but very special promises.

The covenant promises are unconditional. God committed Himself to keep these promises whatever human beings might do. Under no circumstances would the covenant promises be set aside or changed.

The covenant promises are cosmic promises. These promises shape the flow of history itself. They look forward to the time when Christ returns, for they find their ultimate fulfillment in Him.

The covenant promises are restated again and again. Many Bible promises restate or amplify God's covenant commitments. The prophets es-

pecially returned to the covenants again and again to give hope to Israel in times of distress. For example, God through Isaiah looked forward to a day when "your people shall all be righteous; they shall inherit the land forever" (Isa. 60:21). This, like many similar promises woven through the Old Testament, is nothing less than a reminder of the covenant that God had made with Abraham.

So while the covenant promises of God are first stated in key passages (Gen. 12; 2 Sam. 7; Jer. 31), fresh expressions of these cosmic and unconditional promises are woven throughout the Bible, and especially through the Old Testament.

When we read the Old Testament, it is important to set many of its promises in this covenant context. These covenant-linked promises are not ours to claim for ourselves, but they are for us to count on. They remind us that God is in full control of His universe, and that He has chosen to offer us His redemptive love.

GOD'S OTHER WONDERFUL PROMISES

The cosmic, covenant promises are not the only promises in the Bible. There are many more. Most believers have found these other wonderful promises a rich source of personal comfort and hope.

Most of us have claimed Bible verses as if they were promises made to us personally. At one time in my life, when I was facing a critical decision, one of God's promise verses kept coming up. I saw the verse on a billboard outside a Christian business. Whenever I turned on my car radio, I seemed to run across a preacher speaking on this verse. I stopped at a motel, and the Gideon Bible there was open to the very page on which the verse was printed.

It became clear that God was inviting me to apply the wonderful promise of that verse to my own life. Through that verse, He was pointing me toward the decision He wanted me to make. The verse was Jeremiah 29:11:

———————— ❖ ————————

For I know the thoughts that I think toward you, says the LORD, thoughts of peace and not of evil, to give you a future and a hope.

There are several things about that experience that helped me understand how to read the promises of God and how to claim them.

HOW TO CLAIM GOD'S PROMISES

Jeremiah 29:11 was spoken originally to a particular generation of Israelites, reassuring them that God would be faithful to His covenant commitment. But God the Holy Spirit applied it to my own situation. This can be the experience of every Christian as we explore God's Word with both understanding and faith. Here's how to claim the promises that God's Spirit calls us to apply to our own lives.

First, examine the context of the promise. Jeremiah was speaking to the people of Judah in a time of national disaster. The Babylonians were about to take Jerusalem and destroy the holy city. The people who heard Jeremiah's words would soon be carried from their homeland and resettled in pagan Babylon. Yet through Jeremiah, God promised that one day the Jews would return to their homeland. The national disaster was not a sign that God had abandoned them, nor should His present discipline make them give up hope. Instead, the people of Judah could take comfort in the fact that God planned to do them good. In spite of the present distress, in God they had hope and a future.

Next, identify the critical elements in the promise. There are several important questions we need to ask about any Bible promise.

To whom is the promise made? Is this a promise made to everyone? Or is this a promise made to a specific person or group? Most important, is this a promise God is making to *me, today?*

In the case of Jeremiah 29:11, the promise was made to the Jewish people of Jeremiah's time. When it was written, it certainly was not a promise that God was making to me in my moment of decision several centuries later. Even so, this ancient promise was one through which God did speak to me. It was a promise He clearly expected me to claim.

Is the promise conditional or unconditional? The promise in Jeremiah 29:11 is stated without any conditions. God simply says He has plans for His people, and that He intends to do them good. In Him they have hope and a future.

Some promises are conditional. For instance, Jesus said, "If you abide in Me, and My words abide in you, you will ask what you desire, and it shall be done for you" (John 15:7). This is a conditional promise. Jesus promises that we will be given what we ask—if . . .

So before we claim a promise, we should note whether the promise is conditional or unconditional—and if conditional, what the conditions are.

What does the promise reveal about God? This is one of the most important questions we can ask, and it is critical in claiming promises for ourselves.

In the case of Jeremiah 29:11, this verse shows a great deal about who our God is. He is a God who disciplines His sinning people. Yet He is a God who does not abandon them. Even when His people deserve a devastating punishment like the Babylonian invasion, God still has plans to do them good. What a loving, forgiving, wonderful God this verse reveals! How great His kindness is; how steadfast His commitment to His people. Surely this God wants what is best for His own—for you and me and all His people. Surely when we follow His leading, our own hope and future are assured.

It is this aspect of the promise—what it tells us about our God and His relationship to His own—that transforms the ancient promise from a word directed specifically to the Jews of Jeremiah's day to a word for you and me and in our day. It's important to examine Bible promises not just for special circumstances but for their revelation of the character and nature of God. Who God was for those of Jeremiah's time, He is for us today. And thus this promise is for us, too!

Does the Holy Spirit intend me to claim this promise? This question is critical for personal application of the promises we find in God's Word. God the Holy Spirit, who gave us His Word, lives within us to make that Word real to us.

In my experience with Jeremiah 29:11, the Holy Spirit used a variety of means to make me aware that I was to claim it as a promise made to me. God's Spirit used that billboard, radio preachers, and even a Gideon Bible in a motel to keep my thoughts focused on that one verse. God then used the verse to help me sense His will and to make a decision which shaped my future.

None of us can say ahead of time what God's Spirit will use to impress a promise on our hearts. But because the Holy Spirit is with us, we can rely on Him to guide us. In claiming promises, we need to rely consciously on the Holy Spirit and seek His guidance in prayer.

How am I to respond to the God who makes this promise to me? In my experience with Jeremiah 29:11, God used the verse to guide me in making a specific decision. Once the Holy Spirit had made this clear, the Lord expected me to act on the promise. I was to make the decision indicated and to stand by it.

One of the most exciting things about God's promises is that they provide guidance and motivation for action. Whenever God's Spirit impresses any Bible truth on our hearts, He expects us to respond with faith. We are to rely so completely on God's Word that we will joyfully put it into practice. This is as true for God's promises as for any other word from God.

The wonderful thing is that Christians throughout the ages have sensed the Spirit speaking to them through God's Word. They have claimed promises given to us in God's Book, acted on those promises in faith, and found Him faithful and true to His word.

STUDYING GOD'S PROMISES TOGETHER

In this major section on God's covenants and promises, we will look at the "other promises of God" that are found in the Old and New Testaments. That is, we will not comment on the many promises that are essentially restatements of God's covenants. Instead, we will focus on the other promises of God—promises which God has made to individuals or in special circumstances—promises which are ours to claim as well.

In our look at the other wonderful promises of God, we examine:

1. the promise itself;
2. the context of the promise;
3. understanding the promise;
   - To whom is it made?
   - Is it conditional or unconditional?
   - What does it reveal about God?
4. claiming the promise; and
5. responding to the promise.

It will be up to you to rely consciously on the Holy Spirit as to how and when you should claim these promises for yourself.

Coming to understand and claim God's wonderful promises holds untold blessings for believers. In this study, you will draw nearer to God and sense His closeness. There is no better way to know Him than by learning and claiming the promises found in His Word.

CHAPTER 9

CREATION'S COSMIC PROMISES:

PERSONAL PROMISES IN GENESIS

The first five books of the Old Testament are called the Pentateuch. The first of these, Genesis, describes the origin of the universe and all living creatures in God's creative acts. In Genesis we also find the wonderful covenant promises which God made to Abraham and confirmed to Isaac, Jacob, and their descendants.

Exodus, Leviticus, Numbers, and Deuteronomy record events that took place thousands of years later in the time of Moses, whom the Lord called and empowered to free Abraham's descendants from slavery in Egypt. God also used Moses to give the Israelites a law that showed them how to live in harmony with Him and others. Moses led Israel for 40 years. During that time God purified His people and finally brought a generation that was fully committed to Him to the borders of the land He had promised to Abraham many years before.

It's not surprising that these seminal books of the Old Testament are rich in promises that express God's loving intent for His people. Those promises have been thoroughly explored in the section of this book on God's covenants. But God was concerned with individuals as well as the developing nation. And so we find in these great Bible books many personal promises as well.

GOD'S PERSONAL PROMISES IN GENESIS

The book of Genesis begins with answers to the most basic questions humans can ask. These answers, found in the first three chapters of Genesis, express implicit promises made to all humankind. Genesis then moves on to focus our attention on the three patriarchs: Abraham, Isaac, and Jacob. To each of these leaders God made very explicit promises.

GOD'S UNIVERSAL PROMISES
(Genesis 1—3)

PROMISES IN CREATION

The promise: "In the beginning God created the heavens and the earth" (Gen. 1:1).

The context of the promise. At first glance, Genesis 1:1 doesn't look like a promise. Grammatically it's a statement. And yet there are few verses in Scripture so rich in promissory intent. This first verse in the Bible introduces us to God, placing His work of creation in promise perspective. In a unique way these promises are presented to every human being, affirmed again and again in the creation that this verse describes.

Understanding the promise. The promises implied in this verse are universal. They are made to every human being who enters the world.

How is it that all hear these promises? Romans 1:20 reminds us that "since the creation of the world His invisible attributes are clearly seen, being understood by the things that are made." And Psalm 19 says,

> The heavens declare the glory of
> God;
> And the firmament shows His
> handiwork.
> Day unto day utters speech,
> And night unto night reveals
> knowledge.
> There is no speech nor language
> Where their voice is not heard.
> Their line has gone out through all
> the earth,
> And their words to the end of the
> world (Ps. 19:1–4).

The promises implicit in the story of creation are thus broadcast through the creation to the whole world, and through all time! The living heart of the creation promises is found in what this verse and creation itself reveals about God.

"In the beginning" (Genesis 1:1). These simple words remind us that matter is not eternal. There is more to this universe than fiery stars and stony planets whirling through space. This simple truth—that the universe had a beginning—opens the soul to look for life's meaning in origins. If there were no beginning—if matter existed eternally and life somehow derived from it—the universe would be cold and impersonal. Mute nature would be unaware and untouched by our birth or death, much less by our joys and sorrows.

But the universe *did* have a beginning. Even those who deny the existence of God admit that the material universe is constantly expanding. Moving back along the track of racing stars, scientists have been forced to conclude that the universe did have a beginning—a theory which has been nicknamed the "Big Bang." But for the cause of that cosmic event, science has no answer.

Whatever else we know about the universe we live in, we know that it is not eternal. It had a beginning. Within the universe there is progress: everything is in motion toward some unstated end.

One theory proposed by the ancient Greeks was that over the span of 10,000 years the universe blossomed, reached full flower, and then collapsed upon itself, only to blossom again in an unending cycle of cosmic birth and death. Each human being was thus destined to relive his or her life exactly as before; to know the same joys and sorrows, to make the same decisions, to be visited with the same tragedies, all in meaningless repetition. This is not the universe that Genesis invites us to contemplate. In the fact of a beginning, we sense progress toward some end. The universe—and thus our lives—is not directionless and without meaning.

"God" (Genesis 1:1). While science can make no statement about the source of the event through which the universe sprang into existence, the Bible simply says, "In the beginning, God." And what meaning this adds to the fact that there was a beginning.

One of the great fictions of the ancient world and of much contemporary science is that the universe "just happened." According to this assumption, a chain of material causes and material events extends endlessly back into time, and is destined to extend forward just as endlessly. This kind of universe, a mindless juggernaut, rolls on uncaring and unaware of human hopes and dreams, untouched by our disappointment or despair.

But then we hear and see what creation as well as Scripture affirms—God—and everything changes. The universe is not impersonal! Behind the material causes lies a Person—a being who is completely and fully aware.

No one can relate personally to mindless matter. But we human beings can relate to a Person! Creation reveals in its wonderful design the existence of such a Person, and the universe takes on a different hue. We are persons within a world whose origin is personal!

The message of a beginning is that this universe is marked by progress. The fact that the universe was designed by a Person holds out hope that we might possibly come to know Him. And, through a relationship with the Creator, we might discover meaning and purpose in the universe and for our own lives!

"God created the heavens and the earth" (Genesis 1:1). To say as Genesis does that God created the heavens and the earth is not limited to the often expressed meaning, "to make something out of nothing." To say that God created means also that He gave the universe and our earth its shape and form. God designed all that exists with a clear purpose in mind. The prophet Isaiah declared,

> For thus says the LORD,
> Who created the heavens,
> Who is God,
> Who formed the earth and made it,
> Who established it,
> Who did not create it in vain,
> Who formed it to be inhabited:
> I am the LORD, and there is no other
> (Isa. 45:18)

The story of how God designed and shaped the universe, told in Genesis 1 and reflected in creation itself, fills us with hope. In the whole, we sense God's power. In the regularity of the seasons, we sense His faithfulness. In the stability of the heavens, we sense His

trustworthiness. The shape of God's creation affirms the fact that God did make our world to be inhabited. Everything about the universe we live in assures us. He whose power launched all that is intends to do us good!

Thus, the first verse in the Bible is full of promise, just as creation is. Both point us to the Creator. Both promise us that there is meaning to our existence. And both promise us that we can discover meaning for our lives in a personal relationship with God.

Claiming the promises. The promises implied in Genesis 1 are repeated endlessly through creation itself. God speaks to all through what He has made, and His message is one of promise. Anyone may claim these promises by responding to God's voice with faith. The Bible tells us how, describing the response that expresses faith in this universal promise.

Responding to the promise. Romans 1 describes two possible responses to God's creation promises. One response is summed up

❖

From the beginning, God's creation was good and purposeful.

in Romans 1:21: "Although they knew God, they did not glorify Him as God, nor were thankful." That response, ignoring both the promise and promisemaker, leads to ignorance, depravity, and despair (cf. Rom. 1:21–32).

The response of those who hear and respond to God's creation promises is so different. Those persons in whom His promises awaken faith praise God joyfully. The psalmist portrayed this response of believers in Psalm 96:

> For the LORD is great and greatly to
>   be praised;
> He is to be feared above all gods.
> For all the gods of the peoples are
>   idols,
> But the LORD made the heavens.
> Honor and majesty are before Him;
> Strength and beauty are in His
>   sanctuary.
> Give to the LORD, O families of the
>   peoples,
> Give to the LORD glory and strength.
> Give to the LORD the glory due His
>   Name (Ps. 96:4–8).

The promises implicit in creation answer one important question. If we ask how human beings who have never heard of Christ can be held responsible for their unbelief, one answer is that God has revealed Himself to all. Romans argues that "they are without excuse" because in fact "what may be known of God is manifest in them, for God has shown it to them" (Rom. 1:19, 20). The fact that human beings have not responded to the promises implicit in creation underlines the impact of sin. It also highlights God's grace, in that He continued to reach out to humankind by giving us His special revelation in Scripture and in Jesus Christ.

But believers are aware of the God who makes promises to us in creation. Like the psalmist, we respond to His wonderful promises by giving the Lord the glory which belongs to Him.

THE PROMISE OF SIGNIFICANCE

The promise: "So God created man in His own image; in the image of God He created him; male and female He created them" (Gen. 1:27).

The context of the promise. The culminating act of creation was the formation of human beings. This event is so significant that after providing an overview of the creative days in Genesis 1, the Lord returned in Genesis 2 to examine in detail the creation of Adam and Eve. The brief statement in chapter 1, "So God created man," is expanded, and we see the Lord for the first time abandon creating by simply speaking a word (cf. Gen. 1:3, 6, 9, 14, 20, 24). He bent over Adam and touched the dust from which Adam's body was formed, before gently breathing into Adam the breath of life.

Understanding the promise. Here as in Genesis 1:1, we have a promise expressed in the form of a statement: "So God created man in His own image." What a wonderful promise is implicit in this declaration. Human beings, created in God's image, have a value and significance far greater than anything else in God's universe!

The psalmist recognized this truth and expressed his wonder. Considering the vastness of the created universe, how amazing it is that God focuses His attention on human beings! The psalmist David wrote,

> When I consider Your heavens,
>   the work of Your fingers,
> The moon and the stars, which You
>   have ordained,
> What is man that You are mindful of
>   him,
> And the son of man that You visit
>   him?
> For You have made him a little lower
>   than the angels,
> And You have crowned him with
>   glory and honor (Ps. 8:3–5).

What promises are implicit in God's creation of human beings in His image?

The promise of personal worth and value. The Hebrew Bible linked the words *image* and *likeness* (Gen. 1:26), creating a special theological concept, "image-likeness." It is this which God shared with human beings when He created Adam and Eve. This unique character was passed on to their offspring, in spite of Adam's subsequent sin.

The fact that human beings bear the image-likeness of God provides the rationale for capital punishment, instituted in Genesis 9:6. Throughout the Old Testament era, a money payment served as compensation for an injury one person might inflict on another. But no amount of money can compensate for the taking of a human life. Each person's life is precious beyond measure. God instituted capital punishment for the sake of justice—to make it clear to all that no individual has the right to take another's life without forfeiting his or her own.

The promise of personal relationship. The exact nature of the image-likeness which God shared with human beings has been debated by Jewish and Christian theologians. It cannot be holiness, for after the Fall Scripture continued to portray human beings as possessing this God-given quality (Gen. 9:6; James 3:9). It is best to take our clue from Genesis itself. This image-likeness is best understood as personhood—the sum of those qualities which made both God and human beings persons. Like God, we human beings can appreciate beauty. We can find satisfaction in meaningful work, can invent and create, can communicate in language, can think and remember, can experience emotions, and can make moral choices. How significant that the Genesis 2 description of Eden emphasizes the opportunities that God provided there for Adam to use all the capacities of his personhood.

What is most significant, however, is that in sharing His image-likeness, God made it possible for human beings to have a true personal relationship with Him. We may love our pets, but there is no way to have a personal relationship with them. Animals lack many of the traits that make us persons, so they cannot relate to us on the personal level. In creating us in His image, God lifted human beings far beyond the animal realm. His gift of image-likeness carries a promise of personal relationship with Him.

The promise of eternal life. When God breathed into Adam the breath of life, more than biological life was imparted. The gift included spiritual life. In this gift, the promise of eternal life is implicit. While human beings must die biologically, our individual identity survives and we will exist, self-conscious and aware, forever. God's decision to give human beings the breath of life is reflected in the Scripture's later revelation that there is a heaven to win and a hell to avoid. With the decision to give humankind the gift of spiritual life, the Lord committed Himself to the Cross.

Each of these promises—the promise of worth and value, the promise of personal relationship, and the promise of eternal life—is implicit in the Genesis statement, "God created man in His own image."

Claiming the promise. At the 1997 Women of Faith Conference, a young woman who had co-hosted "The 700 Club" shared her experience. Although successful as a Christian singer and TV personality, she felt empty inside. Her depression and sense of worthlessness deepened until one day she began to sob uncontrollably on the set.

Later a Christian psychiatrist asked her, "Who are you?" She answered that she was a Christian singer. "No," he said, "I didn't ask what you do. I asked, 'Who are you?'" She said, "I'm a co-host on 'The 700 Club.'" Again he said, "No. Who *are* you?"

Through God's grace, her depression led her to discover who she truly is: a child of the King. A person made in God's image and likeness. An individual who has infinite worth and value because God had shared so much of Himself with her, and then given her the gift of salvation.

Many people today sympathize with this woman in her depression. They also have what we call a "low self-image." Whatever the cause, that sense of worthlessness seems epidemic. So many are unaware of the answer to the question, "Who am I?" Yet for every human being born into our world the answer is, "I am a person of worth and value, because God created me in His image. I am special, gifted with unique capacities that make it possible for me to succeed in this world and to have a personal relationship with God. I am special, for eternity is my destiny. Long after this world has been folded up and put away, I will continue to exist."

The fact that God created human beings in His image makes me—and every other person—significant. By faith, we are to agree with God's assessment of who we are and claim the promise of significance as our own.

Responding to the promise. We are to respond to the promise of individual human significance on many levels.

The promise of significance reminds us of the value of human life and should cause deep concern over the direction of our society. Life is increasingly being cheapened. The criminal justice system has abandoned the biblical principle that a life must be taken for a life. The unborn, genetically distinct from the mothers who carry them, are lightly disposed of. The medical community now debates when taking an adult life is justified. In all these ways, God's promise of significance for every person is being ignored. As a result, every person's life is gradually being devalued. The rabbis taught that "Man was first created a single individual to teach the lesson that whoever destroys one life, Scripture ascribes it to him as though he had destroyed a whole world; and whoever saves one life, Scripture ascribes it to him as though he had saved a whole world" (Sanh. IV. 5).

On a personal level, God's promise in Genesis 1:26 is to shape our sense of personal worth and value. A low self-image is simply not appropriate for any person who bears the image-likeness of God.

On an interpersonal level, we are to respond to the promise of significance by treating others as God sees them—as persons of worth and value. When we view people in this way, we begin to grasp how important it is to give every person the respect he or she deserves and to be concerned about their needs.

For the Christian, the promise of personal relationship with God encourages us to share the good news of Jesus' redemptive work with all people.

THE PROMISE OF PLACE

The promise: "Then God blessed them, and God said to them, "Be fruitful and multiply; fill the earth and subdue it; have dominion" (Gen. 1:28).

The context of the promise. This promise is imbedded in a command to the first pair. God created Adam and Eve in His own image (Gen. 1:26), and He gave them a role to play in His creation. The psalmist, who stood

Concern for others prompts believers to share the good news of Jesus.

amazed as he contemplated God's concern for human beings (Ps. 8:3, 4), continued his train of thought with these words:

> You have made him [man] to have
> dominion over the works of
> Your hands;
> You have put all things under his
> feet.
> . . .
> O LORD, our LORD,
> How excellent is Your name in all the
> earth! (Ps. 8:6, 9).

Understanding the promise. Like the two earlier implicit promises, this promise is made to all humankind. God established humanity's place in the creation order—a place higher than and distinct from all other living creatures. The significance of this promise is summed up in the word *dominion.*

The Hebrew word is *radah,* and it is used 25 times in the Old Testament. It is used of man's rule rather than God's, or rather of man's rule under the authority of God. Here in Genesis 1, this word implies both the right to utilize the earth's resources and responsibility to care for them. Man's place is one of both privilege and responsibility.

Claiming the promise. This promise, like the one in the verse before it, is claimed as we accept God's word about man's significance. Human beings are over, not among, the plants and animals with which we share this planet. We are to accept the fact that God has defined our place in the creation order. Glorying in His gift of dominion, we should accept the responsibility that goes with it.

As the Scripture gives human beings dominion, it also tells us to "subdue." It is not unusual for some in the ecology movement to claim that Scripture is at fault for the damage human beings have done to our planet. They see the source of every ecological problem in God's gift of dominion, and in the command to "fill the earth, and subdue it." But in this context, "subdue" does not mean to plunder

the earth. It means to bring order and fruitfulness to the wilderness. Genesis actually provides a biblical basis for ecological concern in that human beings are to care for all which has been placed under them.

While this command has been misunderstood, it is important to remember that man's first concern is the well-being of others. To tilt the balance in God's world toward animals at the expense of people is unjustified.

Responding to the promise. We human beings respond to this promise of God when we look ahead to determine what is best for humankind, while giving careful consideration to the lives placed in our charge.

Genesis 1 contains implicit promises which are made to all humankind. Genesis 1:1 reminds us that creation itself witnesses to the Creator, and carries a promise of meaning to human life. Genesis 1:26 with its teaching that God created man in His image-likeness contains the promise of personal significance. And Genesis 1:27, which describes the gift of dominion given to humankind, contains the promise of a unique place in the creation order—a place of privilege and responsibility.

How great and wonderful are these promises!

GOD'S PROMISES TO OUR FALLEN RACE *(Genesis 3:1, 9)*

The story of man's creation in Genesis 1 and 2 is followed immediately by the account of the Fall of humankind in Genesis 3. While creation in God's image explains all that is bright and beautiful in human nature, the story of the Fall explains man's dark side. Genesis 3 relates the disobedience of Adam and Eve to God's command, outlining the consequences of the spiritual death that followed (see Eph. 2:1–3).

In the Fall, sin gained a grip on the human personality, alienating us from God and setting mankind on a course that leads to idolatry, crime, violence, and immorality. This course leads to eternal separation from God.

Against this terrible background, two promises to Adam and Eve stand out, offering hope.

THE PROMISE OF REDEMPTION

The promise: "Also for Adam and his wife the LORD God made tunics of skin, and clothed them" (Gen. 3:21).

The context of the promise. Once again, we see a promise implied in a statement—this time a statement of the initiative God took on behalf of Adam and Eve.

Adam and Eve had sinned in disobeying God. God's verdict, that "the day that you eat of it you shall surely die" (Gen. 2:17) had been executed. The processes that lead to biological death were instituted, and spiritually Adam and Eve died the day they sinned. "And thus death spread to all men" (Rom. 5:12).

Without God's intervention, the destiny of Adam and Eve and all their descendants was fixed.

But God still loved the first pair, so He chose to intervene. God clothed Adam and Eve with tunics of skin, symbolically covering their sins so they could continue to have a relationship with Him.

Understanding the promise. The meaning of this act is easy to miss. To clothe Adam and Eve with tunics of skin, some animal had to give its life. Several centuries later, God explained the significance of sacrifice such as this to Moses, who recorded what God said in Leviticus 17:11. "For the life of the flesh is in the blood, and I have given it to you upon the altar to make atonement for your souls; for it is the blood that makes atonement for the soul."

The simple statement in Genesis 3:21— that God clothed Adam and Eve in skins— relates history's first sacrifice. The blood of a substitute was shed in order that the sin of human beings might be covered and a sinner might enter the presence of God. In the brief report in this verse in Genesis, we have the promise of a redemption that God would make available to all humankind.

Understanding the promise. The covering was provided for Adam and Eve, and the promise was made first of all to them. But throughout Scripture, Adam is viewed not only as the first human being but as the representative human being. In the Fall, Adam stands for everyman, explaining our inner propensity to sin. In Genesis 3:21, Adam is also mankind's representative, so the promise of redemption to come is made to all.

But clearly this promise is conditional— the first conditional promise in the Scripture. We know that it is conditional because of the story of Adam's sons, Cain and Abel. Genesis 4 tells us that each of them brought an offering to God. Abel brought an offering from his flocks and sacrificed it to God. Cain "brought an offering of the fruit of the ground to the LORD" (Gen. 4:3). Abel's offering was accepted but Cain's was rejected, and Cain became angry.

The key to understanding this story is found in Genesis 4:6, 7. God asked Cain why he was angry. He told Cain, "If you do well, will you not be accepted?"

Those words, "if you do well," can be explained only if we assume that Adam and Eve had taught their sons that they must approach God with a blood offering. Cain *knew* that only a blood sacrifice could cover his sins, but Cain chose instead to approach God without acknowledging his need for redemption.

The rabbis explained Cain's rejection by teaching that he brought rotted fruit, thus insulting the Lord. It is far more likely that Cain chose the best of what his labors had produced. But the best that sinful human beings can do has no merit in God's eyes. In the Scripture's verdict that "all have sinned and fall short of the glory of God" (Rom. 3:23), God dismisses every human effort to win His favor. Only by relying on the grace of God and by placing our faith in the promise that God will accept the death of a substitute in place of our own death can anyone be accepted by God.

Cain's refusal to come to God by way of blood sacrifice foreshadows the tragic decision of all who refuse to come to God by way of

Christ's cross. In His sacrificial death, Jesus won salvation for all who trust Him. But we must trust the promise of redemption given us in Christ, or His death will have no value for us.

This first promise of salvation is a conditional promise. But how much it tells us about God! It reveals His continuing love for human beings, His grace to us, and His power to save. The God who clothed Adam in skins is eager to clothe us as well, in that great exchange in which Jesus Christ takes our sins and gives us His righteousness. When we place our trust in Him, we are clothed indeed.

Claiming the promise. Abel claimed the promise of redemption by coming to God with sacrificial blood. Cain rejected the promise by coming to God with nothing but the fruit of his own labor. We can claim the promise of redemption today only by coming to God through Jesus, who told us plainly, "I am the way, the truth, and the life. No one comes to the Father except through Me" (John 14:6).

Responding to the promise. The promise of redemption is the one promise to which we *must* respond if we are to have a relationship with the Lord. Only by accepting Jesus as Savior, and thus placing our confidence in the blood He shed for us on Calvary, can we be redeemed.

THE PROMISE OF RESTORATION

The promise: "He placed cherubim at the east of the garden of Eden, and a flaming sword which turned every way, to guard the way to the tree of life" (Gen. 3:24).

The context of the promise. This is another statement that implies a promise. After Adam and Eve had sinned, God drove them from the Garden of Eden. Genesis explains that God's motive was to prevent them from taking the

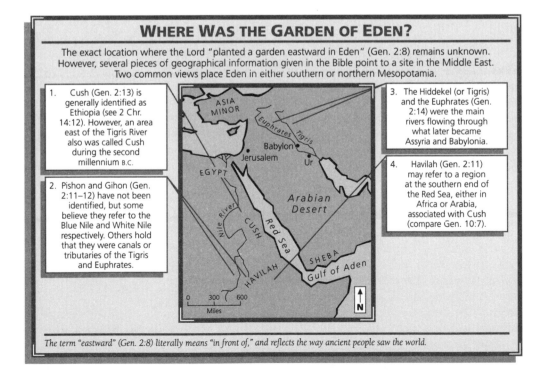

WHERE WAS THE GARDEN OF EDEN?

The exact location where the Lord "planted a garden eastward in Eden" (Gen. 2:8) remains unknown. However, several pieces of geographical information given in the Bible point to a site in the Middle East. Two common views place Eden in either southern or northern Mesopotamia.

1. Cush (Gen. 2:13) is generally identified as Ethiopia (see 2 Chr. 14:12). However, an area east of the Tigris River also was called Cush during the second millennium B.C.

2. Pishon and Gihon (Gen. 2:11–12) have not been identified, but some believe they refer to the Blue Nile and White Nile respectively. Others hold that they were canals or tributaries of the Tigris and Euphrates.

3. The Hiddekel (or Tigris) and the Euphrates (Gen. 2:14) were the main rivers flowing through what later became Assyria and Babylonia.

4. Havilah (Gen. 2:11) may refer to a region at the southern end of the Red Sea, either in Africa or Arabia, associated with Cush (compare Gen. 10:7).

The term "eastward" (Gen. 2:8) literally means "in front of," and reflects the way ancient people saw the world.

fruit of "the tree of life, and eat, and live forever" (Gen. 3:22).

At first glance, this seems to be a punishment. But how tragic it would have been for Adam and Eve to be doomed to an endless life on earth, witnessing in every generation the injustice and the anguish caused by their act of disobedience! God's driving the first pair from the garden was actually an act of grace. The hurt they must have felt after Cain killed Abel, knowing that their sin had tainted their children, would not be repeated endlessly. Adam and Eve would be allowed to die.

Understanding the promise. The key to understanding this promise is in the placement of the cherubim and flaming sword to "guard" the way back to Eden. The cherubim and flaming sword were not placed there to keep human beings out of Eden, but *to keep the way home open!*

In Genesis 3:21, we saw the promise of redemption acted out in the slaying of animals to provide covering for Adam and Eve. Now, just three verses later, we see the promise of a restoration to innocence and perfect fellowship with God which Eden symbolizes. With the whole Bible in our hands, we now know that God will one day raise the saved to eternal life, and at that time will remove every taint of sin. Innocence will be restored and perfected. Once again, human beings will enjoy the most intimate relationship with the living God.

Until that day arrives, cherubim and a flaming sword guard the way to the tree of life. No hostile power can close the highway which Christ has opened through His death. In Christ, we can return to Eden and our fellowship with God is assured.

This is also a conditional promise—one made only to those who by faith approach God in the way He has ordained. Only by following the path stained by the sacrificial blood of Christ can we find our way back to our true home.

How amazing is the love of God! He chose to suffer for us, taking on Himself the penalty of our sin, that we might return to Him.

Claiming the promise. The promise of return is the possession of every person who responds to God's promise of redemption through the blood of Christ.

Responding to the promise. The apostle John invited us to look ahead to Christ's return and all this means. When Jesus returns, we will be raised and we will be home at last. And John declared, "It has not yet been revealed what we shall be, but we know that when He is revealed, we shall be like Him, for we shall see Him as He is." And then John added, "And everyone who has this hope in Him purifies himself, just as He is pure" (1 John 3:2, 3).

While we rejoice in the prospect of our return to Eden and a perfected innocence, the prospect creates a desire in us to live in holiness and purity. In the promise of restoration we see our true selves, as God created us to be. Drawn to that true self, we are motivated to live for God here and now.

GOD'S PERSONAL PROMISES TO ABRAHAM

In the first part of this book, we looked at covenant promises which God made to Abraham. We saw how these promises gave shape to history, as God set out in the form of promises the goals which He intends to accomplish in our world.

These promises were precious to Abraham, and his faith that God would fulfill every word was credited to Abraham as righteousness. While God's covenant promises spelled out what the Lord intended to accomplish through the patriarch and his descendants, God also gave Abraham personal promises to claim in his own day. It is these personal promises to Abraham that we examine now.

A PROMISE OF PROTECTION AND REWARD

The promise: "Do not be afraid, Abram. I am your shield, your exceedingly great reward" (Gen. 15:1).

The context of the promise. Abraham had just rescued his nephew Lot, who had been taken captive with the citizens of Sodom. After the defeat of the raiding kings and the rescue, the king of Sodom offered Abraham the material goods that the raiders had looted from Sodom as a reward. Abraham refused to accept anything at all, "lest you should say, 'I have made Abram rich'" (Gen. 14:23).

BIBLE BACKGROUND:

THE KINGS OF GENESIS 14

The antiquity of the account is shown by the addition of later names to aid in identification of the places mentioned (cf. Gen. 14:7, 8). While the kings named have not been identified by archaeology, the invasion route is known. The kings approached along what is known as the King's Highway. The itinerary faithfully describes the main centers of known occupation along the highway, in correct sequence. The fact that the settlements there were abandoned about 1950 B.C. fits the Bible's dating of Abraham's life. (See H.H. Rowly, *From Joseph to Joshua*, 1950, pp 61ff).

Understanding the promise. At first glance, the words *don't be afraid* seem out of place. One would think that God would speak them to encourage Abraham before the battle was fought, not after it was won! But the verb *be afraid* deals with the future. It invites Abraham to look ahead and to dismiss future fears *on the basis of the victory God has just given him.*

When God said "I am your shield," He was expressing a proven reality. God's protection of His servant is the explanation for Abraham's victory as well as a promise of future protection.

The phrase "I am . . . your exceedingly great reward" (Gen. 15:1) stands in contrast to the king of Sodom's offer to reward Abraham with booty taken by the raiders (Gen. 14:21–23). In rejecting the offered wealth,

Abraham showed his intent to accept only what the hand of God disperses. But when God spoke to Abraham, the Lord reminded him and us that the most rewarding thing in this life or beyond is a relationship with God in which He becomes our treasure.

It is clear that the promise of protection and reward was made to one man, Abraham, in a specific historical setting. And it was an unconditional promise. It was a promise expressed as a simple statement of who God is, and who God will be for the patriarch. The promise affirmed both God's power to intervene on behalf of His servants, and the fact that knowing Him is a far greater treasure than any human beings can assemble here on earth.

Claiming the promise. While this promise was made specifically to Abraham, it can be claimed by any believer. The reason is that the roots of the promise are not anchored in who Abraham was, but in who God is for His own people. The God who loved Abraham loves us. The God who spread His protective wings over Abraham spreads them over us today. The psalmist said,

> But let all those rejoice who put
> their trust in You;
> Let them ever shout for joy,
> because You defend them;
> Let those also who love Your name
> Be joyful in You.
> For You, O LORD, will bless the
> righteous;
> With favor You will surround him
> as with a shield (Ps. 5:11, 12).

In the same way, we can find in God the treasures that satisfy our hearts. In another prayer, David contrasted himself with "men of the world who have their portion in this life" (Ps. 17:14), and said,

> As for me, I will see Your face in
> righteousness;
> I shall be satisfied when I awake in
> Your likeness (Ps. 17:15).

How do we claim the promise God made to Abraham? We claim it by facing each day with renewed confidence that God is a shield around us. We claim the promise by choosing, as Abraham did, not to be distracted by material treasures from the true riches that are to be found in our relationship with the Lord.

Responding to the promise. We often find ourselves afraid to do something we know is right. What will others think? What do we risk if we choose to speak out? When we remember that God is a shield for His own people, we can set aside our fears and speak and act boldly for what is right.

But to be free of fear, we must also keep our attention focused on the Lord. He must be more important to us than any reward we might gain. No friendship, job, or promise of wealth should distract us from a passionate desire to love God and glorify Him in all we do. When we make loving God our primary goal, we learn by personal experience how great is the reward we have in Him.

PROMISE TO A PAINED PARENT

The promise: "Yet I will also make a nation of the son of the bondwoman, because he is your seed" (Gen. 21:13).

The context of the promise. After ten years in Canaan, when Sarah still had no children, she urged Abraham to take her maid Hagar. Ancient documents reveal that it was accepted practice for childless women to have their slaves serve as surrogates and that children born to such slaves were considered to be children of the wife.

However, when Hagar became pregnant, conflict erupted between the two women. Years later, after Sarah had given birth to Isaac, Sarah insisted that Abraham cast out both Hagar and Ishmael. Even by the standards of the time, to do so would be wrong, and Abraham refused. There is no doubt that Abraham also cared for his son Ishmael, then a teenager. But then God intervened, telling Abraham to do as Sarah had said. We can imagine the anguish

Abraham felt. How terrible to turn out one's own flesh and blood! It was then that God made Abraham His promise to bless Ishmael, "because he is your seed."

This was actually the second promise that God had made to Abraham concerning Ishmael. The earlier promise is found in Genesis 17:20: "And as for Ishmael, I have heard you. Behold I have blessed him, and will make him fruitful."

Understanding the promise. Genesis 21:13 is one of the clearest examples in Scripture of a personal promise. It grew out of a pain-filled situation as an anguished father was compelled to give up his child. This promise reveals a great deal about the God who made that promise unconditionally.

The promise showed God's sensitivity to our pain. God fully understood all that Abraham was experiencing. And God responded compassionately.

The promise showed God's control of the future. God alone could look ahead and tell what would become of the child Abraham loved but was about to lose. And God graciously shared His knowledge of the future with Abraham.

The promise showed the extent of God's commitment to His own. God promised to be gracious to Ishmael "because he is your seed" (Gen. 21:13). God's love reaches out, in some sense, to shelter our loved ones as well as us. The promise given to Abraham concerning Ishmael suggests that when we are forced to surrender our children, God Himself takes over the parents' protective role.

The Tosifta (Sot. IV. I) has an interesting comment on this point, suggesting that "the attribute of [God's] grace exceeds that of punishment by five-hundred fold." The saying is based on Exodus 20:5, in which God describes Himself as "visiting the iniquity of the fathers upon the children to the third and fourth generations of those who hate Me, but showing mercy to thousands, to those who love Me." The Hebrew suggests that "thou-

Even though Abraham sent Hagar and her son away, God promised to bless Ishmael.

sands" refers to generations rather than persons, and the plural convinced the rabbis that at least two thousand generations must be in view. By dividing the 2,000 generations that would experience God's mercy by the four generations that would be visited by His justice, the principle that God's grace exceeds His justice 500-fold was derived.

We need not adopt this reasoning. But the conclusion is valid. In dealing with His own, God's grace rules.

Claiming the promise. Too many families these days are torn apart by divorce. Some parents simply don't care about their offspring. But in many divorce cases, at least one parent is torn by the emotions that wracked Abraham as he contemplated the loss of his son. While the predictive element of the promise given to Abraham was made to him alone, the concern that God expressed reveals His heart of concern for all. The promise reminds us that God not only cares for us; He also cares for those we love. And this is something we can rely on completely when we are torn from our loved ones as Abraham was.

There is a confirming principle stated in the New Testament. The apostle Paul wrote to worried Christians in Corinth who were married to non-Christian spouses. He told them, "The unbelieving husband is sanctified by the wife, and the unbelieving wife is sanctified by the husband; otherwise your children would be unclean, but now they are holy." In this comment, Paul built an analogy on the Old Testament concepts of "sanctified" and "holy." When even one parent believes, the unbelieving spouse and the children are placed in proximity to the holy, where they can experience the love of God through the believing partner. Whether a spouse or child will respond to that love with saving faith is an individual decision. But God does grant special exposure to His love to the children of those who know Him.

Responding to the promise. If we should ever find ourselves in the position of Abraham, we can respond to God's promise by trusting our children into His hands. We can respond by remembering that it is through our lives that our boys and girls first perceive the love and grace of God. And we can live our faith in Him before our children.

A PROMISE CLAIMED

The promise: "The LORD, before whom I walk, will send His angel with you and prosper your way, and you shall take a wife for my son from my family and from my father's house" (Gen. 24:40).

The context of the promise. When it was time for Abraham's son Isaac to marry, Abraham sent a servant to arrange a marriage within his extended family. When the servant expressed concern that no young woman would be willing to leave her home to travel hundreds of miles to marry a man she had never seen, Abraham reassured him. Abraham told the servant that God would "send His angel before you" (Gen. 24:7).

When the servant arrived in Haran, where Abraham's relatives lived, God answered the prayer for guidance and showed the servant His choice for Isaac's bride: Rebekah.

Understanding the promise. Genesis 24:7, 40 report a promise relayed by Abraham to his servant. These verses expressed Abraham's confidence that God's angel would guide his servant to the woman whom God had chosen to become Isaac's wife. The text does not say whether God communicated this promise to Abraham, or whether Abraham inferred what God would do based on God's earlier revelations. The Jewish sages tended to argue for the latter, suggesting the verse means, "In the light of His many promises to me, I am confident that He will grant you His Special Providence and aid you in finding a suitable mate" (Rabbi Meir Zlotowitz, *Bereishis*, 1969, p. 901).

In any case, the promise relayed here is one made to or inferred by Abraham. It is a promise that angels would prepare the hearts of those to whom the servant was sent—a promise that angels would accompany and lead the servant on his way. As Genesis reports, the promise made or inferred was kept.

Claiming the promise. The experience of the servant raises a significant question. Can we *infer* promises, and then act on them, as if God had actually spoken them to us? It should be clear that no inferred promise has the credibility of a promise expressed in God's Word. Since even the Bible's words can be misunderstood, we should hesitate before claiming a promise inferred by anyone.

At the same time, one phrase in verse 40 should give us pause. That phrase is "before whom I walk." Abraham was a man of faith who did walk with God. In the intimacy of that relationship, Abraham came to know God well, perhaps sensing His unspoken will. It may well be that the Holy Spirit speaks in the hearts of those who walk with God and that silent promises which we can count on do pass between God and man.

In a significant passage on the role of the Holy Spirit in communicating and interpreting God's will, Paul asked, "Who has known the mind of the Lord that he may instruct Him?" Then Paul added, "But we have the mind of Christ" (1 Cor. 2:16). Paul's point is that while we cannot penetrate God's mind, God has in the Spirit given us access to the mind of Christ, *that He may instruct us!*

The guidance which Paul described is personal—not general—and for the individual rather than the church. That general guidance, like general promises, are revealed in Scripture. Thus, the verse reminds us that as we walk with God, His Spirit may breathe special promises into our hearts, as the Genesis text suggests He breathed into the heart of Abraham.

Responding to the promise. No special guidance given by the Spirit will ever contradict the revealed Word of God. And no special guidance is given to believers *for others.* A mother told a young man that God had told her he was to marry her daughter. The young man replied, "Let's wait until God tells *me.*"

A passage in 1 Corinthians on the role of the Spirit contains this statement: "He who is spiritual judges all things, yet he himself is rightly judged by no one" (1 Cor. 2:15). This text reminds us that the gift of God's Spirit enables us to evaluate situations for ourselves

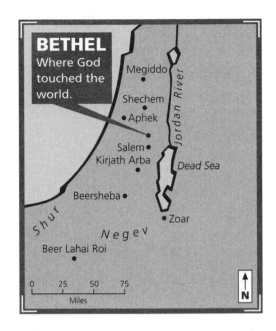

BETHEL
Where God touched the world.

Megiddo
Jordan River
Shechem
Aphek
Salem
Kirjath Arba
Dead Sea
Beersheba
Zoar
Shur
Negev
Beer Lahai Roi

0   25   50   75
Miles
N

and to sense the Spirit's direction. In cases of such private leading, we are not to judge others. And when we sense God's leading in our lives, we are not to let others dissuade us from what we believe to be God's will.

GOD'S PERSONAL PROMISES TO JACOB

Jacob, who was renamed Israel in his later years, was the grandson of Abraham and inheritor of the covenant promises transmitted to him through his father, Isaac. As a young man, Jacob defrauded his older brother Esau and tricked their father into giving him the blessing which Isaac intended for Esau. The deceit was unnecessary, for God had announced His intention to channel the covenant promises through Jacob, not his brother (cf. Gen. 25: 23). Jacob's actions so angered Esau that he planed to kill Jacob. Under this threat, Jacob fled to the extended family back in Haran. As Jacob journeyed, God appeared to him with several personal promises.

THE FIRST PROMISE OF GOD'S PRESENCE

The promise: "Behold, I am with you and

will keep you wherever you go, and will bring you back to this land; for I will not leave you until I have done what I have spoken to you" (Gen. 28:15).

The context of the promise. In his flight to his mother's relatives, Jacob stayed overnight at Bethel, a wilderness area at the time. He was given a vision of God and of angels passing between heaven and earth. In this vision, God announced that the covenant promises given to Abraham would pass to Jacob and his descendants. With this restatement of the covenant promises, God gave Jacob this personal promise.

Understanding the promise. This was a personal promise made without any conditions. God announced that He was with Jacob and (1) would keep Jacob wherever he might go, and (2) would bring Jacob back to the land. During Jacob's years away from Canaan, God also promised, "I will not leave you until I have done what I have spoken."

❖

In a dream, God promised Jacob to always be with him.

The promise revealed an aspect of God which underlines the differences between Him and pagan gods. The peoples of the ancient world identified their gods with the territory which the gods were supposed to "own." It was common practice for a traveler to show respect for the gods of the lands through which he passed, as those gods were thought to influence events within their territories.

A rabbinic parable reflects this reality. When a storm struck a ship at sea, everyone on board prayed to his gods, with no relief. A young Jewish traveler was then asked to pray, and the storm ceased. Upon coming to land, the wealthy merchants who had been on board exclaimed, "We are the poor aliens; for some of us are here and have our gods in Babylon; others have them in Rome; others have their gods with them but they are no benefit to us. As for you, however, wherever you go your God is with you!" (p. Ber. 13b).

This was the wonderful promise given to Jacob as he rested in Bethel. God would keep Jacob *wherever* he might go, and would bring him safely back to Canaan. And God would not leave Jacob before all His promises to him were fulfilled. This promise is rooted in the nature of our everywhere-present God and in God's unshakable commitment to His own.

Claiming the promise. While this promise was given to Jacob, it surely applies to us as well. The psalmist David claimed the promise of God's presence in awed wonder:

> Where can I go from Your Spirit?
> Or where can I flee from Your
> presence?
> If I ascend into heaven, You are
> there;
> If I make my bed in hell,
> behold, You are there.
> If I take the wings of the
> morning,
> And dwell in the uttermost parts of
> the sea,
> Even there Your hand shall lead me,
> And Your right hand shall hold me
> (Ps. 139:7–10).

The God who is everywhere is with us as He was with Jacob. God will not leave us until He has done all He has promised us in Christ.

Responding to the promise. It's wonderful to note that the promise of God's presence involves both space and time. Wherever we may travel, our God is by our side. And whatever the future holds for us, God will be there. We can place our hand in His with confidence, finding peace in the certainty that His presence goes with us.

A SECOND PROMISE OF GOD'S PRESENCE

The promise: "Then the LORD said to Jacob, 'Return to the land of your fathers, and to your family, and I will be with you' " (Gen. 31:3).

The context of the promise. During twenty years in Haran, Jacob gained two wives, many children, and large flocks. God was with him just as He had promised. But then, as God sent Jacob back to Canaan, the Lord added, "And I will be with you."

Why add this word of promise? Because going home was not something Jacob viewed with joy. He had left home hurriedly about 20 years before because his brother Esau threatened his life. In order to gain a blessing, Jacob had also deceived his father. Even more, during Jacob's absence, his mother Rachel had died. She had been his fierce supporter in Jacob's rivalry with his brother. With her gone, Jacob had no one in the family on his side. So the thought of going home was hardly a comfort to Jacob.

God's word of encouragement was just what Jacob needed. He couldn't count on the reaction of other family members, but he could count on the Lord. Whatever was waiting for him at home, God promised "I will be with you."

Understanding the promise. The promise of Genesis 31:3 was made by God to Jacob. It was a personal promise, stated unconditionally. Like the earlier promise of God's presence, this promise was also given at a time when Jacob needed to hear just this word from the Lord.

Claiming the promise. This promise was made specifically to Jacob. But we can sense situations in which it may be claimed and applied by us today. For Jacob, the call to return home aroused fear and uncertainty. We may also find ourselves called to face situations in which we are uncertain and fearful. Whatever stress we experience in our own lives, there is the certainty that we never have to face an uncertain future alone. The God who was with Jacob is with believers today. And the promise "I will be with you" is ours indeed.

Responding to the promise. The writer of Hebrews stated well the principle of God's presence and showed us how to apply it in our lives.

He Himself has said, *"I will never leave you nor forsake you."* So we may boldly say:

> *"The Lord is my helper;*
> *I will not fear.*
> *What can man do to me?"* (Heb. 13:5, 6).

We can confront our fears and live victoriously when we claim the promise of God's presence with boldness and commit ourselves to living His will.

A THIRD PROMISE OF GOD'S PRESENCE

The promise: "I will go down with you to Egypt, and I will also surely bring you up again; and Joseph will put his hand on your eyes" (Gen. 46:4).

The context of the promise. Jacob returned to Canaan and was welcomed by the brother whom he had feared. But tragedy awaited the patriarch. Jacob's favorite son, Joseph, was sold into slavery by his brothers. For years, Jacob mourned for his lost boy. Then Jacob learned that Joseph was alive and serving as a ruler in Egypt and that Joseph had sent for his father and the other members of his family to join him in that land.

Jacob was 130 years old (Gen. 47:9) and near death when God told him to go to Egypt (Gen. 46:3) and gave him this promise. The phrase "Joseph will put his hands on your eyes" (Gen. 46:4) meant that Jacob's dearly loved son Joseph would be with Jacob when he died, to close his eyes.

Understanding the promise. This was the third promise of God's presence given to Jacob. Like the first, this was a promise that God would accompany the patriarch beyond the borders of Canaan. It is significant that what was essentially the same promise was repeated to Jacob three times. So we need to ask when were the promises given and in what circumstances.

The promise was first given when Jacob was young, was repeated when he was a mature adult, and then was repeated again in his old age. God was with Jacob throughout his life, as He is with us.

This promise was also given and repeated at crisis points in Jacob's life. God promised Jacob His presence when he fled from home toward an uncertain future, again when he prepared to return home to an uncertain future, and again when he was about to go to Egypt, with an equally uncertain future. How reassuring it is to know that in the crises of our own lives—when we most need to sense God's presence—He is with us.

Claiming the promise. This third promise of God's presence was also given to Jacob in a specific historical situation. It was an unconditional promise given to one man. But from Jacob's experience, we learn that we also are always in the presence of our God.

To claim the promise given to Jacob, we need not ask God to be with us, for He always is. We simply need to remember that He is always near.

Responding to the promise. The familiar Twenty-third Psalm expresses a peace and confidence that can be ours as we live in God's presence.

The LORD is my shepherd;
    I shall not want.
He makes me to lie down in green
    pastures;
He leads me beside the still waters.
He restores my soul;
He leads me in the paths of
    righteousness
For His name's sake.

Yea, though I walk through the
    valley of the shadow of death,
I will fear no evil;
For You are with me;
Your rod and Your staff, they comfort
    me.

You prepare a table before me
    in the presence of my enemies;
You anoint my head with oil;
My cup runs over.
Surely goodness and mercy shall
    follow me
All the days of my life;
And I will dwell in the house of the
    LORD
Forever (Ps. 23:1–6).

He is ours, and we are His. Forever.

A PERSONAL PROMISE TO JOSEPH

As a young lad, Joseph was the favorite son of his father, Jacob. The favoritism stimulated the jealousy of Joseph's brothers. When Joseph was a teenager, his brothers sold him into slavery, and Joseph was taken to Egypt. The familiar story of Joseph's rise to become vizier of Egypt is told in Genesis 37—50.

When Joseph was young and still at home, he was given two prophetic dreams which may be construed as promises.

THE PROMISE OF PREEMINENCE

The promise: "There we were, binding sheaves in the field. Then behold, my sheaf arose and also stood upright; and indeed your sheaves stood all around and bowed down to my sheaf" (Gen. 37:7).

The context of the promise. In the ancient world, dreams were considered a source of revelation. When Joseph had a dream in which he saw the sun, moon, and eleven stars bowing down to him, even his father took it seriously. The text says that "his father rebuked him and said to him, . . . 'Shall your

Joseph's dream of preeminence angered his brothers.

INTERPRETATION OF DREAMS

The Egyptians among whom Joseph lived placed great importance on dreams. One Egyptian dream book, which dates back to the time of Joseph (2000–1800 B.C.), listed dream interpretations. Here are samples, translated by Alan H. Gardiner, *Hieratic Papyri in the British Museum, Third Series, Chester Beatty Gift,* 1935, I, 9–23; II, Plates 5–8.

IF A MAN SEES HIMSELF IN A DREAM:

shooting at a mark	*good:* good things will happen to him.
with a bow in his hand	*good:* great office will be given to him.
looking out a window	*good:* his cry will be heard by a god.
copulating with his sister	*good:* possessions will be decreed unto him.
writing on a papyrus	*bad:* it means the tallying of his misdeeds by his god.
seeing people far off	*bad:* his death is near.
fire spreading over his bed	*bad:* this means driving out his wife.

The list of good and bad omens stretches on and on, testifying to the Egyptian's belief that dreams foretold the future. It is not surprising that in such a culture Joseph's later interpretation of pharaoh's dreams should lead to his promotion as the wisest of men.

mother and I and your brothers indeed come to bow down to the earth before you?' " (Gen. 37:10).

Understanding the promise. Neither Joseph, his father, nor his brothers had to appeal to a book of dream interpretations to understand Joseph's dream. They agreed that it foreshadowed Joseph's promotion above everyone in the family, including his own father! While the rest of the family took the dream as an expression of Joseph's arrogance, the dream may have had additional meaning for Joseph. Perhaps Joseph even took it as a promise. If he did, that promise must have sustained him in Egypt until it was finally fulfilled.

Claiming the promise. If we take Joseph's symbolic dreams as promises, the promises were made specifically to Joseph and not to us today. But we need to consider this incident seriously because it raises an important question. Does God make promises to us through *our* dreams? Do we have any basis to assume that our dreams might convey a message from God?

Dreams in Scripture. Dreams are mentioned in Scripture a total of 115 times, with 106 occurrences in the Old Testament. Some of these are a context for divine revelations.

Revelatory dreams. Many of the dreams reported in Scripture served as the vehicle for a vision, in which God or an angel spoke plainly to an individual (cf. Gen. 28:11–15; Matt. 1:20–24). Through these dream visions, God gave a revelation of Himself, His will, or the future.

Symbolic dreams. Some dreams reported in Scripture are highly symbolic. Pharaoh dreamed about ears of corn that ate one another and of cattle that ate other cattle (Gen. 41). Nebuchadnezzar dreamed about a giant statue made of different metals (Dan. 2). Daniel dreamed about strange animals that fought with one another (Dan. 7, 8). Each of these symbolic dreams had at least two things in common. Each was prophetic, and *each was interpreted.* No one was left to speculate about the meaning of these dreams.

Revelatory dreams today? The fact that Scripture's symbolic dreams are followed in the text with an interpretation should make us hesitate to read too much into our own dreams. The Egyptian Dream Book mentioned above reminds us that for at least 4,000 years human beings have struggled to understand the meaning of their dreams. But the interpretations offered in the dream book show us how subjective dream interpretations are. It would be wrong to deny the possibility that God might grant a person a promissory symbolic dream today. But it is not wrong to suggest that this is unlikely, simply because the interpretation of such a dream is so uncertain.

Responding to the promise. If Joseph's dream can be considered a promise, it was a promise made to him alone. To those who would try to apply the event to their own experience and treat their symbolic dreams as divine promises, a word of warning from Jeremiah is appropriate. Jeremiah warned the people of Judah not to let their prophets and diviners deceive them. Then he added, "Nor listen to your dreams which you cause to be dreamed" (Jer. 29:8). Those words, "which you cause to be dreamed," are significant. Our dreams are far more likely to reflect our doubts and desires than to be a message from the Lord.

CHAPTER 10

PROMISES GIVEN AND FULFILLED:

PERSONAL PROMISES IN EXODUS—DEUTERONOMY

The book of Exodus picks up the story of the descendants of Abraham, Isaac, and Jacob about 400 years after Jacob's death. The Israelites had multiplied in Egypt, but they had also been enslaved. Exodus opens with the introduction of Moses, a unique personality whom God used to win the release of His people, to give them His Law, and to lead them back to the promised land.

Exodus is a book filled with promises given and promises fulfilled. Again and again, Exodus recalls or restates the commitments God made in the Abrahamic Covenant. Yet within this great book there are many additional promises: personal promises given to Moses, and promises made to God's distressed people. These additional promises are the ones we explore here.

PERSONAL PROMISES GIVEN TO MOSES

Moses was an Israelite adopted as a baby by the daughter of Pharaoh. In spite of the advantages he enjoyed growing up in the royal court, Moses dreamed of freeing his own people from their servitude. At age 40 Moses killed an Egyptian taskmaster who was abusing an Israelite, and was forced to flee. He spent the next 40 years in the Sinai desert herding sheep. There his youthful dreams were forgotten. But God had not forgotten Moses. When Moses was 80, God called him to the mission that once had been dear to his heart. But 40 years in the desert had changed Moses and drained his self-confidence. Moses responded to God's call by begging the Lord to send someone else. But Moses was God's choice. Many of the personal promises God made to Moses were designed to strengthen him for the task ahead.

THE PROMISE OF GOD'S PRESENCE

The promise: "I will certainly be with you."

The context of the promise. When God called Moses to return to Egypt, Moses objected: "Who am I that I should go to Pharaoh, and that I should bring the children of Israel out of Egypt?" (Ex. 3:11). Moses was not being humble. Moses had lost all confidence in himself and his abilities. In his own eyes, Moses was a failure. When the door of opportunity suddenly opened, Moses was unwilling to enter.

Understanding the promise. The promise "I will be with you" is repeated to different individuals a dozen times in the Old Testament. It is one of the most basic of the commitments that God makes to individuals. The same promise is expressed in a variety of ways. For instance, several times in the Old Testament God stated, "I will never leave you or forsake you" (Deut. 31:6, 8; Josh. 1:5; 1 Chron. 28:20). Thus, while the promise in the text was made specifically to Moses, it is a promise that we can claim as well.

In this promise, no condition is laid down. In Moses' confrontation with the leader of his world's greatest power, God would always be at his side.

In earlier considerations of promises of God's presence, we emphasized God's omnipresence. Here we need to emphasize an aspect of God: His commitment to personal involvement on our behalf. God did not expect Moses to do God's work on his own. He would undergird Moses with His personal presence as Moses confronted the pharaoh of Egypt.

Claiming the promise. The fact that the promise of God's presence is found so frequently in the Scripture underlines its importance. This is a promise God wants us never to forget and always to claim. When God calls us to any task, He never leaves it to us alone. God stays with us so the power we need to accomplish His purpose is always available.

Responding to the promise. Moses felt overwhelmed by the task to which God was calling him. We can understand his reaction. How often have you and I hesitated, wondering "who am I?" But like Moses, we ask the wrong question. The question we should ask is, "Who is *God*?" If we ask that question, and in our hearts answer that He is the all-powerful, we will hesitate no longer. The all-powerful will certainly be with us, so we can face our challenges with confidence.

THE PROMISE OF SUCCESS

The promise: "Then they will heed your voice."

The context of the promise. Moses' first challenge was to win acceptance by the elders of his own people. He wondered how he could, for Moses would seem to be a simple old man from the desert with a wild tale of being called by God to free the Israelites.

Understanding the promise. When we undertake any task, the outcome is uncertain. We never know if we will find success or failure. But God left no room for doubt when He encouraged Moses to go to Egypt. As for the elders of His people, "They will heed your voice" (Ex. 3:18). Success was assured.

God also told Moses that success with the pharaoh would not be *easy*. The king of Egypt would refuse to release his slaves. But even this warning was accompanied by the promise of ultimate success. "I will stretch out My hand and strike Egypt . . . after that he will let you go" (Ex. 3:20). God's presence, promised in Exodus 3:12, was a guarantee of God's involvement in Moses' mission! And this guaranteed success.

Claiming the promise. This promise of success to Moses was unconditional. While the promise was made to Moses and not to us, nevertheless we are reminded that where God is present He is also involved. In one sense, this reality is a blanket promise of success given to every Christian.

Our problem is that we often fail to measure success as God does. Moses undoubtedly would be judged a success by everyone. He saw the Israelites freed, given God's Law, and led to the border of the promised land. But consider the prophet Jeremiah. He also ministered for forty years. But few would consider him a success. In spite of Jeremiah's faithful preaching of God's word, king and people remained rebellious and Jerusalem was destroyed. Yet, was Jeremiah really unsuccessful? He faithfully conveyed God's message. It was hardly his fault if the people of his own day refused it. Perhaps even more significantly, out of the prophet's tears emerged the bright hope of a New Covenant that God would make with His sinning people at a future time. And that message, found in Jeremiah 31, brought hope to generations of Jews. It also placed in perspective the significance of Jesus' death.

Jeremiah, like Moses, *was* a success. God was with each of these great men, actively involved in their ministries. Jeremiah, like Moses, accomplished what God intended.

Responding to the promise. It is important that our own measure of "success" be that used by the Lord. The prophet Isaiah reminds us,

> So shall My word be that goes forth
> from My mouth;
> It shall not return to Me void;
> But it shall accomplish what I please,
> And it shall prosper in the thing for
> which I sent it (Isa. 55:11).

Whatever task God sets before us, His presence will be with us, and He will be involved. Whatever we do for Him is sure to succeed. As Paul reminds us, "Therefore, my beloved brethren, be steadfast, immovable, always abounding in the work of the Lord, knowing that your labor is not in vain in the Lord" (1 Cor. 15:58).

A PROMISE OF GUIDANCE

The promise: "I will be with your mouth and teach you what you shall say" (Ex. 4:12, 15).

The context of the promise. In spite of God's reassurance, Moses continued to resist returning to Egypt. One of Moses' last excuses was, "I am slow of speech and slow of tongue" (Ex. 4:10). Moses did not see himself as a gifted speaker.

In some irritation, the Lord asked Moses, "Who made man's mouth?" Moses had raised a foolish objection. If God were personally involved, the maker of Moses' mouth would give him the words to say.

Understanding the promise. Jesus made this same point in speaking with His disciples. He warned that His disciples would be persecuted and brought before kings and rulers, but that "it will turn out for you as an occasion for testimony." Jesus went on,

Therefore settle it in your hearts not to meditate beforehand on what you will answer; for I will give you a mouth and wisdom which all your adversaries will not be able to contradict or resist (Luke 21:13–15).

Jesus' point was that we are to rely on the Lord to *guide us in the situations in which we find ourselves.* We cannot predict the future, so we cannot prepare for it. Our approach to life must be to cultivate our relationship with the Lord, expecting Him to guide us whenever the need arises.

This principle was just as true in Moses' time. Knowing that God shaped the mouth, Moses should have recognized the promise implicit in God's creative act. The God who made Moses' mouth and who had promised to be with him would give Moses the words to say when the time for words arrived. Even so, God restated the obvious as a fresh promise. "I will be with your mouth and teach you what you shall say."

Claiming the promise. Promises like the one given to Moses and expressed by Jesus are implicit in God's commissioning to any task. Whatever God asks, God provides. Whenever God commands, God enables.

In making the implicit promise explicit, the Lord revealed one of His most beautiful traits. Rather than berate us when we are foolish, God stoops to spell out carefully what we should have known all along.

Many wonderful promises that are implicit in who God is and in His commitment to His own have been spelled out in Scripture. God expects that as we come to know Him better, we will claim many promises that are implicit in who He is.

Responding to the promise. The promise made to Moses reminds us that we are to expect God to lead us today. He may or may not lead us through specific or implicit promises given us in Scripture. But we can be sure of one thing: If we want to do the will of God, God will reveal His will to us—when the time for decision arrives.

THE PROMISE OF GREATER INTIMACY

The promise: "I will make all My goodness pass before you, and I will proclaim the name of the LORD before you" (Ex. 33:19).

The context of the promise. Moses responded to God's call and went to Egypt. He went as God's representative, and God spoke through him. Later, on Mt. Sinai, God gave Moses His Law for Israel. After their initial meeting, God often met with Moses in the tabernacle. The text says, "So the LORD spoke to Moses face to face, as a man speaks to his friend" (Ex. 33:11). The phrase "face to face" indicates intimacy, not that God appeared in visible form. But Moses' experience with God aroused a desire for even more intimacy, and Moses begged, "Please, show me Your glory" (Ex. 33:20).

In the Old Testament, the "glory" of God is linked with His revelation of Himself. There is much imagery: God's glory appeared as the blazing flame that often marked His presence (cf. Ex. 16:10; 40:34, 35; 2 Chron. 7:1, 2). But what Moses asked was to see God in His *essential* glory—to see God as He really is. God rejected this request for Moses' benefit: "No man shall see Me, and live" (Ex. 33:20).

What God did was to promise to show Moses as much of Himself as Moses could bear. In a beautiful act, God placed Moses in a rocky cleft and covered him as His glory passed by. God then permitted Moses to see not His face, but His back.

Understanding the promise. The promise that God gave Moses was in response to Moses' request. While the promise was made to Moses and not to all believers, we do have access to the blessing which Moses received! We can come to know God more intimately.

In Moses' case, God first revealed truth about Himself (Ex. 33:19), and then the Lord permitted Moses a greater personal experience with Him (33:22, 23). The truth God revealed was: "I will be gracious to whom I will be gracious, and I will have compassion on whom I will have compassion" (Ex. 33:19). This means God revealed that He is sovereign and free to act as He chooses, but that His choice is to be gracious and compassionate. Just like Moses, we should evaluate our experiences in the light of this truth about God.

God then permitted Moses to see more of Him than he had experienced before, while protecting Moses from seeing more than he could bear.

Claiming the promise. One of Paul's prayers for believers, recorded in Colossians 1:9–11, is reminiscent of Moses' experience. In his prayer, Paul outlined a path we can follow to experience greater intimacy with God.

Paul's prayer begins with truth about God. He asks that we might "be filled with the knowledge of His will." The Greek language says a knowledge of "that which God has willed," a reference to what He has revealed in Scripture. This knowledge is to be held in all "wisdom" or "spiritual insight." Each of the two Greek words so translated emphasize the practical application of truth to daily life. When we apply Scripture in daily life, we become "fruitful in every good work." And, Paul promises, we also increase "in the knowledge of God."

This last phrase indicates something different from the "knowledge of what God has willed." "What God has willed" is objective truth. The "knowledge of God" is personal and experiential. What Paul indicates is that we can know God more intimately by hearing and doing His Word.

It is this reality to which God's promise to Moses points. And it is this which Jesus spoke of also, saying "He who has My commandments and keeps them, it is he who loves Me. And he who loves Me will be loved by My Father, and I will love him and *manifest Myself to him* (John 14:21; italics mine).

We claim the promise of greater intimacy with God by loving Him and showing our love by keeping His Word. As we do so, Jesus "manifests Himself" to us, becoming more and more real to us each day.

Responding to the promise. One day we will see the Lord in His essential glory. Until then, we are promised a growing intimacy with and personal experience of the Lord. But this is a conditional promise. We must search out God's will in His Word and permit Scripture to shape our lives. As we do, Jesus will manifest Himself to us.

PROMISES GIVEN TO THE ISRAELITES

During the Exodus period, the people under Moses faced crisis after crisis. In spite of their persistent grumbling and rebellion, God made many promises to the Exodus generation.

THE PROMISE OF REDEMPTION AND JUDGMENT

The promise. "I will rescue you from their bondage, and I will redeem you with an outstretched arm and with great judgments" (Ex. 6:6).

The context of the promise. Moses came to the enslaved Israelites with word that God was about to act. Promises given to the patriarchs would be fulfilled in their day. God would use His power to break the Egyptians' grip on His people and set them free.

Understanding the promise. This promise was made to the Israelites in Egypt. God committed Himself not only to free them, but also to judge the Egyptians. The promise reflects a truth about God expressed throughout Scripture. The God who saves also judges.

Claiming the promise. In the experience of the Exodus generation, deliverance and divine judgment were combined into a single act. The plagues that won Israel's freedom also exacted vengeance on the oppressing Egyptians.

Today deliverance and vengeance are isolated. God has acted in Christ to deliver human beings, but He has delayed passing judgment on sinful humanity for thousands of years. The New Testament warns those who refuse to repent that "you are treasuring up for yourself wrath in the day of wrath and revelation of the righteous judgment of God" (Rom. 2:5). The promise of judgment is not one that we are to claim. But it is one that we count on.

The psalmist felt the tension between redemption provided and judgment delayed. He wrote,

> O LORD God, to whom vengeance
> belongs;
> O God, to whom vengeance belongs,
> shine forth!
> Rise up, O Judge of the earth;
> Render punishment to the proud.
> LORD, how long will the wicked,
> How long will the wicked triumph?
> (Ps. 94:1–3).

While judgment is delayed, it is as certain as the redemption God has provided for us in Christ. The God who redeemed us has said, "Vengeance is Mine, and recompense; their foot shall slip in due time; for the day of their calamity is at hand, and the things to come hasten upon them" (Deut. 32:35; cf. 2 Thess. 1:8–11).

Responding to the promise. It should comfort us to know that whatever inequities there are in this life, all will be balanced out by our just and loving God. The promise that God will repay releases us from the burden of feeling that we must exact personal revenge. In its place we discover a freedom to love even those who make themselves our enemies, and thus be more like our God, who makes His sun shine on both the evil and the good (Matt. 5:44, 45).

A PROMISE OF SECURITY

The promise: "When I see the blood, I will pass over you" (Ex. 12:13). "The LORD will pass over the door and not allow the destroyer to come into your houses to strike you" (Ex. 12:23).

The context of the promise. Egypt's pharaoh refused to let his Israelite slaves go, in spite of a series of plagues which devastated his land. Then the culminating judgment was announced: God would execute the firstborn in every Egyptian household. But the Israelites were instructed to sprinkle sacrificial blood on the door frames of their houses. They were promised that He would "pass over" them.

Understanding the promise. The root of the Hebrew word *pasah* is uncertain. Exodus 12:33 suggests that it should be understood as "hover over" rather than "pass over." When the death angel came, the Lord Himself hovered over the homes to protect those sheltered by the sacrificial blood.

Whatever the image conveyed by the verb, the intent is clear. God Himself guaranteed the security of those sheltered by the blood.

❖

Blood sprinkled on the doorpost signaled the destroyer to "pass over."

The New Testament draws an analogy from this historical event and applies it to Christians. Paul wrote that "Christ, our Passover, was sacrificed for us" (1 Cor. 5:7). As the blood of the Passover lamb kept Israel secure when God judged Egypt, so the blood of Christ will keep us secure when God judges the world.

Claiming the promise. With Christ as our Passover lamb, and sheltered by His blood, we also rest secure. Christ has taken the punishment we deserve, and God Himself will shelter us when the day of judgment comes.

THE PROMISE OF DIVINE INTERVENTION

The promise: "The LORD will fight for you, and you shall hold your peace."

The context of the promise. The Israelites left Egypt and set out toward the Sinai wilderness. The cloudy-fiery pillar led them into what seemed to be a trap. The people's way was blocked on three sides and a pursuing Egyptian army closed in. Moses encouraged the terrified Israelites to "stand still and see the salvation of the LORD" (Ex. 14:13).

Understanding the promise. God Himself had led His people into this impossible situation. God was about to impress upon His people that their safety and success did not depend on them but on Him. Israel was told to "stand still." God would fight "and you shall hold your peace."

Claiming the promise. This promise was specific to its time and place. God does not generally expect us to do nothing. In contrast, God called on the Israelites when they invaded Canaan to be courageous in battle (cf. Josh. 1:5, 9). We can hardly generalize from this promise to our difficult situations today. But there are two significant lessons for us in this story.

First, God may lead us into difficult situations. It's natural to expect everything to turn out well if we have made a choice that we believe is God's will. It's also natural to wonder when that choice turns out badly. Did we misinterpreted God's will? The Israelites' experience reminds us that God does not always lead His people in pleasant pathways. He may lead us into situations that challenge our faith. We should not assume that we have missed God's path if a choice or an event doesn't turn out as we expected.

Second, God has His own purposes in choosing a path for us. In the case of Israel at the Red Sea, His purpose was to show Israel more of His power and to increase their faith. We often grow more spiritually during a week of stress than an entire year of ease.

Responding to the promise. Let's follow God's will as best we can, without second-guessing if things should go wrong. When we do what is right and troubles follow, we can look with confidence to the Lord, certain that He has a good purpose in the experience.

THE PROMISE OF GOOD HEALTH

The promise: "If you diligently heed the voice of the LORD your God and do what is right in His sight, give ear to His commandments and keep all His statutes, I will put none of the diseases on you which I have brought on the Egyptians" (Ex. 15:26).

The context of the promise: Three days after God opened the Red Sea for the Israelites, the people needed water. Rather than appeal to the Lord, the Israelites turned against Moses. In response to Moses' prayer, God made bitter waters in the area drinkable. A conditional promise of good health was introduced—as a test!

Understanding the promise. This particular promise is conditional, made to a rebellious generation of Israelites. Exodus 15:26 called this a "statute and an ordinance" and a "test." Israel's freedom from the diseases of Egypt depended on their response to the Lord rather than on His grace.

MARAH
Where bitter waters turned sweet.

It is important to note the context of this conditional promise. God had acted for His people, freeing them from Egypt and miraculously rescuing them from a pursuing Egyptian army. His visible presence had accompanied them in the cloudy-fiery pillar that led them. Yet in spite of grace after grace, Israel had not responded to God with trust or gratitude. In this situation, a conditional promise was introduced, to teach Israel that they *couldn't presume upon His love.* If Israel was to continue to experience blessing, the people must respond to God appropriately. Soon this principle would be imbedded in the Law that Moses gave Israel at Sinai (see the Mosaic Covenant, pp. 40–54).

Claiming the promise. Many Christians are concerned about health and healing. Some are convinced that healing is promised to believers and that the promise is to be claimed by faith. There is no basis for this assumption in this passage. If God were to grant us good health on the condition that we should "keep *all* His statutes," we would be a sickly people indeed!

Responding to the promise. This promise, seen in the context of Israel's unresponsiveness to the Lord, reminds us how important it is for us to appreciate God's grace. When we focus on His goodness, He will have no need to test us or make our blessings conditional.

THE PROMISE OF PROVISION

The promise: "Behold, I will rain bread from heaven for you" (Ex. 16:4).

The context of the promise. The food that the Israelites brought from Egypt ran out before they reached Mt. Sinai. Once again, the people turned against Moses, accusing him and God of bringing them into the wilderness to kill them! God's response was to provide manna, a bread substitute, which appeared each morning except the Sabbath, and which continued to appear until the Israelites crossed into Canaan nearly 40 years later.

Understanding the promise. Probably some two million Israelites followed Moses out of Egypt. They traveled into the Sinai wilderness, where there were no natural food sources. For nearly 40 years God miraculously provided the daily food required to sustain them.

Looking back on these years, Moses said, "So He humbled you, allowed you to hunger, and fed you with manna ... that He might make you know that man shall not live by bread alone; but man lives by every word that proceeds from the mouth of the LORD" (Deut. 8:3).

Understanding the promise. This promise was made to the Exodus generation. While unconditional, the promise was limited to the years the Israelites spent in the wilderness areas outside of Canaan. The experience was intended to teach Israel to rely completely on God. The Lord promised Moses that the manna would be supplied daily. Each day the people relearned the truth that they could depend on God's word.

Claiming the promise. The meaning of the promise is explained in Deuteronomy 8:3. God humbled Israel (made them completely dependent on Him) to teach them to rely on His promise. Their experience shows us that we need to rely and act on God's Word.

Responding to the promise. Two New Testament incidents reflect on this incident. When Jesus was tempted by Satan, He turned back Satan by quoting Deuteronomy 8:3 (see Matt. 4:4). Jesus would not act on Satan's suggestion but only on the Word of God. We should also look to God's Word for guidance in every situation.

Some time later Jesus fed a large crowd. They recalled God's provision of manna and wanted to make Jesus king. Christ refused. Israel had missed the message of the manna. While Christ was the true bread from heaven—God's provision for our spiritual lives rather than our biological needs—He must be appropriated by faith in God's Word about Him. He should not be sought because He can meet material needs.

For us too, God's Word and spiritual blessings are to have priority. We are to love and serve God not because of what He can do for us, but because He is God.

THE PROMISE OF LONG LIFE

The promise: "Honor your father and your mother, that your days may be long upon the land which the LORD your God is giving you" (Ex. 20:12).

The context of the promise. The promise is linked with one of the Ten Commandments which God gave Israel. It is the only commandment with which a promise is associated.

Understanding the promise. In Ephesians the apostle Paul told children to "obey your parents" and mentions this commandment, calling it the "first commandment with promise" (Eph. 6:2). What specifically is the promise, and in what sense is it the "first"?

The promise, like the commandment, was given to Israel as a people. This was not a promise of individual long life, but a conditional promise of national continuity on the land. As such, it was considered very important by the rabbis.

But in what sense is this the "first commandment with promise"? In both testaments "first" emphasizes priority—in time, sequence, or rank within a class. Exodus 19:5, 6 contains

RABBINICAL COMMENTS ON HONORING PARENTS

It was generally understood in Judaism that "honoring" one's parents meant "he provides him with food, drink, clothing, and shelter, helps him in and helps him out" (Kid. 31b). The following passage from the Talmud show how important honoring parents was considered to be.

> Great is the precept to honor parents since the Holy One, blessed be He, attached to it still greater importance than the honoring of Himself. It is written, "Honor thy father and thy mother," and also "Honor the Lord with thy substance." With what do you honor God? With that which He has bestowed upon you, as of the field, tithes, charity to the poor, etc. If you possess the means of fulfilling these commandments, do so; but if you are destitute, you are not under the obligation. With the honoring of parents, however, no such condition is made. Whether you have means or not, you must fulfill the commandment, even if you have to go begging from door to door (P. Peah 15d).

a commandment and associated promise, so Exodus 20:12 clearly is not the first commandment God gave Israel that had a promise linked to it. It is best to understand the commandment as having priority *in human experience.*

As a child grows up, the first commandment he or she must obey is that of honoring and showing respect to parents. The child who learns respect for parents early will generally find it easier to transfer that respect to God. The child who is rebellious and unwilling to respond to parental guidance will find it far more difficult to submit to God. It is no wonder that this commandment is linked to national continuity in the promised land. Blessing in the land was only for those generations of Israelites who honored the Lord and

kept His commandments. Honoring parents is still the doorway through which children walk as they learn to honor God.

Claiming the promise. This promise made to Israel is not ours to claim today. But the underlying principle—that children who honor parents will find blessing—does apply. While parents are to be concerned with the needs and wants of their children, parents must insist that their children respect them. Without respect for parents, respect for God and submission to Him will be learned late, and painfully.

Responding to the promise. Honoring parents is not simply for children but for adults as well. We are to honor our parents even when we are aware of their flaws. At the same time, the parent who permits a child to be disrespectful is not showing love but an unwillingness to do what is best for the child.

THE PROMISE OF AID

The promise: "Behold, I send an Angel before you to keep you in the way and to bring you into the place which I have prepared" (Ex. 23:20).

The context of the promise. God through Moses gave Israel laws to live by when they possessed the land of Canaan (cf. Ex. 23). How could Israel, then in the Sinai wilderness, know they would possess the land? God promised to send an angel before them, to protect and to aid. (See also Ex. 32:34; 33:2.)

Understanding the promise. The promise of divine aid is followed immediately by a warning not to disobey the Lord. The generation to which this promise was made later refused to attack Canaan when God commanded them to do so (see Num. 14). As a result, all in that generation except two, Joshua and Caleb, died in the wilderness. Some 38 years later their descendants, who were obedient, did enter and conquer Canaan. Yet the promise which the first generation to leave Egypt failed to claim remained good. And it was claimed by their children. God remained faithful in spite of His people's unfaithfulness.

Claiming the promise. This promise of aid was given specifically to ancient Israel and related to the conquest of Canaan. At the same time, the incident gives us insight into the ministry of angels to believers of every era. Angels are described in the Bible as "ministering spirits sent forth to minister for those who will inherit salvation" (Heb. 1:14). They help us today even as they aided ancient Israel. [For answers to your questions on this topic, see the companion volume, *Every Good and Evil Angel in the Bible.*]

Perhaps the most wonderful lesson contained in the passage is that God's promises remain open. The Exodus generation failed to obey God, and the promise was not fulfilled for them. Their children did obey God, and God's angel brought them into the promised land (cf. Judg. 2:1). Although disobedience may keep us from claiming a promised blessing at one time in our lives, when we return to the Lord we may find that the promise is still ours to claim.

Responding to the promise. We should respond in faith to God's word so that His blessings may fall on us.

GOD'S PROMISES IN LEVITICUS

The book of Leviticus contains rules for holy living that God gave to Israel through Moses. The first seven chapters cover regulations for offerings and sacrifices. The rest of the book covers a number of lifestyle issues, ranging from appropriate foods to laws regulating marriage and Israel's religious festivals. Aside from references to God's covenant commitments, there are few promises found in Leviticus.

THE PROMISE OF FORGIVENESS

The promise: "So the priest shall make atonement for his sin that he has committed, and it shall be forgiven him" (Lev. 4:35).

The context of the promise. The law code which God gave to Israel defined sins and condemned those who violated the laws. Leviticus established a system of sacrifices through which sins could be covered and the sinner could find forgiveness. But the sacrifices established in the first seven chapters of Leviticus were only for sins committed *unintentionally* (cf. Lev. 4:2, 13, 22, 27; 5:15). But forgiveness was provided even for intentional sins. Once a year on the Day of Atonement, the high priest made a prescribed sacrifice:

For on that day the priest shall make atonement for you, to cleanse you, that you may be clean from all your sins before the LORD (Lev. 16:30).

Understanding the promise. The sacrifices provided for God's Old Testament people teach many truths. They show that God is eager to forgive sinning people. They teach that the punishment of sin is death, but that God will

The priest offered sacrifices for his own sins and the sins of the people.

accept the death of a substitute. The sacrifices of the Old Testament foreshadowed Jesus' death on the Cross and helped to define its meaning. Jesus died as our substitute, paying the penalty for our transgression against God.

Claiming the promise. The promise of forgiveness acted out in the Old Testament is ours to claim today. The book of Hebrews says of Christ's sacrifice:

We have been sanctified through the offering of the body of Jesus Christ once for all. And every priest stands ministering daily and offering repeatedly the same sacrifices, which can never take away sins. But this Man, after He had offered one sacrifice for sins forever, sat down at the right hand of God. . . . For by one offering He has perfected forever those who are being sanctified (Heb. 10:10–12, 14).

The forgiveness that is ours when we trust Christ as our sacrifice and Savior is perfect and complete.

Responding to the promise. We respond first to the promise of forgiveness by humbling ourselves to accept it as God's gift. We respond, second, by giving ourselves to the One who gave Himself for us. And we respond, third, by sharing the promise with others.

THE PROMISE OF PROVISION

The promise: "Then I will commend My blessing on you in the sixth year, and it will bring forth produce enough for three years" (Lev. 25:21).

The context of the promise. Every seventh year the Israelites were commanded to leave their fields uncultivated. God promised that He would make up for the possible loss of crops by multiplying the harvest of the sixth year. That year would produce enough for three years—the sixth and the seventh, with seed for the eighth year, plus food until the new crops matured.

Understanding the promise. The fascinating thing about this promise is that it was fulfilled before God's people were asked to respond! Israel could let the land lie fallow the seventh

year, for the sixth-year harvest would already be in their barns!

Claiming the promise. The striking thing about this promise is that the Israelites failed to act on it. Second Chronicles 36:21 indicates that one reason the Babylonian exile lasted for seventy years was to permit the land to "enjoy her Sabbaths." The verse goes on to say that "as long as she [the land] lay desolate she kept Sabbath, to fulfill seventy years." Thus for at least 490 years the Israelites had not used the excess they were given as God intended! In the end, the price paid for greed was a terrible one indeed.

Responding to the promise. Israel's experience raises the practical issue of how *we* are to use the excess which God gives us. Will we use it to honor Him, or will we use it selfishly?

PROMISES OF BLESSINGS AND PUNISHMENTS

The promise: "If you walk in My statutes and keep my commandments, and perform them . . ." (Lev. 26:3).

The context of the promises. In our study of the Mosaic Covenant (pp. 40–54), we saw that Israel's blessing was conditioned on obedience. A generation which loved and obeyed God would experience in their time the blessings the Abrahamic Covenant promised for history's end. This reality served as the foundation for the promised blessings and punishments spelled out in Leviticus 26 and Deuteronomy 28.

Understanding the promises. These promises are promises of blessings in this life. They are conditional promises, claimed by our obedience.

Claiming the promises. It is important that we not view these Law-linked promises as something we can claim. Our blessings are spiritual blessings, which we experience independently of material well-being or even good health.

It is also important to keep in mind that God's blessing depends on His grace. We cannot earn God's blessings, nor does anything we do give us a "right" to His blessings. The notion that if we believe strongly enough, then God must heal—or provide riches—may grow out of a misunderstanding of such Scriptures as Leviticus 26.

Responding to the promises. As we move on to the New Testament, we will learn that God's blessings are rooted in grace. To enjoy all He is eager to give, we must live in fellowship with Him.

Blowing the silver trumpets sent a signal to the people and to God.

GOD'S PROMISES IN NUMBERS

The book of Numbers continues the story of the Exodus. Moses organizes the camp for travel (chs. 1—10). Upon reaching Canaan, the Israelites rebel against God and refuse to enter (chs. 11—14). God condemns the rebels to wander in the wilderness until the arrival of a new generation which will trust and obey Him (chs. 15—25). The last part of the book traces the progress of the new generation to the borders of the promised land (chs. 26—36). The entire book shows the impact of the Abrahamic and Law Covenants as they are worked out in the experience of two generations of Israelites. The book contains several special promises given to Moses and the Israelites.

THE PROMISE OF DELIVERANCE

The promise: "When you go to war in your land against the enemy who oppresses you, then you shall sound an alarm with the trumpets, and you will be remembered before the LORD your God, and you will be saved from your enemies" (Num. 10:9).

The context of the promise. God commanded the making of two silver trumpets. Blowing the trumpets was a signal for Israel to assemble or move on. Blowing the trumpets was also to signal the Lord, when Israel went to

war, and when the people offered sacrifices during religious holidays. God promised that when Israel called on Him by sounding the alarm with the silver trumpets, He would save them from their enemies.

The use of "remember" in this verse does not imply that the Lord forgets His people. In Hebrew idiom, to remember is to act, usually to punish sins or to save.

Understanding the promise. While there is no condition expressed with this promise, Israel was under the Law. God had linked deliverance from enemies with a generation's faithfulness to Him and obedience to His law (cf. Lev. 26:7, 16, 17). Thus, this promise is conditional.

The promise was one that Israel had to claim by blowing the trumpets. Blowing the trumpets expressed dependence on the Lord as well as faith in Him.

Claiming the promise. God is willing to help us. But we must express faith by turning to

Him. Today we have no silver trumpets to blow. But we can express our faith—for example, by asking others to pray for us.

THE PROMISE OF SHARED BURDENS

The promise: "I will take of the Spirit that is upon you and will put the same upon them; and they shall bear the burden of the people with you, that you may not bear it yourself alone" (Num. 11:17).

The context of the promise. In spite of God's miracles on behalf of the Israelites, the Exodus generation continued to grumble and complain. Moses was driven to despair, his leadership an affliction rather than a blessing! God responded by promising Moses that He would give others the Spirit, that they might share the burden of leadership with Moses. The promise was fulfilled when God anointed seventy elders of Israel (Num. 11:24–25).

BIBLE BACKGROUND:

THE ORIGIN OF THE SANHEDRIN

In Jesus' day this incident was viewed as the basis for the establishment of the Sanhedrin. The body was to have seventy-one members, and "sat in Moses seat"—it was the supreme legislative and judicial body in Judaism. Lesser courts in biblical times were composed of either three or twenty-three judges.

Understanding the promise. Earlier at Sinai Moses had followed the advice of his father-in-law Jethro and established a series of courts (Ex. 18:13–23). These courts dealt with lesser disputes, allowing Moses to deal only with the most difficult cases. The specific responsibilities of the seventy mentioned here are not defined. But it is clear that God's endowment of them with the Spirit equipped them to share leadership with Moses, answering Moses' com-

plaint that he carried the entire burden of Israel alone.

The incident introduces a principle reflected in both testaments. While God has raised up individuals to lead the nation Israel and to serve the whole church, leadership in the communities of ancient Israel and in local congregations of New Testament times was provided by teams of elders. The people of faith are not to be lorded over by autocrats. They are a community guided by elders who share responsibility and spiritual authority. God will put His Spirit upon members of such teams so they may bear the burden of leadership together.

Responding to the promise. The promise made to Moses established a pattern which we are to follow. God expects no one to bear the burden of leadership alone. In every setting—from the family to the church—we are to share with partners the responsibilities and authority of leadership.

THE PROMISE OF TENURE

The promise: "Behold, I give to him My covenant of peace; and it shall be to him and his descendants after him a covenant of an everlasting priesthood, because he was zealous for his God, and made atonement for the children of Israel" (Num. 25:12, 13).

The context of the promise. Moabite women had seduced a number of Israelite men and led them into idolatry. Phinehas, a priest, saw an Israelite bring one such woman into his tent, and he killed them both. His action stopped a plague that God had sent to punish the people for this sin. God rewarded Phinehas's zeal with the promise of perpetual priesthood.

Understanding the promise. Hebrew writing used consonants only. The vowels had to be supplied by the reader. The meaning of a word can differ, depending on which vowels are supplied. Here the word translated "peace" would, with different vowels, read "reward," and the phrase "my covenant of peace" would read "my covenant as a reward." This is probably the meaning here. Phinehas was rewarded with the promise that his descendants would serve God as priests throughout Israel's history.

Claiming the promise. The promise given to Phinehas cannot be applied directly to us today. But the incident does reveal something of God's grace toward those who are fully committed to Him.

Responding to the promise. The experience of Phinehas calls to mind a study of two New England families traced through five or six generations. The patriarch of one family was a minister. Across the years, this family produced missionaries, pastors, professional people, and college presidents. The patriarch of the other family was a criminal. Across the years, his descendants produced thieves, swindlers, and murderers. Maintaining zeal for the Lord is one of the most significant gifts a parent can give to his or her children.

GOD'S PROMISES IN DEUTERONOMY

The book of Deuteronomy contains a series of sermons or messages given by Moses. The structure of the book follows the form of an ancient suzerainty covenant (see page 51). In this powerful restatement for the new generation of Israelites, Moses emphasized God's loving motive in giving them His Law to follow. While many of the promises expressed in Deuteronomy restate commitments God made in the Abrahamic Covenant, special promises are also recorded in this great Old Testament book.

A PROMISE REMEMBERED

The promise: "This day I will begin to put the dread and fear of you upon the nations under the whole heaven, who shall hear the report of you, and shall tremble and be in anguish because of you" (Deut. 2:25).

The context of the promise. God had promised to send His angel ahead of Israel to protect and fight for them (Ex. 23:27). One element of that promise is remembered here, in an extended passage in which Moses reviews God's faithfulness to the Israelites (Deut. 1—4).

Understanding the promise. The promise was made as Israel advanced toward the promised land. God had been faithful to this promise in earlier struggles east of the Jordan River. Moses now reminded the Israelites that what God had promised, *He had fulfilled.* Partial fulfillment of the promise is recalled as a reminder of God's faithfulness and as a stimulus to continuing confidence in Him.

Claiming the promise. This promise does not apply directly to us today, but it does teach us a valuable lesson. As we look to the future, we also need to remember God's faithfulness to us in the past. The God who kept promises to us yesterday will surely be with us as we face new challenges.

Responding to God's promises. It's easy to accept what God gives—and then forget His goodness. Moses kept a record of God's faithfulness to Israel. We would be wise to keep a written record of His faithfulness to us. What an encouragement reviewing such a record can be.

THE PROMISE OF GUIDANCE

The promise: "I will raise up for them a Prophet like you from among their brethren, and will put My words in His mouth, and He shall speak to them all that I command Him" (Deut. 18:18).

The context of the promise. In this chapter, God commanded the Israelites not to look to any of the occult practices engaged in by the surrounding nations when seeking guidance. God knows that situations will arise in which the nation or individuals will need special guidance not available through the written Word. God promises to guide in these situations—through prophets whom He will raise up.

This promise has dual reference. As the capitalization of "He" in Deuteronomy 18:15 and 18 indicates, the passage refers to a particular prophet whom God would send to Israel. Jewish and Christian commentators alike have interpreted this as a reference to the Messiah.

This promise is also understood to imply the sending of other spokesmen whom God would send His people in time of need. This aspect of the promise is made clear in verses 19–22. These verses provide for tests by which the claim of any person who says he speaks for God can be substantiated.

Understanding the promise. The Old Testament contains stories of many prophets whom God raised up for Israel. These prophets advised kings, confronted sin, and interpreted current events in the light of God's covenants. When the need arose for special guidance, God provided it through the prophets.

The role of the prophet in providing guidance is seen in an incident that took place after the Babylonians destroyed Jerusalem (Jer. 42—43). The governor left by Nebuchadnez-zar was assassinated, and the remaining Jewish population was terrified. Nothing in God's Word told the people what they should do in this situation. So the leaders begged Jeremiah to ask the Lord whether they should stay in their homeland or flee to Egypt. God through Jeremiah told them to stay. But the people rejected the prophet's guidance and went to Egypt anyway. God did provide guidance through His prophets. But the prophets' words were often ignored.

Claiming the promise. Should we take this job, or that? Should we marry, or wait? Should we send our children to a private or a public school? Questions like these call for special guidance. And God still guides us, though not through prophets. God has given us the Holy Spirit as a leader and guide (John 16:13; Gal. 5:18). He will show us God's will as we look to Him today.

Responding to the promise. As the Israelites were to consult prophets when seeking God's guidance, so we are to turn to the Holy Spirit. Neither prophets nor the Spirit will lead us to violate the written Word of God (cf. Deut. 13:1–5). How wonderful that through the

Prophets such as Jeremiah were often ignored by the people.

Holy Spirit we have access to the mind of Christ, who does guide His own even today (1 Cor. 2:16).

THE PROMISE OF AID

The promise: "The LORD your God is He who goes with you, to fight for you against your enemies, to save you" (Deut. 20:4; see the discussion of Ex. 23:20, page 117).

PROMISES OF BLESSINGS AND PUNISHMENTS

The promise: "If you will diligently obey the voice of the LORD your God . . . the LORD your God will set you high" (Deut. 28:1; see the discussion of Leviticus 26, page 119).

THE PROMISE OF RESTORATION

The promise: "The LORD your God will bring you back from captivity, and have compassion on you, and gather you again from all the nations where the LORD your God has scattered you" (Deut. 30:3).

The context of the promise. In his final speech to the Israelites, Moses reviewed the promises and penalties defined in Mosaic Law (Deut. 28—29). Looking ahead, Moses realized that Israel would turn from God and that the ultimate penalty of expulsion from the land loomed ahead. Thus, some 800 years before

the Babylonian Exile, and nearly 1,500 years before the Roman destruction of Jerusalem in A.D. 70, Moses predicted the scattering of the Jewish people among the nations.

But the broad context of Israel's experience is the Abrahamic Covenant. Under that covenant, God promised that Abraham's descendants would exist as a nation in their own homeland. How did exile—an exile that has seen a majority of the Jewish people living outside Canaan for the last 2,600 years—fit in? According to Moses' words in Deuteronomy 30, God knew what His people would do. Through Moses, He announced that one day He would bring them home. That day of final return still lies ahead. But God's promise remains, permanently etched in the words of Scripture.

Understanding the promise. This promise is linked in the text with the original promise to Abraham that his descendants would occupy the promised land (Deut. 30:5). That promise is for Israel, not for Christians, and it is unconditional. What is fascinating is that Deuteronomy 30 adds information not explained in the Abrahamic Covenant. Spiritual renewal and a return to the Lord will be associated with—or perhaps trigger—Israel's return to the land. In the words of the apostle Paul, the day will come when "all Israel will be saved" (Rom. 11:26). God still cares for His

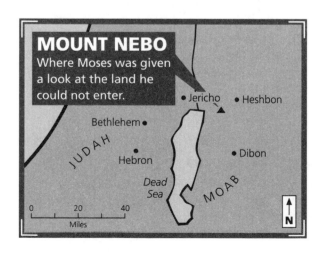

MOUNT NEBO
Where Moses was given a look at the land he could not enter.

Jericho •   • Heshbon

Bethlehem •

JUDAH

• Hebron

• Dibon

Dead Sea

MOAB

0   20   40
Miles

N

ancient people, who are "beloved for the sake of the fathers. For the gifts and the calling of God are irrevocable" (Rom. 11:28, 29).

Claiming the promise. This promise is not ours to claim. But it is ours to contemplate. How amazing the love of God is, and how great His compassion. He was rejected by many Old Testament generations and decisively rejected by Israel when He came to them through Jesus the Messiah. But our God still remains committed to His ancient promises. How confident we can be that we are truly saved in Him through the sacrificial death of His Son.

THE PROMISE OF GOD'S CONTINUING PRESENCE

The promise. "Be strong and of good courage, do not fear nor be afraid of them; for the LORD your God, He is the One who goes with you. He will not leave you nor forsake you" (Deut. 31:6; cf. Deut. 31:8).

The context of the promise. The promise of God's presence was often extended to the Exodus generation and their children (Ex. 10:10, 24; 33:14; Deut. 2:7; 4:31; 20:1, 4). Why is it repeated here? The reason undoubtedly is that Moses was about to die. The man who had led Israel for 40 years—the only leader this generation had known—would no longer be with them. How appropriate for Moses to reassure God's people. Moses will be gone, but God will never leave them. Moses will be gone, but the God who acted through him will be present and continue to act on their behalf.

Claiming the promise. This promise made to the Israelites is rooted in God's commitment to His own. God will not leave or forsake us. His presence gives us the courage to face each day with boldness and confidence.

CHAPTER 11

LIVING IN THE PROMISED LAND:

PERSONAL PROMISES IN THE HISTORICAL BOOKS

Joshua—2 Chronicles

The historical books contain narrative accounts of Israel's experience beginning with the conquest of Canaan (ca. 1400 B.C.) and continuing through approximately 400 B.C. These books make frequent references to God's covenant promises, but they also contain special promises.

GOD'S PROMISES IN THE BOOK OF JOSHUA

The book of Joshua relates the story of the conquest of Canaan under Moses' successor, Joshua. The conquest was a partial fulfillment of God's promise to Abraham that his descendants would possess that land. In this book, the Abrahamic Covenant is referred to as the basis of Israel's claim to the land (Josh. 1:3–6), and is mentioned again after organized Canaanite resistance is put down (Josh. 23:5). In his final address, Joshua reminded Israel that under the Mosaic Covenant the people must continue to honor and obey the Lord if they expect to remain in the promised land (Josh. 23:15).

The promises:

- "No man shall be able to stand before you all the days of your life; as I was with Moses, so I will be with you. I will not leave you nor forsake you" (Josh. 1:5).
- "Do not be afraid, nor be dismayed, for the LORD your God is with you wherever you go" (Josh. 1:9).
- "Do not fear them, for I have delivered them into your hand; not a man of them shall stand before you" (Josh. 10:8).
- "Do not be afraid because of them, for tomorrow about this time I will deliver all of them slain before Israel" (Josh. 11:6).
- "One man of you shall chase a thousand, for the LORD your God is He who fights for you, as He promised" (Josh. 23:10).

Understanding the promise. These verses in Joshua promise God's active aid, for this is the meaning of the phrase, "I will be with you." The basic promise is repeated five times—at the beginning, during, and following the conquest of Canaan. The promises encouraged Joshua and the Israelites as they struggled to occupy Canaan.

As Israel then lived under Moses' Law, the promise of aid was conditional. An incident highlights this fact. A man named Achan took booty from Jericho after the Lord had specifi-

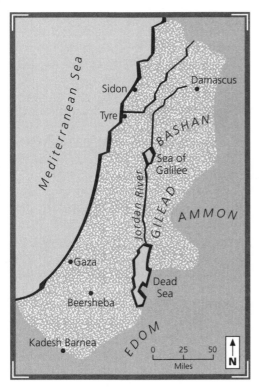

The Promised Land

cally commanded the people not to do so. This led to a defeat of Israel at the little town of Ai, and to a stern warning. God warned Israel, "Neither will I be with you anymore, unless you destroy the accursed from among you" (Josh. 7:12). Achan was identified and executed, and God then continued to aid His people.

Claiming the promise. God is always present with us. And God is eager to be involved on our behalf. But disobedience can cut us off from His aid. When we deal with our sin and return to Him, the promise of God's involvement in our struggles is ours to claim again.

It's fascinating to note that this particular promise to Joshua was repeated so often. Some might say once was enough—and it was. Yet God graciously kept on encouraging Joshua as new situations arose. We also may need to return to God's promises again and again as new situations arise in our lives. God, who kept on encouraging Joshua, will never rebuke us for returning to His promises to claim them over and over again.

Joshua led the Israelites in conquering Canaan.

GOD'S PROMISES IN THE BOOK OF JUDGES

The book of Judges spans several hundred years of Israel's experience in Canaan, from the successful conquest up to the time just before establishment of the Hebrew monarchy. During these centuries, God's people often abandoned Him and turned to idolatry. When the Lord brought foreign enemies to oppress them, the Israelites repented and prayed for relief. Again and again the Lord answered their prayers by raising up judges—military, political, and spiritual leaders—as deliverers.

The promises recorded in the book of Judges were made to the individuals whom God called to deliver His people. Like the promises given to Joshua, the promises in Judges are of God's assistance.

The promises:

- "Go in this might of yours, and you shall save Israel from the hand of the Midianites . . . Surely I will be with you, and you shall defeat the Midianites as one man" (Judg. 6:14, 16).
- "I will deliver them into your hand" (Judg. 20:28).

Understanding the promises. Each of these promises was given before a battle, to encourage those whom God was sending into battle. God never sends His people into battle expecting a defeat!

GOD'S PROMISES IN 1 SAMUEL, 2 SAMUEL, AND 1 CHRONICLES

The books of 1 and 2 Samuel trace the transition of the Israelite tribes from a loose confederation governed by judges into a unified nation governed by a king. The books are organized around the stories of three key figures: Samuel, Saul, and David. The most significant promise found in these books is one made to David: the Davidic Covenant. This promise and its implications are explained in the chapter on the Davidic Covenant (see pages 55–67).

These books contain a few prophetic announcements by the Lord which stated His intent (1 Sam. 2:30, 35; 6:19) as well as incidents in which David asked for and was given divine guidance (1 Sam. 30:8; 2 Sam. 5:19; 1 Chron. 14:10). Other than these, the experience of Israel during these years reflects the conditions imposed by the Mosaic Covenant. When God's people were faithful and obedient, God blessed. When they were unfaithful and sinful, God punished.

The book of 1 Chronicles parallels 2 Samuel's account of David's life, developing David's accomplishments even further. It also reports the incident in which David was given God's covenant promise. Associated with that commitment was an immediate promise to David that "I will subdue all your enemies" (1 Chron. 17:10). Another striking personal promise made to David concerned Solomon. Before Solomon's birth, God told David, "A son shall be born to you, who shall be a man of rest; and I will give him rest from all his enemies all around. His name shall be Solomon, for I will give peace and quietness to Israel in his days" (1 Chron. 22:9). As God promised, Solomon's rule was marked by great prosperity and an absence of war. And the Davidic Covenant passed from David through Solomon to Solomon's descendants (1 Chron. 22:10).

The lesson we learn from this period is an important one. While the basic principles incorporated in the Mosaic Covenant governed the experience of the nation, God did reach out to touch individual lives with special blessings. In the promises God made to individuals, you and I find encouragement, for the God who directed David's life is just as deeply involved in our own.

GOD'S PROMISES IN 1 KINGS, 2 KINGS, AND 2 CHRONICLES

These narrative books record the history of God's people during the era under ruling kings. For forty years after the death of David, King Solomon ruled a united Hebrew kingdom. On Solomon's death in 930 B.C. the nation was divided. A Northern Kingdom—Judah—and a Southern Kingdom—Israel—existed side by side. The kingdom of Israel ceased to exist in 722 B.C., but Judah survived until 586 B.C. The books of Kings record the turbulent history of the two kingdoms, surveying the reign of kings and the ministries of prophets.

The same period is covered from a slightly different perspective in 2 Chronicles. While the books of Kings provide a straightforward historical account, 2 Chronicles serves as a divine commentary on the age. This book pays special attention to the reign of the godly kings of Judah, and especially to the role of infrequent spiritual revivals.

The history of these times reflects the operation of the Mosaic Covenant (cf. 2 Chron. 15:2) and the Davidic Covenant (1 Kin. 11:11–13) in national life. A number of special promises linked to specific situations are also reported in these books of history.

THE PROMISE OF WISDOM

The promise: "I have given you a wise and understanding heart . . . and I have also given you what you have not asked: both riches and honor, so that there shall not be anyone like you among the kings all your days" (1 Kin. 3:12, 13; cf. 2 Chron. 1:11, 12).

The context of the promise. When Solomon took the throne, God invited him to make a request. Solomon asked for "an understanding heart to judge Your people, that I may discern between good and evil" (1 Kin. 3:9). This unselfish response pleased the Lord, who granted it and added the blessings of wealth and long life.

Understanding the promise. Solomon was not asking for intelligence. He was asking for wisdom to discern what would be beneficial for the nation he led ["good"] and what would be harmful ["evil"]. This distinction between intelligence and wisdom is made throughout

Scripture. While Solomon was given vast intelligence (cf. 1 Kin. 4:29–34), what he was promised by the Lord was *wisdom*.

Claiming the promise. While this promise was made specifically to Solomon, there are parallel promises in the New Testament which should encourage us. James tells us that "if any of you lacks wisdom, let him ask God, who gives to all liberally and without reproach, and it will be given to him" (James 1:5). And Jesus encouraged us to set priorities similar to Solomon's when He said, "Seek first the kingdom of God and His righteousness, and all these things shall be added to you" (Matt. 6:33).

Solomon's story is especially encouraging. How richly God blesses those who make His priorities their own!

Responding to the promise. Seeing the promise God gave Solomon should fill us with expectation. How confidently we can make God's priorities our own! We cannot lose by putting God first. We can only gain.

THE PROMISE OF AVAILABLE GRACE

The promise: "If My people who are called by My name will humble themselves, and pray and seek My face, and turn from their wicked ways, then I will hear from heaven, and will forgive their sin and heal their land. Now My eyes will be open and My ears attentive to prayer made in this place" (2 Chron. 7:14, 15; cf. 1 Kin. 9:3).

The context of the promise. Solomon dedicated the temple at Jerusalem that he had constructed in honor of the Lord. At the dedication, Solomon asked God to be available to His people, so that should they pray at or toward the temple, God would hear and answer them. Unlike pagans, who assumed that their gods lived in the temples built for them, Solomon acknowledged God's transcendence. God would not "live" in the temple (1 Kin. 8:27). But the temple could serve as faith's fo-

The dedication of the temple in Jerusalem was the highlight of Solomon's reign.

cal point for Israel: it would serve as a place of meeting where sacrifices and prayers could be presented to God.

Understanding the promise. The promise of available grace was made to all God's people. This was a conditional promise. God's people could come to God with their requests. But they could not expect God to bless them while they pursued wicked ways. God is always ready to forgive. But God cannot be taken advantage of or treated with disrespect.

Claiming the promise. This magnificent promise is frequently quoted by Christians. This is appropriate, because its Old Testament expression beautifully states basic principles of personal relationship with God. God is a for-

giving God, always ready to restore us. His eyes are open and His ears are attentive to our prayers. Yet God is God, and if we are to know His richest blessings we must be committed to Him.

Responding to the promise. The writer of Hebrews restated the ancient promise, with one significant change. Israel approached God by coming to the temple. The Christian comes boldly to the very throne of grace in heaven (Heb. 4:16). The Hebrews verse tells us that at God's throne "we may obtain mercy and find grace to help in time of need." The forgiveness promised Israel is always available to us. And in addition there is grace, that in our time of need we might find strength to remain faithful to the Lord.

A PROMISE OF SATISFIED DESIRE

The promise: "I will take you, and you shall reign over all your heart desires, and you shall be king over Israel" (1 Kin. 11:37).

The context of the promise. In Solomon's old age, pagan wives led him away from the Lord into idolatry. As a consequence, God divided the Hebrew kingdom, taking ten of the twelve tribes from Solomon's descendants. The promise in 1 Kings 11 was made to Jeroboam, who was to be the first king of the northern Hebrew kingdom, Israel. The promise to give these tribes to Jeroboam was unconditional. But a conditional promise was added. If Jeroboam would keep God's statutes as David had, God would give him an "enduring house" and his descendants would rule permanently in the north.

Understanding the promise. God did make Jeroboam king in the north, as He had promised. Jeroboam received from the hand of the Lord what he had wanted. But Jeroboam feared that if he permitted his subjects to worship in Jerusalem, as God's Law required, eventual reunion with the south would follow. So Jeroboam ignored God's instructions and set up a counterfeit religious system with its own worship centers, sacrifices, priesthood, and religious festivals. As a result, Jeroboam's dynasty fell, and many subsequent northern dynasties ended in assassinations.

The promise given to Jeroboam is exceptional in that it was made to an ambitious individual without a real faith in God. God is often gracious to those who do not believe or to believers we might consider undeserving. But those who do receive God's grace become responsible for how they use God's gifts. Those

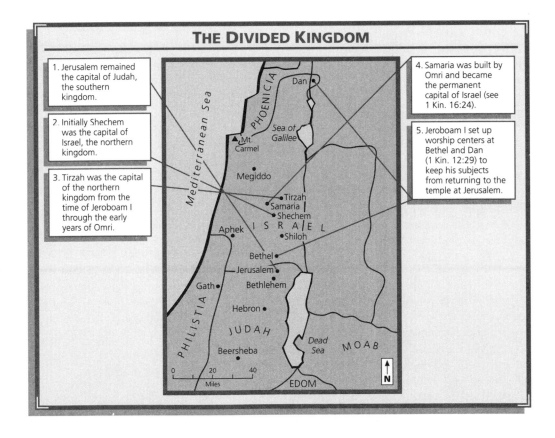

THE DIVIDED KINGDOM

1. Jerusalem remained the capital of Judah, the southern kingdom.

2. Initially Shechem was the capital of Israel, the northern kingdom.

3. Tirzah was the capital of the northern kingdom from the time of Jeroboam I through the early years of Omri.

4. Samaria was built by Omri and became the permanent capital of Israel (see 1 Kin. 16:24).

5. Jeroboam I set up worship centers at Bethel and Dan (1 Kin. 12:29) to keep his subjects from returning to the temple at Jerusalem.

who respond by turning to Him can expect continued blessing. Those who respond by ignoring or rejecting Him will bear the consequences of their choice.

THE PROMISE OF PROOF

The promise: "Behold, I will deliver it into your hand today, and you shall know that I am the LORD" (1 Kin. 20:13, 28).

The context of the promise. Ahab was one of the most wicked of Israel's kings. Ahab and his wife Jezebel worked to replace worship of the Lord with the worship of Baal and persecuted God's prophets. Yet when Israel was threatened by Syria, God sent a prophet to Ahab to promise deliverance. This happened not once but twice, and each time God engineered the defeat of the enemy. Each promise contained the formula, "And you shall know that I am the LORD."

Understanding the promise. God displayed His power to serve as proof of His power. After the two victories against overwhelming odds, Ahab could have no doubt that the Lord was the true God. The promises and their fulfillment was compelling evidence: Ahab *knew* that God truly is the all-powerful Lord.

But this knowledge did not result in any change in Ahab's heart. Immediately after these incidents, 1 Kings 21 reported Ahab's desire to have a vineyard owned by a man named Naboth. Jezebel arranged for his murder, and Ahab took possession of the property. Confronted there by the prophet Elijah, Ahab heard the prophet say, "You have sold yourself to do evil in the sight of the LORD" (1 Kin. 21:20).

Responding to the promise. God's promises in Scripture are rich sources of insights into His love for and commitment to us. How eager God is to reveal Himself and His goodness to human beings. But each fresh revelation lays an obligation on the one who receives it: an obligation to respond appropriately to the Lord.

THE PROMISE OF JUDGMENT DELAYED

The promise: "Because he [Ahab] has humbled himself before Me, I will not bring the calamity in his days" (1 Kin. 21:29).

The context of the promise. Ahab had been given proof of God's presence and power. Rather than repent, he continued to act wickedly. Elijah confronted Ahab in Naboth's vineyard and announced God's judgment. Ahab's descendants would die, and his blood would stain the vineyard which murder had obtained.

Understanding the promise. This time Ahab was terrified. He showed that he believed God's word by tearing his clothes, wearing sackcloth, fasting and mourning (1 Kin. 21:27). This was the traditional way an easterner showed remorse and sorrow. God then sent Elijah to Ahab again, noting "how Ahab has humbled himself before Me." By his actions Ahab showed that he believed God would punish as He had said. Even this dim glimmer of belief in God's Word was enough to move God to delay the punishment. The ordained calamity would come, but not in Ahab's lifetime.

The incident gives us an amazing insight into God's grace. Even the most wicked people who humble themselves before the Lord will be treated more kindly than their actions deserve. If God was so kind to Ahab, whose entire life was dedicated to wickedness, He will certainly be gracious to us when we sin.

Responding to the promise. Those who let sins drive them away from God make a tragic mistake. God knows our failings, but He loves us anyway. Any believer who humbles himself and returns to the Lord will be welcomed and fully restored.

THE PROMISE OF VICTORY

The promise: "You will not need to fight in this battle. Position yourselves, stand still, and see the salvation of the LORD, who is with you, O Judah and Jerusalem" (2 Chron. 20:17).

The context of the promise. Jehoshaphat was one of Judah's godly kings. When a coalition army of Moabites and Ammonites attacked Judah, Jehoshaphat turned to God and called on his people to fast and pray. In his prayer, Jehoshaphat honored God by expressing confidence in His ability to save. He also claimed the promise the Lord had made to Solomon to hear the prayers of those who appealed to Him at His temple. Jehoshaphat then appealed to God to judge the enemy. God then sent a messenger to Jehoshaphat with His promise, along with instructions to "go down against them" the next morning.

The response to this promise was significant. The king and the people worshiped and praised the Lord, and "early" the next morning marched out of the city, still singing praises. When the Jews reached a rocky overlook, they saw the bodies of the enemy spread across the valley. The Ammonites and Moabites had turned on each other, and all that was left for the Jews to do was collect the spoil.

Understanding the promise. This promise to Jehoshaphat was fulfilled the very next day. Like other fulfilled promises in the Bible, this one also testifies to the faithfulness of God.

Responding to God's promises to us. What is most impressive about this story is the response of king and people to God's promise. They worshiped, praised God, and the next morning marched out to battle still singing

Not one Israelite arrow was shot in God's victory over the Ammonites and Moabites.

praises. How often we remain skeptical until a promise is fulfilled. To these Israelites, promise and fulfillment were one. They rejoiced in the promise given as we often rejoice in the fulfillment.

To honor God, we need to view His promises as Jehoshaphat did. We are to rejoice in God's promises and act on them, assured that God's promises *will* be fulfilled.

A PROMISE OF HEALING

The promise: "Go and wash in the Jordan seven times, and your flesh shall be restored to you, and you shall be clean" (2 Kin. 5:10).

The context of the promise. Naaman, the commander of Syria's armed forces, had been told by a young Jewish slave that there was a prophet in Israel who could heal his leprosy. When that prophet, Elisha, told Naaman to wash in the Jordan River, the Syrian was in-

Naaman, the Syrian general, found healing when he followed Elisha's instructions to wash in the Jordan River.

sulted. He had expected the prophet to heal him personally, waving his hand and calling on his God. His attendants talked Naaman into doing what the prophet said, and Naaman's leprosy was cured. Naaman acknowledged the Lord and worshiped only Him from then on.

Understanding the promise. This promise was made to a specific individual, not to everyone. And it was conditional; it depended on Naaman's willingness to wash in the Jordan River. The story reminds us that God is gracious to those who have no claim on His goodness. Naaman was even an enemy of God's covenant people. This incident also reminds us that many of God's promises can be claimed only by those who humble themselves and reach out to grasp what God is eager to give.

Claiming the promise. Naaman is often compared to an unconverted person who hears the gospel. Naaman's leprosy is compared to sin. The promise of healing if Namaan would wash in the Jordan is compared to the promise of salvation if we trust Christ as Savior. Naaman's reluctance to accept such an easy healing is compared to the assumption of many that salvation must involve more than belief and acceptance. The analogy does hold true on at least one point. The gospel promise, like that given to Naaman, is one on which we must act if we are to be saved.

THE PROMISE OF A MIRACLE

The promise: "Tomorrow about this time a seah of fine flour shall be sold for a shekel, and two seahs of barley for a shekel, at the gate of Samaria" (2 Kin. 7:1).

The context of the promise. The city of Samaria was besieged by the Syrians. The Israelites were literally starving when Elisha the prophet made this announcement. That night God panicked the Syrians, who fled and left vast stores of food behind. The prophecy/promise was fulfilled.

Understanding the promise. The promise was an unconditional statement of what God intended to do. It was not made to a people of faith, but it was given in spite of a people's unbelief! Their attitude was reflected by their ruler. In utter frustration, the king blamed God for the calamity, and said, "Why should I wait for the LORD any longer?" When Elisha uttered the promise, one high official even ridiculed. What a difference we note between this response to God's promise and that of King Jehoshaphat and the people of Judah in his time (see p. 133)!

Yet this promise was not conditional. It did not depend on the faith of the Israelites, nor were they asked to do anything to claim it. Just as God promised, the next day there was so much food available that the finest wheat sold at a reduced price.

On the one hand, the promise and its fulfillment shows the mercy of God, which He showered on a starving city. On the other hand, the prediction and its fulfillment testified to the power of the God whom the Northern Kingdom had abandoned.

What of the official who ridiculed God's promise? Elisha announced that he would see the promise fulfilled but he would not eat any of the grain. The next day he was trampled by the people who rushed out of the city to gather food from the Syrian camp.

God may not require us to believe His promises before they are fulfilled. But God will not deal kindly with those who ridicule them.

A PROMISE AS A REWARD

The promise: "Because you have done well in doing what is right in My sight, and have done to the house of Ahab all that was in My heart, your sons shall sit on the throne of Israel to the fourth generation" (2 Kin. 10:30).

The context of the promise. Jehu was an officer in the army of King Ahab. A prophet anointed Jehu to be Israel's next king. Jehu was aware of the judgment God had decreed against Ahab (cf. 2 Kin. 9:36, 37). When his fellow officers proclaimed him king, Jehu proceeded to exterminate the family of Ahab. Then he executed all of the most dedicated followers of Baal in the nation. His actions may have been motivated by self-interest. By leaving none of Ahab's descendants alive, Jehu made sure no one could challenge his claim to the throne. By killing the followers of Baal, Jehu wiped out a cult that might have provided a base of support for a rival. Whatever Jehu's motive, God promised a four-generation dynasty.

Understanding the promise. The biblical text makes it clear that Jehu was not motivated by any zeal for the Lord. Immediately after quoting the promise, the text tells us, "But Jehu took no heed to walk in the Law of the LORD" (2 Kin. 10:31). As an immediate discipline, "In those days the LORD began to cut off parts of Israel" (2 Kin. 10:32).

The promise made to Jehu was unconditional—a gracious reward for serving God's purposes. The promise was never taken back. But when Jehu failed to respond appropriately to the gracious reward given him, God punished King Jehu and the nation.

God is gracious and faithful to His promises. God may choose to reward even those who are not of the household of faith, but who do His will from selfish reasons. Yet no one who receives God's grace can treat Him with contempt.

Responding to God's promise. A general principle stated in Proverbs 14:34 is that "righteousness exalts a nation." A nation whose laws reflect high standards of morality tends to be stable and strong. This is a reward God graciously gives to all citizens of the country. But a nation that strays from those standards will surely fail.

Christians concerned for their society need to call for righteousness and justice in public policy—not for religious reasons but because righteousness truly does exalt a nation. God often grants rewards in this life even to the unsaved.

A PROMISE OF PROTECTION

The promise: "For I will defend this city, to save it for My own sake and for My servant David's sake" (2 Kin. 19:34).

The context of the promise. In 722 B.C. the Assyrians swept over the northern Hebrew kingdom, Israel. They exiled and resettled its population. By 701 B.C. the Assyrians had destroyed the fortified border cities of Judah and threatened Jerusalem itself. When an Assyrian officer appeared outside the city walls and shouted out his demand for Jerusalem's surrender, King Hezekiah turned to the Lord. God then promised that He would defend the city.

Understanding the promise. The situation here parallels an earlier situation in which Jehoshaphat was threatened by a powerful enemy (see page 133). In Hezekiah's case, an angel of the Lord struck a large portion of the Assyian army dead, and King Sennecharib was forced to return to Assyria, where he was assassinated.

This promise, made and fulfilled in a specific historical situation, is not ours to claim. But it is ours to contemplate. God can and will keep His promises, even if it takes a miracle to do so.

Claiming the promise. The story of Hezekiah's prayer and God's answer is so significant that it is repeated three times in the Old Testament: here, in 2 Chronicles 32, and in Isaiah 37—39. We do well to explore this story carefully for guiding principles.

- Hezekiah led his people back to God before the crisis arose. He and they were spiritually prepared.
- The Assyrians ridiculed Hezekiah's reliance on the Lord. They dismissed God as being as powerless as the idols of the lands they had already overcome.
- Hezekiah looked to God's prophets for guidance, as we today look to God's written Word.

- Hezekiah brought the Assyrian's threat to the Lord in prayer, asking God to act to defend His honor.

God still performs miracles for persons who are spiritually prepared, who seek His guidance, and who are concerned with His honor.

THE PROMISE OF EXTENDED LIFE

The promise: "I have heard your prayer, I have seen your tears; surely I will heal you. . . . And I will add to your days fifteen years" (2 Kin. 20:5, 6).

The context of the promise. When Hezekiah became ill, the prophet Isaiah was sent to tell the king he would die. Hezekiah prayed, reminding the Lord of his loyalty. God relented and sent Isaiah back to tell the king he had been given fifteen additional years.

❖

Faced with a terminal illness, Hezekiah prayed and had fifteen years added to his life.

Understanding the promise. While the story of Hezekiah's healing follows the story of Jerusalem's deliverance in the Bible, the healing actually took place before the Assyrian invasion. The speed with which Hezekiah's prayer was answered is notable. The prophet Isaiah left after telling King Hezekiah that he would die. The text indicates that before Isaiah "had gone out into the middle of the court," God sent him back to the king with the news that his prayer had been answered!

This promise of extended life undoubtedly helped to prepare Hezekiah for the national crisis that followed. Through this experience Hezekiah learned that God answers prayer with promises which He quickly fulfills.

Responding to God's promise. Our own experiences with answered prayer prepare us for future crises in our own lives. Each answer to prayer is in a sense a promise that the next time we call on Him, He will surely hear.

A PERSONAL PROMISE

The promise: "Surely, therefore, I will gather you to your fathers, and you shall be gathered to your grave in peace; and your eyes shall not see all the calamity which I will bring on this place" (2 Kin. 22:20; cf. 2 Chron. 34:27, 28).

The context of the promise. Josiah became king as a child. His father, Manasseh, had abandoned worship of God during his 55-year rule, closing the temple and getting rid of copies of Old Testament books. But Josiah dedicated himself to God. While the temple was being repaired, a lost book of the Bible was found. Most believe this was the book of Deuteronomy, which in chapter 28 details the promises and penalties associated with keeping or breaking God's Law. When the book was read to Josiah, the king realized how seriously the people of Judah had violated God's Law for decades. Josiah tore his clothes, humbled himself, and sent officials to consult a

prophetess named Huldah. Through her the Lord told Josiah that the nation was destined for calamity. But because Josiah's heart had been touched and he had humbled himself before God, the calamity would be delayed. The godly young king would live out his life in peace.

Understanding the promise. This promise was given to Josiah. Although it was a personal promise, it had great impact on others. If calamity for the nation was delayed during Josiah's lifetime, all who lived in Judah benefited! In a real sense, the righteousness of Josiah preserved his people.

Claiming the promise. This promise was made to Josiah alone and is not for us. But once again we see principles of God's dealings with human beings displayed. God is gracious to those whose hearts are responsive to Him. And in blessing such individuals, God often blesses others as well.

Responding to the promise. From his youth Josiah had been dedicated to the Lord. At age 16 he began to purge Judah of idolatry, systematically destroying the centers where pagan deities had been worshiped (cf. 2 Chron. 34:3–7). At age 26 Josiah began to repair the temple, and it was there that the lost book of the Law was found. Clearly Josiah was far better than his father and most of the people of Judah. He was a person who was truly committed to the Lord.

Yet when Josiah learned from the lost book of the Law what God expected from His people, the king identified himself with his people and accepted responsibility for the state of society. Like Isaiah, Josiah realized, "I am a man of unclean lips, and I dwell in the midst of a people of unclean lips" (Isa. 6:5).

It is a temptation for any believer to disassociate himself or herself from the sins of the time. Yet like Josiah and Isaiah, we share at least some responsibility. Josiah reminds us to accept our responsibility and to repent before the Lord.

CHAPTER 12

POETRY, NOT PROMISES:

THE SPECIAL FOCUS OF THE BOOKS OF POETRY

Job—Song of Solomon

Five Old Testament books are classified as poetry. These are Job, Psalms, Proverbs, Ecclesiastes, and the Song of Solomon. Each has unique characteristics that govern our reading. While many contemporary compilations of "God's promises" feature quotes from the poetical books, in most cases the verses quoted are not promises at all. To know how to understand verses from these books, we must be clear about the nature of each book and its role in the Bible.

PROMISES IN THE BOOK OF JOB

The book of Job may be the oldest book in the Bible. Job is a penetrating exploration of the problem of suffering, addressed through the situation of a man named Job. At the beginning of the book, God Himself announces that Job has lived a blameless life. He is a good man. Yet God permits Satan to torment Job.

The book consists mostly of Job's conversations with three friends, all of whom struggle to understand why he is suffering and to determine what Job can do about it. These friends believe God must be punishing Job for some secret sin, and they urge their friend to repent. Job agrees that suffering is punishment. But he knows in his own heart that he has not consciously violated God's standards. Surely he has done nothing to merit the terrible things that have happened to him.

Job and his friends make statements that reflect their own viewpoints. None of their statements can be taken as a promise given by God, although several of Job's comments display exceptional faith.

When Job and his three frustrated friends finally realize they have no solution to his problems, a younger observer notes that not all suffering need be viewed as punishment. God may use suffering to instruct or to warn as well as to punish. Thus, Job should not be charged with sin or God with injustice!

Then God speaks. He does not explain the reason He permitted Job to suffer, but He does point out the difference between His understanding and that of human beings. Man's only appropriate response to mystery is to worship God and trust Him.

The book concludes with God doubling Job's original wealth and providing additional blessings.

Given the nature and content of this book, we can understand why we should not treat any of its sayings as promises.

PROMISES IN THE PSALMS

The psalms are a treasure house for believers. The 150 poems included in this book range in tone from pleas for deliverance to testimonials to God's goodness. The psalms display the deepest emotions of believers who freely express their emotions to the Lord, confident that He hears and cares.

Only a few psalms quote God's words to human beings. A few others contain prophetic insights concerning the coming Messiah (see Pss. 22, 89, 91, 132). Most of the psalms express the confidence of believers in the Lord that have grown out of their personal experiences with Him.

There is no question that the psalms, like the rest of Scripture, are the inspired Word of God. But these are words addressed to God rather than a report of words spoken by Him. This means we need to be careful about treating the psalmists' beautiful expressions of faith as promises made to believers.

In reading the psalms, then, we need to distinguish between promises made by God and the psalmist's expressions of confidence in the Lord.

GOD'S PROMISES IN THE PSALMS

The writers of the psalms often quote God's words to His people. In three psalms these quotes include promises which the Lord makes.

A PROMISE OF GUIDANCE

The promise: "I will instruct you and teach you in the way you should go; I will guide you with My eye" (Ps. 32:8).

Understanding the promise. This promise was given to David as he contemplated his sins and God's forgiveness. The imagery is striking. In the future David is to stay so close to the Lord, gazing into God's face, that David can be guided by God's eye. That is, David is to keep his eyes on the eyes of the Lord, so he will

sense where God is looking and move in that direction.

Claiming the promise. God is also eager to guide us. When we keep our attention fixed on the Lord, we will also be able to sense His will.

Responding to the promise. For too many of us, decision-making is nothing but a rational process. We balance pros and cons, try our best to predict outcomes, and take a chance. Yet God does have a plan for our lives, and our first concern should be to seek His will. This promise reminds us that if we look to the Lord for guidance, He *will* direct our paths.

A PROMISE OF AID

The promise: "Call upon Me in the day of trouble; I will deliver you, and you shall glorify Me" (Ps. 50:15).

The context of the promise. The pagan peoples of biblical times viewed their deities as dependent on worshipers for the offerings which "fed" them. In this psalm, God reminded His worshipers that the cattle on a thousand hills are His. He is not dependent on them; they are dependent on Him. God then invited His people to call on Him when they are in trouble, promising that He would deliver them.

Understanding the promise. This promise reminds us that God graciously permits us to serve Him. Just as God did not require the sacrifices of Israel, He is not *dependent on* anything that we do for Him. We have no claim on God's goodness and no right to demand mercy.

When we remember this, we remain grateful and humble. And humility—recognition of our utter dependence on the Lord—leads us to call on Him in our time of trouble. When we do so, God will deliver us—not because we have earned His mercy—but because in displaying His goodness to us He is glorified.

Claiming the promise. Let's remember that God is glorified in what He does for us, not by what we do for Him. Remembering this reality will help us remain humble and dependent on His grace and goodness.

A PROMISE OF DELIVERANCE

The promise: "Oh, that My people would listen to Me, that Israel would walk in My ways! I would soon subdue their enemies, and turn My hand against their adversaries" (Ps. 81:13, 14).

The context of the promise. This psalm was written as a lament by God over His unresponsive people. The larger context was the Mosaic Covenant. This covenant demonstrated that Israel's disobedience to God had made it impossible for Him to bless and deliver His people. Perhaps the most striking feature of the psalm is its expression of God's pain. Because of Israel's sin, the Lord had not been able to deliver them.

Understanding the promise. This expression of God's conditional promises to Israel in the Law reveals the Lord's compassion for us, even when we sin against Him. God is eager to bless us. Only our own unresponsiveness keeps us from experiencing His best.

Responding to the promise. In 1 Corinthians 10:11, the apostle Paul reminded us that the experiences of Israel were written for our instruction. We are to learn truths about our own relationship with God by studying the relationship of God with Israel. What a vital truth we learn from the tragic consequences of Israel's failures to walk in God's ways. How eager we should be to respond to Him so He could subdue our enemies and act on our behalf.

EXPRESSIONS OF CONFIDENCE IN THE LORD

In addition to the three direct promises found in the psalms, many expressions of faith by the psalmists have been taken as promises by believers. A number of such expressions are quoted below. While these are not promises *per se,* these expressions of others' experiences with God do encourage us. Their testimonies enrich us and reveal the God who has remained faithful to His own through the ages.

"But I know that the LORD has set apart for Himself him who is godly; the LORD will hear when I call to Him" (Ps. 4:3).

"For the needy shall not always be forgotten; the expectation of the poor shall not perish forever" (Ps. 9:18).

"Wait on the LORD; be of good courage, and He shall strengthen your heart; wait, I say, on the LORD!" (Ps. 27:14).

"Many sorrows shall be to the wicked; but he who trusts in the LORD, mercy shall surround him" (Ps. 32:10).

"The angel of the LORD encamps all around those who fear Him, and delivers them" (Ps. 34:7).

"Delight yourself also in the LORD, and He shall give you the desires of your heart" (Ps. 37:4).

"Commit your way to the LORD, trust also in Him, and He shall bring it to pass" (Ps. 37:5).

> Blessed is he who considers the
>   poor;
> The LORD will deliver him in time
>   of trouble.
> The LORD will preserve him and
>   keep him alive,
> And he will be blessed on the earth;
> You will not deliver him to the will
>   of his enemies.
> The LORD will strengthen him on
>   his bed of illness;
> You will sustain him on his
>   sickbed (Ps. 41:1–3).

"For this is God, Our God forever and ever; He will be our guide even to death" (Ps. 48:14).

"Cast your burden on the LORD, and He shall sustain you; He shall never permit the righteous to be moved" (Ps. 55:22).

"You, who have shown me great and severe troubles, shall revive me again, and bring me up again from the depths of the earth" (Ps. 71:20).

"For He will deliver the needy when he cries, the poor also, and him who has no helper" (Ps. 72:12).

"For the LORD God is a sun and shield; the LORD will give grace and glory; no good thing will He withhold from those who walk uprightly" (Ps. 84:11).

"He will bless those who fear the LORD, both small and great" (Ps. 115:13).

"The LORD is your keeper; The LORD is your shade at your right hand. . . . The LORD shall preserve your going out and your coming in from this time forth, and even forevermore" (Ps. 121:5, 8).

"Those who sow in tears shall reap in joy. He who continually goes forth weeping, bearing seed for sowing, shall doubtless come again with rejoicing, bringing his sheaves with him" (Ps. 126:5, 6).

> The LORD is near to all who call
>   upon Him,
> To all who call upon Him
>   in truth.
> He will fulfill the desire of those
>   who fear Him;
> He will also hear their cry and
>   save them.
> The LORD preserves all who love
>   Him,
> But all the wicked He will
>   destroy (Ps. 145:18–20).

GOD'S PROMISES IN PROVERBS

The third book of poetry in the Bible is the book of Proverbs. It is also classified as "wisdom literature," for it sets down general principles intended to guide our choices.

Solomon's continuing pursuit of wisdom is reflected in the gems in Proverbs.

To interpret the Proverbs correctly, we need to understand several things about this unique book of Scripture. One authority pointed out:

The Book of Proverbs is a collection of advice and counsel intended to guide the reader's practical and moral choices. . . . While the general principles captured in the proverbs have universal application, their significance in Scripture is defined by the Bible's unique view of God. The God of the Old Testament is a living, active Person, who as the moral Judge of the universe supervises the consequences of human moral choices. Thus the individual who does what is right and good can expect to be blessed, and the individual who does what is wrong or evil can expect disappointment and disaster (Richards, *The Bible Reader's Companion,* 1991, p. 385).

While recognizing God's hand in the proverbs and in the moral universe which the proverbs assume, we are not to take these statements of general principles as binding promises. According to Richards,

You can profitably use the Book of Proverbs as a practical handbook to living wisely in modern times, but keep its nature and characteristics in mind. The sayings found here express general and universal principles which are relevant to all people of all times. These guidelines apply to everyone, not just to believers. The sayings are generalizations, and all general statements have exceptions. Don't mistake a proverb for a promise God is giving to you to claim by faith. If you think on the proverbs and follow their advice, you'll find them a wonderful source of insight into your daily life (Richards, *The Bible Reader's Companion,* p. 385).

Understood in this way, we can see that there are no promises, as such, in Proverbs. In fact, we will be deeply disappointed if we mistake the book's general statements as promises.

AN EXAMPLE: PROVERBS 22:6

A classic example of mistaking a general principle for a promise is Proverbs 22:6, which says, "Train up a child in the way he should go, and when he is old he will not depart from it." Taken as a general principle, this proverb provides guidance and encouragement. Hebrew scholars C.F. Keil and F. Delitzsch explain:

The instruction of youth, the education of youth, ought to be conformed to the nature of youth; the matter of instruction, the manner of instruction, ought to regulate itself according to the stage of life, and its peculiarities; the method ought to be arranged according to the degree of development which the mental and bodily life of the youth has arrived at (*Commentary on the Old Testament,* Vol. 6, Book 2, pp. 86, 87).

When we understand that Proverbs 22:6 expresses a general principle of wise child-rearing, we find its guidance helpful. But if we take this verse as a promise, we set ourselves up for terrible disappointment. The fact is that there are no guarantees in child-rearing. Every human being is free to make his or her own choice. We cannot "program" children like computers. We can do our very best as parents, and our children may still make tragic life decisions. More than one godly parent has read this proverb and wrongly assumed responsibility for his or her child's decisions. Before we assume responsibility for our children's behavior, we should remember that even perfect parents cannot guarantee their children will be godly. Even God, the ideal parent, saw His children Adam and Eve disobey His commands.

So proverbs are not promises. Nor are results of the choices they describe guarantees of what will happen. Instead, the proverbs encourage us to make wise moral choices. They describe what will *usually* follow when we do.

CHOICES AND USUAL CONSEQUENCES

Here are a number of Proverbs which are frequently mistaken as promises. Taken as they are intended, these proverbs are helpful guides to godly living. But they are not promises guaranteed by the Lord.

"Trust in the LORD with all your heart, and lean not on your own understanding; in all your ways acknowledge Him, and He shall direct your paths" (Prov. 3:5, 6).

"Honor the LORD with your possessions, and with the firstfruits of all your increase; so your barns will be filled with plenty, and your vats will overflow with new wine" (Prov. 3:9, 10).

"Hear, my son, and receive my sayings, and the years of your life will be many" (Prov. 4:10).

"The fear of the LORD prolongs days, but the years of the wicked will be shortened" (Prov. 10:27).

"The righteousness of the upright will deliver them" (Prov. 11:6).

"The posterity of the righteous will be delivered" (Prov. 11:21).

"No grave trouble will overtake the righteous" (Prov. 12:21).

"Commit your works to the LORD, and your thoughts will be established" (Prov. 16:3).

"When a man's ways please the LORD, He makes even his enemies to be at peace with him" (Prov. 16:7).

"He who has pity on the poor lends to the LORD, and He will pay back what he has given" (Prov. 19:17).

"The fear of the LORD leads to life, and he who has it will abide in satisfaction; he will not be visited with evil" (Prov. 19:23).

"Foolishness [moral evil] is bound up in the heart of a child; the rod of correction will drive it far from him" (Prov. 22:15).

"Correct your son, and he will give you rest; Yes, he will give delight to your soul" (Prov. 29:17).

GOD'S PROMISES IN ECCLESIASTES

Tradition tells us the book of Ecclesiastes was written by Solomon. It is a philosophical treatise—an authentic report of the efforts of the world's wisest man to find life's meaning apart from God.

When reading this book, we need to understand several things about it. The writer tells us that he has chosen to search for life's meaning "by wisdom" (Eccl. 1:13). He also tells us that he will limit his search to things that are done "under heaven" or "under the sun" (Eccl. 1:13, 14). Solomon consciously chose *not* to look to revelation for information. Instead, Solomon determined to consider only data he could gather from human experience and observation.

But doesn't the fact that Scripture is the inspired Word of God require that Solomon's statements are true? It's important here to make a distinction between revelation and inspiration. Revelation has to do with truth that

God makes known to us. Such truth has been communicated in the creation (see pages 89–95) and is recorded in the Bible. Inspiration has to do with Scripture. Inspiration is the guarantee that the words of Scripture as originally given contain exactly the message the Holy Spirit intended them to convey. So the fact that Ecclesiastes is inspired—conveying the message God intended it to express—does not necessarily mean that its content is true. After all, Genesis 3 and Matthew 4 record the words of Satan, and no one would argue that what Satan said is true!

Why then is a book like Ecclesiastes found in Scripture? It was placed here to show us the limits of human reason and to drive home the truth that human life has no meaning apart from God. Solomon's conclusion, "All is vanity" [literally, "meaningless"], is the conclusion reached by all who seek meaning apart from a personal relationship with God.

With this understanding of the book, we can see why nothing in Ecclesiastes should be taken as a promise from the Lord.

GOD'S PROMISES IN THE SONG OF SOLOMON

The last book of poetry in the Bible is a love poem, which was also written by Solomon, according to tradition. The poem has been interpreted in several ways. Taken literally, it is a celebration of human love between husband and wife. It reflects on the meeting of the lovers, their attraction to each other, and finally their marriage.

The Jewish sages interpreted the Song of Solomon as an allegory celebrating the relationship between God and Israel. This approach has also been followed by a number of Christian commentators, who have seen it as an allegory celebrating the relationship between Christ and the church. However, even if the Song of Solomon is treated as an allegory, one must strain to find phrases in this poem which might be taken as promises.

The poetical books of Scripture are not vehicles through which God expresses His promises to humankind. Only in three psalms, in which God Himself is quoted by the psalmist, are promises expressed. Each of these books makes its own unique contribution to the Bible and to our personal relationship with the Lord. But we should be hesitant to take any of their expressions as promises that God wants us to claim.

CHAPTER 13

LOOKING AHEAD IN HOPE:

PROMISES IN THE PROPHETS

Isaiah—Malachi

INTRODUCTION TO THE PROPHETS

The prophets of the Old Testament were men and women chosen by God to convey His messages to their contemporaries. Deuteronomy 18:10–14 commanded the Israelites not to turn to the occult as a source of guidance as the peoples of Canaan did. The roots of pagan religion and its practices are explored in the companion volume, *Every Good and Evil Angel in the Bible,* which traces occult practices to demons.

While forbidding Israel to look to the occult, God did promise supernatural guidance. He would raise up prophets and guide Israel Himself (Deut. 18:18–22). We know many such men and women by name through the Scriptures.

Categories of prophets and their writings. God's prophets fall into two categories, not based on their fame, but on their mode of communication. Many prophets only communicated God's word orally. These are called the "speaking" prophets. Some of their briefer messages may be recorded in the Old Testament historical books (see 1 Kin. 17:1; 2 Kin. 9:1–13), but we have no lengthy written materials representing their ministry.

The other category is "writing" prophets. While most preached their messages, a significant body of what God called them to say was also recorded in writing. These written works of the prophets have been preserved, and they appear as books of the Old Testament. The writings of the prophets also fall into two categories: The major prophets (Isaiah, Jeremiah, Ezekiel, and Daniel) and the minor prophets (the other twelve). The so-called major prophetic books are longer; the so-called minor prophetic books are shorter.

The mission of the prophets. The prophets whom God sent to His people had as their main mission interpreting the experiences of their generation in light of God's promise covenants and the Mosaic Covenant, and calling their generation back to loyalty to the Lord. In most cases, the prophets were either ignored or persecuted by their contemporaries. But their writings stand as a monument

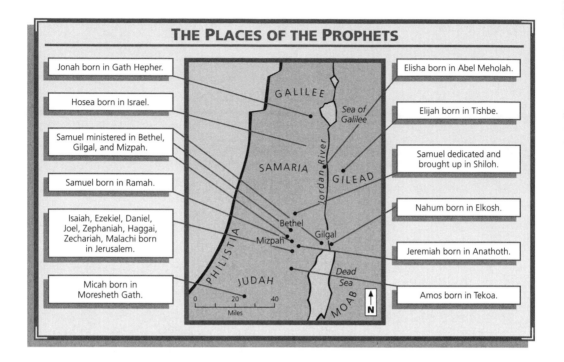

THE PLACES OF THE PROPHETS

Jonah born in Gath Hepher.

Hosea born in Israel.

Samuel ministered in Bethel, Gilgal, and Mizpah.

Samuel born in Ramah.

Isaiah, Ezekiel, Daniel, Joel, Zephaniah, Haggai, Zechariah, Malachi born in Jerusalem.

Micah born in Moresheth Gath.

Elisha born in Abel Meholah.

Elijah born in Tishbe.

Samuel dedicated and brought up in Shiloh.

Nahum born in Elkosh.

Jeremiah born in Anathoth.

Amos born in Tekoa.

GALILEE

Sea of Galilee

SAMARIA

Jordan River

GILEAD

Bethel

Mizpah

Gilgal

PHILISTIA

JUDAH

Dead Sea

MOAB

0   20   40
Miles

N

to God's continuing loyalty to His people, and to His firm commitment to His covenant promises.

Promises in the prophets. As we survey the prophetic books of the Old Testament, we discover that the great bulk of the unconditional promises they contain are restatements or amplifications of the covenant promises given to Abraham or David. In the same way, the majority of the conditional promises are restatements of blessing/cursing promises found in the Mosaic Law, as stated in Leviticus 26 and Deuteronomy 28.

There are also what we can call special promises recorded in the prophets. These promises may be linked to the covenants, but they so clearly express universal principles of God's relationship to His people that they can be claimed by believers of all times. In this chapter, we will work book by book to list the promises which are restatements of those already given in the promise covenants or in Moses' Law, and then look closely at the special promises which we may claim today.

GOD'S PROMISES IN ISAIAH

Isaiah ministered in Judah during the reigns of Uzziah, Jotham, Ahaz, and Hezekiah (Isa. 1:1). During these critical years, the northern Hebrew kingdom, Israel, was crushed by Assyria. Judah itself was invaded. Only God's intervention kept the Assyrians from taking Jerusalem and deporting its population along with those of Israel.

The first part of the book of Isaiah (chaps. 1—35) is full of dire predictions that God will judge Judah as He has judged Israel. Interspersed with these predictions of disaster are bright promises of the coming of a Messiah, a descendant of David, in whose days God's people will enjoy peace. In perspective the first half of Isaiah looks forward to the Babylonian captivity of Judah, which occurred about a hundred years after Isaiah's time.

Following a historical interlude (chaps. 36—39), the second half of Isaiah (chaps. 40—66) changes perspective. From a viewpoint beyond the Babylonian captivity, the second half of Isaiah looks toward the glorious future God has in store not only for Israel but also for the entire world. The perspective of this half of the book, with a shift in vocabulary, has led some to assume there were two or more "Isaiahs." Most conservative scholars reject this view, pointing out that Hebrew prophets were not limited to a single historical perspective (see Joel 1 with Joel 2). It is hardly unreasonable to believe that such a visionary leap was possible for Isaiah. As for the change in vocabulary, any writer who deals with different subjects can be expected to adopt a different vocabulary, and even a different style.

In looking at Isaiah, then, we are wise to see the entire book as the product of one of Israel's greatest prophets, who—inspired by God—conveyed a message of warning and hope, and whose words speak powerfully to us today.

COVENANT-LINKED PROMISES IN ISAIAH

Many of the promises recorded in the prophets are restatements or amplifications of covenant promises given to Abraham or David, or of principles expressed in the Mosaic Covenant.

Major covenant-linked promises found in Isaiah are: Isaiah 1:19; 2:2–4, 12; 7:14; 9:6, 7; 10:20–22; 11:1–6, 10–12; 14:1; 19:23–25; 25:8; 26:19; 30:19, 23, 24; 32:1, 2; 35:1, 5, 6; 37:33–35; 40:4, 5, 10–12; 41:9, 10, 15, 16; 42:1–3, 6, 7; 43:1, 2, 5, 6, 25; 44:26; 48:9; 49:11, 12, 25; 51:3, 11; 52:15; 54:3, 4; 55:4; 58:9–11; 59:1–3, 20, 21; 60:13, 14, 19, 20; 61:4–9; 65:9, 10, 20–25; and 66:12–13.

SPECIAL PROMISES TO CLAIM IN ISAIAH

While often reflecting principles seen in the covenants, Isaiah records a number of promises which believers can claim or respond to today.

A PROMISE OF CLEANSING

The promise: "Though your sins are like scarlet, they shall be as white as snow; though they are red like crimson, they shall be as wool" (Isa. 1:18).

The context of the promise. Isaiah's first sermon is an indictment of God's people as evildoers. Yet God calls His people back to Him and promises that they can be cleansed. The reference to scarlet and crimson is significant. Many of the ancient dyes did not fix well, and so faded. But crimson/scarlet dyes were the most permanent known in the ancient world. What a stunning promise—that God is able to make the permanently stained "white as snow!"

Understanding the promise. Isaiah framed this promise within the context of Moses' covenant (Isa. 1:15–17, 19, 20). Yet promise of forgiveness and cleansing from sin is extended throughout Scripture to all people on the basis of faith. Abraham believed, and his faith was credited to him as the righteousness he did not have (Gen. 15:6). Anyone who wishes to establish a relationship with the Lord must come to Him as one stained with sin, yet with faith in God's promise of forgiveness.

Claiming the promise. This promise is not just a call to saving faith. It is a call to straying believers to repent and return to God's ways. However great our sins, God will cleanse us when we turn back to Him.

Responding to the promise. Some have assumed that a blanket promise of restoration is a license to sin. But love begets love. Sensing God's forgiving love, we have more motivation to want to please Him.

As for those who have sinned, the certain knowledge that our heavenly Father will welcome us when we return to Him is strong motivation for repentance and change. If sinning believers had only God's anger to look forward to, they might keep on running from Him. Knowing that we will be welcomed and forgiven encourages us to come home.

So the promise of cleansing is for every believer. As the promise draws the sinner back to God, its expression of God's unending love keeps the faithful near to Him.

PROMISES OF RESURRECTION JOY

The promise: "He will swallow up death forever, and the LORD God will wipe away tears from all faces" (Isa. 25:8).

"Your dead shall live; together with my dead body they shall arise. Awake and sing, you who dwell in dust; for your dew is like the dew of herbs, and the earth shall cast out the dead" (Isa. 26:19).

The context of the promise. These are two of the Old Testament passages that teach the resurrection of the dead. While the Sadduccees of Jesus' time rejected this doctrine, the Pharisees, the forerunners of rabbinic Judaism, held fast to it. There is no doubt that a belief in resurrection rooted in the Old Testament Scriptures was a basic tenet of first-century Judaism.

Understanding the promise. Biological death is not the end for any human being. For believers, there is the promise that "God will wipe away tears." For all others, there is the certain prospect of judgment.

Responding to the promise. The vision of resurrection which Scripture shares with believers is a beautiful one. We shall "awake and sing." This future is guaranteed to us. Rather than being a promise we claim, it is a promise God has claimed for us in Christ.

How are we to respond to the promise of resurrection? We are to respond with a joy that brightens our darkest nights. That joy fills us even as we or our loved ones walk through the valley of the shadow of death. As we respond to this promise with faith, death loses its sting, and the grave loses its power to terrify.

A PROMISE OF INNER PEACE

The promise: "You will keep him in perfect peace, whose mind is stayed on You, because he trusts in You" (Isa. 26:3).

BIBLE BACKGROUND:

RESURRECTION IN JUDAISM

The following story is told in an early rabbinic commentary on Genesis, and illustrates the sages' belief in resurrection.

It happened that a man who resided in Sepphoris lost his son and a heretic was sitting with him. R. Jose b. Chalaphta went to pay him a visit; and on seeing him, he sat down and laughed. The bereaved father asked, "Why do you laugh?" He answered, "We trust the Lord of Heaven that you will again see your son in the World to Come." The heretic said to him, "Has not this man suffered enough anguish that you come to inflict further pain upon him? Can pieces of potsherd be mended? And is it not written, 'Thou shalt dash them in pieces like a potter's vessel'?"(Ps. 2:9). He replied, "With an earthenware vessel, its creation is from water and its completion in fire; with a glass vessel, both its creation and completion are in fire. If the former is broken, can it be mended? But if the latter is broken, can it not be repaired?" The heretic answered, "Glass can be repaired because it is made by the process of blowing." The Rabbi retorted, "Let your ears take note of what your mouth utters. If something which is made by the blowing of a human being can be repaired, how much more so with that which is made by the breath of the Holy One, blessed be He!" (Genesis Rabbah. xiv.7).

The context of the promise. Isaiah 25 and 26 is one of those passages which looks ahead and envisions a future shaped by God's presence. That future hardly seemed likely in Isaiah's time. Judah was threatened by a terrible enemy—an enemy which in Hezekiah's day battered down the fortified cities protecting Judah's borders and took over two hundred thousand of Judah's citizens captive. It hardly seemed appropriate to speak of "peace" in such dark days, much less to promise it as a present experience.

Yet the Hebrew word for "peace" (*shalom*) *is* very special. It speaks of harmony and wholeness as much as of security. The serenity expressed in the phrase "God's in His heaven and all's right with the world" conveys some sense of the meaning of *shalom,* peace.

So Isaiah's promise of "peace" is a promise of an inner serenity which exists whatever one's circumstances.

Claiming the promise. The promise of inner serenity is available to any believer "whose mind is stayed on" God. The verb implies dependence, and is passive. The person who leans on God and rests on Him will have peace. While Isaiah 25 and 26 look forward to God's action in the future, this promise is for the present moment. Serenity of heart and mind can be ours in the most stressful of times.

A PROMISE OF DELIVERANCE

The promise: "In returning and rest you shall be saved; in quietness and confidence shall be your strength" (Isa. 30:15).

The context of the promise. Some of God's people will urge reliance on a military alliance with Egypt (Isa. 30:1–5). They will despise God's promises and turn instead to human allies in place of the Lord. Isaiah called for a return to the Lord, for He alone is truly able to help.

Understanding the promise. The invitation to rely on the Lord will be rejected by Judah. Because of this, disaster awaited.

Responding to the promise. Isaiah's words in 30:15 are not so much a promise to claim as a truth to act on. Like God's ancient people, when we are threatened we are too quick to rely on resources other than the Lord. It is not wrong to go to doctors when we're sick, but we are to *rely* on the Lord. It is not wrong to seek counsel for problems in our marriages, but we are to *rely* on the Lord.

We also need to be aware that panic often leads to hasty and unwise choices. A quiet confidence in the Lord frees us to consider all our options, enabling us to live through the stress in our lives in quietness and confidence.

A PROMISE OF UNEXPECTED AID

The promise: "Do not be afraid of the words which you have heard . . . he shall hear a rumor and return to his own land" (Isa. 37:6, 7).

The context of the promise. An Assyrian officer called for Jerusalem's surrender. He ridiculed both the military weakness of Hezekiah and the king's reliance on the Lord. When the king appealed to the Lord, God sent him this promise through Isaiah.

Understanding the promise. This unconditional promise was given to Hezekiah in a specific situation. It shows the faithfulness of God—and also His creativity and sense of humor. The Assyrian ruler hurled threatening words at Hezekiah. So God would use words—a rumor!—to send the Assyrian king back to his own land. There, history tells us, the Assyrian monarch was assassinated by two of his sons.

Responding to the promise. How vulnerable we are to words. So often the mere threat of ridicule, or concern for what others may think or say, is enough to keep us from speaking out or acting on what we believe is right. The promise given to Hezekiah reminds us that God uses words, too. We need not fear the threats or ridicule of others; God can use words to thwart their intent.

He may even use our words, if we are bold enough to speak up.

A PROMISE OF EXTENDED LIFE

The promise: "Surely I will add to your days fifteen years" (Isa. 38:5). See the discussion of this promise on page 136.

A PROMISE OF INNER STRENGTH

The promise:

He gives power to the weak,
And to those who have no might
    He increases strength.
Even the youths shall faint and be
    weary,
And the young men shall utterly
    fall,
But those who wait on the LORD
Shall renew their strength;
They shall mount up with wings
    like eagles,
They shall run and not be weary,
They shall walk and not faint (Isa.
    40:29–31).

The context of the promise. With Isaiah 40 the tone of this great prophecy changes. Earlier chapters were colored by the threat of impending judgment. Now, suddenly, a note of joy is introduced which will echo throughout the rest of the book. God—Israel's God—loves His chosen people and holds their future in His loving hand.

Understanding the promise. This exquisite passage expresses one of Scripture's universal promises. The promise is not made to a specific individual or relegated to a specific time. This is a promise made to all who "wait on the LORD."

Claiming the promise. If we want to claim this promise, there is one condition we must meet. We must be weak and "have no might."

The person who is confident of his or her ability will never experience the blessing offered here. The person who relies on God-given talents will soon reach the limit of these natural gifts and fail.

This is one of the great paradoxes of our faith. To be strong, we must be weak. To soar, we must faint. Only when we give up can we succeed. We must rely so completely on God that whatever we accomplish is clearly His work and not our own.

"Those who wait on the LORD . . . shall mount up with wings like eagles."

What these verses promise is that when we do acknowledge our weakness, and turn to Him, God will provide us with His strength. When we rely on Him in our exhaustion, He enables us to run and not be weary. When our last resources are gone, He enables us to walk on. Only in our weakness can we experience the fullness of His strength.

A PROMISE OF GOD'S PROTECTIVE PRESENCE

The promise: "When you pass through the waters, I will be with you; and through the rivers, they shall not overflow you. When you walk through the fire, you shall not be burned, nor shall the flame scorch you" (Isa. 43:2).

The context of the promise. These words were spoken to Israel as a people whom God created and formed, whom He redeemed, named, and chose to be His own (Isa. 43:1). This litany clearly describes the covenant relationship which God established with Abraham and which He faithfully maintained through the millenniums.

Understanding the promise. Strikingly, each element of the relationship which God established with Israel is reflected in the Bible's picture of the Christian's relationship with God today.

God created Israel. Ephesians 2:10 says, "We are His workmanship, created in Christ Jesus for good works."

God redeemed Israel. 1 Peter 1:18, 19 says that we "were not redeemed with corruptible things, like silver or gold . . . but with the precious blood of Christ."

God called Israel by name. Revelation 17:8 indicates that our names have been "written in the Book of Life from the foundation of the world."

"When you walk through the fire, you shall not be burned."

God said of Israel "You are Mine." John 10:29 says that Christians have been given to Jesus by the Father, "and no one is able to snatch them out of My Father's hand."

Because the God who made this promise to Israel is our God too, and because He has established the same kind of relationship with us in Christ, this promise truly is ours to claim.

Claiming the promise. Relationship with God is no guarantee of an easy life. The promise implies that in the course of our lives we *will* pass through waters and walk through fire. Life will not treat us kindly simply because we belong to Jesus. We too are descendants of Adam and subject to all the ills of mankind. We can lose our employment, be crippled in an automobile accident, contract cancer, see loved ones die.

What is different is that *when* we pass through the deepest waters or tread in the hottest fires, God is with us. The tragedies of our lives will test us, but they will not *harm* us. We will hurt, but we will heal. And during the time of greatest pain, we will sense the comforting presence of a God who stays with us, who feels our pain, and who will bring us safely through.

A PROMISE OF CONSTANT SUPPORT

The promise: "Even to your old age, I am He, and even to gray hairs I will carry you!" (Isa. 46:4).

The context of the promise. God called a stubborn Israel to look back, and then to look ahead. Unlike the idols that the pagans carried, God has carried His people from their birth. Surely the God who has never abandoned Israel in the past will continue to carry them "even to your old age."

Understanding the promise. Isaiah adopted man's life span as an analogy to show God's commitment to Israel. As God upheld Israel from "birth," surely God will continue to carry

"Even to gray hairs I will carry you!"

his people into their "old age." His goal for history and for Israel will surely be realized (see Isa. 46:9, 10).

Claiming the promise. Isaiah 46 portrays God as one who declares the end from the beginning, saying "My counsel shall stand, and I will do all My pleasure" (Isa. 46:10). God sees our lives as a whole—from birth to old age—and has planned our end even before our beginning. You and I must travel through life one day at a time. But surely we can trust the God who has carried us from birth to be with us into our future.

God, who knows and has planned our future, is the guarantee that His good pleasure for us will be fully realized.

Responding to the promise. When the days ahead appear dark, we are to look back and remember all that God has done for us. Surely His past goodness is a promise that good things lie ahead.

GOD'S PROMISES IN JEREMIAH

Jeremiah is frequently called the "weeping prophet." He ministered during the last forty years of Judah's existence as a nation. His mission was to warn of the coming Babylonian victory, to portray it as a divine judgment. Jeremiah then urged his contemporaries to surrender to Babylon and so lighten the blow about to strike Judah and Jerusalem.

The people of Jeremiah's day not only rejected his ministry; they accused him of being a Babylonian agent and plotted to murder him. Jeremiah's love for his nation and the pain of his rejection often drove him to despair. Yet he remained faithful to his mission, and he lived to see his predictions fulfilled.

While most of Jeremiah's prophecies emphasized the judgment which God was about to bring upon Judah, the prophet was given a great gift. He was chosen as the Old Testament prophet to announce that God would one day make a New Covenant with his people. Under the New Covenant, God's forgiveness would flow unchecked, and rebellious hearts would be tamed. Thus, in the darkest of Judah's bleak days the brightest light began to shine.

COVENANT-LINKED PROMISES IN JEREMIAH

In spite of the judgment emphasis in Jeremiah, there are frequent references to the Abrahamic, Davidic, and Mosaic Covenants, as well as the promise that God would one day make a New Covenant with Israel. The following passages contain significant covenant-linked promises.

Jeremiah 3:14–18; 7:1–7, 23; 11:1–14; 15:19–21; 16:6, 7, 14, 15; 23:4–8; 30:3, 10, 11, 19, 22; 31:3–9, 16, 17, 27–34; 32:37–41; 33:6–9, 15, 16, 21, 22; 39:17–18.

SPECIAL PROMISES TO CLAIM IN JEREMIAH

Jeremiah lived a stressful life. He was under constant pressure from a people who resented and resisted his message. Yet Jeremiah remained faithful and spoke out fearlessly for the Lord. Special promises given to him and through him during the years of his ministry must have been precious indeed.

A PROMISE OF DELIVERANCE

The promise: " 'Do not be afraid of their faces, for I am with you to deliver you,' says the LORD" (Jer. 1:8).

The context of the promise. Jeremiah was called by God to serve as a prophet. The prospect frightened Jeremiah, who protested that he was just a youth. God rejected the plea and told Jeremiah to speak all that He commanded. With this command, God gave Jeremiah the promise quoted above.

Understanding the promise. It is difficult for anyone to speak out while looking into hostile faces. We can hardly imagine how hard it would be to continue speaking out year after year. For Jeremiah, the hostility was not simply on his contemporaries' faces. It was expressed in their angry words, threats, and even plots to kill the prophet. God encouraged Jeremiah by telling him that he need not be afraid. For all their hostility, his enemies would not be able to harm him, "for I am with you to deliver you."

God did deliver Jeremiah, again and again. The city fell as he predicted, but the prophet survived.

Claiming the promise. This promise was given to Jeremiah, not to us. How Jeremiah must have been encouraged when he remembered it during the years of his ministry. Yet many a martyr has fallen since Jeremiah's time who was just as faithful but who was not delivered. In many parts of the world today, Christians are still being martyred. While we believe that God is with us and with them, we cannot be sure that God is present "to deliver you."

And yet perhaps we can claim the promise, if we understand deliverance in a broader perspective. Our biological life is not so precious that we must grasp it at the cost of surrender to the threats of those who are hostile to us and to our faith. The glorious promise of the gospel is one of *ultimate* deliverance, and this promise is ours indeed. With this in mind, we can gladly affirm, "the LORD is my helper; I will not fear. What can man do to me?" (Heb. 13:6).

A PROMISE OF WELCOME

The promise: "Return, you backsliding children, and I will heal your backslidings" (Jer. 3:22).

The context of the promise. Jeremiah 3 is an extended appeal to the people of Judah to return to the God who loves them. Woven into the invitation is a reminder of the Abrahamic and Davidic promises concerning their national future. But the fate of the people of Jeremiah's time depended on their response to the Lord.

Understanding the promise. There is an urgency to Jeremiah's words. The future of God's people is assured. But their fate depended on their willingness to return, now, to the Lord.

It is so easy to backslide. The tendency to sin is always with us. But God has the power to heal our tendency if we turn to Him.

Claiming the promise. We hear a lot these days about addictions. There is addiction to drugs, tobacco, alcohol, sex, and gambling. Anyone in the grip of one of these addictions knows how powerful its pull is. A whole "recovery" literature has been developed to help those with addictions and their families. One principle of most recovery programs is to urge the addict to rely on a "higher power."

Scripture personalizes this principle, presenting a God who is Creator and Redeemer, and who alone is able to heal our backsliding. The steps which recovery programs offer can be helpful. But ultimately only God can do in our lives what He promised to do for Israel when Jeremiah announced, "I will heal your backslidings."

A PROMISE OF REST

The promise: "Stand in the ways and see, and ask for the old paths, where the good way is, and walk in it; then you will find rest for your souls" (Jer. 6:16).

The context of the promise. Chapter 6 contains one of Jeremiah's predictions of disaster. Because of Judah's sins, national destruction had become certain. The only hope for Judah was to return to the traditional values in God's Law, and to walk in these values. But Judah rejected this appeal, and said, "We will not walk in it."

Understanding the promise. This promise was addressed to the nation, and it is conditional. If God was to bless the nation, there had to be a return to what we today might call "traditional" values. Here the "old paths, where the good way is" are the paths defined in God's Law. Loyalty to God and commitment to His values are essential to national health and well being.

Two principles underlie this promise. The first is that under the Mosaic Covenant God was obligated to bless when a generation walked in the "old paths." The second is that because God's moral laws function in any society, any nation which strays far from God's values will experience serious social breakdown. In our society today, the call to return to the old paths, as rooted in our Judeo-Christian heritage, can be expressed with the same urgency.

Claiming the promise. The promise as given has a national focus. Society itself must turn back to the old ways if the nation is to survive. Yet there are implications for the individual as well. Any individual seeking rest must choose God's ways as his or her own. And if we do not? Isaiah reminds us that "'the wicked are like the troubled sea, when it cannot rest. . . . There is no peace,' says my God, 'for the wicked'" (Isa. 57:20, 21).

A PROMISE OF INNER STRENGTH

The promise:

Blessed is the man who trusts
    in the LORD,
And whose hope is in the LORD.

"The man who trusts in the LORD . . . shall be like a tree planted by the waters."

For he shall be like a tree planted
  by the waters,
Which spreads out its roots by the
  river,
And will not fear when heat
  comes;
But its leaf will be green,
and will not be anxious in the
  year of drought,
Nor will cease from yielding fruit
  (Jer. 17: 7, 8).

The context of the promise. In chapter 17, Jeremiah announced God's sentence of exile upon the nation. But then Jeremiah had a message for "the man who trusts in men" and another for "the man who trusts in the LORD."

Understanding the promise. The nation was doomed to experience the searing heat of judgment and the withering of its hopes. Jeremiah tells us that when this happens, an individual's relationship with the Lord will make a difference. The person who trusts in man will dry up like a shrub in the desert. The person who trusts God will remain strong and vital, like a tree with its own source of water. However barren the situation, the person who trusts in the Lord will remain vital and alive and will bear fruit.

Claiming the promise. Although Jeremiah was speaking to the people of Judah in his own time, the promise is addressed to those "who trust in the LORD." Clearly this promise is for us today. It reminds us that our true well being does not depend on circumstances but on maintaining our trust in the Lord. If we maintain our focus on the Lord as one who is in sovereign control of our lives—and who intends to work good for our lives—we will be able to trust Him, no matter what happens.

A PROMISE OF GOOD HOPE

The promise: "For I know the thoughts that I think toward you, says the LORD, thoughts of peace and not of evil, to give you a future and a hope" (Jer. 29:11). See the discussion of this promise on page 87.

A PROMISE OF REJUVENATION

The promise: "Call to Me, and I will answer you, and show you great and mighty things, which you do not know" (Jer. 33:3).

The context of the promise. This promise was addressed to the two fallen Hebrew houses [kingdoms]. Israel had fallen long before Jeremiah prophesied. Jerusalem and Judah were about to be crushed by the Babylonians as a divine punishment. Yet even as judgment threatened to fall, God spoke to His people and invited them to call on Him. What "great and mighty things" will the Lord do when His people call on Him? God said through Jeremiah, "I will bring it [Jerusalem] health and healing; I will heal them and reveal to them the abundance of peace and truth" (Jer. 33:6).

The prospect of a complete restoration of God's people to their land is rooted in the Abrahamic Covenant and the New Covenant. Because God had promised, the descendants of Abraham would build a lasting nation in what was ancient Canaan. But this promise tells us more of *when* this will happen. One day God's people will call on Him. When they do, God will answer with great and mighty acts.

Understanding the promise. The covenant-linked promise was made to God's Old Testament people. Yet it speaks powerfully of God's universal mercy and grace. When things are darkest in our own lives, God is the one on whom we can call with confidence. He not only cares, but He has the ability to do great and mighty things for us.

Claiming the promise. To claim this promise, we need only remember who God is and then call on Him. We cannot begin to know beforehand what great and mighty things He will do for us. But we need only know that He will. He who will bring a dead nation back to life is surely able to breathe life into our dead hopes.

A PROMISE OF FAVOR

The promise: "Jonadab the son of Rechab shall not lack a man to stand before Me forever" (Jer. 35:19).

The context of the promise. Jeremiah called members of a nomadic tribe into the temple and offered them wine. They refused, because one of their ancestors had commanded, "You shall drink no wine, you nor your sons, forever" (Jer. 35:6). The family had shown greater respect for the commandment of a long-dead ancestor than Judah had shown for the commandments of the living God!

Understanding the promise. God through Jeremiah gave this promise as a reward for the family's loyalty to their ancestor. In that culture, this was a very precious promise, just as in the East having sons to carry on the family line was of vital concern.

We cannot claim this same promise for ourselves today. But we are reminded that Hebrews 11:6 declares that anyone who comes to God must believe that He exists and that "He is a rewarder of those who diligently seek Him." God's point in having Jeremiah call the Rechabites was to emphasize this very truth: God rewards and repays our loyalty to Him.

Responding to the promise. Let us be sure to be loyal to God and to our brothers and sisters. This loyalty will never go unrewarded.

GOD'S PROMISES IN LAMENTATIONS

The book of Lamentations contains a series of funeral, or dirge, poems. Tradition says it was written by Jeremiah, who traveled to Babylon some time after the destruction of Jerusalem. These poems reflect the crushing sense of loss felt by the Jewish exiles after their resettlement in Babylon. No promises from God are incorporated among the many expressions of remorse in this book.

GOD'S PROMISES IN EZEKIEL

The prophet Ezekiel was a contemporary of Jeremiah. Ezekiel prophesied in Babylon, where he had been resettled with other mem-

bers of the Jewish elite after the Babylonians invaded Judah in 597 B.C., some eleven years before Jerusalem's destruction. Between July of 593 B.C. until Judah's fall in 586 B.C., Ezekiel echoed Jeremiah's message of certain judgment.

Some years after the fall, Ezekiel began to minister again, this time to share a vision of national restoration. Although no nation then existed in the Holy Land, God would keep the ancient covenant promises made to Abraham and David. Ezekiel promised that the Messiah would come and that another great temple would be built in a restored Jerusalem. Then, at last, God would be worshiped by all, and the world would know lasting peace.

COVENANT-LINKED PROMISES IN EZEKIEL

Five themes are repeated again and again in Ezekiel:

1. God is transcendent, not limited to the temple or the Holy Land.
2. Judah is sinful. There is no way that God's people can justify themselves.
3. Judgment is certain and imminent. God will be patient no longer.
4. Individuals are responsible. While the Law and earlier prophets emphasized the corporate responsibility of God's people to love Him and keep His laws, Ezekiel emphasized that each individual will be treated in accordance with his or her response to the LORD.
5. Restoration lies ahead. The disaster which has overtaken Judah does not mean that God has set aside His covenant promises.

Given these themes, we can see that everything Ezekiel said was linked with the Abrahamic, Davidic, and Mosaic Covenants. The following passages make this link especially clear: Ezekiel 5:5–17; 11:15–20; 14:1–14; 16:60–63; 20:33–44; 28:25, 26; 34:11–26; 36:23–30; 37:22–28; 39:23–29; 40:1—46:35.

SPECIAL PROMISES WE CAN CLAIM IN EZEKIEL

The book of Ezekiel is so deeply rooted in the covenants that only one passage may imply special promises we might claim. In Ezekiel 18, the prophet emphasized individual responsibility and reward. Even here Ezekiel applied principles incorporated in the Mosaic Covenant. Under that covenant, God is committed to bless the loyal and obedient citizens of Israel and to punish the disobedient.

Ezekiel applied this principle to individuals and to the coming Babylonian invasion of his homeland. The nation would fall and its population would be deported. But during the invasion, God promised to make a distinction between the righteous and the wicked. The person ["soul"] who sins will be killed when the Babylonians come, while the life of the righteous will be preserved. [In this chapter the phrase "the soul who sins shall die" means "the person who sins will be killed." The Hebrew word translated "soul" is often used in the sense of "person," and the death in view in the passage is biological.]

The promise of preservation for those who walk in God's statutes (Ezek. 18:9) was made specifically to the inhabitants of Jerusalem and Judah about six hundred years before Christ. It is not a general promise of preservation which believers today can claim. Yet it reminds us of two great truths.

First, each individual is responsible to God for his or her choices. And second, God can and does so govern His universe that the fate of individuals may be determined by Him. Ezekiel 18 reminds us that God does not need to perform miracles to guard the righteous. Our God is so great that He is able to work through what appears to be normal cause and effect to keep His promises to His own people.

GOD'S PROMISES IN DANIEL

Daniel was taken as a captive to Babylon as a teenager in 605 B.C. There he was enrolled in a school that Nebuchadnezzar had established to train promising youths from all over his empire to serve in his bureaucracy. As an adult, Daniel filled important positions in the administration of both the Babylonian and Medo-Persian empires.

COVENANT-LINKED PROMISES IN DANIEL

The first six chapters of Daniel contain familiar stories of Daniel's adventures with rulers of the ancient world empires. Chapters 7 through 12 report Daniel's prophetic visions.

The visions of chapters seven through nine contain predictions concerning the course of history from Daniel's day to the time of Christ. The most important of these visions—in Daniel 9:23–27—identifies the specific time the promised Messiah will appear and predicts His death and the subsequent destruction of Jerusalem by the Romans (Dan. 9:26).

Chapters 10 through 12 of Daniel look ahead and describe events to take place at history's end. Prophecies recorded in these chapters were quoted by Jesus in His teachings about the future (Matt. 24). These prophecies are also reflected in the last book of the Bible, Revelation. These chapters are related to the time when God will act to fulfill His covenant promises, defined in the first part of this book.

GOD'S PROMISES IN HOSEA

The prophet Hosea was called to share God's anguish. As God's people were unfaithful to Him, so Hosea's wife was unfaithful to God's prophet. Hosea lived and ministered in Israel, the Northern Kingdom, between 753 B.C. and 723 B.C. The first three chapters of his book tell Hosea's personal story of continuing love for his unfaithful wife, Gomer. Chapters 4 through 14 contain sermons that the prophet must have preached many times during his thirty-year ministry.

COVENANT-LINKED PROMISES IN HOSEA

Like the other Old Testament prophets, Hosea interpreted Israel's present experience and future in light of the Mosaic Covenant. A notable theme in his and the other prophets' writings is the reaffirmation of God's commitment to His earlier covenant promises. Passages in Hosea which emphasize this commitment are 2:16–23; 11:1–11; and 14:4–9.

GOD'S PROMISES IN JOEL

Joel's undated prophecy emphasizes the role of God as Judge, both in history and at the time of the end. A plague of locusts symbolizes God's present judgment on sin, stimulating a prophetic vision of a dreadful judgment to come at history's end.

COVENANT-LINKED PROMISES IN JOEL

Joel's call to repentance (2:12–17) reflects the promises made by Moses to bless any generation of Israelites which is loyal and obedient. But Joel looks beyond the present moment and foresees a day when God will fulfill the promises that He made to Abraham and David. Several passages in Joel reveal more about how God will keep these promises as history draws to a close. These powerful covenant-linked promises are found in Joel 2:18–27. The same chapter includes a powerful prophecy related to the promised New Covenant. Peter quoted Joel 2:28–32 in his first evangelistic message (Acts 2). The book concludes with a vision of God's people restored to the promised land (Joel 3:18–21).

GOD'S PROMISES IN AMOS

Amos was a shepherd in Judah whom God called to deliver a prophetic warning to neighboring Israel. Amos visited Israel during a time of exploding prosperity in the Northern Kingdom. But the period was also marked by social injustice, as the wealthy exploited the poor, seeking to build large estates on lands taken from small farmers. Amos' message of justice and judgment reaffirmed the old Mosaic laws, warning of imminent divine punishment. But Amos also concluded with a vision of the future promised in the covenants that God had made with Abraham and David. These great covenant-linked promises are found in Amos 9:11–15.

GOD'S PROMISES IN OBADIAH

This brief one-chapter book announces judgment on the Edomites for supporting an enemy attack on Jerusalem. The book reflects God's commitment to Abraham to bless those who blessed him and his descendants, and to curse those who cursed them (Gen. 12:3).

GOD'S PROMISES IN JONAH

Jonah was a prophet who lived in Israel. He predicted military victories that led to his nation's prosperity under Jeroboam II (see 2 Kin. 14:25). When God called him to go to the capital of Assyria and announce its destruction, the patriotic prophet ran away. Jonah feared that the people of Nineveh would repent and that God would withhold judgment from them.

Every Sunday school student is familiar with the story of Jonah being swallowed by a great fish and carrying out his mission after his deliverance from the fish. As Jonah had feared, Nineveh did repent, and the threat of God's judgment was withdrawn.

The link of this story to God's covenants is subtle, but very real. The Mosaic Covenant provided for repentance and subsequent blessing. By treating Nineveh graciously and accepting the repentance of its citizens, God provided a graphic demonstration of this principle. Surely Israel, God's own, would repent under the preaching of contemporary prophets like Amos. God would also withhold the punishment they deserved.

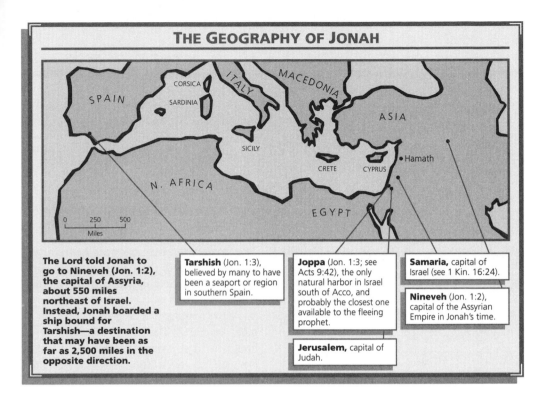

THE GEOGRAPHY OF JONAH

The Lord told Jonah to go to Nineveh (Jon. 1:2), the capital of Assyria, about 550 miles northeast of Israel. Instead, Jonah boarded a ship bound for Tarshish—a destination that may have been as far as 2,500 miles in the opposite direction.

Tarshish (Jon. 1:3), believed by many to have been a seaport or region in southern Spain.

Joppa (Jon. 1:3; see Acts 9:42), the only natural harbor in Israel south of Acco, and probably the closest one available to the fleeing prophet.

Samaria, capital of Israel (see 1 Kin. 16:24).

Nineveh (Jon. 1:2), capital of the Assyrian Empire in Jonah's time.

Jerusalem, capital of Judah.

But Israel did not repent. Within half a century of Jonah's mission, the Assyrians crushed Israel and carried its citizens into exile.

The experience of both nations is a message for us today. We can repent after sinning and find God's blessing. Or we can persist in sin and experience His discipline.

GOD'S PROMISES IN MICAH

Micah was a prophet in Judah and a contemporary of Isaiah. The message of the two prophets is similar, which is not surprising in view of the fact that both spoke God's message to the same generation. Each prophet emphasized sin, repentance, and renewal.

Micah like Isaiah looked ahead to a future fulfillment of the promises to Abraham and David, in spite of the judgment due the Judah of his day. Passages which reflect these great covenant promises include Micah 4:1–8; 5:1–5; and 7:8–20.

GOD'S PROMISES IN NAHUM

Nahum's words were hurled against Nineveh, describing graphically the coming fall of the Assyrian capital. The prophecy, given probably between 663 B.C. and 655 B.C., announced the doom of a people who had oppressed God's people for centuries. Underlying the prophecy is God's promise to bless those who bless Abraham's descendants and to punish those who curse them (Gen. 12:3).

GOD'S PROMISES IN HABAKKUK

Habakkuk prophesied during the reign of King Josiah (639–609 B.C.) or King Jehoiakim (608–597 B.C.). The prophet's basic concern was God's holiness, and he pondered how the Lord could permit a sinful Judah to go unpunished. God showed Habakkuk that He would soon send the Babylonians [the "Chaldeans"] against His people. The coming invasion would be God's punishment, serving to vindicate His justice and to discipline His straying people. When Habakkuk wondered how God could use a more wicked people to punish the less wicked, the Lord responded by revealing principles of divine judgment (chap. 2). Habakkuk accepted God's verdict. In spite of the anguish which the Babylonian invasion would cause the nation, Habakkuk determined that he would live by faith.

The book reflects the Mosaic Covenant under which God is responsible to punish generations that stray from His paths. It also illuminates an unusual way in which God fulfills His commitment to Abraham to curse the one who curses [harms] his descendants (Gen. 12:3).

GOD'S PROMISES IN ZEPHANIAH

Zephaniah was a contemporary of Habakkuk. Like Habakkuk, Zephaniah was concerned with vindicating the holiness and justice of God. While Habakkuk was shown principles of present judgment that operate in human history, the grand visions of Zephaniah focused on the future, when God would judge all people and all nations in a great "day of the LORD."

This day of judgment is specifically linked to God's fulfillment of His covenant promises. Only then would the hearts of God's people be changed and the people restored to their land (Zeph. 3:9–19).

GOD'S PROMISES IN HAGGAI

The prophet Haggai ministered in Judea to the Jews who returned to their homeland from Babylon. His sermons are unusual, in that they can be dated specifically: The sermon in chapter 1 was given 29 August 520 B.C.; in chapter 2:1–9, 17 October 520 B.C.; in chapter 2:16–19 and 2:20–23, 18 December 520 B.C.

The ministry of Haggai was also atypical, in that the returned exiles actually responded to his preaching! Through Haggai, God urged His people to finish rebuilding the temple, and they did!

Like the other prophets, Haggai concluded by predicting the ultimate fulfillment of God's covenant promises (Hag. 2:20–23).

Two specific promises included in these sermons deserve special attention.

THE PROMISE OF MESSIAH'S PRESENCE

The promise: "I will fill this temple with glory" (Hag. 2:7).

The context of the promise. God through Haggai promised that although the rebuilt temple would be half the size of Solomon's and far poorer in gold and silver, "the glory of this latter temple shall be greater than the former" (Hag. 2:9). The temple that the exiles rebuilt was later expanded and beautified. In fact, under Herod the Great the Jerusalem temple became one of the wonders of the ancient world.

Understanding the promise. Strikingly, the promise to "fill this temple with glory" had nothing to do with its later beautification. The promise was fulfilled hundreds of years later when Jesus, the Son of God, entered the temple area and ministered. What Haggai spoke of was the glory of God's presence in the person of Jesus Christ (see John 1:14).

A PROMISE OF BLESSING

The promise: "But from this day I will bless you" (Hag. 2:19).

The context of the promise. When Haggai began his ministry, Judah was in the midst of an economic depression. Although the temple foundations had been laid 18 years earlier, no additional work on the temple had been done, as the little community struggled to survive. In his preaching, Haggai linked the depressed economy to the people's failure to give God priority.

Understanding the promise. The promise was in no way a bribe. But it was a reward—a reaffirmation of the principle in Mosaic Law that God would bless any generation of His people who honored Him.

Claiming the promise. This promise was made to a specific generation of God's Old Testament people after they had responded to God's Word. While this promise is not ours to claim, it does remind us of a wonderful truth. No one can out-give God. Those who put God first and give Him their best will receive God's blessings.

GOD'S PROMISES IN ZECHARIAH

Zechariah was a contemporary of Haggai. Some of his sermons can be dated between 520–518 B.C. While Zechariah also urged loyalty to God and the rebuilding of the Jerusalem temple, his sermons and visions had a different focus. Zechariah looked ahead and spoke to the Jewish people about the centuries of Gentile domination that lay ahead—and about history's end. It is no surprise that his picture of the future was built on the great covenant promises given earlier by God.

Specific links to the covenant promise are found in Zechariah 6:12, 13; 8:7, 8, 12, 13; 9:14–17; 10:6, 10; 12:8–10; 14:3–11.

GOD'S PROMISES IN MALACHI

Malachi is the last book in the Old Testament. It was written as a series of charges made by God against His people. Each segment began with a statement by God, to which His people responded with a scornful and challenging question. While the book of Malachi reflects the low spiritual condition of God's people some four hundred years before the birth of Christ, it also reflects God's continuing commitment to His covenant promises. This is seen particularly in Malachi 1:11; 3:1; and 4:1–6.

Old Testament prophets spoke God's words to their contemporaries. They interpreted the experiences of their generation through the lens of the Mosaic Covenant, calling God's people back to a closer walk with Him. While their words often contained stern warnings of judgments about to strike Israel or Judah, the prophets were also messengers of hope. No matter how dark the present, no matter how severe the judgment God was to bring upon His people, the Lord would one day fulfill the promises He had given to Abraham and David. At history's end Israel, God's Old Testament people, would surely be blessed.

Nearly all the promises in the prophets thus have a direct link to the covenants. While other, special promises are at times given to individuals or to a specific generation, these too are essentially Israel's promises, and not directly applicable to us. Yet through every promise in the Old Testament, we learn more about the Lord. Often these promises encourage the development of a closer relationship with Him—a relationship in which we may find His promises kept in our own lives.

CHAPTER 14

COMMITMENTS OF THE KING:

JESUS' PROMISES IN MATTHEW AND MARK

Each Gospel writer had a special audience in mind as he told the story of Jesus. Matthew addressed his Gospel to the Jews, who had waited for centuries for God to send the promised Messiah. According to the Davidic Covenant, the Messiah was expected to establish God's kingdom on earth.

Although Jesus had presented Himself as the fulfillment of the Messianic promises, He had died a shameful death. How could he possibly be the Messiah? And if He were, what of the kingdom that He promised? These are the issues that Matthew's Gospel was written to address.

Matthew's Gospel presented Jesus as a king, but as a servant king. Numerous quotes in Matthew from the Old Testament show that Jesus of Nazareth fulfilled the prophecies intended to identify the Messiah. He alone performed the specific kinds of miracles linked with the messianic age (cf. Isa. 35:5, 6).

Matthew also answered questions about what had happened to the expected kingdom. Matthew showed that before the promised kingdom could be instituted, the human heart must be transformed. Part of the Messiah's mission was to pay the penalty for mankind's sins, in order that the New Covenant promises of forgiveness and renewal might be offered to humankind.

Matthew presented the resurrection of Jesus as God's seal on the Messiah's saving work and as a guarantee that when the risen Christ returned, the other kingdom prophecies would be fulfilled. Meanwhile, Jesus the Messianic King would rule in the hidden kingdom of believers' hearts.

Thus, the Gospel of Matthew is a link between the Old and New Testament revelations. It harmonizes in the person of Jesus the Old Testament's prophecies of salvation and triumph with the realities of cross and kingdom.

A PROMISE OF SALVATION

The promise: "You shall call His name JESUS, for He will save His people from their sins" (Matt. 1:21).

The context of the promise. While Mary was betrothed to Joseph, she became pregnant. Joseph intended to break the relationship quietly. But an angel appeared to him in a dream, told him to wed Mary, and instructed him to name the child "Jesus."

Understanding the promise. The promise is implicit in the name, *Jesus.* "Jesus" is the Greek

THE LAND OF THE GOSPELS

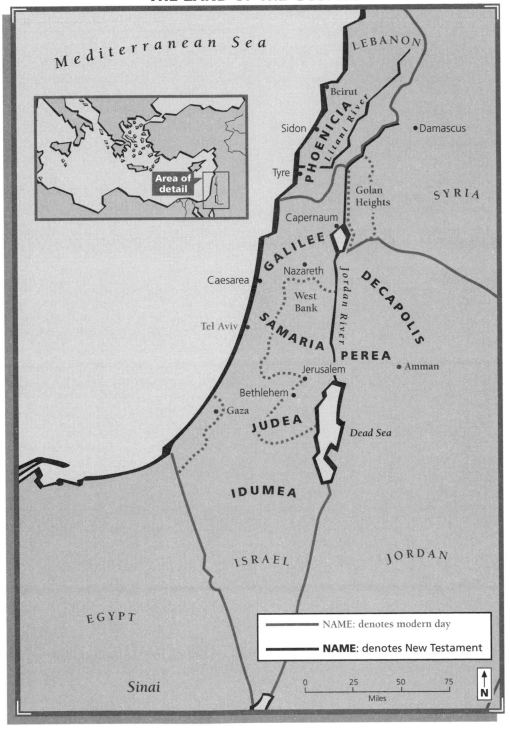

Mediterranean Sea

LEBANON

Beirut

PHOENICIA

Litani River

Sidon

•Damascus

Tyre

Golan
Heights

SYRIA

Capernaum

GALILEE

Caesarea

Nazareth

DECAPOLIS

West
Bank

Jordan River

Tel Aviv

SAMARIA

PEREA

Jerusalem

• Amman

Bethlehem •

JUDEA

• Gaza

Dead Sea

IDUMEA

ISRAEL

JORDAN

EGYPT

Area of
detail

—— NAME: denotes modern day

—— **NAME**: denotes New Testament

Sinai

0   25   50   75
Miles

N

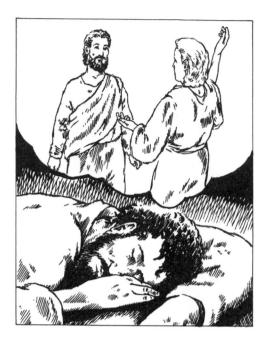

An angel came to Joseph in a dream.

form of "Joshua," which means "Yahweh saves." First-century Jews looked forward to the coming of the Messiah. They were convinced this deliverer would save Israel from the Roman oppressors and establish a glorious Hebrew kingdom like that of his ancestor David. The angel's announcement shifted the focus of this expected salvation away from deliverance from earthly enemies to deliverance from the power and penalty of sin.

This aspect of the Messiah's ministry, although taught in the Old Testament (cf. Isa. 53:4–12), was not emphasized in Judaism. Jewish theology taught that God had created human beings with both a "good impulse" and an "evil impulse." It was up to each individual to overcome the evil impulse and to gain personal salvation by repentance, good works, and careful observance of God's Law.

The message of the angel to Joseph redefined the significance of the name *Jesus* and refocused the concept of salvation. Far more important to human beings than salvation from earthly enemies is salvation from sin. For sin is no mere "evil impulse." It is a corruption of human nature—a corruption which turns our hearts away from God and separates us from God while making us liable to judgment.

One of the great gaps between Judaism and Christianity is their respective views of sin. The Jews had no felt need for deliverance from sin. We can understand why they saw no need for the Messiah to suffer and pay for their sins.

God, however, knew the need. And in sending His angel to Joseph, God expressed in the very name of "Jesus" a promise that was fulfilled on the Cross. He "will save His people from their sins."

Claiming the promise. When God spoke to Abraham hundreds of years before Christ's birth, He promised that "in you all families of the earth shall be blessed" (Gen. 12:3). With the angel's words to Joseph, just how this ancient covenant promise was to be fulfilled began to dawn. Today we realize that the promise that is implicit in the name *Jesus,* "Yahweh saves," truly is for all to claim. Whoever comes to Jesus with faith in Him as the living Son of God is saved and becomes "His people" indeed.

Responding to the promise. Jacob Neusner, perhaps today's most respected Jewish scholar, commented on the tendency of both Christian and Jewish theologians to cast Jesus as a first-century rabbi and to debate whether His teachings were unique. In a letter in a biblical publication, Neusner wrote: "What makes a Christian a Christian is that he or she believes Jesus is Christ, unique, God, son of God, risen from the dead. To those profound, Christian beliefs the issue of whether or not Jesus taught this or that which Judaism also taught is simply, monumentally irrelevant" (*Bible Review,* June 1991).

Neusner is absolutely right. The angel's message to Joseph, and the promise implicit in the name Jesus, means that the issue for every human being is to decide who Jesus is. On that decision and on our response to Jesus as Son of God, our eternal salvation depends.

THE PROMISE OF A BETTER BAPTISM

The promise: "I indeed baptize you with water unto repentance, but He who is coming after me is mightier than I. . . . He will baptize you with the Holy Spirit and fire" (Matt. 3:11).

Understanding the promise. John the Baptist spoke these words. He described his own ministry as calling Israel to national repentance. John's baptism in water was connected with this repentance. John, speaking as God's prophet, made this promise of Jesus: "He who is coming after me" will provide a far better baptism "with the Holy Spirit and fire."

The Jewish sages relied heavily on repentance for salvation. John's promise that Jesus would baptize with the Holy Spirit and with fire conveys a far different message. In the Greek language of the New Testament, both "Holy Spirit" and "fire" are governed by the preposition, *en.* Normally this indicates a unified concept: i.e., "Spirit-fire." Only the purifying presence of the Holy Spirit can transform a person from within.

The best efforts of a human being cannot bring about such an inner transformation. We can be sorry for our sins, but we cannot purify ourselves from them. How wonderful the promise that, as Jesus' gift to His people, the Holy Spirit will do in us what we could never do for ourselves.

Claiming the promise. When we accept Jesus as our personal Savior, we open our lives to the purging fire of the Holy Spirit, who alone can cleanse us within.

A PROMISE OF FUTURE REWARD

The promise: "Blessed are you when they revile and persecute you, and say all kinds of evil against you falsely for My sake. Rejoice and be exceedingly glad, for great is your reward in heaven, for so they persecuted the prophets who were before you" (Matt. 5:11).

THE TALMUD ON REPENTANCE

In *Everyman's Talmud* (1949), Abraham Cohen described the place of assigned repentance by the Jewish sages.

Inasmuch as God created man with the evil impulse, by reason of which he is prone to sin, justice demanded that an antidote should likewise be provided for his salvation. If wickedness is a disease to which the human being is susceptible, it was necessary for him to have a medium of healing. Such is to be found in repentance.

First place is assigned to repentance, because without it mankind could not endure and would be overwhelmed by a flood of wickedness. Not only has it the power of stemming the tide of evil; it is capable of neutralizing it and making life wholesome after it has been tainted by wrongdoing. 'Great is repentance, for it reaches the Throne of Glory. Great is repentance, for it makes the Redemption (by the Messiah) to come near. Great is repentance, for it lengthens the years of a man's life' (Joma 86a *et seq.*). 'The place which the penitent occupy the perfectly righteous are unable to occupy' (Ber. 34b).

With the fall of the Temple and the cessation of the atonement offerings, the importance of repentance as a means of expiation became inevitably enhanced. . . . There is the explicit teaching: 'Neither sin-offering nor trespass-offering nor death nor the Day of Atonement can bring expiation without repentance' (Tosifta Joma v. 9). . . . 'Whence is it derived that if one repents, it is imputed to him as if he had gone up to Jerusalem, built the Temple, erected an altar and offered upon it all the sacrifices enumerated in the Torah? From the text, "The sacrifices of God are a broken spirit" (Ps. Li.17)' (Lev. R. VII.2).

In placing this emphasis on repentance, the Jewish sages robbed the temple sacrifices of their significance. Far more significantly, the sages denied the necessity of the purging which could come only through the sacrificial death of the Messiah, Jesus Christ.

The context of the promise. This statement of Jesus concludes the Beatitudes, a series of "blessed are" statements which express the unexpected values of His kingdom. These values are so radical, according to Jesus, that the world would revile, persecute, and slander His followers.

In Judaism, such a reaction by society would be taken as proof of the sufferer's sin, as "there is no suffering without iniquity" (Shab. 55a). But Jesus pointed out that the prophets, later honored in Judaism, were treated like this by their own contemporaries.

Understanding the promise. This promise is made to those who hear and respond to the call of Israel's Messiah-King by following Him through adopting a radical lifestyle. Those who do respond will be so out of step with society that others will revile, persecute, and say all kinds of evil against them.

This happened to the early Christian community. At first the Christians were considered a sect within Judaism, but soon they were viewed as heretics [*minim* in rabbinic literature]. No contact with *minim* was permitted, and the Christian poor were cut off from access to food provided for the needy of Jerusalem.

Yet Jesus said that His followers who were treated like this were to rejoice and "be glad" not because of their earthly suffering but because of their heavenly reward.

Claiming the promise. The fact that discipleship may lead to suffering should not surprise us. After all, Christ's total commitment to God's will took Him to the Cross. Peter pointed this out in his first letter, reminding believers that "to this you were called, because Christ also suffered for us, leaving us an example that we should follow His steps" (1 Pet. 2:21). When discipleship results in suffering, we are to focus on Christ and His heavenly kingdom. Then we will realize that such suffering is a grace gift from God, and His joy will fill our hearts.

A PROMISE OF OPEN REWARD

The promise: "But when you do a charitable deed, do not let your left hand know what your right hand is doing, that your charitable deed may be in secret; and your Father who sees in secret will Himself reward you openly. . . . But you, when you pray, go into your room, and when you have shut your door, pray to your Father who is in the secret place; and your Father who sees in secret will reward you openly" (Matt. 6:3, 4, 6).

Understanding the promise. The context of this promise sets up a contrast with the "hypocrite" who does his giving or praying in public to gain a reputation for piety. This was *not* characteristic of Judaism. In fact, the Talmud defined the best kind of almsgiving as where "a person gives a donation without knowing who receives it, and a person receives it without knowing who donated it" (B.B. 10b).

Yet what is significant in Jesus' teaching is His emphasis on an "in secret" relationship with God the Father. Our motive should be to please and serve Him, without any thought of how others might perceive our actions.

Jesus encouraged praying in private.

A promise is associated with this call to nurture an "in secret" relationship with God. "Your Father, who sees in secret, will reward you openly." While we would place no limit on God's grace, the clear tendency of the New Testament is to locate rewards in the future when Jesus Himself will be revealed as Lord (Matt. 5:12; 1 Cor. 3:18).

Claiming the promise. The promise is conditional. Those whose primary concern is the praise of people and who do their acts of piety to impress others "have their reward" (Matt. 6:2, 5). If our primary concern is to please God the Father, we do our good deeds quietly, confident that when Christ's kingdom comes, the truth about our "in secret" relationship with God will be made known.

A PROMISE OF FORGIVENESS

The promise: "For if you forgive men their trespasses, your heavenly Father will also forgive you. But if you do not forgive men their trespasses, neither will your Father forgive your trespasses" (Matt. 6:14, 15).

Understanding the promise. Several approaches have been taken to explain this difficult saying of Jesus.

- The "you" is plural, and so the saying applies to the believing community. When forgiveness is not exercised in the local community, God will not overlook the community's flaws.
- The "you" is "everyone," and the issue is eternal salvation. The one who forgives will be saved. This, of course, denies the clear teaching of the Bible that God forgives those who believe in Jesus on the basis of Christ's sacrificial death on Calvary (Acts 5:1; Rom. 4:7; Eph. 1:7).
- The saying is addressed to believers individually, and is both a promise and a warning. God wants us to experience now the release that comes with assurance of forgiveness. But when our hearts are hard toward others and we refuse to forgive them, that release is denied to us as well.

Forgiveness is like a coin. To be genuine, a coin has both heads and tails. For forgiveness to be genuine, it must also have two dimensions—a receiving side and an extending side.

Claiming the promise. These verses are best taken as a commentary on that part of the Lord's Prayer which says, "And forgive us our debts [trespasses] as we forgive our debtors" (Matt. 6:12). Jesus does not make our forgiveness *dependent on* our willingness to forgive others. Rather, He forges a link in our thinking between forgiving others and experiencing forgiveness. No matter how we understand Jesus' saying, it is clear that a failure to be forgiving is harmful to our spiritual growth, while a willingness to extend forgiveness nurtures a deeper personal relationship with our forgiving Lord.

A PROMISE OF DIVINE PROVISION

The promise: "But seek first the kingdom of God and His righteousness, and all these things shall be added to you" (Matt. 6:33).

The context of the promise. Jesus had been expounding principles to guide those who would acknowledge Him as sovereign, who would live as citizens of His kingdom. In Matthew 6:25–32, He described those whose focus in life is on meeting physical needs. Note that Jesus speaks here of necessities, not luxuries. Most people in Jesus' time struggled to meet their most basic needs for food, clothing, and shelter. Workmen were paid daily, so that they would have money to buy food for their families the next day. It is difficult for us today, with our social safety nets, to understand how precarious life was for most people of the first century.

Jesus urged those who would live as citizens of His kingdom to give priority to spiritual matters. They were to *seek first* the kingdom of God and His righteousness, confident that the God who knew their needs would provide for their daily needs.

Understanding the promise. This promise should also be interpreted in the context of

Matthew's emphasis on Jesus as the promised Messiah-King. King Jesus is laying out principles for living as citizens of His hidden kingdom—a kingdom that for a time will exist alongside and within the kingdoms of the world. Those who own Him as sovereign Lord are to put priority on living as His followers, even at the cost of an emphasis on necessities.

Giving Jesus' kingdom and righteousness priority is reasonable, in view of the nature of God as our heavenly Father. The God who feeds the birds and clothes the flowering grasses of the field has a far deeper concern for the followers of His Son than for anything in nature. Knowing God as heavenly Father frees us from the burden of worry over necessities, releasing us to give God priority in our lives.

Claiming the promise. To claim this promise, we must give the Lord's kingdom and righteousness first place in our lives. But let's remember that the test says seek "first," not "only." There is no warrant in this verse for those who refuse to work (see 2 Thess. 3:10–12).

A PROMISE OF RESPONSE

The promise: "Ask, and it will be given to you; seek, and you will find; knock, and it will be opened to you" (Matt. 7:7).

The context of the promise. The broad context of this prayer promise is the Sermon on the Mount, in which Jesus explained the righteousness, mercy, sincerity, humility, and love expected of a kingdom citizen. The promise itself is more closely defined by the illustration of the good human father, and by Jesus' observation that God surely knows how to give "good gifts" to those who ask Him (Matt. 7:11).

Understanding the promise. The limits of this prayer promise are defined by both the larger context and the immediate context. Those who actively approach God seeking humility, love, etc., will surely be given these gifts by a loving heavenly Father.

Claiming the promise. God does not answer selfish or sinful prayers. James wrote, "You ask and do not receive, because you ask amiss, that you may spend it on your [sinful] pleasures" (James 4:3). Yet when we actively approach God seeking His *good* gifts, we can be sure that He hears and responds.

A PROMISE OF GUIDANCE
(Matthew 10:19)

(See the commentary on Ex. 4:12–15, page 111.)

A PROMISE OF ACKNOWLEDGMENT

The promise: "Therefore whoever confesses Me before men, him I will also confess before My Father who is in heaven" (Matt. 10:32).

The context of the promise. Jesus had just urged His followers not to fear those who would persecute them because of Him (Matt. 10:25–31). In spite of the pressure, Jesus' true followers would confess Him, and would in turn be confessed by God the Father. The Greek verb translated "to confess" is *homologein,* meaning "to acknowledge."

Calvin pointed out that there will be differences in the way in which believers acknowledge the Lord, even as our boldness, fluency, wisdom, and sensitivity differ. But Jesus' point and promise are unmistakable. The future of human beings in the world to come depends on their relationship with and attitude toward Jesus here and now. Fear of others must not keep anyone from coming to Jesus for salvation and from acknowledging Him as Savior and Lord.

Claiming the promise. This promise is for all, as "whoever" is an inclusive term. But with the promise, there is a threat or consequence. Whoever denies Jesus before others, Jesus will also deny before His Father in heaven (Matt. 10:33). Jesus is not only the pivot on which history turns, but the hinge on which individual destiny turns as well. When we acknowledge Him as Scripture's Messiah and Savior, we take sides with Him and He takes sides with us as well.

Responding to the promise. Some promises in Scripture may or may not be claimed, as we choose. This is a promise which *must* be claimed, or we will inherit the consequences.

A PROMISE OF A NEW SELF

The promise: "He who finds his life will lose it, and he who loses his life for My sake will find it" (Matt. 10:39).

The context of the promise. Throughout Matthew 10, Jesus explained the dangers and rewards of discipleship. While in most cases the dangers are here on earth—from those who are hostile to Jesus—the rewards are in the world to come. Yet this promise of Jesus points to a significant danger here and now as well as to a present reward.

This promise is recorded at least four additional times in the Gospels (Matt. 16:24; Mark 8:34; 10:21; Luke 6:22, 23). In each case, it is linked with Jesus' call to His disciples to take up their crosses and follow Him. In several of the passages, it is also associated with denying oneself.

Understanding the promise. The disciple's cross is not martyrdom, as some in the early church assumed. Just as His Cross was God's will for Jesus, so in Christian theology the cross can serve as a symbol of God's will for each believer. We are to meet each new day committed to doing God's will, whatever that may be. In doing so, we take up our crosses and follow the example set by Jesus.

To understand the implications of this choice, we need to look at Matthew 16:25, 26, which expands the thought expressed in Matthew 10.

For whoever desires to save his life will lose it, but whoever loses his life for My sake will find it. For what profit is it to a man if he gains the whole world, and loses his own soul? Or what will a man give in exchange for his soul?

The Greek word translated both "life" and "soul" is *psyche,* and it should be understood

in the sense of "his very self." Jesus is telling us that the person who holds on to his old self—fearful of what it might cost to take up his cross and follow Jesus—loses the new "very own self" which he or she might become. Commitment to living as a disciple of Jesus is the secret to becoming all we can be!

How strongly this promise of Jesus reminds us that God always has our best interests at heart. When He calls us to surrender all to Him, what we give up is nothing, compared to what we gain.

Claiming the promise. We will find a new, rich life when we turn our old selves loose in order to live for Jesus.

A PROMISE OF REST

The promise: "Come to Me, all you who labor and are heavy laden, and I will give you rest" (Matt. 11:28).

The context of the promise. Jesus had just announced judgment on the cities in which many of His miracles were performed. In spite of the evidence, the cities of Bethsaida, Chorazin, and Capernaum refused to acknowledge Jesus as the Messiah (Matt. 11:20–24). At the same time, Jesus thanked God for revealing His true identity to individuals, extending an invitation to anyone who was burdened and heavy laden. To all such who come to Jesus, He promised, "I will give you rest."

Understanding the promise. In the first century, the term *yoke* was used metaphorically for whatever controlled people's lives. Jesus' saying is made more vivid when we realize that in first-century Judaism the Law was spoken of as a yoke. Thus the daily repetition by the pious Israelite of the Shema (Deut. 6:4) was defined as "the acceptance of the yoke of the Kingdom of Heaven" (Ber.II.2), that is, as submission to the divine law.

The Jewish rabbis also taught that "whoso receives upon himself the yoke of the Torah, from him the yoke of the kingdom and the yoke of worldly care will be removed; but

Exhausted? Frustrated? Jesus promises to "give you rest."

❖

whoso breaks off from him the yoke of the Torah, upon him will be laid the yoke of the kingdom and the yoke of worldly care."

The rabbis' point was that there must be something which controls and gives direction to a person's life, and it was better that this be the divine law rather than man's law (the kingdom) or materialism (worldly care).

In contrast, Jesus offered another yoke: "My yoke." It is clear that this yoke was very different from the yoke of God's Law, especially as interpreted by the Pharisees of Jesus' day. Jesus' yoke was designed to lighten one's heavy burden rather than to increase it. Jesus' yoke was designed to give the weary rest, rather than to define another burdensome duty.

What follows in Matthew 12 illustrated this truth well. When Jesus' disciples ate grain on the Sabbath, the Pharisees condemned Christ's hungry followers (Matt. 12:1–8). Jesus then healed a man with a withered hand, and

the Pharisees plotted to destroy Him. What a contrast these men of the Law were with Jesus, who explained that God was concerned with mercy and meeting human needs. No wonder Jesus' yoke was to be preferred to that of the Law as Israel interpreted it.

Claiming the promise. To claim this promise of Jesus, we should abandon a legalistic approach to life in favor of the principles of Jesus' ministry—mercy and grace. We find rest in claiming the mercy Jesus brings us in His cross. We also find rest in making mercy and grace controlling principles of our relationships with others.

A PROMISE TO PETER

The promise: "And I also say to you that you are Peter, and on this rock I will build My church, and the gates of Hades shall not prevail against it. And I will give you the keys of the kingdom of heaven, and whatever you bind on earth will be bound in heaven, and whatever you loose on earth will be loosed in heaven" (Matt. 16:18, 19).

The context of the promise. Jesus had just heard the disciples' report that the crowds believed Him to be among the greatest of Israel's prophets. Peter then expressed the belief of the disciples that Jesus was "the Christ, the Son of the living God" (Matt. 16:16).

Understanding the promise. Jesus' statement to Peter, "On this rock I will build my church," has been used by the Roman Catholic Church as the basis of the doctrine that Peter was the first pope. The promise of "the keys to the kingdom of heaven" has also been interpreted as the grant of papal authority.

However, many of the early church fathers did not understand the rock to be Peter. The foundation-stone of the church was seen as either Peter's confession of Jesus as the Christ, or the one whom Peter confessed: Jesus, truly the Christ, truly the Son of God. This last interpretation seems correct, especially in view of 1 Corinthians 3:11: "No other foundation can anyone lay than that which is laid, which is Jesus Christ."

There is no doubt that "keys" in Scripture are a metaphor of authority. But what authority is in view? The rabbis claimed the right to "bind" or "loose" things and people. In reference to things, this was the right to legislate which actions were forbidden and which were permitted. In reference to people, this was a judicial right to declare a person guilty or innocent.

However, another reference made by Jesus to keys helps us understand His point here. Jesus condemned Israel's law teachers because of their misuse of the "key of knowledge," neither entering God's kingdom themselves nor permitting others to do so (Luke 11:52).

It is best to understand Jesus' words to Peter as a promise that Peter would be privileged to use the knowledge of who Christ is that he had just professed. In using that key, Peter would open the door of salvation to all, loosing those willing to enter, and binding [condemning] those who reject the gospel message.

Claiming the promise. Peter did use the keys to the kingdom of heaven. Peter was the first to preach the gospel to the Jewish people (Acts 2:14–39) and also the first to bring the gospel to a Gentile (Acts 10:30–43). That door which Peter opened in his preaching of the gospel remains open wide today. And it is the decision made by persons who hear the truth which Peter first proclaimed that binds or looses them for eternity.

A PROMISE OF A NEW SELF
(Matthew 16:25–27)

(See the commentary on Matt. 10:39, page 169.)

A PROMISE OF DIVINE PARTICIPATION

The promise: "Assuredly, I say to you, whatever you bind on earth will be bound in heaven, and whatever you loose on earth will be loosed in heaven" (Matt. 18:18).

The context of the promise. This verse follows Jesus' explanation of a judicial process by which believers are to deal with conflict. What should we do if a brother sins against us? We should go to him alone (Matt. 18:15). If he does not hear, we should take others with us and try to be reconciled again (Matt. 18:16). If he refuses to listen, we should bring the matter to the church (Matt. 18:17). If he refuses even then to work toward a resolution of the conflict, he is to become "like a heathen and a tax collector" (i.e., cut off from fellowship).

Immediately after outlining this judicial process, Jesus assured believers that in using this community process (the "you bind" and "you loose" is plural here, unlike the singular "you" in Matt. 16:19), their joint action would be confirmed in heaven.

In following this process, believers will be doing heaven's will, and the outcome of following the process will be guided and confirmed by God Himself.

Understanding the promise. This promise is made to the believing community. It is conditional, and it depends on following Jesus' instructions for resolving conflicts and dealing with hurts within the church. It is an especially precious promise, as we tend to draw back from confrontation, hoping that hurts and the damage caused by interpersonal sins will "go away."

Jesus reminds us that the impact of such sins on the believing community is serious and should be addressed. God's promise that He will be involved in the process is great encouragement, especially when we remember that the goal of the process is not punishment but the restoration of harmony and fellowship (cf. 2 Cor. 2:5–8 with 1 Cor. 5:1–5).

Claiming the promise. Is there someone who has hurt you deeply enough to block the flow of mutual love between you? We can experience God in the process of reconciliation if we take the steps which Jesus outlined in this passage.

A SECOND PROMISE OF GOD'S INVOLVEMENT

The promise: "Again I say to you that if two of you agree on earth concerning anything that they ask, it will be done for them by My Father in heaven. For where two or three are gathered together in My name, I am there in the midst of them" (Matt. 18:19, 20).

The context of the promise. These verses have been treated as if they were unconnected to what precedes and follows. However, the phrase "again I say to you" suggests that a connection exists with the preceding instructions for resolving conflict in the Christian community. Indeed, that "again" seems to make an immediate connection with the preceding verse, treated above. If so, these verses do not contain a prayer promise, as they are typically understood, but a promise that God will be actively involved in the process by which conflict in the church is resolved.

Understanding the promise. The verb *aiteisthai,* which can mean "asking in prayer," is used in judicial contexts with the sense of "pursuing a claim." In this setting, the promise is that the solution accepted by the disputants (the "two of you" who agree) will succeed, or "work out" (Matt. 18:19). The reason is given in verse 20. Whenever two or three (asked by the church to serve as judges to suggest a resolution) gather in Jesus' name, Jesus is with the judges. Jesus will provide the wisdom needed to arrive at an appropriate solution.

These verses, then, contain additional promises made by Jesus to those willing to address conflict within the church. When the church asks two or three to gather in Jesus' name to find a solution to any disputed matter ("anything," v. 19), Jesus will be present to guide them. And when the disputants accept the solution they suggest, it will work out successfully.

Claiming the promise. How important it is that Christian communities deal with interpersonal sins and interpersonal disputes of all sorts. We are not to let hurts fester or to allow sin to corrupt our fellowship. How wonderful that our Lord gave us a process for dealing with such matters, including His promise to be in the process Himself. Christ's living, active presence is His guarantee to those communities willing to obey.

A PROMISE OF TREASURE IN HEAVEN

The promise: "Jesus said to him, 'If you want to be perfect, go, sell what you have and give to the poor, and you will have treasure in heaven; and come, follow Me'" (Matt. 19:21).

The context of the promise. A wealthy young man came to Jesus, asking what he had to do to gain eternal life. Jesus' demand—that he sell all—called for a greater sacrifice than we can imagine. In the Mediterranean world, to "sell all" would mean the sale of the family home and land. This would mean a rejection of his identity as defined by his position and his family's in the community. And to top it off, Jesus required that he reject his family in favor of a relationship with Jesus and a surrogate family formed by Jesus' followers!

The wealthy young man turned away regretfully, unwilling to make this kind of sacrifice, even for a place and treasure in the world to come.

Understanding the promise. Jesus' words are not a demand for the radical discipleship some have seen in this verse. First, Christ's words are directed to one young man—not to all Christians. Second, Jesus had a unique purpose in view in presenting this young man with a dilemma.

Jesus had already asked the young man if he had kept the commandments, and he quoted only from the second tablet of the Law. Second tablet commandments dealt only with human interpersonal relationships, and the young man said he had always kept these laws. But when Jesus told the young man to sell all and follow Him, the focus shifted to the first tablet of the Law, which governs relationship with God. Jesus, Himself the God in whom the young man believed, gave him a command: Go and sell, and follow me. And that command was disobeyed!

The young man's response revealed that his heart was far from God. In a choice between wealth and Jesus, money won. And in choosing his wealth, the young man broke the first and greatest of the commandments—to have no other God than the one supreme Lord.

The incident was an effort by Jesus to reveal to the young man his lostness. It was also a warning to us that nothing must be allowed to take Christ's place in our hearts.

Claiming the promise. Later, Jesus was asked by His disciples what they would gain. After all, they had turned their back on all they held dear to follow Christ. Jesus replied there was a special place reserved in eternity for the Twelve (Matt. 19:28). And for all who follow Jesus, there is not only treasure in heaven, but also greater rewards in this life than we would have experienced had we chosen not to become His followers (Matt. 19:29).

A PROMISE OF ANSWERED PRAYER

The promise: "And whatever things you ask in prayer, believing, you will receive" (Matt. 21:22).

The context of the promise. Just the day before Jesus had cursed a fig tree, whose leaves promised a fruit it did not deliver. The disciples marveled, wondering how the tree could have withered so soon. Jesus told them that "if you have faith and do not doubt, you will not only do what was done to the fig tree, but also if you say to this mountain, 'Be removed and be cast into the sea,' it will be done" (Matt. 21:21). The prayer promise quoted above immediately followed this saying.

Understanding the promise. Jesus also used the image of the moving of a mountain in Matthew 17:20. The image is a metaphor of the humanly impossible—of a miracle which is possible only for God. Christ's point is that we have access through prayer to the super-

A withered fig tree became an object lesson in faith.

natural, for the One to whom we pray is the God of miracles.

In verse 21 a tension is set up between faith and doubt. God's supernatural power is available to those who have faith and do not doubt.

Some people interpret this verse as "condition" for answered prayer. They reduce "belief" in Jesus to forcing ourselves to "believe" that God will do what we do not really believe He will do. Then, if our prayers are unanswered, the fault can be laid to our lack of faith!

In fact, this verse does not lay down a condition, but it commends a genuine trust in God and discernment of God's will. As we rest the full weight of our trust in God, seeking to know and do His will, our Lord's power will flow, and our prayers will be answered.

Claiming the promise. God calls us to trust Him and to seek His will in all things. As our discernment of God's will increases, we will pray with confidence, and our prayers *will* be answered.

A PROMISE CONCERNING JESUS

The promise: "Nevertheless, I say to you, hereafter you will see the Son of Man sitting at the right hand of the Power, and coming on the clouds of heaven" (Matt. 26:64).

The context of the promise. Jesus was on trial before the Jewish Sanhedrin, which had condemned Him for claiming to be the Christ, the Son of God. Jesus promised those men who treated Him as a blasphemer that one day the truth would be visible to all: they themselves would see Jesus standing beside the Father, and coming in glory.

Understanding the promise. Jesus had come to Israel and fulfilled key prophecies about the promised Messiah. But God's own people had rejected His Son, condemning Him to death. Yet in the world to come, all would know the truth about Jesus. All would see Jesus in His glory; all would bow before Him at His return (cf. Phil. 2:10).

For those who believe, this promise evokes joy. Jesus will reign as King of kings and Lord of lords, and we will reign with Him. But for those who refuse to acknowledge Jesus as God's Son and Savior, Christ's promise can evoke only dread.

Claiming the promise. This is not a promise to claim, but a promise to consider carefully. When we see Jesus in His splendor, will that great revelation fill us with joy or fear? Joy will be ours if we claim Him now.

PROMISES IN MARK'S GOSPEL

While Matthew shaped his Gospel to present Jesus as the promised Jewish Messiah, Mark's Gospel shows Jesus as a person of authority and action. He portrayed Jesus as the kind of person who would appeal to action-oriented Romans. The content of Mark's and Matthew's Gospels parallel each other. Mark's shorter Gospel contains fewer promises, and many of these promises closely resemble promises recorded in Matthew.

A PROMISE OF SIGNIFICANCE

The promise: "Follow Me, and I will make you become fishers of men" (Mark 1:17).

The context of the promise. This call and promise was addressed to fishermen whom Jesus had chosen as His disciples. In first-century Judaism, "disciples" lived and traveled with a rabbi to master his teachings and copy his lifestyle. Becoming a disciple meant making a significant commitment.

Understanding the promise. Fishing was an occupation that helped meet the need of Palestine's population for protein. But fishers of men were called to meet the deepest need of every human being—the need of a personal relationship with God. Jesus' call of these fishermen to discipleship thus connected making the significant choice of discipleship with a significant future. The disciples chose the future that Jesus held out to them, and "immedi-

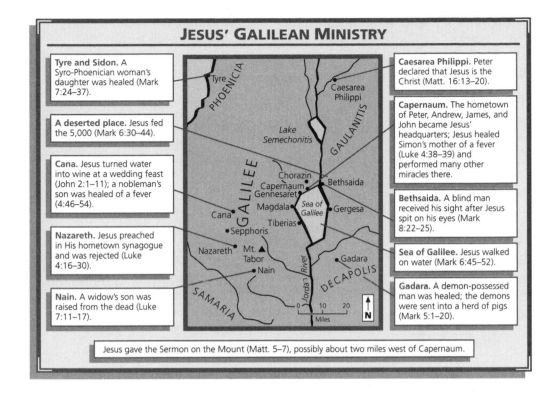

JESUS' GALILEAN MINISTRY

Tyre and Sidon. A Syro-Phoenician woman's daughter was healed (Mark 7:24–37).

A deserted place. Jesus fed the 5,000 (Mark 6:30–44).

Cana. Jesus turned water into wine at a wedding feast (John 2:1–11); a nobleman's son was healed of a fever (4:46–54).

Nazareth. Jesus preached in His hometown synagogue and was rejected (Luke 4:16–30).

Nain. A widow's son was raised from the dead (Luke 7:11–17).

Caesarea Philippi. Peter declared that Jesus is the Christ (Matt. 16:13–20).

Capernaum. The hometown of Peter, Andrew, James, and John became Jesus' headquarters; Jesus healed Simon's mother of a fever (Luke 4:38–39) and performed many other miracles there.

Bethsaida. A blind man received his sight after Jesus spit on his eyes (Mark 8:22–25).

Sea of Galilee. Jesus walked on water (Mark 6:45–52).

Gadara. A demon-possessed man was healed; the demons were sent into a herd of pigs (Mark 5:1–20).

Jesus gave the Sermon on the Mount (Matt. 5–7), possibly about two miles west of Capernaum.

ately left their nets and followed him" (Mark 1:18).

Jesus' promise was made to several first-century fishermen by the Sea of Galilee. They met the one condition that they choose to follow Jesus. And history makes it clear that Jesus kept His promise. These ordinary men did become fishers of men, and indeed launched the church that Jesus founded with His blood. In following Jesus, they truly became significant people.

Claiming the promise. The promise was given to the first disciples, not to us. But throughout history those who have chosen to follow Jesus have been used by God to touch others with the good news of His Son, and thus have become significant indeed.

We can make the choice of those first disciples. And we can be sure that if we do, our lives will also become significant.

A PROMISE OF A NEW SELF
(Mark 8:35–36)

(See the commentary on Matt. 10:39, page 169.)

A PROMISE OF VISIBILITY

The promise: "Assuredly, I say to you that there are some standing here who will not taste death till they see the kingdom of God present with power" (Mark 9:1).

Understanding the promise. This promise serves as a transition statement. It takes us from Mark's report of a time when Jesus taught a crowd and His disciples to a unique experience which happened about six days later.

Jesus took three of His disciples up on a high mountain and "was transfigured before them." Only on that occasion was Jesus seen in something like His essential splendor. Only then was He joined by Elijah and Moses. So this was the visible expression of the kingdom's power which Jesus had promised some of His listeners would see. And thus the promise was made, and kept, within the seven days.

You and I will see Jesus in His glory. We do not know exactly when this will be. But we know He will return, and perhaps soon— maybe even before we taste death.

A PROMISE OF FUTURE TREASURE   (Mark 10:21)

(See the commentary on Matt. 19:21, pages 172–173.)

A PROMISE OF REWARD   (Mark 10:30)

(See the commentary on Matt. 19:21, page 173.)

A PROMISE OF ANSWERED PRAYER   (Mark 11:23–24)

(See the commentary on Matt. 21:22, pages 173–174.)

A PROMISE OF FORGIVENESS (Mark 11:25–26)

(See the commentary on Matt. 6:14, 15, page 167.)

A PROMISE OF GUIDANCE (Mark 13:11)

(See the commentary on Ex. 4:12, 15, pages 111–112.)

CHAPTER 15

PROMISES TO FOLLOWERS OF JESUS:

PROMISES IN LUKE AND ACTS

GOD'S PROMISES IN LUKE

The Gospel of Luke portrays Jesus as the ideal human being. While taking nothing from Christ's deity, Luke's portrait of Jesus establishes a new standard for human excellence.

Excellence, *arete,* was a Greek ideal. But in the Hellenistic world, excellence was essentially selfish, viewed as the fullest possible development of an individual's gifts. In Jesus, Luke displays a new standard of excellence. In Jesus, the ideal human is shown to be compassionate and sensitive, able and willing to respond to the needs of others while remaining fully committed to God.

The basic structure of Luke parallels that of the other two synoptic Gospels, Matthew and Mark. A number of promises found in the first two Gospels are also recorded by Luke. But Luke records several promises that the others do not.

A PROMISE OF MESSIAH'S BIRTH

The promise: "And behold, you will conceive in your womb and bring forth a Son, and shall call His name JESUS. He will be great, and will be called the Son of the Highest; and the Lord God will give Him the throne of His

father David. And He will reign over the house of Jacob forever, and of His kingdom there will be no end" (Luke 1:31–33).

The context of the promise. These were the words of the angel sent to inform Mary that she had been chosen by God to bear the Messiah. The angel's announcement identified Jesus as the one promised in the Davidic Covenant, who is also the key to fulfilling God's promises to Abraham.

Understanding the promise. The Abrahamic Covenant and the Davidic Covenant contained unconditional promises defining what God intended to do in history. The covenants revealed God's heart of love, stating His firm commitment to redeem and bless the lost human race. The angel's announcement to Mary that she would bear the Messiah marked Mary's son, Jesus, as the one through whom God's ancient covenant promises would be fulfilled.

The significance and content of the covenant promises are discussed in the first part of this book.

A PROMISE OF REWARD

The promise: "But love your enemies, do good, and lend, hoping for nothing in return;

The Annunciation: The angel Gabriel tells Mary she is to bear God's Son.

and your reward will be great, and you will be sons of the Most High. For He is kind to the unthankful and evil" (Luke 6:35).

The context of the promise. This chapter contains Jesus' "sermon on the plain" (cf. Luke 6:17). It contains much of the same material included in His more famous Sermon on the Mount (Matt. 5—7). In Jesus' three-year ministry, Christ must have often repeated the themes found in these two sermons, which emphasized the way of life to be adopted by those who follow Him.

Understanding the promise. Jesus promised those who imitate God in the way they deal with enemies that they would be given a great reward. The promise is conditional; the reward is for those who love their enemies, do good, and who "lend, hoping for nothing in return." This last phrase refers to some benefit in addition to repayment of the principal. Je-

sus was saying that a person should help the helpless as well as make interest-free loans to friends who can later do favors in return.

But rewards are the reason we should love enemies. The reason believers should act in this way is that it is appropriate for children to resemble their fathers. Jesus does not imply that a person can earn sonship (cf. John 1:12, 13). He simply says that God's children ought to pattern their lives on the example set by their heavenly Father.

Claiming the promise. Jesus' call to believers to be like God lies within a well-established rabbinic tradition. Yet it is one thing to recognize a moral obligation and quite another to fulfill it. What sets Jesus' teaching apart is the realization that only those who become sons of God through faith in Christ can become like the Father. Christ is not telling sinners to try to be like God. He is reminding sons of God to be who they are!

Responding to the promise. The promise of reward is ours to claim today. We do so by relating to others as God in mercy and love relates to us.

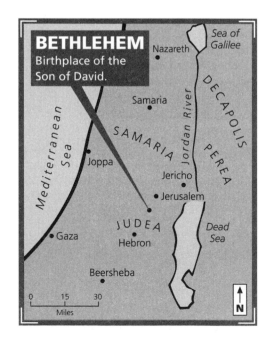

BETHLEHEM
Birthplace of the Son of David.

MAN'S MORAL OBLIGATION TO BE LIKE GOD

God Himself is the standard of morality. The rabbis recognized that God's Law called His people not simply to obedience but to likeness. Concerning the words of Deuteronomy 10:12, "Walk in all His ways," the oldest Jewish commentary on that book says:

> These are the ways of God, "The LORD, a God merciful and gracious . . . " (Ex. 34:6). "All who are called by the name of the LORD shall be delivered" (Joel 3:5). How can a man be called by the name of God? As God is called merciful, you too must be merciful. The Holy One, blessed be He, is called gracious, so you too must be gracious . . . and give presents freely. God is called righteous . . . so you too must be righteous. God is called *hasid* (loving, devoted) . . . so you too must be *hasid* (*Sifre* on Deuteronomy 11.22).

Similarly *Targum Ps. Jonathan* on Leviticus 22:28 says, "My people, children of Israel, as your Father is merciful in heaven, so you must be merciful on earth." Throughout history, the people of God have been chosen to be like Him.

A PROMISE OF INITIATIVE REWARDED

The promise: "Judge not, and you shall not be judged. Condemn not, and you shall not be condemned. Forgive, and you will be forgiven. Give, and it will be given to you; good measure, pressed down, shaken together, and running over will be put into your bosom. For with the same measure that you use, it will be measured back to you" (Luke 6:37, 38).

The context of the promise. These verses are part of a sermon Jesus gave on the interpersonal relationships appropriate to children of God. As this subject both precedes (Luke 7:27–36) and follows (Luke 7:39–42) these

two verses, we must assume that these "promise" verses also deal with relationships.

Understanding the promise. Some people assume these verses are about God's treatment of individuals. If we do not judge others, God will not judge us, etc. This view rests on two faulty assumptions:

1. The subject of Jesus' discourse is human interpersonal relationships, not the relationship between God and Jesus' followers.
2. The form of Jesus' expression indicates that these sayings were proverbs—brief, easy-to-remember sayings intended to sum up practical principles of godly living. If this were the case, Jesus' sayings would not be promises at all!

If we reject these two faulty assumptions, we can see how these verses fit into the flow of Jesus' teaching. Christ's call in this context to love our enemies seems to make us terribly vulnerable. If we respond lovingly, won't people take advantage of us? Doesn't simple self-defense require us to act *against* others as others act against us?

Jesus' answer to these questions is a decisive "no." Rather than respond to others as they act toward us, God's children are called to establish new patterns of relationships. Rather than judge, condemn, and withdraw from others, God's children are to withhold judgment, to refuse to condemn, and to forgive. What will happen if we consistently treat others—even enemies—in this way? Jesus says, "With the same measure you use, it will be measured back to you."

Claiming the promise. Social psychologists call the principle Jesus expressed the "norm of reciprocity." All this means is that people tend to treat others as others treat them. Invite someone to dinner, and they will probably invite you in return. Smile when you meet someone, and they will most likely smile too. If someone shouts at us angrily, our tendency is to make an angry retort. But Jesus' call to love our enemies (see Luke 6:35, above) rules this behavior out for God's children. It is up to

us to break old patterns of hostility by showing love instead of anger, by forgiving rather
than condemning.

The wonderful message expressed in
these verses is that such responses are far less
risky than we imagine. In most cases, loving
responses will establish new patterns of reciprocity. Jesus is stating an old and wonderful
truth. We can overcome most enemies with
love and transform them into friends in the
process.

Responding to the promises. We need to examine our relationships with others. If un-
healthy patterns exist, we need to obey Jesus
and take the initiative of love.

A PROMISE OF A NEW SELF
(Luke 9:24, 25)

(See the commentary on Matt. 10:39,
page 169.)

A PROMISE OF RESPONSE   *(Luke 11:9–13)*

(See the commentary on Matt. 7:7, page
168.)

Note that in Luke, Jesus' teaching concludes with the promise of the Holy Spirit
rather than the "good gifts" in Matthew's report. This is not a conflict. Christ must have
preached this basic message many times to
different crowds during His three-year public
ministry. He probably varied His words and
expressions from time to time. At the same
time, there is real harmony between the report
of the two Gospel writers. After all, it is the
Holy Spirit's empowering presence that enables the believer to receive the "good gifts" of
righteousness, humility, love, etc. of which
Matthew wrote.

A PROMISE OF ACKNOWLEDGMENT
(Luke 12:8, 9)

(See the commentary on Matt. 10:32,
pages 168–169.)

A PROMISE OF GUIDANCE
(Luke 12:11, 12)

(See the commentary on Ex. 4:12, 15,
pages 111–112.)

A PROMISE OF PROVISION
(Luke 12:28)

(See the commentary on Matt. 6:33,
pages 167–168.)

A PROMISE OF POWER

The promise: "If you have faith as a mustard seed, you can say to this mulberry tree,
'Be pulled up by the roots and be planted in
the sea,' and it would obey you" (Luke 17:6).

The context of the promise. Jesus had just instructed His disciples to forgive a brother who
repents, no matter how often he might sin
against them (Luke 17:1–4). The disciples
were taken aback by this instruction, so they
asked Jesus to "increase our faith" (Luke
17:5).

Understanding the promise. Jesus' initial response to the disciples' request for increased
faith is our "promise" verse. As the mustard
seed was the smallest of garden seeds, Jesus
was clearly *dismissing* their request for "more"
faith. That is, He was saying, "You need hardly
any faith at all to perform miracles!" But why
dismiss a request for increased faith? Because
"faith" had nothing to do with what Christ
had just told His disciples!

This point is brought out in the story that
follows in Luke 17:7–10. When a master told
a servant (literally, a slave) to do something,
the servant did it. The servant didn't expect
praise, because it was a slave's place to obey
his master. In the same way, the Lord Jesus
commanded His disciples to forgive. He did not
say, "If you have enough faith, forgive." The issue was obedience. If Jesus truly is Lord, it is a
disciple's place to obey.

In this context, then, Jesus' saying about
faith and the mulberry tree is seen for what it
is. It is *not* a promise of the powers that believ-

ers with enough faith can possess. It is not a promise at all, but a hyperbolic way of dismissing the disciples' request for increased faith as irrelevant.

Claiming the promise. Jesus did not expect His followers to display their faith by moving mulberry trees. Nor does He expect us to ask for more "faith" in order to keep His commandments. What God expects is that we who acknowledge Jesus as Lord will choose to obey Him, confident that as we take each step God will provide the strength we need.

A PROMISE OF REWARD *(Luke 18:29–30)*

(See the commentary on Matt. 19:21, pages 172–173.)

A PROMISE OF GUIDANCE *(Luke 21:14, 15)*

(See the commentary on Ex. 4:12, 15, pages 111–112.)

A PROMISE OF PERSONAL ATTENTION

The promise: "And you will be hated by all for My name's sake. But not a hair of your head shall be lost" (Luke 21:17, 18)

The context of the promise. Luke 21 contains special instructions which Jesus gave to His disciples shortly before His crucifixion. Together these constitute realistic warnings about dangers that lie ahead, along with encouragement to persevere. In 21:17–19, Jesus warned that the disciples would be hated for their commitment to Him. He urged them to be patient and persevere.

Understanding the promise. A saying of Jesus already reported in Luke 12:7 helps us understand the nature of this promise. In this verse, Christ told His followers that "the very hairs of your head are all numbered. Do not fear therefore; you are of more value than many sparrows."

Neither Luke 12:7 nor 21:8 teach that believers will be protected from all harm. What these verses do teach is that God gives His *personal attention* to His own. We are so important to the Lord that each hair of our head is numbered and precious in His sight.

We know from Scripture and from the thousands of martyrs recorded in church history that Christians who were committed to Jesus have been brutalized and murdered. But from this and many other promises in Scripture, we know that those martyrs were not abandoned by God. God was with them in their suffering, and when death came He welcomed them into His presence.

Responding to the promise. We may be uncertain about the future. But we can never be uncertain about whether God is giving us His personal attention. He is involved in the most minute details of our lives.

A PROMISE OF PERSEVERANCE

The promise: "Assuredly, I say to you, this generation will by no means pass away till all things take place" (Luke 21:32).

The context of the promise. Luke 21, like Matthew 24 and Mark 13, contains Jesus' prophecies concerning the end of history. The prophecies in each Gospel passage incorporate many prophetic themes found in the Old Testament.

Understanding the promise. The promise Jesus made in this passage has been misunderstood by many people, who assumed that "this generation" means "a generation" of 70 or 80 years. In fact, the Greek word *genea* can refer to either a span of time or a race of people. If used in the sense of a period of time, no fixed number of years is implied.

If a period of time is in view here, it is most likely that period which follows the events which Jesus said would initiate the time of the end. In this case, Jesus' promise would be that once the sequence of end-time events begins, they will quickly be carried through to their conclusion.

The other possibility is that *genea* refers to a group or class of people. If this is the meaning, then Jesus' promise was that the Jewish race would be preserved throughout the ages until history's consummation. The Jews have been preserved as a distinct race. God has been faithful to His covenant promises to Abraham. At history's end, the Jewish people will at last inherit all that God committed Himself to do for the descendants of Abraham.

Some who have read the passage superficially have argued that Jesus was wrong, because the generation to which He spoke has died. But when we understand what the word translated "generation" actually meant in Jesus' day, it's clear that this objection is simply wrong. Jesus is and always will be faithful to His promises. As He reminds us in the next verse in Luke, "Heaven and earth will pass away, but My words will by no means pass away" (Luke 21:33).

Claiming the promise. This is not a promise for any of us to claim. It is a statement of truth by the One who is master of truth. And this unusual statement of truth by Jesus reminds us that it is our role always to take Jesus at His word.

A PROMISE OF PARADISE

The promise: "Assuredly, I say to you, today you will be with Me in Paradise" (Luke 23:43).

The context of the promise. Jesus was crucified between two criminals. Both ridiculed

In response to his faith, Jesus promised a criminal Paradise.

and mocked Him at first (cf. Matt. 27:44; Mark 15:32). But after a time, one of the criminals acknowledged Jesus as the Messiah by calling Him "Lord" and asking to be remembered when Jesus came into His kingdom. It is likely that the phrase "into Your kingdom" implies that the criminal expected Jesus to come down from the cross and begin to reign immediately. Whatever the man on the cross expected, his request to Jesus was an expression of true faith. And it was treated as such by Jesus.

Understanding the promise. Jesus made no comment on the criminal's request to be remembered when Jesus came into His kingdom. Instead, Jesus promised "today you will be with Me in paradise." "Paradise" is a Persian word which had been taken into Greek. It indicated a place of joy and delight.

Jesus' kingdom will surely come. But faith had won the criminal paradise "today."

Claiming the promise. The promise to the criminal on the cross contains an implicit promise to everyone. If faith in Christ could win this man a last-minute reprieve from punishment and a place in heaven, surely anyone who calls on Jesus will also be saved.

GOD'S PROMISES IN ACTS

The book of Acts is a narrative history of the spread of the gospel. It was written by Luke, the author of the Gospel which carries his name. Acts traces the spread of the gospel from its initial presentation in Jerusalem, on to Judea, to Samaria, and ultimately to the major population centers of the Roman world. Luke told this story primarily through the ministry of two men, the apostles Peter and Paul.

While Acts is a distinct New Testament book, the earliest Christian sermons as recorded in Acts make it very clear that God remains faithful to the covenant promises made to Abraham and David in the earlier era. Specific reference to these covenants is made in Acts 3:19–24; 7:5–17, 37, 45; 13:22–39; 15:15–17; and 26:23.

While Luke also reported several special promises of God given during the 30-year span which his book covers, we should not expect Acts to contain many promises directed to believers today.

A PROMISE OF POWER

The promise: "But you shall receive power when the Holy Spirit has come upon you, and you shall be witnesses to Me in Jerusalem, and in all Judea and Samaria, and to the end of the earth" (Acts 1:8).

The context of the promise. The resurrected Jesus was about to return to heaven. During this final meeting with His followers, Jesus reminded them of His earlier promises concerning the Holy Spirit (Acts 1:5). When the disciples wondered aloud if Jesus was about to establish the kingdom promised in the Old Testament (Acts 1:6), Jesus redirected their attention. The kingdom lay in the future; they were to be concerned about a more immediate issue (Acts 1:7).

Understanding the promise. Luke concluded his Gospel with a report of Jesus' instructions to His disciples. They were to wait in Jerusalem until filled with power (Luke 24:49). During this final meeting, Jesus explained that they would receive power when the Holy Spirit came upon them.

The word for power which Jesus used is *dunamin.* In this context, the word refers to the spiritual power needed for effective Christian witness. How encouraging that our witness for Jesus does not depend on our speaking skill, our knowledge, or on saying "just the right words." All depends on the power provided by the Holy Spirit, who alone can take the words we speak and plant faith in the heart of the hearer.

With the coming of the Holy Spirit, the mission of the disciples would begin. And that mission—to spread the good news of Jesus to all—remains our mission today.

Responding to the promise. The promise of the Spirit's coming was kept on the day of

Pentecost. Since that time, the Holy Spirit has been given to all who trust Christ as Savior (cf. Acts 11:15–17). His presence means that we also have the power needed to witness to others about Jesus.

You and I need not hesitate when prompted by the Spirit to speak to someone about Jesus. We may have many reasons not to be confident in our own ability to share Christ, but we can still speak up with assurance. We have the Holy Spirit, and He will speak through our life as well as our words.

A PROMISE OF THE SPIRIT POURED OUT

The promise: "And it shall come to pass in the last days, says God, that I will pour out of My Spirit on all flesh" (Acts 2:17).

The context of the promise. When the Spirit whom Jesus had promised came on the day of Pentecost, His coming was marked by miraculous signs. These caused confusion among onlookers. So Peter stood up to explain. He began by quoting a passage from the prophet Joel which all associated with the messianic era.

In quoting this passage, Peter was not arguing that every sign Joel mentioned had been or would be fulfilled immediately. Peter was given a *peshur,* an interpretation of the relevance of the passage in Joel to the present situation. In using Joel in this way, Peter was following a well-established rabbinic approach to the exegesis of the Old Testament.

Peter used the passage to provide a context for the events his listeners had observed. He also announced the *initiation of* the age of the Spirit. And finally, Peter used the passage to highlight the report in verse 21, that "whoever calls on the name of the Lord shall be saved."

In Joel, the prophecy related to the initiation of the final phrase of God's program, which is compared to the appearance of the Messiah. It was appropriate for Peter to quote this passage, for Jesus was the Messiah!

Peter used the emphasis in Joel on the pouring out of God's Spirit to explain the phenomenon which everyone had observed. According to Joel, the coming of the Messiah would introduce an age of the Holy Spirit. And, Peter proclaimed, the Spirit had now come!

Peter continued to quote Joel up to his climactic promise, that whoever calls on the name of the Lord will be saved.

Understanding the promise. The resurrection of the Messiah provided the perspective needed to see added significance in Joel's prophecy. God had inaugurated the last days with the resurrection of his Son.

Most significant, in the fulfillment of one promise, God had extended a new promise to all humankind—whoever called on the name of the Lord would be saved.

A PROMISE OF SALVATION

The promise: "And it shall come to pass that whoever calls on the name of the Lord shall be saved" (Acts 2:21).

The context of the promise. (See the discussion of Acts 2:17, above.)

Understanding the promise. Peter used the promise originally expressed in Joel as a bridge to an evangelistic sermon. Luke recorded Peter's sermon to the visitors and inhabitants of Jerusalem in Acts 2. This sermon defined what it means for a person to "call on the name of the Lord."

How would a person call on the name of the Lord? Peter first drew attention to Jesus, whom all knew as the crucified wonder-worker, who had been raised from the dead by God. Peter then went on to show that what had happened was in harmony with the Old Testament Scriptures. Through Jesus' resurrection, God had declared Jesus to be both Lord and Christ.

Thus it was necessary for Peter's listeners to repent (that is, change their minds about Jesus) and to be baptized in His name for the remission of their sins. Peter concluded his sermon by promising that those who called on Jesus in this way would receive the Holy Spirit.

Claiming the promise. The gospel which Peter preached on the day of Pentecost is the same gospel preached throughout the world today. The gospel promise has never been rescinded. The gospel facts have never been changed. Jesus the crucified wonder-worker who was raised from the dead is Lord. All who call on Him will be saved.

A PROMISE OF SALVATION

The promise: "Believe on the Lord Jesus Christ, and you will be saved, you and your household" (Acts 16:31).

The context of the promise. After several weeks of preaching the gospel in Philippi, Paul and Silas were imprisoned. That night as they sang hymns and praised God, an earthquake jolted open the doors of the prison and loosened their chains. When the jailer discovered the open door, he prepared to commit suicide.

Under Roman law, a person to whom prisoners had been delivered was subject to the punishment decreed for any who might escape. The jailer apparently felt he was in danger of execution. By committing suicide, the jailer would have avoided an additional penalty—the forfeiture of his home and wealth. Suicide would preserve an inheritance for his heirs. This is likely the reason for the jailer's hasty decision to kill himself.

Before the jailer could act, Paul called out that all the prisoners were still present. It is clear from the text that the jailer was aware of Paul and his message. He called for a light, bowed before Paul and Silas, and asked "What must I do to be saved?"

Understanding the promise. Acts 16:31 is one of the most misunderstood verses in Scripture. It has been taken by some as a guarantee that God will save the children of believers. This teaching does not suggest that children are saved by their parents' faith. But it does suggest that God in grace bound Himself to cause the children of Christians to believe. Yet this teaching cannot be substantiated by this verse, promise though it may be.

First, in New Testament times, one's "household" was not the nuclear family. A person's household did include children and

Two prisoners point their jailer to salvation.

other relatives, but it also included family slaves. The household of influential men also might include their "clients." In the Roman world, *clients* were persons who owed political or other allegiance to the head of a house, and who in turn were helped financially and in other ways by him.

Since Philippi was a Roman colony, settled by discharged Roman soldiers, Luke's reference to the jailer's "household" must be taken in the Roman sense of the word.

Second, Paul did not promise that if the jailer believed, his household would be saved. What Paul said was, "Believe on the Lord Jesus and you will be saved." The added phrase simply indicated that the same promise of salvation by faith was extended to the jailer's household.

In fact, many people in the Roman world would likely follow the example of the head of the house to which they owed allegiance by adopting his faith. Yet that decision was one each person had to make for himself or herself.

Why then did Paul add the phrase, "you and your household?" One possibility is that Paul was reassuring this influential citizen of Philippi that in becoming a Christian he would not upset the social order. The fabric of society, as rooted in the Roman household, would not be violated by the new faith.

In fact, the salvation offered the head of the house was offered to the whole household. To become a Christian did not require a change in a believer's role in society or in his social status. Paul wanted people everywhere to know Jesus; he had not set out on a crusade to change the existing social order.

Claiming the promise. God does show Himself most gracious to the children of believers. Children living with godly mothers and fathers are exposed to the Lord and to the difference that a personal relationship with God makes in a person's life. The familiarity our boys and girls have with the gospel and the instruction in biblical truth which they get at home and in the church give the children of believers great

advantages. Yet each person is responsible for making his or her own choices.

In spite of the advantages of growing up in a Christian home, there is no guarantee that every child of believers will make a personal commitment to Jesus Christ.

Acts 16:31 is a promise. Each person who believes in the Lord Jesus Christ surely will be saved. In New Testament times, this promise was for the jailer and for every member of his household. Today this promise is for you and me and for our children as well. But to be saved, each of us must claim the promise by making a personal decision to trust in Christ.

A PROMISE OF PROTECTION

The promise: "Do not be afraid, but speak, and do not keep silent; for I am with you, and no one will attack you to hurt you; for I have many people in this city" (Acts 18:9, 10).

The context of the promise. The apostle Paul had arrived in Corinth. A brief ministry in the local Jewish synagogue led to the conversion of a group of believers and the establishment of a separate Christian church. It had been Paul's practice to visit a city, stay long enough to see a small group of believers established, and then to move on to another city. But Paul was told by the Lord to remain in Corinth. God also promised Paul that no one would "attack you to harm you."

Understanding the promise. This was a special promise given to Paul in a specific situation. We can understand how gracious this promise was by noting Paul's experience in cities he had visited earlier. In Philippi, Paul had been beaten and imprisoned (Acts 16:19–24). In Thessalonica, Paul's life was threatened by jealous Jews, who started a riot (Acts 17:5–9). Even in Corinth, significant opposition had begun to develop (Acts 18:5, 6). Paul was always willing to suffer for the sake of the gospel. But it must have been a relief to realize that he could minister for a time at least without threat of harm!

In fact, an incident happened while Paul was in Corinth which may have contributed to the spread of the gospel. The Jews brought charges against Paul before the Roman procounsul, Gallio. Their goal was probably to have Paul's faith declared an illicit (illegal) religion. Instead Gallio decided that the dispute was "a question of words and names *and your own law*" [italics mine].

Gallio's legal finding was that Christianity was a sect *within* Judaism. Since Judaism was a licit (legally recognized) faith, the Roman provincial government recognized Christianity as a legal faith as well, refusing to interfere in its propagation!

While Gallio's judgment was not binding on Roman governors of other provinces, it may well have been referred to as a precedent. Some decades later a sharp distinction was made between Christianity and Judaism, and Christianity lost its legal status. Rome persecuted Christians not for crimes but simply for holding to their faith in Jesus. Yet during the years Paul ministered in Corinth, God's promise spread its protective shield over Paul and the church as well.

Claiming the promise. God's promise was made to Paul in a specific situation for a limited period. Later Paul himself was arrested and twice tried in Rome. Tradition tells us that he was convicted at his second trial and eventually executed. Yet we need to remember that God's protective hand was never removed from His servant, even as it is not removed from us. When our trials are greatest, we can still experience His peace.

A PROMISE OF DELIVERANCE

The promise: "Do not be afraid, Paul; you must be brought before Caesar; and indeed God has granted you all those who sail with you" (Acts 27:24).

The context of the promise. Paul was being taken under guard to Rome to be tried on charges made by the Jewish leaders in Jerusalem. Although it was late in the season, the centurion guarding a number of prisoners took passage on a ship heading for Crete. A storm arose, driving the ship unmercifully for two weeks.

At last an angel brought Paul the promise quoted in verse 24. Paul took the angel at his word. He encouraged the ship's company to eat and prepare to run aground on an island.

All happened as the angel had promised, and everyone on board lived through the shipwreck.

Responding to the promise. This is another specific, situational promise give by God to an individual. It does not apply to us. However, Paul's response to God's promise *does* apply. When Paul told those on board of the angel's visit, he announced, "I believe God that it will be just as it was told me" (Acts 27:25).

Paul's confidence in the promise of God is a model for us, as we respond to every promise given to us in the Word of God.

PROMISES FOR ALL TIME:

PROMISES IN JOHN'S GOSPEL

John's Gospel has been called the "universal Gospel." Unlike the synoptic Gospels, which take a chronological approach in telling the story of Jesus, John organized his Gospel around a series of Jesus' miracles and related teachings. While the other Gospel writers shaped their accounts to fit specific audiences in the first-century world, John appealed to all in his presentation of Jesus as God the Son, the Savior of all who believe.

A PROMISE OF FULL REVELATION

The promise: "Jesus answered and said to him, 'Because I said to you, "I saw you under the fig tree," do you believe? . . . Most assuredly, I say to you, hereafter you shall see heaven open, and the angels of God ascending and descending upon the Son of Man' " (John 1:50, 51).

The context of the promise. After spending a day with Jesus, Philip hurried to tell his brother Nathanael that he had discovered the Messiah. As the two approached, Jesus commented on Nathanael's spotless character. The surprised Nathanael asked how Jesus knew him. Jesus replied, "Before Philip called you, when you were under the fig tree, I saw you."

Nathanael immediately grasped the implications of Christ's supernatural knowledge, and said "You are the Son of God! You are the king of Israel!" (John 1:49). In response to this confession of faith, Jesus promised that Nathanael would see greater things than these—that is, greater than the knowledge He had displayed of Nathanael.

Understanding the promise. Jesus promised future supernatural revelation. Nathanael would see heaven open and the angels ascending and descending upon Jesus as the Son of Man.

The image of angels ascending and descending goes back to a vision in which Jacob saw a ladder, or stairway, linking heaven and earth. Angels were going up and down this ladder. The Lord stood above this bridge between heaven and earth and spoke to Jacob (Gen. 28:12f). Jesus' promise was that one day Nathanael would see the reality that lies alongside our material universe. He would see

Jesus revealed as the true bridge between heaven and earth.

The promise was eschatological. The revelation was for the future, when Nathanael would see Jesus come from heaven with His mighty angels. Then Christ will appear as Son of Man, a title drawn from Daniel 7:13, 14. This mysterious figure will be invested by God with universal authority.

What Jesus was saying is that the one whom Nathanael recognized by faith would one day be revealed to all, and that Nathanael would witness that great day.

Claiming the promise. The promise given to Nathanael is ours as well. There is nothing we need to do to claim it: it is ours by right of faith. Today we recognize Jesus as the Son of God. Tomorrow, when Jesus returns, we will witness and share in His final triumph.

THE PROMISE OF ETERNAL LIFE

The promise: "For God so loved the world that He gave His only begotten Son, that whoever believes in Him should not perish but have everlasting life" (John 3:16).

The context of the promise. Jesus had been speaking with Nicodemus, a leading Pharisee and member of the Jewish ruling council, the Sanhedrin. Nicodemus had admitted that he and his associates knew that Jesus was "a teacher come from God" (John 3:2). But they remained confused.

Jesus told Nicodemus that He had come from heaven to become the focus of Israel's faith.

Understanding the promise. John 3:16 has been called "the gospel in a nutshell." It establishes God's motive in sending His Son: love. It establishes the identity of Jesus: God's Son. It establishes God's goal in sending Jesus: to provide everlasting life to a perishing humankind. And it defines the promise implicit in Jesus' coming: whoever believes in Him will not perish but have everlasting life.

Claiming the promise. The word *believe* can be confusing. We believe that Augustus Caesar was the Roman emperor when Jesus was born. But there is a vast difference between this kind of belief and believing in the Jesus who lived in Augustus's time.

The difference is expressed in two prepositions. We believe what history tells us *about* Augustus. We agree that certain things in the historical record are probably accurate and true. But we believe *in* Jesus Christ. While we agree that certain things history tells us about Jesus are accurate and true, we go beyond this kind of belief. What believing *in* means is that we *trust ourselves to* the Jesus of history. We rely completely on Him and His sacrifice on Calvary. In doing so, we accept the gift of eternal life which He offers.

There's another difference too. Our beliefs about Augustus Caesar make no real difference in our lives. But our belief in Jesus Christ will make a profound difference. When we trust ourselves to Jesus, God enters our hearts and begins to work a wonderful transformation. Our motives and desires change, and with them our behavior changes also. Belief *in* Jesus initiates an inner transformation which gradually reshapes believers toward Jesus' likeness.

Responding to the promise. Too many people don't know the difference between belief about the facts of Jesus' life and death and belief *in* Jesus. To claim God's promise of everlasting life, we are to come to a conscious decision to rely on Jesus for forgiveness of our sins and so accept God's wonderful gift of eternal life.

A PROMISE OF WRATH

The promise: "He who believes in the Son has everlasting life; and he who does not believe the Son shall not see life, but the wrath of God abides on him" (John 3:36).

The context of the promise. John had reported Jesus' conversation with Nicodemus in which Christ presented the "gospel in a nutshell" (see above). John had also quoted the testimony of John the Baptist about Jesus. In this verse the apostle John sums up the choice that faces each individual: believe in Jesus and have everlasting life, or do not believe and face God's wrath.

Understanding the promise. We often think of promises as positive, welcome words. But in truth a promise is simply a commitment which a person makes to behave in a certain way. A father who says "If you're late, you'll be grounded" is no less making a promise than a father who says, "I'll be at your game tonight."

Thus this verse, which sets out the two choices given every person who hears of Jesus, is a promise. The promise is preceded by a simple statement. "He who believes . . . has everlasting life." There is no promise here for believers; none is needed. We have, now, as our present possession, eternal life.

No, the promise in this verse is a dread one. "He who does not believe the Son shall not see life, but the wrath of God abides on him." The person who does not believe has no hope. All that lies ahead for the unbeliever is an eternal experience of God's wrath.

Responding to the promise. Some people put off making a decision about Jesus, thinking they will make a commitment to Him in the future. But Scripture gives us only two choices. We either believe in Him, or we do not. "Later" is a choice not to believe.

If we truly believe God's promise of wrath ahead, we will decide for Jesus *now*.

A PROMISE OF ENDLESS REFRESHMENT

The promise: "Whoever drinks of the water that I shall give him will never thirst. But the water that I shall give him will become in him a fountain of water springing up into everlasting life" (John 4:14).

The context of the promise. Jesus was speaking to a Samaritan woman who had come to draw water from a well. Jesus had struck up a conversation by asking her for a drink. In the

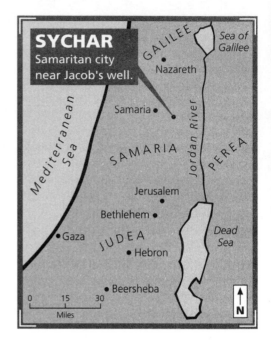

SYCHAR
Samaritan city near Jacob's well.

conversation, Jesus remarked that if she had known who He was, she would have asked Him for "living water."

Understanding the promise. In Judaism a distinction was made between water standing in a pool and "living" (running) water. Only running water could be used in the *mikvah,* or purifying bath used to make a Jew ritually clean after having become ritually unclean. It is possible that Jesus was drawing an analogy to this practice. If so, His teaching was that one who accepts Christ has a purifying spring of water that flows from within.

Some commentators focus on the contrast between well water, which the woman had to draw again and again to quench physical thirst, and Jesus' reference to a spring (*pege*) of bubbling water within which quenches man's inner thirst.

In either case, the spring of water within satisfies a person's deepest spiritual needs. The implicit promise is that in giving us eternal life, Jesus provides us with a source of inner refreshment that meets our most basic needs.

Responding to the promise. Jesus' promise was made without conditions. The spring of inner refreshment exists within us. One commentator has written, "Christ satisfies a man not by banishing his thirst, which would be to stunt his soul's growth, but by bestowing upon him by the gift of His Spirit an inward source of satisfaction which perennially and spontaneously supplies each recurrent need of refreshment" (G. H. C. Macgregor).

Too often in times of pain or pressure we look everywhere for relief—except within, to Him, where Jesus' refreshing spring still bubbles up.

A PROMISE OF LIFE

The promise: "Most assuredly, I say to you, the hour is coming, and now is, when the dead will hear the voice of the Son of God; and those who hear will live" (John 5:25).

The context of the promise. Jesus was condemned by the religious leaders for healing a man on the Sabbath (John 5:16). Christ responded by claiming equality with God (John 5:17, 18), and insisting that trust in Him not only honors God but also gains the believer everlasting life (John 5:21–24).

Understanding the promise. The life in view here is spiritual life, and it is offered to the spiritually dead (cf. Eph. 2:1–3) who "hear" His voice. In Scripture, "to hear" is more than an auditory event. To hear implies an appropriate response. The person who "hears" Jesus recognizes Him as the Son of God and places his trust in Him.

Claiming the promise. This promise of life is made to all who are spiritually dead. There is only one condition. The one who hears is to trust Jesus as the Son of God and by doing so to trust the Father who sent Jesus. Every person who hears and responds to Jesus' claim will live eternally.

A PROMISE OF ETERNAL LIFE

The promise: "I am the living bread which came down from heaven. If anyone eats of this bread, he will live forever; and the bread that I

shall give is My flesh, which I shall give for the life of the world" (John 6:51).

The context of the promise. Jesus had miraculously fed 5,000 people by multiplying a few loaves of bread. The miracle motivated the crowd to acclaim Jesus as king, not because they believed in Him but because He could feed them. They justified this action by pointing out that God had miraculously fed their forefathers with manna in the desert.

Jesus then preached what is called His "sermon on the bread of life." Building on the metaphor, Jesus presented Himself as the "true bread from heaven," which God has now miraculously provided to give and sustain spiritual life. Continuing with the metaphor, Jesus reminded His listeners that their fathers ate manna in the desert—and died. In contrast, God has now provided a "bread" which "one may eat and never die."

The promise expressed in John 6:51 sums up Jesus' message. He identified His flesh as the "bread" that He would give in order that those who "eat" might live forever.

Understanding the promise. Christ's listeners did not understand the analogy, which seems clear to us today. John indicated that many who had considered themselves Jesus' followers "went back and walked with Him no more" (John 6:66).

Yet Jesus was using the language of sacrifice. After offering up an animal, the offerer and his family ate part of the sacrificial animal. Through the sacrifice, the sinner had returned to God, and in the sacrifice God provided a meal that affirmed a protective relationship with Him. In His teaching, Jesus thus presented Himself as a sacrifice for humankind's sin, promising that those who symbolically partook of His sacrifice would be given everlasting life.

Claiming the promise. Saint Augustine summed up the meaning of "eating" Christ's flesh in three Latin words: *Crede, et manducasti*— "Believe, and you have eaten" (*Homilies on John*, 26:1). Through faith, men and women throughout the ages have participated in Christ's sacrifice. In return, they have been given God's gift of everlasting life. In the same way we may participate in Christ's sacrifice today.

A PROMISE OF DISCERNMENT

The promise: "If anyone wills to do His will, he shall know concerning the doctrine, whether it is from God or whether I speak on My own authority" (John 7:17).

The context of the promise. Opposition to Jesus by the leaders finally hardened to the point where they planned to kill Him. Yet when Jesus showed up in Jerusalem in the middle of the week-long tabernacles festival and began to teach, the Jews [a phrase which John uses to refer to religious leaders, not the race] were frustrated by His evident knowledge of the Scriptures.

Christ initiated a challenge by stating, "My doctrine [teaching] is not Mine, but His who sent Me." He continued to express His challenge by identifying the source of their hostility. A person committed to do God's will would know that Jesus' teaching was from God. Clearly then, the leaders' failure to acknowledge the authenticity of Jesus' teaching was rooted in their failure to submit to God and their unwillingness to do His will.

Understanding the promise. There is an implicit promise in Jesus' statement. Christ located the issue of recognizing truth not in the intellect but in the heart. If there is a readiness to do God's will, discernment follows.

Claiming the promise. While Jesus' words were addressed to the skeptics of His day, they have application to us today. God wants us to know Him, and to understand both His revelation and His will for our lives. Our ability to discern both truth and God's daily guidance hinges not so much on our intellect as on our heart attitude. If we are committed to doing God's will, whatever that will may be, we will be able to discern God's will.

BIBLE BACKGROUND:

WATER AND THE HOLY SPIRIT

During the Feast of Tabernacles, a priest drew water from the Pool of Siloam in a golden pitcher and poured it out each day at the west side of the altar during the morning sacrifice. Some rabbis connected this water-pouring ceremony with the future outpouring of the Holy Spirit. The Jerusalem Talmud, *Sukkah* 5.1.55a, explained that the ceremony was called "water-drawing" because "from there they will draw the inspiration of the Holy Spirit, as it is written, 'With joy you will draw water from the wells of salvation' " (Isa. 12:3).

On the eighth and most holy day of the Feast of Tabernacles, no water was drawn or offered. And it was the eighth day that Jesus invited all to come, not to the waters, but to Him. The invitation was a promise. Those who did come to Jesus would receive the Holy Spirit of whom the water-drawing ceremony spoke!

THE PROMISE OF THE SPIRIT

The promise: "He who believes in Me, as the Scripture has said, out of his heart will flow rivers of living water" (John 7:38).

The context of the promise. Jesus issued an invitation to anyone who thirsts. The invitation echoed an invitation extended by God through the prophet Isaiah, which was intimately associated with the dawning of the messianic age: "Ho! Everyone who thirsts, come to the waters" (Isa. 55:1). To those familiar with the Old Testament, Jesus' words constituted a claim to being the Messiah, provoking a debate in the crowd as to who Jesus was (cf. John 7:40–43).

Understanding the promise. John explained Jesus' promise of living water flowing from the heart. "This He spoke concerning the [Holy] Spirit, whom those believing in Him would receive" (John 7:39).

Claiming the promise. Some promises must be claimed. Other promises automatically become ours when we trust Christ as Savior. This is one of those promises that God gives us with His Son. How do we know?

First, the Spirit is promised to "those believing in" Jesus. Romans 8:8 makes it very clear that every Christian is given the Holy Spirit. The text says that "if anyone does not have the Spirit of Christ, he is not His."

Second, the giving of the Spirit was contingent on Jesus being glorified. The use of this term in John 12:16 makes it clear that John was referring to Christ's resurrection. Today Christ is risen, and the Spirit is given to all who believe.

Responding to the promise. Many Christians today thirst for a deeper, more significant spiritual life. Too many cast about for an experience or for leaders who offer more if the believer will only pray harder or give more. Jesus reminds us that if we have come to Him for salvation, the Holy Spirit has already taken up residence in our lives. And the Spirit is the source of a veritable river of living waters.

If we want a deeper spiritual life, we are to look within our own hearts. Is your personal relationship with the Lord such that the channels through which the Spirit's waters flow are open wide? Do you take time to worship, to pray, to listen to God's Word, to love others? The secret to quenching our thirst lies within our own hearts.

A PROMISE OF LIGHT

The promise: "I am the light of the world. He who follows Me shall not walk in darkness, but have the light of life" (John 8:12).

The context of the promise. In writing his Gospel and his epistles, the apostle John relied frequently on contrasts. Life was contrasted with death. Faith was contrasted with unbelief. Truth was contrasted with falsehood. Light was contrasted with darkness.

The contrast between light and darkness in John is especially significant. Light is neces-

sary to know reality as God sees and knows it. Darkness depicts our human condition, with all our distorted notions about reality and right and wrong. As the light of the world, Jesus is the one who strips away mankind's illusions and reveals righteousness as well as reality.

Understanding the promise. Implicit in the image of walking in darkness is immense danger. The person who walks in darkness cannot see where he or she is going, and as a result is unable to avoid life's pitfalls. In contrast, a person who has the "light of life"—the life-giving light—can see clearly. He or she can make wise and right decisions which keep one secure.

Claiming the promise. Proverbs 14:12 declares, "There is a way that seems right to a man, but its end is the way of death." How vital that we rely on God's Word and not our own unaided judgment in choosing what is right in God's eyes. Jesus is the Light of the World. We who follow Him truly have the life-giving light.

A PROMISE TO EXPERIENCE

The promise: "If you abide in My word, you are My disciples indeed. And you shall know the truth, and the truth shall make you free" (John 8:31, 32).

The context of the promise. This statement appears in a passage which described a heated conflict. Jesus warned some Pharisees that if they did not believe, they would die in their sins (John 8:13–29). He also stated that the physical descent from Abraham which they considered important was actually meaningless (John 8:33–59). The lengthy confrontation concluded with Jesus' assertion that He was the "I AM"—the Yahweh of the Old Testament whom the Pharisees claimed to worship as God.

Even as the harsh words were exchanged, some listeners put their trust in Jesus (John 8:31a). It was to these believers that Christ's promise was addressed.

Understanding the promise. The promise is conditional. These new believers must "abide in My word." The phrase means to live in accord with, to keep, or to obey, Jesus' word. What benefit does abiding in Jesus' word bring? Those who abide in Jesus' words will "know the truth," and this will "make you free."

Knowing the truth. In biblical thought, there is a vast difference between truth and accurate information. The masthead of the *New York Times,* which carries John 8:32, clearly takes the truth that sets free as accurate information. Nothing could misrepresent Jesus' words more. In John, "to know" means "to know by personal experience." When we live by Jesus' words, we learn the truth of what Jesus taught by personally experiencing what His words reveal.

No matter how much accurate information one may have about the Bible or Jesus' teachings, only the person who practices what Jesus taught can know the truth.

Make you free. People tend to think of "freedom" as license to do whatever they want to do when they want to do it. But in Scripture, freedom is far different. Freedom is a release from that which holds man in bondage. Freedom is extrication from the inner drives which pull toward what is wrong and harmful. Freedom is emancipation from all that prevents us from becoming our true and ideal self.

To find this kind of freedom, we surrender what we want to do in favor of choosing what God wants us to do. When we make this daily surrender and commit ourselves to keeping Jesus' words, we discover that Jesus truly does free us and make us whole.

Claiming the promise. This promise is held out to every believer. But it is conditional. If we are to enjoy the freedoms which relationship with Jesus makes possible, we must abide in Jesus' word and experience God's truth in a personal way.

Responding to the promise. How important is freedom to us? How much do we want to avoid those choices which harm us and others? How eager are we to become all that we can be in Christ? The commitment we show to reading, understanding, and living by God's commands reveals our priorities.

A PROMISE OF SALVATION

The promise: "I am the door. If anyone enters by Me, he will be saved, and will go in and out and find pasture" (John 10:9).

The context of the promise. In John 10, Christ used the image of a shepherd and his sheep to communicate spiritual truths. This imagery is rooted in the Old Testament, and not only in Psalm 23. Both Jeremiah and Ezekiel used the shepherd as a metaphor for spiritual leadership. Both prophets pictured Israel's leaders, charged by God with watching out for His people, as flawed and selfish. The prophets then looked forward to a time when God Himself would shepherd His people. Through Ezekiel God promised, "I will establish one shepherd over them, and he shall feed them— My servant David. He shall feed them and be their shepherd" (Ezek. 34:23). In presenting Himself as Shepherd, Jesus again claimed to be the promised Messiah.

Understanding the promise. The sheepfold of biblical times was a corral made of rocks or thorns. It had only one opening. At night the shepherd led his sheep into this enclosure, and then he himself lay down across the opening as its "door." No thief or wild animal could harm the sheep without passing their protector.

In Jesus' teaching, "anyone who enters" through Christ becomes one of His sheep. Such a person is not only saved, but throughout life he or she will be shepherded by Jesus and led in and out to find pasture.

Claiming the promise. In this brief parable, Jesus presented Himself as the one through whom we gain access to salvation and the world to come. In the context of Christ's reference to Himself as the true Shepherd, Jesus

Lying across the entrance to the sheepfold helped the good shepherd protect his flock.

called for His hearers to recognize Him as the promised Messiah of the Old Testament.

This promise of Jesus remains open to people today. Jesus is still the door of the sheep. And all people are invited to enter.

A PROMISE OF ETERNAL SECURITY

The promise: "And I give them eternal life, and they shall never perish; neither shall anyone snatch them out of My hand. My Father, who has given them to Me, is greater than all; and no one is able to snatch them out of My Father's hand" (John 10:28, 29).

The context of the promise. John 10 continued to build on the analogy of sheep and shepherds that has such deep roots in the Old Testament (see the comments on John 10:9, above).

Understanding the promise. Jesus spoke here of those who are His own "sheep." They *have been* given eternal life, and "they shall never perish."

This is a blanket, unconditional promise. It is made even stronger by a series of additional remarks:

- "neither shall anyone snatch them";
- "out of My hand";
- the Father "has given them to Me";
- "no one is able to snatch them";
- "out of His hand."

The idea of "eternal security" bothers some Christians. They are concerned that if believers know their salvation is guaranteed, they will have no motivation to live holy lives.

Jesus did not deal with this concern in this passage. But Jesus did teach eternal security when He said that His own have been given eternal life and "they shall never perish." This is an unconditional promise: a commitment made by Jesus. Its certainty is underscored by Christ's additional remarks. Those whom Jesus has given eternal life shall never perish because they are in His hand and the Father's hand.

Believers are the Father's gift to Jesus—and once given, God's gifts are not taken back (Rom. 11:29). Finally, salvation is guaranteed by both the Son and the Father, and no one is strong enough to tear a believer from their grip.

This series of grand affirmations reminds us that salvation is God's work from first to last. We are saved on the basis of what Jesus did for us at Calvary. Nothing we have done contributed to our salvation. Nothing we do can maintain us in a saved state. All depends on Jesus' sacrifice for us. Nothing depends on what we do for God.

Claiming the promise. This is not a promise that we claim, but one in which we are to find rest. Jesus has promised those whom He has given eternal life that "they shall never perish." As we took God at His word concerning His offer of salvation, so we are to take Him at His word concerning His promise of preservation.

Responding to the promise. Those who are uncomfortable with the concept of eternal security argue that this verse says nothing about the believer *taking himself* out of God's hand! They suggest that while no one else can put our salvation in jeopardy, we ourselves may.

But this argument ignores the original promise: "they shall never perish." *Never* remains *never*, and no argument based on what Jesus did *not* say can change that fact.

But what of the concern that underlies the hesitation of some to rest in Jesus' promise of eternal security? The concern arises from confusing the basis of salvation with motivation for holy living. We are saved because of Jesus' work on the Cross, from first to last. Nothing we do can add to or subtract from the efficacy of Jesus' self-sacrifice.

When we come to the crucified Christ and recognize His overwhelming love, God's Spirit begins to create a love response in our own hearts. As John wrote in another place, "We love Him because He first loved us" (1 John 4:19). The motivation to live a holy life is not fear that we may lose our salvation, but love for the one who has saved us at such a cost.

How then are we to respond to the promise of eternal security? With awed amazement at the love of God. And with a love for Him which moves us to please the Lord in all we do.

A PROMISE OF RESURRECTION

The promise: "I am the resurrection and the life. He who believes in Me, though he may die, he shall live. And whoever lives and believes in Me shall never die" (John 11:25, 26).

By calling Lazarus back to life, Jesus demonstrated His power over life and death.

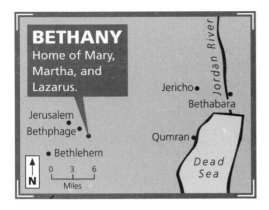

BETHANY
Home of Mary, Martha, and Lazarus.

Jordan River
Jericho
Bethabara
Jerusalem
Bethphage
Qumran
Bethlehem
Dead Sea
0   3   6
Miles
N

The context of the promise. Lazarus, a close friend of Jesus, had died. When Jesus arrived several days later, the sisters of Lazarus expressed their belief that if Christ had been there, Lazarus would not have died. Christ responded by affirming that He Himself *is* the resurrection and the life (John 11:25, 26). A few moments later, Jesus demonstrated the truth of this affirmation by calling Lazarus back to life.

It is important to make a distinction here between resurrection and resuscitation. Resurrection involves the spiritual transformation of the believer; resuscitation is the restoration of biological life. Resurrection will occur at history's end, when Jesus returns, and those raised will never die. Resuscitation takes place in history. Those who were restored to biological life by Jesus in this life would die again.

Understanding the promise. Jesus stated a fact: "I am the resurrection and the life." The truth of this statement was proven when Jesus called Lazarus back to biological life and later when He Himself was raised from the dead (see Rom. 1:4). As the source of life, Christ has authority to promise eternal, resurrection life to those who believe in Him.

Claiming the promise. Trust in Jesus unites us to the source of life, so that while we are still subject to biological death, our future resurrection is guaranteed.

A PROMISE OF EFFICACY

The promise: "And I, if I am lifted up from the earth, will draw all peoples to Myself" (John 12:32).

The context of the promise. The crisis point of Jesus' ministry had arrived, as reflected in His contemplation of His coming death (John 12:23–27). When some Greeks approached one of Christ's disciples with the request to see Jesus, Jesus turned them away. That was not the time, although the time would come soon enough.

Understanding the promise. The "if I am lifted up" in this promise should be understood as "when I am lifted up." The expression *lifted up* has a dual reference. First, it refers to the Cross (John 12:33). But the Greek preposition *ek* means "out from" the earth, and not merely away from it. Thus, Jesus' words about being lifted up also imply His resurrection and exaltation to God's right hand.

Shortly after making this statement, Jesus was lifted up—first on the Cross and then to heaven itself after His resurrection. Thus, the condition Jesus stated had been met, and the promise "I will draw all peoples to Myself" was now in force.

Some scholars have suggested that this promise was Jesus' true response to the request of the Greeks. For His promise was that the gospel message would be addressed to all peoples, without reference to race or nationality. Through His Cross and resurrection, Jesus even now draws all people to Him.

Responding to the promise. The fact that the gospel is for all people places a special obligation on Christians. If the gospel is for all, it must be carried to every tongue, tribe, and nation. Even those who are not summoned to go as missionaries are called to support missions with gifts and their prayers.

A PROMISE OF CHRIST'S RETURN

The promise: "And if I go and prepare a place for you, I will come again and receive you to Myself; that where I am, there you may be also" (John 14:3).

The context of the promise. Chapters 14 through 17 of the Gospel of John contain what is called Christ's "Last Supper Discourse." John welcomes us into the little group which gathered the night before Jesus was crucified to listen to what Jesus taught that fateful night.

This passage has been called the "seedbed of the New Testament," because many important doctrines developed in the New Testament epistles were expressed by Jesus in these chapters in John's Gospel.

A number of promises given by Jesus appear in these chapters. These promises are especially precious, inviting us to enter into a deeper and closer relationship with our Lord.

Understanding the promise. The "if I go" in this verse should be read as "since I go." In the Greek language, this is first class conditional, in which the condition is assumed to be fulfilled. Jesus was going to go away to "prepare a place for you" (John 14:2). But His leaving did not mean abandonment. Jesus promised to return. And when Jesus returns, He will take His followers to Himself, to be with Him forever.

Claiming the promise. This is another of those promises which we do not claim, but which are ours because of our relationship with Jesus. Christ will not abandon us. We are always in His thoughts. Even now He is preparing a place for us in the world to come. And when the time is right, Jesus will come back to claim us as His own.

Responding to the promise. In his first letter, John looked ahead to Christ's second coming. He wrote, "Beloved, now we are children of God; and it has not yet been revealed what we shall be, but we know that when He is revealed, we shall be like Him, for we shall see Him as He is" (1 John 3:2). When Jesus returns, He will transform us to make us like I Iimself.

But this promise has present implications. John adds, "And everyone who has this hope in Him purifies himself, just as He is pure" (1 John 3:3).

How eagerly we should look for Christ to come back. The more we focus on Jesus' return, the greater our motivation will be to live for Jesus now, that we might greet Him with joy rather than shame.

A PROMISE OF ANSWER TO PRAYER

The promise: "If you ask anything in My name, I will do it" (John 14:14).

The context of the promise. (See the comment on the Last Supper Discourse under "context" above.)

Understanding the promise. On the one hand, "anything" would seem to make the promise very wide indeed! We are invited to ask anything—and are thus reminded that there are no limits to what God can do in response to our prayers. On the other hand, the phrase "in My [Jesus'] name" narrows and focuses the promise.

In biblical times, one's "name" was more than an identifier. One's name was considered to capture the essence—the very nature or character—of the person or thing. Thus when Jesus invited the disciples to pray in His name, He called for prayers which are in harmony with all that Jesus Himself is. One authority observed:

When Jesus encouraged the apostles to pray in his name (John 14:13, 14; 15:16; 16:23, 24, 26), he was not referring to an expression tacked on to the end of a prayer. To pray "in Jesus' name" means (1) to identify the content and the motivations of prayers with all that Jesus is and (2) to pray with full confidence in him as he has revealed himself (*The Expository Dictionary of Bible Words*, 1985, 454).

We can be confident that prayers which are in harmony with the character and nature of Jesus will be answered.

Responding to the promise. Rather than puzzle over why God may say "no" to some of our most heartfelt prayers, we may be wise to spend the time considering the content and motivation of our prayers. When we come to God, let's be sure that we come "in Jesus' name."

At the same time, let's remember that God wants to hear our requests, even those which are foolish or immature. We are, after all, God's children. Yet as we grow in the Lord, our prayers should reflect our growing maturity.

A PROMISE OF THE HOLY SPIRIT

The promise: "And I will pray the Father, and He will give you another Helper, that He may abide with you forever—the Spirit of truth, whom the world cannot receive, because it neither sees Him nor knows Him; but you know Him, for He dwells with you and will be in you" (John 14:16, 17).

The context of the promise. (See the comment on the Last Supper Discourse under "context" on page 198.)

Understanding the promise. The Holy Spirit is the third person of the Trinity, God with the Father and the Son. The identification of the Spirit as God is implicit in John's choice of the word which is translated "another." The Greek word *allos* means "another of the same kind," in contrast to *heteros,* another of a different kind.

Jesus told His disciples that He would not be present with them, but that God would provide a Helper of the same kind: God the Spirit, who would take up the discipling ministry of God the Son. Jesus promised that the Holy Spirit would abide (stay) with His disciples forever, and that He would be *in* rather than *with* them.

Ever since the day of Pentecost, the Holy Spirit has been the permanent companion of the Christian. He is present now as our Helper. The New Testament names or describes a number of ministries of the Holy Spirit. A sampling of these ministries of the Spirit helps us sense how important this promise was.

MINISTRIES OF THE HOLY SPIRIT

Named works of the Holy Spirit

1. Baptism. The Spirit unites believers to Christ and His body (1 Cor. 12:13).
2. Sealing. The Spirit's presence guarantees God's ultimate redemption of believers (Eph. 1:13; 4:30).
3. Filling. The Spirit empowers the believer who is in fellowship with God (Acts 4:31).
4. Indwelling. The Spirit takes up permanent residence in the believer's personality (2 Cor. 1:22).
5. Gifts. The Holy Spirit enables believers to minister to one another in various ways (1 Cor. 12).

Described works of the Holy Spirit

1. The Holy Spirit leads and guides believers (Acts 11:12; Rom. 8:14).
2. The Holy Spirit transforms believers toward Jesus' likeness (2 Cor. 3:17, 18).
3. The Holy Spirit enables believers to live righteous lives (Rom. 8:2–11).
4. The Holy Spirit prays with and for believers (Rom. 8:26).
5. The Holy Spirit enables us to understand Christ's will for us (1 Cor. 2:6–16).
6. The Holy Spirit sets us free from the Law to relate to others in love (Gal. 5:13–25).

Responding to the promise. Jesus' promise of the Holy Spirit has been kept. The Spirit came to dwell within believers on the day of Pentecost (Acts 2). He is now present in everyone who has trusted Christ as Savior (1 Cor. 12:7; Rom. 8:9). Because the Holy Spirit is within us, we have immediate access today to all the power we need to live vital Christian lives.

A PROMISE OF JESUS' MANIFESTATION

The promise: "A little while longer and the world will see Me no more, but you will see Me" (John 14:19).

The context of the promise. (See the comment on the Last Supper Discourse under "context" on page 198.)

Understanding the promise. It is tempting to suppose that Jesus was speaking of His return in this verse. But this cannot be. When Jesus comes again, His return will be public and visible, and "every eye will see Him" (Rev. 1:7).

No, Jesus' promise was addressed to believers, and it relates to the experience of believers during His present stay in heaven. The promise is that believers will sense Christ's presence—a presence that the world cannot see.

In the conversation which followed the promise, Jesus explained that the believer who has His commandments and keeps them dwells in God's love (John 14:21). And, Christ said, "I will . . . manifest Myself to him."

The Greek word translated "manifest" means to make plain. We might paraphrase the promise, "I will become real to him."

This promise of Jesus to be real to believers is conditional. Christ will seem less and less real to any believer who loves this world and wanders out of the pathway marked by Jesus' teachings. But the believer who loves Jesus and keeps His commandments will sense the presence of Jesus with him.

Responding to the promise. All of us have known times when Jesus seemed very real to us. In times of anguish, we have sensed His comforting touch. During moments of worship, we have experienced awe at His nearness. Jesus yearns to become more and more real to His people. What a motive for us to choose to love and obey our Lord. As we draw near to Him, He will draw near to us. And Jesus will make His presence felt in our lives.

A PROMISE OF THE SPIRIT'S PRESENCE

The promise: "But the Helper, the Holy Spirit, whom the Father will send in My name, He will teach you all things, and bring to your remembrance all things that I said to you" (John 14:26).

The context of the promise. This is the second promise concerning the Holy Spirit's presence in the Last Supper Discourse (see pages 197–198).

Understanding the promise. This promise was given to the disciples. As they ministered, the Holy Spirit would stimulate their memories so they would be able to recall appropriate teachings of Jesus to suit every situation.

Responding to the promise. While this promise was given to the disciples, it is applicable to us as well. The same Holy Spirit is present with us. One of God's purposes in giving us the Holy Spirit is that He might bring to our minds truths of the Word of God which we need to apply in our daily lives.

There is one implied condition. If we do not know God's Word—if we do not read and study and memorize it—there will be nothing in our minds *to* recall. How important it is that we make reading and studying the Bible a daily priority.

A PROMISE OF FRUITFULNESS

The promise: "I am the vine, you are the branches. He who abides in Me, and I in him, bears much fruit; for without Me you can do nothing" (John 15:5).

The context of the promise. The image of God's people as a vine goes back to the Old Testament. Isaiah 5 records a complaint that God lodged against Israel. The Lord had carefully planted and tended His vine, Israel, in a vineyard. The Lord had a right to expect from Israel the good fruit of justice and righteousness. But instead Israel produced the sour grapes of injustice and sin.

A similar image is found in Galatians 6. There the apostle Paul described "fruit" produced in the believer by the Holy Spirit. This fruit is also reflected in character. And what God expects of New Testament believers is the fruit of love, joy, peace, longsuffering, kindness, goodness, faithfulness, gentleness, and self-control.

Fruitless branches are thrown into the fire.

These Old and New Testament parallels help us understand the image of the vine and fruitfulness in John 15:1–17. Jesus expects a fruitful life of believers. Jesus is not speaking about fruits or works that produce salvation but of the results of our salvation.

Understanding the promise. Jesus' promise to those who abide in Him lays the foundation for our understanding of fruitful Christian living. No branch which has been separated from its vine can produce fruit. The vine is the source of vitality; nourishment required to produce fruit flows through the vine to its branches. By analogy, believers must live in close connection with Jesus if they are to have fruitful lives. Jesus is the source of the spiritual nourishment we require to produce the fruit of love, joy, peace, and godliness.

As Jesus continued building on the analogy, He explained how believers can "abide in" (stay connected to) Him. We maintain an inti-mate relationship with Jesus when we keep His commandments (John 15:10), and especially when we live by the commandment to love one another as Jesus has loved us (John 15:12).

In the passage, the promise of fruitfulness is clearly conditional. While God has chosen us and appointed us to produce fruit (John 15:16), whether we produce fruit depends on our daily decision to remain obedient to Him.

Claiming the promise. A believer who fails to remain close to Jesus is as useless as the severed branch of a vine. The stringy fibers of the grapevine were worthless as building material, and they could not even be carved into kitchen utensils. All a first-century farmer could do with disconnected branches was toss them in the fire.

It is important to remember that the subject of this teaching is fruitfulness—not salvation. Jesus did not threaten unfruitful believers with eternal punishment. Rather, Jesus made it clear that if we are to become all we can be in Christ, we must live in close fellowship with our Lord.

As we make the choice of obedience to Jesus each day, we can count on Him to keep His promise. Jesus will work in our hearts, and His power will produce the fruit that God longs to see.

A PROMISE OF ANSWERED PRAYER

The promise: "If you abide in Me, and My words abide in you, you will ask what you desire, and it shall be done for you" (John 15:7).

The context of the promise. (See the discussion of the context of John 15:5, above.)

Understanding the promise. The word translated "abide" means to "remain in." In this verse, Jesus' words are His *rhemata,* His individual teachings, rather than His *logos,* His teaching in its entirety. To stay close to Jesus, we are not obligated to obey perfectly all that Christ has taught. If that were the case, only the most knowledgeable and mature believers could hope for their prayers to be answered!

No, Jesus placed His emphasis on our response to specific teachings. As we learn each new truth and respond to that truth with faith and obedience, we maintain a relationship with the Lord in which He is free and answers our prayers.

There is another truth in this verse that relates specifically to the prayer promise. As Jesus' words infuse us and shape our lives, His words will also shape our desires. We will increasingly want what Jesus wants. And, as Jesus' desires were in harmony with the will of God, so His prayers reflected God's will. When we desire what God wants and we make these desires a matter of prayer, we can be confident that "it shall be done for you."

Claiming the promise. Closeness to Jesus maintained by daily obedience to His *rhemata* is the key to fruitfulness. It is also a key to efficacious prayer. This is not because our obedience merits God's blessing. A more intimate relationship with Jesus will shape our thoughts and desires, bringing our prayers into harmony with God's will.

A PROMISE OF GUIDANCE

The promise: "However, when He, the Spirit of truth, has come, He will guide you into all truth; for He will not speak on His own authority, but whatever He hears He will speak; and He will tell you things to come" (John 16:13).

The context of the promise. (See the discussion of the Holy Spirit's coming and ministry, page 199.)

Understanding the promise. This is the fifth reference to the Holy Spirit in the Last Supper Discourse. In this verse, Jesus promised that the Spirit would "guide you into all truth."

This promise has been misunderstood by some, who have argued that since sincere Christians differ on various points of doctrine, this promise has failed. First, of course, there has been and still is a common core of beliefs subscribed to by all true Christians. Second, Jesus did not promise that the Spirit would

lead all Christians to agree doctrinally. Jesus promised that the Spirit would guide believers in *the way of all truth.*

Earlier Jesus had told those who believed in Him that they would "know the truth" and that the truth would set them free (John 8:31, 32). In looking at this promise, we noted that "knowing the truth" means *experiencing* truth by putting Jesus' teachings into practice (see pages 193–194). In John 16:13, Jesus was speaking of the same thing—experiencing God's truth. Thus, the Holy Spirit is charged with the ministry of guiding believers into an experience of the truth revealed in Jesus. The Holy Spirit is not charged with leading all Christians to agree on every point of doctrine.

How wonderful it is that God has sent His Spirit to guide us in the way of all truth. And how we need to rely on the Spirit as we live our lives each day. We need His wisdom that we might understand how God's truth relates to every aspect of our daily lives. And we need the strength He provides to enable us to walk in God's ways.

But what of the added promise, "He will tell you things to come?" F.F. Bruce comments,

The verb "declare" is the same as that used in John 4:25, where the Samaritan woman says that when the Messiah comes, "he will declare (*anangelei*) all things to us." As the Messiah was expected to bring out plainly the fuller implications of the revelation that had preceded his coming, so the Paraclete will bring out plainly the fuller implications of the revelation embodied in the Messiah and apply them relevantly to each succeeding generation (*The Gospel of John,* 1983, 320).

The promise of guidance into all truth and fresh insights into the future is for each generation of Christians. The same Holy Spirit who was within the apostles abides within us. As we commit ourselves to follow the Lord, the Spirit will guide us into God's will.

Claiming the promise. The promised Holy Spirit has come. He continues to speak within our hearts, showing us the way that we are to walk in Jesus' truth. We need only to reach out, relying on God's Spirit to provide the guidance we need.

PROMISES OF ANSWERED PRAYER   *(John 16:23, 26)*

(See the discussion of John 14:14, pages 198–199.)

A PROMISE OF PEACE

The promise: "These things I have spoken to you, that in Me you may have peace. In the world you will have tribulation; but be of good cheer, I have overcome the world" (John 16:33).

The context of the promise. This verse concluded John's account of Jesus' words to His disciples the night before He was crucified (see "context," p. 198). A major theme of Jesus' teaching that night was God's provision of the Holy Spirit as a Comforter who would come to the disciples after Jesus' departure. Christ's concluding promise of peace summed up all He had taught His followers.

Understanding the promise. Jesus' promise reminds us that we can choose to live our lives in one of two realms. We can live "in the world" and be ruled by the values and passions that dominate human society. Or, we can live "in Christ" and be ruled by the desire to do the will of God which gave direction to Jesus' own life on earth.

In view of this, there are two senses in which we have tribulation "in the world." First, we live in a culture shaped by humankind's sinful passions. It is not surprising that a person who seeks to live by God's will should be buffeted by tribulation in a society which is essentially hostile to God. But second, we may have tribulation because we adopt the values and passions of the world. If we do this, we will have tribulation indeed, for there is nothing in this world which can satisfy the human heart.

Christ calls us to live in Him. When we adopt Jesus' values and way of life, other people may trouble us. But by choosing to live our lives in Jesus, we will find an inner peace and wholeness that escapes those who are "of the world." What we experience is the peace that Jesus knew, even in the face of rejection by His own people. We will experience a peace rooted in the knowledge that Jesus in His death and resurrection has overcome the world.

Claiming the promise. Peace is ours in Christ. If we chose to live by the world's values, we will have turbulent and troubled lives. How wonderful that we can choose instead to live in Christ. In following Him, we can find His own perfect peace.

CHAPTER 17

RIGHTEOUSNESS FOR ALL WHO BELIEVE:

GOD'S PROMISES IN ROMANS

The book of Romans is one of the great theological documents of all time. In it the apostle Paul examined righteousness, a quality which no human being possesses but which God in grace has chosen to provide for lost sinners. What does Romans have to say about righteousness?

Human beings need righteousness. Human beings fall short of the absolute righteousness which God requires for fellowship with Him. As a sinner, every person lives under the wrath of God. Yet God loved His fallen creatures and determined to forgive and redeem. With forgiveness God credited His own righteousness to those who believe, not as something a person can earn but as a free gift.

God's righteousness requires Him to punish sin. God is absolutely righteous. His righteousness requires that sin be punished. The only way God could forgive and declare human beings righteous was to take the punishment required by man's sins upon Himself. Christ's death on the Cross was a propitiation—an act which satisfied the demands of divine justice. This payment for sin freed God to offer "by faith" salvation to Jew and Gentile alike.

God both declares believers righteous and makes them righteous. As the book of Romans develops, we will see that God's gift of righteousness is both forensic and practical. That is, in a legal sense God credits Christ's death to our account as payment for our sins. God, the judge of the universe, has declared those who trust in His son "innocent." With that grand verdict, the threat of punishment has passed!

But it was not enough for God to declare us righteous. From the beginning God intended to actually *make* us righteous. God does this by uniting us to Jesus Christ, and giving us the Holy Spirit. Through the link with Jesus maintained by the Holy Spirit, Jesus' own life flows into our mortal bodies, enabling born-again sinners to do God's will.

At the resurrection we will be made perfectly righteous. When Christ returns, we who are believers in Christ will be raised from the dead. At that time we will be totally transformed, freed from the inner tendency toward sin that corrupts us now. We will not simply be declared righteous; we will *be* righteous.

Paul's understanding of righteousness is foreign to those who do not see human beings as

lost sinners. As we read the book of Romans, we will become aware that Paul was conversing with an implied audience to whom his teaching on righteousness was utterly foreign. Paul's implied audience was convinced that human beings are perfectible and that salvation is earned by keeping God's Law. So as Paul developed the theme of a grace-based righteousness which is freely given to those who believe, he also had to answer the objections of those who held that a person can become righteous by keeping Moses' Law.

In developing the contrast between law-based righteousness and grace-based righteousness, the apostle made a number of stunning statements about God's Law. These statements totally reshaped the view of Law once held by Paul himself—a view still firmly held by his Jewish fellow countrymen.

The promises in Romans capture Paul's teaching on salvation by grace. It is not surprising to find that the promises in Romans are rooted in Paul's exposition of righteousness, and that several of these promises reflect his unique understanding of the nature and purpose of God's Law.

In a sense, the promises we will consider in Romans sum up the gospel message itself, explaining how God can be just and still justify—or pronounce innocent—those who believe in Jesus.

God's promises to Jew and Gentile in the gospel are in complete harmony with the Old Testament. The apostle Paul understood Christ and the Christian gospel as being in full harmony with the Old Testament revelation. Grace-based righteousness is not a late invention of Jesus' apostles. It is the underlying principle of all relationship with God, established long ago in the relationship that existed between Abraham and God. The Law, which came centuries later, was never a pathway to salvation.

Throughout history, man's relationship with God has been based on God's covenant promises—not on mankind's performance. As Abraham, who believed in God, was declared

righteous because of his faith (Gen. 15:6), so we are also saved by an Abraham-like faith in God's promise of salvation in Christ.

The covenant promises made to Abraham still stand. But can we count on the promises of God? Didn't God go back on His promise to Israel in presenting Jesus as the object of faith for all people? Several passages in Romans assure us that the gospel of Christ poses no threat to the ancient covenant promises originally given to Israel. God remains faithful to what He has said He will do.

References to the covenant promises and their ultimate fulfillment are found in Romans 1:2, 3; 11:1–5, 25–27; and 16:25, 26. In fact, chapters 9 through 11 of Romans are an exposition of principles underlying God's covenant relationships with Israel and with us—relationships established solely because of His sovereign choice to be gracious. To see the significance of these chapters, and as background to the covenant references in Romans, read the discussion of the Abrahamic Covenant and the Mosaic Covenant in the first section of this book.

With this introduction, we're now ready to look at the specific promises in Romans which God makes to us today.

A PROMISE OF RIGHTEOUSNESS

The promise: "Now to him who works, the wages are not counted as grace but as debt. But to him who does not work but believes on Him who justifies the ungodly, his faith is accounted for righteousness" (Rom. 4:4, 5).

The context of the promise. The apostle Paul has argued that all people have sinned and are guilty before God (Rom. 3:1–3:23). Yet God has graciously chosen to declare men innocent through Jesus Christ. Jesus' blood, shed on Calvary, satisfied the requirements of justice that sin be punished by death (Rom. 3:24–27). God then granted individuals salvation on the basis of their faith in Jesus.

Law operates in a totally different way. Those who see law as a way of salvation as-

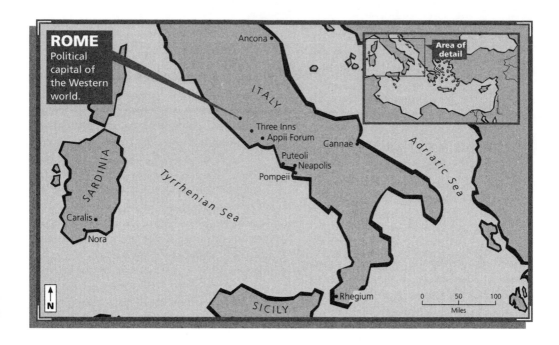

ROME
Political capital of the Western world.

Area of detail

Ancona •

ITALY

Three Inns
• Appii Forum
Cannae •
Puteoli
Neapolis
Pompeii •

SARDINIA

Caralis •
Nora

Tyrrhenian Sea

Adriatic Sea

• Rhegium

SICILY

0   50   100
Miles

N

sume that God's favor is something they can earn by what they do. Yet in Romans Paul argues that the real purpose of God's Law is to serve as a mirror, reflecting mankind's sin and need of a Savior. Does this view fit the Scriptures? Paul's answer is "yes." In Romans 4, Paul showed that man has always established relationship with God on the basis of faith, not works.

Paul's view contradicted the dominant view in the first century, as in contemporary Judaism. The rabbis' view was that relationship with God was a matter of faithfulness to Him and keeping His law. In looking back to Abraham, Judaism emphasized Abraham's readiness to sacrifice Isaac (Gen. 22). It was Abraham's merit, Judaism held, that earned the covenant promises God made to him and his descendants.

This interpretation of the Old Testament is reflected in the writings of Ben Sira, first published about 180 B.C. This pious Jew's reflections on life are typical of the views held in Judaism for the two centuries before Christ. They are also typical of the views of rabbinic Judaism, whose sages laid out the beliefs of Judaism in foundational documents written between the second and fourth centuries A.D.

Ben Sira wrote (44:19–21):

Abraham was the great father of a multitude of nations,
    and no one has been found like him in glory;
he kept the law of the Most High,
    and was taken into covenant with him;
he established the covenant in his flesh,
    and when he was tested he was found faithful.
Therefore the Lord assured him by an oath
    that the nations would be blessed through his posterity;
that he would multiply him like the dust of the earth,
    and exalt his posterity like the stars,
and cause them to inherit from sea to sea
    and from the River to the ends of the earth.

Even more striking is the fact that Sira's phrase "when he was tested he was found faithful" is repeated verbatim in 1 Maccabees 5:52, an apocryphal book incorporated in Catholic Bibles. There this comment is added: "And it [Abraham's faithfulness] was reckoned to him for righteousness!" Judaism thus viewed Abraham's faithfulness as a meritorious act which earned Abraham and his descendants their covenant relationship with God.

Paul turned this interpretation around. He was fully aware that the covenant promises were given to Abraham long before the birth of Isaac, while Abraham lived in Ur (Gen. 12:1–3, 7). Later when God promised the aged Abraham that a son from his own body would inherit the promise, Abraham believed God, and the Bible says that Abraham's *faith* [not his faithfulness!] was counted to him as righteousness (Gen. 15:6).

While the covenant promises were again confirmed to Abraham after he displayed his loyalty to God in the matter of preparing to sacrifice Isaac (Gen. 22:15–18), Abraham had been declared righteous years before on the basis of his faith!

Paul's point was that his co-religionists had made the logical as well as the theological error of reversing cause and effect. According to Jewish doctrine, the supposed effect (the gift of covenant relationship and the declaration of righteousness) preceded the supposed cause (Abraham's faithfulness) by at least 16 years!

Understanding the promise. When the apostle Paul looked back to Abraham to discern the basic principles underlying his relationship with God, he reached a different conclusion than his fellow Jews. Abraham had been justified by his faith—not by his works. The promise implicit in God's relationship with Abraham was that God offers salvation not "to him who works" but "to him who does not work but believes on Him who justifies the ungodly."

To the Jews of Paul's day, the salvation formula was **works = salvation as payment due.** To the apostle Paul and throughout the Scriptures, the true salvation formula was **faith = salvation as a grace gift.** This wonderful promise finds its source in the loving character of our God, who has chosen to be gracious to the ungodly, however little we deserve His favor.

As God declared Abraham righteous on the basis of his faith, so today God will declare anyone righteous who has an Abraham-like confidence in "Him who justifies the ungodly."

Claiming the promise. Two things are essential if any human being is to claim God's stunning promise of a righteousness that he or she does not possess. First, a person must accept God's verdict that nothing we do can earn or merit salvation. Second, he or she must believe in God as one who does justify the ungodly, on the basis of Jesus' sacrifice.

Those who come to God pleading not their own righteousness but the righteousness won for them by Christ are assured of salvation.

THE PROMISE OF IMPUTED RIGHTEOUSNESS

The promise: "Now it was not written for his [Abraham's] sake alone that it [righteousness] was imputed to him, but also for us. It shall be imputed to us who believe in Him who raised up Jesus our Lord from the dead" (Rom. 4:23, 24).

The context of the promise. The entire book of Romans is the context of this promise. (To understand the significance of the "righteousness" theme of Romans, see the introduction to Romans, pages 204–205.)

Understanding the promise. The apostle Paul had shown by argument and by appeal to Scripture that "there is none righteous, no, not one" (Rom. 3:10). Paul then turned to Genesis 15:6 to show that God is willing to accept faith in Him in place of a righteousness which even Abraham did not have.

In saying that this was written "for us," Paul argued that Abraham's relationship with God set the pattern for every individual's relationship with the Lord. Salvation is for all who have an Abraham-like trust in the God who raised Jesus from the dead.

At this point in Romans, Paul was concerned with one special aspect of God's gift of righteousness. This is the forensic, or legal aspect. To understand Paul's teaching, we need to picture God as mankind's judge, which He is. Then picture a person brought before the bar of divine justice, charged with sin. How will he or she plead? What about, "Guilty, but I've done more good things than bad"?

Such a plea would never be heard in a human court. Can you imagine how a human judge would respond to the plea, "Yes, I robbed the store at gunpoint, but I'm kind to animals. I should be let off." Being kind to animals does nothing to change the fact that the defendant is guilty of armed robbery. Yet many think when they are arraigned for their sins before God on judgment day, they will simply say, "Yes, but I did more good than bad." They assume they will be let off and even praised by God! But God's verdict will be, "Guilty as charged."

But what if the sinner pleads, "Guilty, but I believe in the one who raised Jesus from the dead"? What Paul tells us is that God in this case will say, "I find the defendant righteous! Not Guilty."

This is "imputed" righteousness.

It is a legal determination, not based on a person's actions good or bad, but based on the fact that Christ paid for our sins, and in doing so credited His own righteousness to our account.

Claiming the promise. The promise of imputed righteousness is for all who trust in the One who raised Jesus from the dead. We must believe that God will keep His promise to treat us as though we actually were righteous because of what Jesus has done. Then we will be declared righteous by the Lord.

A PROMISE OF DELIVERANCE

The promise: "Much more then, having now been justified by His blood, we shall be saved from wrath through Him" (Rom. 5:9).

The context of the promise. In Romans 1:16–3:23, the apostle Paul showed that all human beings, Jews as well as Gentiles, are sinners who fall short of the glory of God. In Romans 3:24 through Romans 5:11, Paul teaches justification by faith. In view of Jesus'

death for us on the Cross, God has declared the one who believes in Jesus innocent and has credited the believer with Christ's own righteousness.

One authority says of *justification,*

The word "justification" has important judicial meanings. A person whose actions are in question will be justified if those actions are examined and found to have been right. Thus "justify" can mean both "found innocent" and "vindicated" in a particular course of action.

The theological meaning of justification rests heavily on the judicial concept. God is the ultimate judge of all beings in the universe. He will evaluate their actions and will not clear the guilty. Yet David, in Psalm 51, appealed to God for forgiveness. David relied on God's mercy (vv. 1–2), despite the fact that a sentence of condemnation would have been completely justified by the fact of David's sins (vv. 4–5). David faced this dilemma and expressed his conviction that it is God's saving action alone that could free him from guilt and restore his joy (vv. 7–14). Thus, David called on God to justify him—to declare him innocent—despite his sin and his guilt (*The Expository Dictionary of Bible Words,* 1985, p. 372).

In the gospel God announces His willingness to justify those who believe. Indeed, God announces that all who believe *have been justified* by faith (Rom. 5:1). In Romans 5:2–8, the apostle Paul goes on to further explain how this is possible. God can declare believers innocent "in that while we were still sinners, Christ died for us" (Rom. 5:8). It is the death of Christ that serves as the basis for the great gospel promise that Paul proclaims: "Having been justified by His blood, we shall be saved from wrath through Him."

Understanding the promise. Both the Old and New Testaments speak of God's wrath or anger. In the Old Testament, God's anger is closely associated with Israel's rejection of His covenant. In the New Testament, there is a distinctly different focus. God's wrath is reserved for those who refuse to respond to the gospel. These persons are viewed as objects of God's wrath (John 3:36; Rom. 1:18; Eph. 2:3).

Also, in the New Testament God's wrath is linked exclusively with final judgment. The

New Testament places God's expression of His wrath with the future, describing a time at history's end when God will unleash His anger on those who have refused to respond to His love and grace (see Matt. 3:7; Luke 3:7; 21:23; Rom. 2:5, 8; 9:22; 1 Thess. 1:10; 2:16; 2 Thess. 1:6–10).

This is the reason for the future tense in the promise given to us in Romans 5:9. We who believe have been justified (declared innocent) on the basis of Christ's blood. We can therefore *know* that when God's wrath is unleashed against sinners, we will be spared. Having been judicially declared innocent by God Himself, His anger will not be directed against us.

Claiming the promise. This is another of those wonderful promises that is ours automatically when we trust Christ as Savior. We are lifted out of the class of "guilty sinner" against which God's wrath is directed and placed in the class of "justified by His blood." How wonderful to know that the justified will know only the love and grace of Him who has saved us.

Responding to the promise. There are times when we feel that God must be angry with us. Perhaps we have chosen sin and experienced painful consequences. Perhaps we've done nothing wrong that we're aware of, and yet we're suffering. Our spouse wants to leave us; we lose our job; a life-threatening illness strikes.

How important at such times to remember this promise, realizing that God's wrath will be directed against the unsaved, and that we are never its object. What we experience is God's discipline—not His punishment. What is happening to us is a loving Father's way of training us in righteousness. Hebrews 12 reminds us that God disciplines us out of love (12:6), and that while "no chastening seems to be joyful for the present, but painful; nevertheless, afterward it yields the peaceable fruit of righteousness to those who have been trained by it" (12:11).

We have been saved from God's wrath. All that happens to those whom God has justified is filtered not through His anger but through God's love.

A PROMISE OF RELEASE

The promise: "For sin shall not have dominion over you, for you are not under law but under grace" (Rom. 6:14).

The context of the promise. In first-century Judaism, keeping the Law was viewed as a way of gaining merit and earning salvation. In Romans Paul confronted this view. Salvation is a gift of God accessed by faith. Salvation is not a wage that God is obligated to pay those who seek to keep His Law and do good works.

In Romans 3:19, 20, Paul argued that the true function of the Law is to convict human beings of sin. What the Law does is stop every mouth. That is, those who come before God with a list of their good works will be confronted with a list of their violations of His Law—and suddenly they will realize that there is nothing they can say in their defense! Thus the Law was given that "all the world may become guilty before God . . . for by the law is the knowledge of sin."

As Paul continued in Romans to explore grace, faith, righteousness, and the Law, he acknowledged the fact that the Law of God is "holy, and the commandment holy, just and good" (Rom. 7:12). The law has great value as an expression of God's holy character and as a standard against which human beings can measure themselves. But the Law is not a blueprint we follow to become righteous or a list of steps to take to earn God's favor.

In Romans 1—3, Paul had established the fact that every human being sins. We are all sinners, and not one of us is righteous. Whenever a sinner mistakes God's Law as a list of steps to take to earn God's favor, the Law traps that person in his or her sin. No sinner can become righteous by trying to keep the Law. In fact, each time a person tries to do what the Law requires, and fails, the very Law he or she relied on condemns! Man's only hope is to find a way out from under the Law, out from under the dominion of sin.

Understanding the promise. Paul had shown that believers in Christ have been saved from God's wrath (Rom. 5:9). Believers have been justified—declared innocent—and credited with Christ's righteousness. Through faith Christians have entered a realm where grace, not Law, rules.

Yet in saying "you are not under law but under grace," God is *not* implying that Christians are free to sin or to ignore practical righteousness. Just the opposite. In promising "sin shall not have dominion over you" the Scriptures tell us that now, at last, we are free to live righteous lives! God has drawn us into a new relationship with Him. In this relationship we are not to look to the Law to help us live righteous lives, but to God's grace.

As we go on to examine other promises in Romans, we will discover how grace produces a practical righteousness that Law simply could not. It is enough at this point to understand one basic and vital truth. We are freed to live righteous lives *because we no longer try to relate to God through the Law.* For law demands that we attempt to do what is right—in our own strength. As Christians, we are now invited to rest in God's grace and to let Him produce righteousness in us.

Claiming the promise. Once again we have a promise which is already ours. In Christ we have been freed to be righteous and to do righteousness. This freedom has not come to us through the Law, but through the grace of God expressed in Jesus Christ.

Responding to the promise. Imagine a person who has been locked in a prison cell for years. Then one day the door is thrown open. Yet the prisoner behaves as if the door were still locked. Each day he paces back and forth inside the tiny cell; each night he sleeps on his narrow cot. Frequently he stands on his tiptoes, looking out the narrow window overhead to glimpse the treetops.

God's grace frees believers from the restrictions of the law.

The Christian life is like this for too many believers. They stay inside the cell of the Law, even though God in Christ has thrown open the door. They keep on struggling in their own strength to do what is right, standing on their tiptoes to glimpse a freedom they can only yearn for.

Yet all the Christian needs to do is step outside the cell and discover that above and beyond the Law there is God's grace—a grace that frees us from our limitations; a grace that enables us to become more than we could ever be on our own.

A PROMISE OF LIFE, NOW

The promise: "But if the Spirit of Him who raised Jesus from the dead dwells in you, He who raised Christ from the dead will also give life to your mortal bodies through His Spirit who dwells in you" (Rom. 8:11).

The context of the promise. In Romans 1—3 Paul has shown that all human beings are sinners and that they lack the righteousness which God requires. Yet God through Christ has justified—pronounced innocent—those who believe in the risen Christ! What's more, God has imputed Christ's righteousness to us, so that we are saved from God's wrath through Him.

But righteousness is not simply an issue of legal standing before God. Righteousness is a practical issue as well. Those whom God has pronounced righteous are now called to live righteous lives—lives which reflect honor on the Lord who has pronounced us innocent.

In beginning to address this issue in Romans 6:1–11, Paul emphasized the truth that faith unites believers with Jesus. So closely are we bonded to Jesus that in God's sight we died with Him, and we were raised with Him as well.

After promising that through our union with Jesus we would be enabled to live righteous lives, the apostle shared God's promise: "Sin shall not have dominion over you, for you are not under law but under grace" (Rom. 6:14).

Law is no longer relevant in our pursuit of righteousness! In being delivered from sin's dominion, we were also released from the authority of the Law and transported to the realm where God's grace rules.

This statement "not under law but under grace" introduces a mystery. In Romans 7 Paul shared his own experience as a believer eager to please God. Because he truly wanted to please God, he struggled to keep God's Law. But the harder he tried, the more conscious he became that something within him reacted against the Law, perverting even his most valiant efforts.

All of us have experienced this frustration. We want to sing a solo to the glory of God. But even as we praise Him, we find something deep within hoping the congregation will be impressed by our voice.

We develop a personal discipline of prayer and grow closer to the Lord. And unex-pectedly we find ourselves looking down on Christian brothers and sisters who don't rise early like we do to meet with God. Like the apostle Paul, we discover that the harder we try to live righteous lives, the more we become aware of the corrupting taint of sin.

Understanding the promise. To understand this promise, we need to understand the relationship between the Law and the heart. The Law describes not only what a person should do, but also who a person should be.

Many assume that when the Law says, "Love your neighbor," what God requires is that we help neighbors and refrain from harming them. But the real problem pointed out by the Law is that the human heart is corrupt. When the Law says, "Love your neighbor," it means *love* your neighbor. To truly fulfill the Law, we must be *moved by love* to do those things that help and *moved by love* to refrain from things that harm.

The Law does define acts which are both loving and unloving. A person intent on keeping the Law can perform the actions which the Law defines. But the Law cannot transform the heart so that the acts are true expressions of love.

Unless our actions are motivated by love, they are corrupted by selfishness. They are corrupted by a desire to earn praise from God or people, or to compensate for a sense of guilt, or by our intent to merit God's favor. What human beings have always needed is not a clearer definition of the good, but the transformation of our hearts so that we will *be* righteous. Apart from an inner transformation, our best efforts to keep the Law will fall short.

Ultimately Paul learned the secret of Christian living. Paul acknowledged his own sinfulness and mortality. He realized that no matter how hard he tried to keep the Law, his heart was corrupt and his best efforts were tainted. So Paul turned to grace and to the Holy Spirit dwelling in him.

Rather than try to become different by acting differently, the apostle relied on the Spirit to transform him within. And the Spirit's resurrection power began to flow! Without consciously trying to keep God's Law, Paul found himself moved by the Spirit to actions which fulfilled the righteous requirements of the Law (Rom. 8:2–4).

The Spirit so transforms and empowers us within that we spontaneously respond to God and others in loving, righteous ways.

Claiming the promise. What a wonderful promise this is for us to claim today. We are not called to live under the Law, measuring each action against its rules and regulations. We are called to surrender ourselves to His Holy Spirit. As we make this surrender, the Spirit's power is released within us. The Spirit who raised Jesus raises us as well, transforming us from within. And, as we respond moment by moment to the Spirit's prompting, we find ourselves living truly righteous lives.

Responding to the promise. Believers are not under law but under grace. We relate to God by relying on His Spirit rather than by trying to keep His laws. Yet there is great value in searching God's Word to understand the righteous lifestyle to which we are called. Why is this important?

First, the standards of Scripture reveal the character of God. We can come to know God better by studying His Law. Second, the standards of Scripture guard us against self-deceit. If our lives do not display the righteousness expressed in the Law, we can hardly claim—as some do—that we have been transformed!

But most importantly, as we study the Bible's revelation of righteousness in the Law and in the life of Christ, we discover our true selves. In God's Law and in His Son we see a reflection of the person we are becoming through God's grace.

When approaching Scripture in this spirit, law will no longer be a burden we have to bear. It will be a source of joy, as we realize that God's Spirit has come to dwell with us that we might become the kind of person God's Word describes.

A PROMISE OF UNIVERSAL DELIVERANCE

The promise: "The creation itself also will be delivered from the bondage of corruption into the glorious liberty of the children of God" (Rom. 8:21).

The context of the promise. God's Spirit has been given to believers to work an inner transformation. Through His grace, the righteousness lost in the Fall is being restored in us who believe. This is marvelous and wonderful. Yet our progressive transformation pales in view of what the future holds (Rom. 8:23).

Understanding the promise. Paul pointed out that the entire material creation was affected by Adam's sin, being "corrupted" and "subject to futility" (Rom. 8:20, 21). When at the Second Coming we Christians experience the "redemption of the body"—a reference to resurrection—then earth's animal and vegetable creation will be transformed as well.

A PROMISE OF "GOOD"

The promise: "We know that all things work together for good to those who love God, to those who are the called according to His purpose" (Rom. 8:28).

The context of the promise. In the last section of Romans 8, Paul summed up implications of the wonderful salvation he has described. On the basis of Christ's death, lost and helpless sinners have been declared righteous by a loving God. Those who believe have not only been declared righteous; they have been given the Holy Spirit to enable them to actually be righteous by transforming them from within.

What can we say about our relationship with such a wonderful God of grace? One thing we can say with confidence is that "all things work together for good to those who love God."

Understanding the promise. Paul does not ask us to believe that everything that happens to us *is* good. Some things that happen to us are terrible. Rather, Paul assures us that God is so great that He is able to work in any set of circumstances for our good.

There are two common words for "good" in Greek. One word, *kalos,* means beautiful, or pleasant. The other word, *agathos,* means beneficial or profitable. The word in Romans 8:28 is *agathos.* God's commitment to those who love Him is to work in and through every circumstance to our benefit.

Romans 8:29 goes on to define that "benefit." God's intent is that we should be "conformed to the image of His son." To become more like Jesus is the ultimate good. And God is able to work through all experiences we may have to make us more like our Lord.

Responding to the promise. This is a promise which God has made and confirmed. Yet it is clearly a promise to which we are expected to respond. If we slip into despair when trials come, if we doubt God's love, or if we become angry, we are far less likely to experience the good that God intends. On the other hand, if we face our trials in the calm confidence that we are surrounded by the love of God, and if we ask God to teach us what He intends us to learn, we will experience His transforming touch.

A PROMISE OF SECURITY

The promise: "For I am persuaded that neither death nor life, nor angels nor principalities nor powers, nor things present nor things to come, nor height nor depth, nor any other created thing, shall be able to separate us from the love of God which is in Christ Jesus our Lord" (Rom. 8:38, 39).

The context of the promise. In the last section of Romans 8, Paul summed up implications of the wonderful salvation he has described. Lost and helpless sinners have been declared righteous by a loving God, on the basis of Christ's death. Those who believe have not only been declared righteous; they have been given the Holy Spirit who helps them to actually be righteous by transforming them from within.

Paul made it very clear that God is for us (Rom. 8:31). We have been acquitted by God Himself; no one can now bring any charge against us (Rom. 8:33). How clear it should be to all that nothing in this universe can separate us from the love of God in Christ Jesus our Lord.

Understanding the promise. This promise is clear and its intent is unmistakable. The believer who has put his or her trust in Jesus is safe in God's love. Earlier in Romans, Paul pointed out while we were yet sinners, Christ died for us (Rom. 5:6–8). Just as surely, "When we were enemies we were reconciled to God through the death of His Son, much more, having been reconciled, we shall be saved by His life" (Rom. 8:10). If God loved us so much while we were "yet sinners," how much more must He love us now!

This passage points to two realities which should give us confidence that believers will never be separated from God's love.

First, Christ died for us when we were sinners. On the basis of Jesus' death, God has declared us innocent and credited Christ's righteousness to our account. How could we imagine that such a God would turn against us?

Second, even more significantly, it is unimaginable that Christ should have sacrificed Himself for nothing. He shed His blood to save us. Because of Calvary, we have been forgiven and Jesus' righteousness has been credited to our account. If one who has been saved by Christ's blood could later be lost, Jesus' death would have been ineffective. And this is unimaginable.

A PROMISE OF AVAILABLE SALVATION

The promise: "If you confess with your mouth the Lord Jesus and believe in your heart that God has raised Him from the dead, you will be saved" (Rom. 10:9).

The context of the promise. In Romans 10:6–9, Paul quoted Deuteronomy 30:12–14.

That passage emphasizes the availability of God's message. Here the point is the same. Jew and Gentile alike have heard the gospel offer, and each is invited to respond.

Understanding the promise. The inclusion of "confess with your mouth" along with "believe in your heart" has disturbed some. Isn't salvation by faith alone? In mentioning confess along with believe, Paul stays with the "mouth" and "heart" pattern set in Deuteronomy 30:14. How do the two work together?

To "confess" is to agree with God, to say the same thing He says. The believing community is a confessional fellowship: we bear witness to Jesus Christ by confessing Him with our mouths. But the confession originates in a total trust in the God who raised Jesus from the dead. We are saved by faith. Then faith moves us, together with the whole church, to confess Jesus as Lord.

Claiming the promise. We claim the promise of salvation by heartfelt trust in Christ.

Responding to the promise. A true and vital Christianity is confessional. We join with other believers to confess Jesus as Lord publicly. We are not saved because we confess Christ; we confess Christ because we are saved.

A PROMISE OF ENABLEMENT

The promise: "Who are you to judge another's servant? To his own master he stands or falls. Indeed, he will be made to stand, for God is able to make him stand" (Rom. 14:4).

The context of the promise. God's gift of righteousness is to be expressed in relationships within the Christian community. In Romans 14, Paul dealt with an important relationship issue. He warned us against trying to impose our convictions concerning "doubtful things" on other believers.

A "doubtful thing" is any practice not specifically forbidden in Scripture, which some Christians view as a moral issue while other Christians do not. These doubtful things may pose a danger to the unity of the Christian community—a unity which may destroyed by criticism and condemnation.

How are we to deal with doubtful things? Paul reminded believers that Jesus is Lord. He taught that we are not to try to impose our convictions on others or to condemn those whose convictions differ from our own. By giving each other the freedom to respond to Jesus as Lord rather than insisting on conformity, we maintain unity in the body of Christ. We also help others mature as Christians by expecting them to seek God's will for themselves on those matters in which we differ.

Understanding the promise. Paul reminded us that each of us is a servant. Jesus is the Master and Lord of each Christian. What will happen if we stop trying to lord it over our fellow Christians by imposing our standards in a matter of doubtful things? God's promise is that "he [our brother or sister] will be made to stand, for God is able to make him stand."

That is, God is fully able to function as Lord in our brother's life. He does not need us to play God. As Lord, God is able to make our brother stand before Him, as one who will do God's will.

Responding to the promise. There are two ways in which we are to respond to this promise.

First, while we are to listen to the counsel of Christian brothers and sisters concerning doubtful things, we are to relate to Jesus as Lord. We are not to be governed by others' convictions, even though we may weigh them. Ultimately we are responsible to Jesus for what we do, and we are to look to Jesus to reveal His will for us.

Second, while we may be concerned over choices made by a Christian brother or sister, we are not to try to impose our convictions on him or her. If we feel led, we may express our concern. But we are never to try to coerce or force our views on others. Instead, we are to love others and encourage them to be responsive to Jesus as Lord. And then we must honor their decision, whatever it may be.

Jesus is able to make each of us stand. We are to honor Him as Lord in our own lives and in the lives of others.

A PROMISE OF FINAL VICTORY

The promise: "And the God of peace will crush Satan under your feet shortly" (Rom. 16:20).

The context of the promise. The life of grace and love which Paul described in Romans is confronted at every point by our faulty understanding of grace as well as by Satan. As we grow in grace, God will transform our understanding, that we may learn to rely on Him only. Ultimately—shortly—God will crush Satan under our feet.

Understanding the promise. God's final victory has already been won on Calvary. Satan has been judged and sentenced. Before we know it, that sentence will be carried out, and Jesus' promise of total transformation will be fully realized.

CHAPTER 18

PROMISES TO A PROBLEM CONGREGATION:

GOD'S PROMISES TO THE CORINTHIANS

1, 2 Corinthians

The apostle Paul spent about three years in Corinth before moving on to evangelize other areas. His subsequent letters to the Corinthians revealed a troubled church. The Corinthian Christians had numerous spiritual gifts. Yet they were divided—by allegiance to various leaders and by doctrinal disputes as well as by confusion over a number of issues of Christian living. In fact, Paul's first letter to the Corinthians was organized around a series of church problems, with the apostle's teaching on each issue introduced by the Greek phrase *peri dei*, "now concerning."

Paul's first letter to the Corinthians helped the church resolve a number of its problems. But some believers in Corinth continued to resist Paul's authoritative teaching. Paul's second letter was a classic "apology"—a defense of his apostolic authority as well as an explanation of the principles underlying his ministry.

Yet within these epistles, written to confront sins and correct misunderstandings in an early Christian congregation, are wonderful promises which we can claim today.

GOD'S PROMISES IN 1 CORINTHIANS

A PROMISE OF PERSEVERANCE

The promise: [God] "will also confirm you to the end, that you may be blameless in the day of our Lord Jesus Christ" (1 Cor. 1:8).

The context of the promise. This promise is woven into a long sentence expressing Paul's thanks to God for the grace He has shown the Corinthians (1 Cor. 1:4–8). In spite of the fact that the Corinthian church was torn by dissension and far from blameless, Paul remained confident concerning these Christians. His confidence was certainly not based on their behavior. Paul was confident that God was able to accomplish His purposes in the saved (see 2 Cor. 5:15, 16).

Understanding the promise. The key to this promise is the word *confirm*, used twice in this long sentence. One authority points out,

The Greek word for "confirmed" is *bebaios*, which means "sure, reliable, and certain." This word became part of the legal language of the NT world. It not only meant that a transaction or promise was

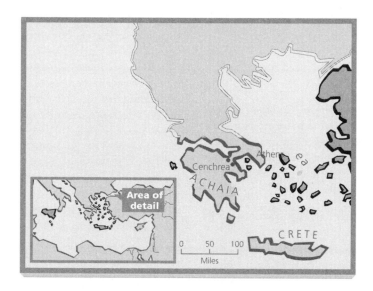

valid but also implied a guarantee—some legally binding confirmation of intentions (The *Expository Dictionary of Bible Words,* 1985, p. 185).

In the past God had confirmed Paul's testimony to Christ by saving the Corinthians. In the future, when Christ returns (1 Cor. 1:7), God's present guarantee of salvation to believers would surely be confirmed. The Corinthians would appear before Christ and be found blameless (1 Cor. 1:8).

Paul's use of legal terminology as well as the reference to Jesus' return explains this promise. Paul made no guarantee that the Corinthians would resolve all their problems. He made no guarantee that they would achieve godliness before Christ returned. But he did promise that God would treat the Corinthians as blameless—because of what Jesus had done for them.

When Jesus returns, the Corinthians will *be* blameless. And so will we.

Responding to the promise. The promise God made to the Corinthians is for all believers. We will also be counted blameless in "the day of our Lord Jesus Christ." This certainty moves true believers to want to live blamelessly in the present. The awesome love of God awakens love in our hearts and makes us want to please Him in all we do (see 2 Cor. 5:14).

It is striking that Paul should express this promise at the beginning of his letter to the Corinthians. This church was so torn by strife and dissension that Paul called them carnal, fleshly rather than spiritual (1 Cor. 3:1). But rather than threaten or warn, Paul chose to reassure. Paul knew, and we need to remember, that only love for the God who counts us blameless can move us to live blameless lives.

A PROMISE OF VICTORY OVER TEMPTATION

The promise: "No temptation has overtaken you except such as is common to man; but God is faithful, who will not allow you to be tempted beyond what you are able, but with the temptation will also make the way of escape, that you may be able to bear it" (1 Cor. 10:13).

The context of the promise. Paul had briefly reviewed the experience of the Exodus generation, noting that most gave in to various temptations and suffered terrible consequences. They lusted after evil things, became idolaters, committed sexual immorality, and complained. And they died in the wilderness. Their experience should give us pause, so Paul warned, "Let him who thinks he stands take heed lest he fall" (1 Cor. 10:12).

The apostle did not want his readers to feel doomed each time they were tempted. In fact, Paul wants all Christians to know that we will be tempted—but we need not surrender to our temptations.

Understanding the promise. God does not exempt any believer from temptation. Nor does God intervene to keep us from surrendering to our temptations. Rather, God makes it possible for us not to surrender to temptation by providing "the way of escape."

Temptation. The Greek word for temptation in this passage is *peirasmos,* meaning "trial." A temptation is not a sin in itself (James 1:12). In fact, temptations can be a source of blessing, for we are strengthened spiritually when we successfully resist them. James argued that we are to see situations in which we are tempted as a good gift from God, through which He intends us to be blessed rather than overcome (James 1:13–17).

Common to man. All human beings are susceptible to temptation. The James passage cited above makes it clear that the source of temptation is our fallen human nature. As all human beings share this nature, all people experience the same kinds of temptations.

We have a tendency to excuse giving in to temptations. We assume that *our* temptations are so much worse, or so much greater, than those experienced by others. First Corinthians 10:13 reminds us that everyone shares our human nature and our human limitations. The temptations which we claim are overwhelming are actually quite ordinary. Everyone experiences them.

God is faithful. As Christians, we never face our temptations alone. We have a relationship with a faithful God, who is with us and who never permits us to be tempted beyond what we are able to bear. Simply put, we do not *have* to give in. We are called to master our temptations—not to be mastered by them.

The way of escape. The Greek text has the definite article "the," although grammatically the phrase may be translated "a way of escape." This way of escape is expressed in the next verse: "flee" (1 Cor. 10:14).

Too often temptations are treated as playthings. We keep them around to entertain us, pretending that we have no intention of giving in. We check out the dessert tray, telling ourselves we only want to look. We watch a sitcom in spite of its immoral assumptions, thinking that we can't be corrupted because we know the difference between right and wrong. This is no way to escape the corrupting influence of the temptations that are common to human beings. God's prescription for escaping our temptations is to escape them by "fleeing," or getting away from them.

Claiming the promise. This is one of those promises which we have to claim. He who knows our limits will not permit us to be tempted beyond our capacity to resist. And God does provide the way to escape temptations. But we can hardly toy with a temptation and then complain that we just weren't able to resist. God's promise concerning temptations is conditioned on our readiness to acknowledge temptations and to avoid them as much as possible.

A PROMISE OF RELEASE

The promise: "For if we would judge ourselves, we would not be judged" (1 Cor. 11:31).

The context of the promise. This promise was given following a discussion of the Lord's Supper. Some factions in the Corinthian church had changed the Lord's Supper from a commemoration of Christ's death into a banquet, like those associated with the pagan deities they once worshiped. It was common at such meals to serve better food and drink to the more important guests while serving poorer food and drink to those lower on the social scale. Paul reminded the Corinthians that the Eucharist is a celebration commemorating the death of Christ, using bread and wine to symbolize His bruised body and shed blood.

The Lord's Supper, or Eucharist, commemorates Christ's death on the Cross.

Paul went on to warn the Corinthians that the church was being disciplined with weakness and sickness because they failed to discern the Lord's body when celebrating communion. The reference to the Lord's body was to the church—the living body of Christ on earth. By turning the Eucharist into a banquet in which individuals were treated according to their social position, the Corinthians were denying a basic reality. The body of Christ is one, and every member is valued and significant.

To avoid God's further discipline, the Corinthians needed to judge themselves and change their practices to reflect the truth of the gospel. When they did this, Paul affirmed, God would no longer need to judge them.

Understanding the promise. The promise, "If we would judge ourselves we would not be judged," was made to the Corinthians. It related specifically to the way in which they practiced the Lord's Supper. Yet the promise expresses a basic principle of life with the Lord which is applicable to all. If we would exercise discernment, sense how our behavior is out of harmony with God's truth, and then correct ourselves, God would not have to discipline us. By judging ourselves, we would avoid the need for correction.

Responding to the promise. Self-examination can be a painful thing. Yet so many of the great saints of the past have written of the benefits of self-examination, confession, and repentance. If we search out our own sins and bring them to Jesus for forgiveness, He will bless us indeed.

THE PROMISE OF SPIRITUAL GIFTS

The promise: "The manifestation of the Spirit is given to each one for the profit of all" (1 Cor. 12:7).

The context of the promise. The Corinthians were overly impressed by the more obvious and noticeable gifts of the Holy Spirit. They assumed that those who possessed such gifts as speaking in tongues were more spiritual than those with more ordinary gifts. Paul took up this issue in 1 Corinthians 12—14.

Paul introduced this section by saying, "Now concerning spiritual *gifts*" (1 Cor. 12:1). The word *gifts* is not in the Greek text, and the verse should be rendered "now concerning *spirituality*." In these chapters, Paul showed the relationship of the gifts of the Spirit to spirituality (ch. 12), identified the marks of true spirituality (ch. 13), and showed how spiritual gifts are to be used in the church (ch. 14).

Understanding the promise. "The manifestation of the Spirit is given to each one" is a stunning gospel promise. God the Holy Spirit expresses His presence in the life of each believer through one or more gifts.

Manifestations of the Spirit. Spiritual gifts are manifestations—expressions or evidence—of the presence of the Holy Spirit in the lives of believers. First Corinthians 12 reminds us that there are many different gifts, some supernatural, some natural and ordinary. Yet each gift is an expression or manifestation of the Holy Spirit's work.

Given to each one. Spiritual gifts are given to each believer. While gifts differ, each one is a manifestation of the Holy Spirit, who is present in every Christian. The Holy Spirit expresses Himself through every gift, and each believer possesses the Spirit. The possession of a particular spiritual gift is not evidence of a special closeness to the Lord.

For the profit of all. Spiritual gifts are not given so that the Christians can identify the "spiritual" among them. Spiritual gifts are given to benefit the entire body of Christ. As each person exercises his or her gift, others are encouraged and built up in the faith.

While the promise as stated was part of Paul's teaching intended to correct the Corinthians' misunderstanding of spirituality, it is a wonderful promise for us. God has given each of us His Spirit, and the Holy Spirit *will* manifest His presence through some gift that he has given us. As the Spirit expresses Himself through each of us, others in Christ's body will grow in the faith.

Responding to the promise. This is another of those special promises that become ours when we trust Jesus. The Spirit has come, and He will manifest His presence in the gifts He gives to each of us.

Yet to fully realize the potential of what God has promised, we need to take several important steps. First, if the Spirit is to minister to "all" through us, we need to be active in some local church. Second, if the Spirit is to manifest Himself through us, we need to build closer personal relationships with other believers. We need to be *connected,* that we might be channels through which the Spirit ministers.

If we become active in our church, build close relationships with other believers, and

seek connectedness, we have God's promise that the Holy Spirit *will* minister through us.

A PROMISE OF TRANSFORMATION

The promise: "Behold, I tell you a mystery: We shall not all sleep, but we shall all be changed; in a moment, in the twinkling of an eye, at the last trumpet. For the trumpet will sound, and the dead will be raised incorruptible, and we shall be changed" (1 Cor. 15:51, 52).

The context of the promise. First Corinthians 15 is Scripture's most detailed exposition on resurrection. Christ's bodily resurrection established the doctrine. That event, in harmony with the Old Testament Scriptures and confirmed by many eyewitnesses, showed that resurrection is a reality. And Christ's resurrection was proof that while Adam's sin condemned human beings to death, Jesus' sacrifice restores to life. The believer's dead body

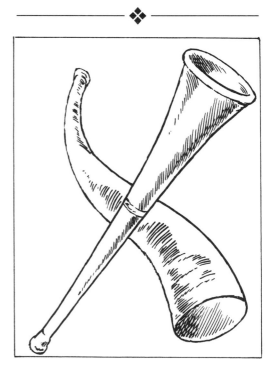

"The last trumpet . . . will sound, . . . and we shall be changed."

will be replaced by a glorious resurrection body, spiritual and incorruptible, recreated on the model of Christ's resurrection body.

Understanding the promise. As Paul's great defense of the resurrection closed, he let us in on a "mystery." In the New Testament, a mystery [Greek, *mysterion*] was an aspect of God's eternal plan which was not revealed in the Old Testament, but is now made known in Christ. Here the "mystery" is that not every believer will experience death. This is the meaning of the phrase, "We shall not all sleep." Paul tells us that believers who are alive when Jesus returns will be transformed and given their resurrection bodies without having to experience death.

This event is described in more detail in 1 Thessalonians 4:15–18:

For this we say to you by the word of the Lord, that we who are alive and remain until the coming of the Lord will by no means precede those who are asleep. For the Lord Himself will descend from heaven with a shout, with the voice of an archangel, and with the trumpet of God. And the dead in Christ will rise first. Then we who are alive and remain shall be caught up together with them in the clouds to meet the Lord in the air. And thus we shall always be with the Lord. Therefore comfort one another with these words.

Responding to the promise. This is one of the many wonderful promises which become ours when we receive Christ as Savior. There is nothing more we have to do to claim it as our own.

But how powerfully the promise speaks to us. Each day we can look forward to the return of Christ and the transformation it will bring. And, when loved ones die, we can comfort ourselves with the knowledge that when Jesus comes we and our loved ones will be reunited forever.

A PROMISE OF REWARD

The promise: "Therefore, my beloved brethren, be steadfast, immovable, always abounding in the work of the Lord, knowing

Work done for the Lord—such as visiting the sick—will not be in vain.

that your labor is not in vain in the Lord" (1 Cor. 15:58).

The context of the promise. This is the final verse in 1 Corinthians 15, the Bible's great chapter on resurrection. One day death will be swallowed up in Christ's victory, and all His own will "put on immortality."

Understanding the promise. This promise is found in the final phrase of this verse: "Your labor is not in vain in the Lord."

There are many goals toward which people work that are truly meaningless. A person can win a vast fortune, only to leave it all at death. A person can develop his or her talents and gain fame. Yet few of our earthly accomplishments will be remembered. But what we do to serve and glorify God is never meaningless. Our labor for Him is never in vain, but it echoes on throughout eternity.

When believers are raised at history's end, we will see the results of our labor for the

Lord reflected in those around us. And God will not forget our labor of love. Second Corinthians 5:10 reminds us that "we must all appear before the judgment seat of Christ, that each one may receive the things done in the body, according to what he has done, whether good or bad."

The "judgment seat" was the *bema*—a raised platform in hellenistic cities from which public proclamations were made. While evil deeds were denounced from the *bema,* honors and praise were also proclaimed for the whole city to hear.

Honors and praise for believers are referred to in 1 Corinthians 15:58. Our labor is not in vain in the Lord. In the day of Christ, all that we have done for Him will be acknowledged. In the words of the apostle, "then each one's praise will come from God" (1 Cor. 4:5).

Responding to the promise. The only rewards with lasting value are those given by the Lord. This realization leads us to set new priorities. If we look ahead eagerly to resurrection and to eternity, we will commit ourselves joyfully to labor for the Lord.

GOD'S PROMISES IN 2 CORINTHIANS

A PROMISE OF PROGRESSIVE TRANSFORMATION

The promise: "But we all, with unveiled face, beholding as in a mirror the glory of the Lord, are being transformed into the same image from glory to glory, just as by the Spirit of the Lord" (2 Cor. 3:18).

The context of the promise. In 2 Corinthians 3, the apostle Paul compared ministry under the Mosaic Covenant with ministry under the New Covenant instituted by Christ. (See the first section of this book for a discussion of these covenants.) Paul pointed out that under the old covenant God's ways were written in stone. But now God is writing His ways on the hearts of living believers. Surely, the apostle argued, the ministry of the New Covenant is more glorious than that of the old covenant.

To illustrate the implications of this truth, Paul reminded his readers that when Moses left the presence of the Lord, his face was radiant. Moses put a veil over his face, not to protect the Israelites, but because this radiance gradually faded away. Moses did not want the Israelites to see the fading glory, "the end of what was passing away" (2 Cor. 3:13).

Understanding the promise. Paul contrasted the Christian's experience with that of Moses. As the Holy Spirit works in our hearts, we become more and more like Jesus! The radiance that marked Moses after being in the presence of God gradually faded away. But now the Lord is *in us,* and we are always in His presence! As a result we are being transformed, from glory to increasing glory.

Responding to the promise. The difference to which Paul draws our attention has practical implications. Paul says that we "use great boldness of speech." Unlike Moses, who hid himself from others, we open our lives to our fellow believers, to live with them in honesty and transparency.

How can we do this? Won't others sense our flaws and weaknesses? Yes. But we can risk honesty because we know that the Holy Spirit is in the process of transforming us. We know that others will see Jesus in us—not because we are perfect but because our imperfections are gradually being transformed. Jesus is displayed in the *process of transformation* that is taking place.

What a burden this promise of transformation removes from our shoulders. We do not have to pretend to be "perfect Christians." We do not have to hide, for fear that others will think less of Jesus because of our failures. Instead we can be our real selves with others, confident that the Holy Spirit is at work in our lives. What a comfort to know that Jesus is seen by others in the changes He makes in us over time.

THE PROMISE OF RESURRECTION

The promise: "We know that if this earthly house, this tent, is destroyed, we have a building from God, a house not made with hands, eternal in the heavens" (2 Cor. 5:1).

The context of the promise. In the last part of 2 Corinthians 4, Paul reviewed the sufferings and the dangers which marked his missionary service. Death seemed near on several occasions. In 2 Corinthians 5, the apostle addressed the comfort available in the Lord at such times.

The first source of comfort is the promise of a spiritual body (2 Cor. 5:1). The second source of comfort is the Holy Spirit, who is God's pledge of our ultimate transformation (2 Cor. 5:4, 5). The third source of comfort is the realization that death takes us from the realm where we walk by faith to that dimension where we walk by sight. Then we will live in Jesus' presence (2 Cor. 5:6).

Understanding the promise. Some people have assumed from 2 Corinthians 5:2–4 that Paul expected God to provide believers with a temporary body between death and resurrection. It is better to understand his remark about being "unclothed" as a rejection of the view that the "resurrection" is spiritual and that it took place at baptism (cf. 2 Tim. 2:17, 18).

It is also possible that Paul was rejecting the assumption of others that after death human beings existed as disembodied souls.

What Paul looked forward to—what God had promised—was a resurrection body that would be like Jesus' body.

Responding to the promise. When we trust Jesus, we are guaranteed a future resurrection. So this is hardly a promise we need to claim. Rather, this is a promise which comforts us as we approach death. Through most of our lives, our hope is focused on the return of Christ. But when death approaches, what a comfort it is to know that laying down this earthly body is a prelude to taking on the immortal body that awaits us in Christ.

THE PROMISE OF A NEW CREATION

The promise. "Therefore, if anyone is in Christ, he is a new creation; old things have passed away; behold, all things have become new" (2 Cor. 5:17).

The context of the promise. The apostle Paul was writing to a troubled congregation, some of whose members still resisted Paul's apostolic authority. In this second letter, Paul defended his authority and explained the spiritual principles which undergirded his ministry.

In 2 Corinthians 3:18, Paul explained that the Holy Spirit was even then at work transforming believers into the image of Christ. Understanding this amazing truth, Paul did not "look at the things which are seen, but at the things which are not seen" (2 Cor. 4:18). What we see is always changing. But the unseen is eternal.

One of the unseen realities on which the apostle counted is that, if anyone is in Christ, he or she truly is a new creation.

The Corinthians, like immature Christians today, appeared to give little evidence of Christ's transforming work in their lives. But anyone who has trusted Jesus as Savior does have Christ in the heart. And Christ is there to work the transformation which He died to make possible.

For this reason, the apostle no longer viewed fellow believers from a human point of view, based on what could be observed in their lives. Instead, Paul looked to the unseen but eternal realities. He saw fellow believers as new creations in Christ. He was convinced that, by God's grace and in time, the immature and the unresponsive would respond to God's love, becoming the Christians they could be in Him.

Understanding the promise. The promise of the new creation is that "old things have passed away; behold, all things have become new" (2 Cor. 5:17). With Jesus in our lives, the grip of sin which once made us helpless has been broken. With Jesus in our lives, everything has become new. Life is filled with possibilities and rich with potential meaning.

Claiming the promise. In one sense, the promise of the new creation has already been fulfilled. When we trusted Jesus, the old was put behind us and everything did become new. Yet you and I, like the Corinthians, have a choice. We can go on living in the old way, moved by old passions and driven by the old values. Or, we can open our lives to the Lord, letting Him give us new desires and engrave His values on our hearts.

The sooner we choose to live as the new creations that we are, the sooner we will experience the joy and meaning that Jesus is eager to bring to our lives.

PROMISES OF RELATIONSHIP EXPERIENCED

The promises:

I will dwell in them
And walk among them.
I will be their God,
And they shall be My people.

Therefore,

Come out from among them
And be separate, says the Lord.
Do not touch what is unclean,
and I will receive you.

I will be a Father to you,
And you shall be My sons and daughters,
Says the Lord Almighty (2 Cor. 6:16–18).

The context of the promises. These verses are a mosaic drawn from a number of Old Testament texts, including Leviticus 26:11, 12, Isaiah 52:11, Ezekiel 20:34, 41, and 2 Samuel 7:14, 27, with possibly Isaiah 43:6. Thus they have an Old Testament as well as New Testament context.

The Old Testament context. The Old Testament mosaic is drawn from passages which encouraged complete commitment to God and separation from idolaters and those whose way of life is "unclean." Such a commitment to the

Lord brings His approval and an experience of His presence.

The New Testament context. This is established in the exhortation expressed in 2 Corinthians 6:14a: "Do not be unequally yoked together with unbelievers." While unequal yoking is not defined here, the series of questions that follows in 6:14b and 15 makes Paul's concern clear. Paul was concerned about any close relationship with unbelievers which might lead to compromising Christian standards or Christian witness.

While application of the principle of unequal yoking to specific situations is left up to the Spirit's leading of individuals, the concept is simple. We are to link our lives only to those who share our Christian standards and goals.

Understanding the promise. The issue raised here is not one of salvation but of Christian experience. We do not *become* sons and daughters by separating from unbelievers. Paul made this clear when he wrote, "You are the temple of the living God" (2 Cor. 6:16). What Paul was concerned about is the quality of our lives as Christians, and the impact that being unequally yoked can have on our relationship with the Lord. As we maintain an undivided commitment to the Lord, we will experience His presence, know His welcome, and be treated as dearly loved sons and daughters.

Claiming the promise. This promise is conditional, dependent on our refusal to be unequally yoked to unbelievers. This verse has traditionally been applied to marriage and business partnerships. However, the passage itself simply states the principle and leaves it up to us for application. For Paul, this seems to involve no great risk.

We Christians have been given the Holy Spirit. He is our Comforter and our Guide. Whenever we consider an enterprise which ties us to unbelievers, we need to seek the Spirit's leading as to whether this principle applies.

Responding to the promise. It is important to balance our response to this principle by being sensitive to another principle. In 1 Corinthians 5:9–13, Paul warned against an overreaction to his warning against association with sinners. Paul told the Corinthians that he was teaching about associating with Christians who were living in sin. Paul did not call for separation from *unbelievers* who were living in sin.

Christians have to associate with sinners, for otherwise we would be unable to live in this sinful world. But even more significantly, a Christian should "keep company with" such sinners, not to judge but to share Christ with them.

So there is a balance to maintain in applying the principle of unequal yoking. We are not to cut off all contact with the unsaved. But we are to avoid partnering with them in any activity which might lead us to compromise our commitment to Jesus Christ.

A PROMISE OF FINANCIAL PROVISION

The promise: "And God is able to make all grace abound toward you, that you, always having all sufficiency in all things, may have an abundance for every good work" (2 Cor. 9:8).

The context of the promise. Chapters 8 and 9 of 2 Corinthians establish New Testament principles of giving. These contrast with principles of giving taught in the Old Testament. In Old Testament times, the believer, who lived on land God had provided for His people, was to pay a tenth of his produce to the Lord. This was "rent," and it was used to support temple worship, to support the Levites and priests who led in worship, and to meet the needs of the poor. The Israelites were also encouraged to bring freewill offerings to God as an expression of their thankfulness.

The New Testament does not require Christians to give a tithe. It calls on us to view all that we have as God's and to respond generously to meet the needs of fellow believers.

Since there were no church buildings or professional clergy in the first century, there is nothing in the New Testament about giving to support "the church." People gave to support itinerant teachers and to aid Christians who were in financial need. Guidelines for this kind of giving are developed in 2 Corinthians 8 and 9. These guidelines include:

"They first gave themselves" (8:5). God wants us—not our money. We are to commit ourselves to the Lord. The giving of money is to grow out of our heart commitment to Him.

"You know the grace of our Lord Jesus Christ" (8:9). Christ is the model of giving, for He gave His all, becoming poor that we might be enriched. Giving is to be a love response to the love that Jesus has showered upon us.

"If there is first a willing mind" (8:12). God does not want any gifts which we give grudgingly. God does not care about the size of our gifts. What God cares about is our heart's desire, the willingness to give awakened by the realization of God's great love for us. While it is true that the amount of our giving will reflect our love, the willingness—the "want to"—comes first with God.

"By an equality" (8:14). In New Testament times, people gave to meet the needs of fellow believers. In fact, the Greek word for giving in 2 Corinthians is *koinonia,* "sharing." The underlying thought is that when we are able, we share with those in need. A time may come when we are in need, and others will then share with us. The goal of giving is a healthy body of Christ, equipped with everything needed to carry out God's will.

"He who sows sparingly will also reap sparingly" (9:6). While God does not *require* giving, He does reward it. A lack of generosity on our part limits the reward we will receive when Jesus returns.

"As he purposes in his heart" (9:7). Each of us is free to decide what to give. In place of the required tithe, God gives us the freedom and the responsibility of setting our own standard.

Giving should be an expression of love.

Whatever that standard is, it must be one that we choose freely, so that our giving will be an expression of love rather than necessity.

Understanding the promise. God's promise of abounding grace was integrated into Paul's discussion of giving. Church leaders may fear to preach the freedom these chapters extend out of fear that Sunday offerings will fall off. Some Christians are hesitant to give generously, fearful that they will be unable to meet their own needs. The promise in 2 Corinthians 9:8 is that God is able. He has abundant grace, and is able to supply what we need so that we always have "all sufficiency in all things."

Claiming God's promise. In Malachi, God challenged His people bring all the tithes into His storehouse: "Try me now in this" (Mal. 3:10). God challenged the Jews and promised to open the windows of heaven and pour out blessings on them.

This New Testament promise echoes this same theme. If we take God at His word and express our trust and love by giving generously, the Lord will see that we have the abundance we need to continue to give "for every good work."

Responding to the promise. In our churches we respond to God's promise of sufficiency by teaching New Testament principles of giving. In our personal lives we respond to God's promise of sufficiency by taking Him at His word and giving generously out of love for our Lord.

A PROMISE OF POWER

The promise: "My grace is sufficient for you, for My strength is made perfect in weakness" (2 Cor. 12:9).

The context of the promise. In 2 Corinthians, the apostle Paul defended his apostolic authority and laid out foundational principles of New Covenant ministry. In chapter 12 Paul shared a personal experience. He was once given a revelation so awesome that there was a danger he might be "exalted above measure." To protect Paul from pride, God permitted Satan to oppress him with a "thorn in the flesh."

The nature of this "thorn in the flesh" has been debated throughout the Christian era. Most scholars now believe that Paul suffered from some sort of physical disability. This view is supported by the association of Satan and demons with physical illness as reflected in the Gospels.

As for Paul's "thorn," a variety of illnesses have been suggested. These range from malaria to a disfiguring eye disease to a speech impediment. Any of these disabilities would help to explain the contempt for Paul expressed by some of the Corinthians, who complained that his "bodily presence is weak, and his speech contemptible" (2 Cor. 10:10; see also 2 Cor. 11:21).

When he was stricken with his thorn in the flesh, Paul turned to God for relief. In spite of Paul's repeated prayers, God turned down his request. Instead the Lord gave Paul the promise quoted in 1 Corinthians 12:9.

Understanding the promise. Rather than remove Paul's thorn, God promised Paul His grace. God also stated a basic spiritual principle. His strength is made perfect in our weakness.

To be "made perfect" is to be fulfilled, to be given full expression. Our weakness clears the way for God's strength to be given its fullest expression. Paul not only accepted God's "no"; he even rejoiced in it. Paul would take pleasure in weaknesses of every sort, since when he was weak he was actually strong!

The paradoxical principle expressed in God's promise to Paul undergirds all ministry. When we see ourselves as strong, we tend to rely on ourselves rather than the Lord. God alone is able to work miracles in the hearts of human beings. When we see ourselves as weak, we rely on Him. Thus our weakness opens channels in our lives through which God's power can flow.

There is another reason why our weaknesses enable God to express His strength. When others see us as strong, they tend to credit us with what God accomplishes through us. Paul was not ashamed that his Corinthians critics viewed him as weak. If they did, it had to be clear even to them that whatever Paul did was due to God's work through him. Thus God was given the glory due Him, and Paul's position as a servant of God was authenticated.

How fascinating that the very weaknesses which the Corinthians pointed out was in fact a powerful confirmation of the apostolic authority which the same Corinthians rejected!

Responding to the promise. When we understand the paradox, we are freed from fear of our own inadequacy. We *are* inadequate. Far from letting our weaknesses keep us from any ministry, awareness of our weakness should encourage us to step out in faith. In our weakness we will rely on the Lord. And as we rely on Him, God's strength will be displayed in us.

PROMISES TO YOUNG
CHURCHES:

THE OTHER EPISTLES OF PAUL
Galatians—Titus

GOD'S PROMISES IN GALATIANS

The book of Galatians contrasts grace and law, faith and works. Paul shows in this epistle that even as a person is saved by faith, so faith is the secret to living a Christian life.

In Galatians as in Romans, Paul looked back to God's Old Testament covenants, showing that the promise principle undergirding them was in complete harmony with His gospel of salvation and sanctification by faith. Specific reference to the Old Testament covenants is made in Galatians 3:7–29.

A PROMISE OF FREEDOM

The promise: "Walk in the Spirit, and you shall not fulfill the lust of the flesh" (Gal. 5:16).

The context of the promise. Paul had argued powerfully that a Christian is not under the law (Gal. 4) and must assert his or her freedom from the law. But this raises a question. Doesn't such liberty mean lawlessness? Won't such "freedom" lead to sin?

Paul's answer was to depict the Christian life as a struggle between the flesh and Spirit.

Here *the flesh* is not the physical body. Theologically, *the flesh* represents our sin nature—a nature that was corrupted and twisted in Adam's fall and which is our inheritance from him. The flesh is the source of such sins as "adultery, fornication, uncleanness, lewdness, idolatry, sorcery, hatred, contention, jealousies, outbursts of wrath, selfish ambitions, dissensions, heresies, envy, murders, drunkenness, revelries, and the like" (Gal. 5:19–21).

Opposed to the flesh is the Holy Spirit. While the flesh is the source of sin, the Spirit energizes the Christian's new nature to produce a totally different kind of fruit. The fruit produced by the Spirit is "love, joy, peace, longsuffering, kindness, goodness, faithfulness, gentleness, self-control" (Gal. 5:22, 23).

As for the law, it condemns the sins produced by the flesh. But the law has nothing to say against love, kindness, or goodness. This is the reason why being free from the law holds no threat for believers. The life of the Christian who walks in the Spirit is filled with the fruit which the Spirit produces—not with sins.

Understanding the promise. The Christian life is frequently characterized in Scripture as a "walk" or way of life (cf. Acts 14:16; 21:24;

Galatia and Surrounding Regions

Rom. 6:4). Thus, to "walk in the Spirit" means to make it our habit to seek and be responsive to the leading of the Holy Spirit. As we take our cue from the Spirit and rely on Him, God promises that we will not fulfill the "lusts of the flesh."

In our society, "lust" is a sexual term. But as used in the New Testament, the Greek word refers to all the motives, desires, and cravings of the sinful human nature. God does not promise that we will no longer feel sinful desires or crave sinful things after we become Christians.

He does promise that if we are responsive to the Holy Spirit in our daily walk, our lives will not be characterized by sin but by a very different fruit. When we produce the fruit of the Spirit, the law will be irrelevant.

Claiming the promise. God will not force us to live holy, happy lives. God's promise of a life in which sins find no room for expression is conditional. We choose between walking in the Spirit and responding to the prompting of our sin nature. When we choose to walk in the Spirit, we truly become free.

A PROMISE OF RELEASE FROM LAW (*Galatians 5:18*)

(See the discussion of Gal. 5:16, above.)

A PROMISE OF FUTURE REWARD

The promise: "And let us not grow weary while doing good, for in due season we shall reap if we do not lose heart" (Gal. 6:9).

The context of the promise. Sometimes living the Christian life seems thankless. Other people seem to have all the fun or make all the money. Too often we seem to have all the trials and troubles. But the apostle Paul wrote, "Do not be deceived, God is not mocked; for whatever a man sows, that he will also reap" (Gal. 6:7).

This principle operates in every life. The person who lives in the flesh—motivated by sinful desires—will ultimately receive what his way of life deserves. And the person who lives in the Spirit—eager to please and respond to God—will eventually receive what his way of life deserves as well.

The problem for some is that the promised rewards are in the future, so they seem unreal. It is easy for the believer to become discouraged and "grow weary" in doing good. And it is also easy for those who live in the flesh to ridicule the notion of repayment for their way of life.

A farmer spent every Sunday working his fields. He harvested a bumper crop, and his barns were full. That fall he wrote a letter to the editor of the local newspaper. He pointed to his prosperity, ridiculing those who had taken Sunday off to honor the Lord. If there really were a God, he wrote, his fields wouldn't have produced such bountiful crops. The editor printed his letter, with a brief comment of his own: "God doesn't necessarily collect his debts in October."

Understanding the promise. God reminds us that "in due season we shall reap." God doesn't promise His people prosperity here on earth. But ultimately, those who have chosen to live for the Lord will be richly rewarded.

This general promise for all Christians is conditional. If we are to reap, we must sow. And if we sow, we will surely reap.

Responding to the promise. Young children don't understand the concept of delayed gratification. As they toddle through a grocery store with Mom or Dad, they point to candy and demand it *now.* But as children grow older, they generally learn the value of delayed gratification. We can't have everything we want "now." God asks all of us to delay the gratification of some desire because, as in the case of sex and marriage, delay is right and best for us.

Whether we respond to the promise in Galatians 6:9 depends on our willingness to live in hope of a future gratification, which is long delayed. The rewards God promises us may never be possessed in this life. No wonder Paul warned us against losing heart or growing weary in doing good. Only the Christian who has learned the value of delayed gratification will remain totally enthusiastic in serving Christ and be satisfied to wait for his or her rewards.

GOD'S PROMISES IN EPHESIANS

Paul's epistle to the Ephesians develops the theme that the church consists of God's people, who are united in Christ as His living body on earth. Ephesians presents Jesus as the living head of His church, and it shows Christians how to live together to promote the growth and ministry of Christ's body here on earth.

A PROMISE OF INHERITANCE

The promise. "In Him you also trusted, after you heard the word of truth, the gospel of

"In due season we shall reap."

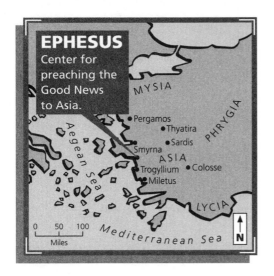

EPHESUS
Center for preaching the Good News to Asia.

ment the seal authenticated the message and conveyed the authority of the one who stamped it. The seal could serve as a signature, recognized by all. . . .

Three times the Holy Spirit is spoken of as a seal. In Ephesians 1:13 and 4:30 the image is commercial. The shipment has been accepted, payment has been made, and the owner's seal stamped on the product to secure it. The presence of the Holy Spirit is God's guarantee that He will accept believers, for whom He has paid the price in Christ. The same thought, the seal of ownership, is found in 2 Corinthians 1:22. God the Holy Spirit is God's guarantee that we will be taken into our Father's house, forever His (The *Expository Dictionary of Bible Words*, 1985, p. 545).

What commitment is expressed in our possession of the "Holy Spirit of promise"? The Spirit has sealed us. We belong to God, and He will take possession of us when Jesus comes. How are we to respond to this awesome gift of God? Perhaps Paul's prayer for the Ephesians best sums it up. After outlining what God the Father, Son, and Spirit had done to provide us with our inheritance, Paul asked that "you may know what is the hope of His calling" (Eph. 1:18). That "hope" is absolute and utter confidence that because we trust in Jesus our salvation is assured.

Responding to the promise. Some are upset when a person says, "I *know* I'll be in heaven." Such a claim seems presumptuous to them. At best, such persons argue, we can only say that we *hope* we'll be in heaven.

But again and again, God gives us promises which show that He expects us to *know* our eternal destiny. Verses such as John 3:36 speak with a clear and certain voice: "He who believes in the Son has everlasting life; and he who does not believe in the Son shall not see life, but the wrath of God abides on him." There is no "I hope," no "perhaps," and no "maybe" in John 3:36. And there is no uncertainty about our sealing by the Holy Spirit of promise, who is Himself God's guarantee of heaven.

Those who are uncertain about eternity have the mistaken notion that human beings contribute in some way to their own salvation. In contrast, our certainty is based on the real-

your salvation; in whom also, having believed, you were sealed with the Holy Spirit of promise, who is the guarantee of our inheritance until the redemption of the purchased possession, to the praise of His glory" (Eph. 1:13, 14).

The context of the promise. Ephesians 1:3–14 outlines the role of each person of the Trinity in carrying out God's plan of salvation. The Father generated and chose the plan by which believers were to become "holy and without blame before Him in love" (1:4). The Son redeemed us through the blood He shed on Calvary (1:7). And the Holy Spirit enters us, serving as the living guarantee that we will inherit all God has provided for us in Christ.

Understanding the promise. This passage calls the third person of the Trinity the "Holy Spirit of promise." The phrase indicates that the Holy Spirit is Himself a promise. He is the "guarantee of our inheritance until the redemption of the purchased possession."

This terminology is drawn from the world of commerce. It explains a unique work of the Holy Spirit by which He "seals" the believer. One authority explained:

In the NT, "to seal" is *sphragizo*. In Greek culture, the seal had great legal significance. When stamped on possessions, the seal indicated ownership and guarded the possession against theft. On a docu-

ization that salvation is a gift, purchased on Calvary. We will be in heaven because of what Christ has done for us—not because of anything we have done. Rather than feeling more holy than others, we who know we will be in heaven are more aware of being sinners who have no hope in ourselves. All the credit and glory for our salvation belongs to Jesus.

A PROMISE OF ACCESS

The promise: "For through Him we both have access by one Spirit to the Father" (Eph. 2:18).

The context of the promise. For thousands of years the human race was divided into Jew and non-Jew. The Jews, descendants of Abraham, had special access to God through the covenant promises made to Abraham and his descendants.

Then Jesus came. Through His death, He instituted the New Covenant which the prophet Jeremiah predicted would replace the Law. Under the New Covenant, the door of access to God was thrown open to all humanity. The old distinction between Jew and Gentile was done away with, and God formed "one new man" from what had been two.

The terms *Jew* and *Gentile* were made irrelevant when both became "Christian." Ephesians says that God reconciled them "both to God in one body through the cross" (Eph. 2:16). Both now have access to the Father by the one Holy Spirit.

Understanding the promise. The Greek word translated "access" in this passage is *prosagoge.* In oriental courts, the *prosagogeis* was the official who brought visitors into the king's presence. Thus, this verse identifies the Holy Spirit as one who conducts all Christians—whatever their ethnic origin—into the presence of God. As Christians, we have direct and immediate access to God's throne.

Claiming the promise. We claim this promise by exercising our right to enter God's presence. We come to Him in prayer—whether in praise, petition, intercession, or meditation on

Through Christ all believers have access to the Father.

who He is. We should take joy from the privilege of visiting the Ruler of the universe—much more so than those who take pride in their access to the powerful people of this world.

Responding to the promise. The promise of access to God by the Spirit made to both Jew and Gentile reminds us of an important reality: All of us are one in Christ. The distinctions so important to ordinary people—differences of race, education, social status, and wealth—are irrelevant to God. The relationship with Jesus which we share with all other believers makes us one. All other distinctions are unimportant.

THE PROMISE OF A UNIVERSAL GOSPEL

The promise: "That the Gentiles should be fellow heirs, of the same body, and partakers of His promise in Christ through the gospel" (Eph. 3:6).

The context of the promise. The apostle Paul had identified a mystery (Eph. 3:3)—an unexpected element of God's plan which was not revealed in the Old Testament but which had now been made known in Christ. The mystery was the fact that Gentiles were to be "fellow-heirs" with Jews, and "of the same body."

The Old Testament made it clear that God had always intended to bless Gentiles as well as Jews (cf. Isa. 11:11; Jer. 16:19). Yet the Jews always thought of themselves as having a closer relationship with God than the Gentiles could have. Gentiles would be blessed, the Jews agreed, but this blessing would come through Israel.

And then after the resurrection of Jesus, God's "promise in Christ" spread through the Roman world. Old distinctions between Jew and Gentile became irrelevant as God formed a single body, the church, that included all people. In this body Gentiles were not subservient to the Jews but were fellow heirs, participating as equals in God's promise.

Understanding the promise. Paul's commission as an apostle was to preach Christ among the Gentiles and "to make all see what is the fellowship of the mystery" (Eph. 3:9). In Christ, God promises us a common salvation as well as a common fellowship. God forms between believers a bond of love which breaks down barriers and makes us one.

Responding to the promise. As Paul developed this thought in Ephesians 3, he identified a cosmic purpose which God had in forming different people into one body. Paul said that God intended that "now the manifold wisdom of God might be made known by [through] the church to the principalities and powers in the heavenly places" (Eph. 3:10).

What is Paul saying? Simply this: The angels, fallen and faithful, observe us daily. They see that the issues that once created hostility between groups of people are set aside in Christ. They notice as Christians live together

in love as God's fellow-heirs. The angels are awed by the wisdom and greatness of our God.

The world is also impressed when Christians live by the truth that we are one with our brothers and sisters in Christ, in spite of our differences.

A PROMISE OF BLESSING

The promise: "'Honor your father and mother,' which is the first commandment with promise: 'that it may be well with you and you may live long on the earth'" (Eph. 6:2, 3).

The context of the promise. The verses "quoted" here are taken from Exodus 20 and Deuteronomy 5, which contain the Ten Commandments. The Old Testament command to honor parents and the associated promise were originally given to Israel as a nation (see page 116).

Paul's "quote" from the Ten Commandments is actually an application of the original

A happy home life involves mutual respect and cooperation.

text. Children are to obey their parents because this is an appropriate way to honor them. The original Old Testament promise was "that your days may be long . . . in the land which the LORD your God is giving you" (Deut. 5:16).

In the Ephesians passage, Paul applied the promise to individuals, writing "that it may be well with you and you may live long on the earth." Thus, Paul indicated that a promise made to the nation Israel could be claimed by Christians and applied to individuals!

In Ephesians the apostle developed what is commonly called a "household code." Beginning in Ephesians 5:22 and extending through 6:9, Paul gave instructions on proper relationships in the Christian household. He touches on the responsibilities of Christian husbands and wives to each other, of Christian parents and children to each other, and of Christian slaves and masters to each other. This promise verse deals with the relationship of children to their parents.

Understanding the promise. The command to honor parents by obeying them is given to each child who lives under the authority of his or her parents. It is important to see this "promise" as a natural consequence of obedience to Christian parents. Christian parents are expected to hold Christian values and to guide their children into a lifestyle in harmony with these values.

There are many kinds of trouble which a child will avoid if he follows Christian values communicated by his parents. And by the very nature of things, such children will live longer lives.

Claiming the promise. Family life is a web of mutual obligations. While children are obligated to obey parents, parents are obligated not to "provoke your children to wrath." Wise, loving guidance rather than multiplied rules and demands should characterize the Christian home. We claim this promise for our children by making it as easy as possible for them to obey. Our children claim the promise by

showing a respect for parents which expresses itself as obedience toward them.

When parents and children live together in mutual respect and love, it is well with them and the blessing of a longer life follows naturally.

Responding to the promise. We should be careful not to read more into this promise than is intended. No particular life span is guaranteed. The text does not promise that obedient youngsters will live 60, 70, or 80 years.

What the text does teach is that when we live together in families in the pattern suggested by this household code, our lives will be longer—longer than we would have expected if we had violated God's principles.

GOD'S PROMISES IN PHILIPPIANS

Paul wrote his letter to the Philippians from prison. In this epistle, Paul shared his feelings about what had happened to him. Throughout his prison years Paul remained joyful and confident. The gospel was being spread, Christ was being exalted, and Paul's goal in life continued—to know Jesus and the power of His resurrection.

Paul shared promises to reassure the Philippians of the future that God had prepared for them. These promises are a source of joy for believers of every generation.

A PROMISE OF GOD'S CONTINUING COMMITMENT

The promise: "He who has begun a good work in you will complete it until the day of Jesus Christ" (Phil. 1:6).

The context of the promise. Paul began his letter with thanksgiving for the partnership of the Philippians in the gospel. He had established the church in their city, and he remained confident that God would continue to work in their lives.

Understanding the promise. The "good work" to which Paul referred was God's transforming work in salvation. This good work begins when we trust Christ as Savior; it continues throughout our lives as God the Holy Spirit gradually transforms us; it will be completed when Jesus comes and we are fully like Him at last.

The word translated "complete" is *epiteleo* in the Greek language. It means to carry to completion. The project once begun will not be abandoned. How wonderful to know that God will not abandon us or the work He set out to do in our lives when we came to Christ.

Responding to the promise. When we trust Jesus, God begins a work of reconstruction in our lives. He has a blueprint to follow: Christ's own perfect character. God is committed to complete our reconstruction in order to make us like Jesus.

This is another of those wonderful promises imbedded in the gospel on which we are to base assurance of our salvation. God wants us to know that He is fully committed to us and to our ultimate transformation. God wants us to be confident, not in ourselves, but in Him.

Later in this letter Paul urged the Philippians to "work out your own salvation with fear and trembling" (2:12). Doesn't this contradict the assurance message of Philippians 1:6? Not at all. Paul did not urge the Philippians to work *for* their salvation, nor was the "fear and trembling" a fear of possible rejection by God. Paul urged the Philippians to let the salvation that had changed them inside change their behavior, and thus be "worked out" in their daily lives. Even this "working out" of our salvation is not done on our own, for "it is God who works in you both to will and to do for His good pleasure" (Phil. 2:13).

All we need to fear is that by some failure to trust Him or some lack of commitment, the *process* of our transformation might be delayed.

A PROMISE OF CERTAIN TRANSFORMATION

The promise: "For our citizenship is in heaven, from which we also eagerly wait for the Savior, the Lord Jesus Christ, who will transform our lowly body that it may be conformed to His glorious body, according to the working by which He is able even to subdue all things to Himself" (Phil. 3:20, 21).

The context of the promise. Earlier in this epistle, Paul had guaranteed that the God who had begun a good work in us would complete it until the day of Christ. While we await our ultimate transformation, God will work in us as we work out the meaning of our salvation through our daily behavior.

Understanding the promise. This promise is unmistakably clear. The phrase *lowly body* [literally, "the body of lowliness"] focuses attention on our mortality, our weakness, and our susceptibility in this life to persecution, sin, and disease. When Jesus returns, He will change this by transforming us into His image. Then the bodies of believers will like the body of the risen Christ. And all this will be done by Him who "is able to subdue all things to Himself."

Responding to the promise. The sequence of transformation promises in Philippians is significant. Paul first assured us that the one who had begun His transforming work in us would continue it until the day of Christ (Phil. 1:6). We are to work out the salvation we have been given, confident that God is at work in us (Phil. 2:12, 13). Now in Philippians 3:21 we are again promised that Jesus will transform our mortal bodies and conform them to His resurrection body. What could be more certain than that we who are saved are saved completely? Our ultimate transformation is guaranteed by God Himself.

A PROMISE OF INNER PEACE

The promise: "Be anxious for nothing, but in everything by prayer and supplication, with thanksgiving, let your requests be made known to God; and the peace of God, which surpasses all understanding, will guard your hearts and minds through Christ Jesus" (Phil. 4:6, 7).

"Be anxious for nothing, but . . . let your requests be made known to God."

The context of the promise. In chapter 4 of Philippians, Paul offered exhortation and encouragement. He spoke from his own experience. Paul had been charged with a capital crime, and he waited in Rome for the verdict. In addition, Paul had a deep concern for the churches he had established in many cities of the Roman Empire. If any person had reason to be anxious, Paul did. And yet his letter conveys a sense of joy and peace—a peace whose secret he shares in Philippians 4.

Understanding the promise. Paul promised the "peace of God" would turn anxieties into prayers. The "peace of God" is a peace which God provides. It surpasses all understanding because it is not dependent on circumstances, but on a relationship with the Lord. Christians and unbelievers alike face situations which create anxiety in most people. When this happens, our first impulse should be to turn the situation over to the Lord, confident of His concern.

Claiming the promise. The promise of peace is ours to claim. We do so by committing ourselves and our problems into the loving hands of the God who loves us in Christ. We trust Him not only as a Father who cares for us, but as the sovereign Lord of the universe who is able and willing to meet our needs. As we turn the problem over to Him, God's Spirit ministers His peace to us. Our emotions and thoughts are calmed and quieted by God Himself.

It is one thing to know in an intellectual sense that God's protective love surrounds us. It is quite another matter to experience His protective love. The promise Paul shares here is that we will know through personal experience a peace which can come only from God.

A PROMISE OF GOD'S PRESENCE

The promise: "The things which you learned and received and heard and saw in me, these do, and the God of peace will be with you" (Phil. 4:9).

The context of the promise. God is the source of peace for believers. To find peace in situations that would cause most people intense anxiety, Paul points us to prayer. By committing such situations to God, we experience an inner peace that only He can give.

But there is more to living in a state of peace than turning to God when we are under stress. A second element in Paul's prescription is to keep our thoughts focused on those things which promote godliness. We are to think on "whatever things are noble, whatever things are just, whatever things are pure, whatever things are lovely, whatever things are of good report"—the virtuous and the praiseworthy (Phil. 4:8).

Understanding the promise. This promise in Philippians 4:9 is the final piece of Paul's puzzle. How can Christians experience an inner peace that is beyond understanding? First, we bring to God in prayer the situations that cause us to be anxious. Second, we keep our minds focused on the noble, just, and pure.

And now, third, we live the Christian life as Paul has taught and modeled it.

Paul's personal ministry and his letters provided instruction in Christian living. These were the things which the Philippians "learned and received." But Paul did more than instruct in Christian living. He modeled it in his own life. Thus the Philippians "heard and saw" the gospel enfleshed "in me." The outcome of this modeling was that the Philippians might "do" as Paul instructed. They were to follow Paul's instruction and example.

How important this is. Only when we *do* the Christian life do we experience the God of peace.

Responding to the promise. This promise is clearly conditional. To claim it, we must take some initiative. Today the apostle Paul still instructs us in Christian living through his letters in the New Testament. But we must look for models of the Christian life elsewhere as well. We can never underestimate the importance of building close personal relationships with committed Christians who can serve as models of Christian commitment. We can also serve as examples for others.

As we "do" what we learn and receive from Scripture and hear and see these principles enfleshed in God's people, the God of peace will fill our lives.

A PROMISE OF SUPPLY

The promise: "And my God shall supply all your need according to His riches in glory by Christ Jesus" (Phil. 4:19).

The context of the promise. The Philippians had sent a gift of money to Paul while he was in prison. The word *prison* is deceptive. Paul was in Rome, awaiting trial. As a Roman citizen, Paul was not placed in a jail cell. He was under "house arrest." He was responsible for renting the house where he was staying and purchasing his own necessities. Since the apostle had no independent means of support, the money gift the Philippians sent must have met a real need.

So Paul thanked the Philippians for their generosity. He was particularly thankful for the concern which the gift reflected, and he called it "an acceptable sacrifice, well pleasing to God." God would reward the Philippians, and this gave Paul joy.

Understanding the promise. Paul made this promise not for himself but for the Lord. Paul had known times of plenty as well as destitution. He knew what it meant to be full as well as hungry. Through it all, God had been faithful. The same God who had met Paul's needs many times would provide for the needs of His other children—even as He will meet our needs today.

Responding to the promise. This promise brings freedom, especially in a materialistic society, where people tend to seek meaning in things. Paul had learned that life cannot be measured in the abundance of things that we possess. In fact, Paul wrote, "I have learned in whatever state I am, to be content."

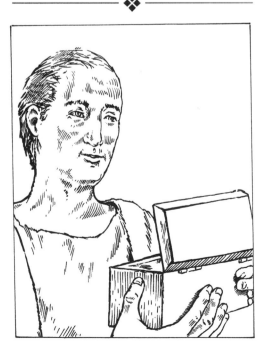

Philippian Christians gave generously to meet the needs of others.

When we commit to the spiritual values that motivated Paul, we will also find a contentment that doesn't depend on our earthly possessions.

GOD'S PROMISES IN COLOSSIANS

Colossians, like Ephesians, is a Christological document; it focuses on who Jesus is, what Jesus has done for us, and how we are to respond to Him. Most agree that in Colossians Paul corrected notions about God and the world that later developed into the Gnostic heresy. This heresy held that God, as perfectly good, could have nothing to do with the material universe, which the Gnostics saw as evil.

Paul countered this heresy by teaching that Jesus, who created the visible and invisible universe, lived on earth as a real human being. Paul also emphasized that Jesus redeemed humankind through His bodily death on the Cross. God did not isolate Himself from the material world, Paul affirmed, but He expressed Himself in it.

And what Jesus did in the material world had implications for eternity. In the same way, believers are called to express God's character in the way they live in this world. The lives we live on earth also have eternal implications.

A PROMISE OF GLORY

The promise: "When Christ who is our life appears, then you also will appear with Him in glory" (Col. 3:4).

The context of the promise. We live in a material universe which consists of things. John described the materialist, who sought the meaning of life in this universe, as "loving" the world. But John warned that "all that is in the world—the lust of the flesh, the lust of the eyes, and the pride of life—is not of the Father but is of the world" (1 John 2:16).

Here in Colossians Paul reminded Christians that we have been raised with Christ. Thus we are to "set [our] minds on things above, not on things on the earth" (Col. 3:2). A passion for wealth, honor, power, or plea-

sures is not worthy behavior for those who have been raised in Christ to a higher level.

The wellspring and source of our new life "is hidden with Christ in God" (Col. 3:3). What motivates us cannot be seen or understood by people of the world.

Understanding the promise. One day Jesus will return to earth. His return is called an appearance, because then He will be visible to all. When Jesus returns, "you also will appear with Him in glory."

Today the world may scoff at Christians. The world may ridicule Christian values or condemn Christian commitment to what God says is just and right. The realities which guide us are hidden from the people of the world, even as we are misunderstood. But, Paul tells us that when Jesus returns and is revealed to all, we will appear with Him in glory. Our true identity and splendor as children of God will be displayed to all when we appear with Jesus in glory.

Responding to the promise. When we look to God as the source of the values we live by, we will be misunderstood. As Peter says, others will "think it strange that you do not run with them" and will speak "evil of you" (1 Pet. 4:4). At such times, we need the reassurance of this promise. When Jesus comes, we will appear with Him in glory. Our choice of Christ and His ways will be vindicated. And those who ridiculed "will give an account to Him who is ready to judge the living and the dead" (1 Pet. 4:5).

A PROMISE OF REWARD

The promise: "And whatever you do, do it heartily, as to the Lord and not to men, knowing that from the Lord you will receive the reward of the inheritance; for you serve the Lord Christ" (Col. 3:23, 24).

The context of the promise. The apostle Paul had shown that what happens in this world has eternal implications. Christ entered our world as a human being, and He died to reconcile us to God. Because of what Jesus did in this world, we have a welcome in the world to come.

In the same way, how we live our lives in this world has implications for eternity. In Colossians 3 and 4, the apostle outlined some of the ways that Christians, whose lives are hidden in Christ, were to live in first-century society. In this passage, Paul looked at the most significant of the "household" relationships a person could have—relationships with others in the church, relationships with one's spouse and children, and relationships between masters and slaves (called "bondservants" in our text).

The promise in Colossians 3:24 was addressed to slaves, who were told to obey their human masters. Christian slaves were not to serve their masters half-heartedly or out of fear, but they were to give earnest service. They were also to see their work for their masters as a way of serving Jesus.

Understanding the promise. The promise to slaves was associated with a charge.

"Whatever you do"—that is, "in all that you do"—"do it heartily, as to the Lord." Slaves were to think of the service they rendered their human masters as service to Jesus, and they were to serve with enthusiasm and joy.

The word translated "reward" is an unusual term. In other New Testament passages, the word *misthos,* "wage," is used. Only here in the entire New Testament do we find *antapodosis,* a word which indicates a full return on one's investment. No first-century slave worked for wages, so *misthos* would have been inappropriate. But no Christian slave who invested his or her life in seeking to please God would be denied a full return on this investment.

Furthermore, the reward would not be given as wages but as an inheritance. Although under Roman law a slave could not inherit property, those who served the Lord Christ would have an inheritance in eternity. Although they were slaves, they were also the children of God.

Responding to the promise. We seldom get a full return in this world on our investment in other people. The things a parent does out of love are generally taken for granted by their children. The hard work of a faithful employee is often overlooked by an employer. Teachers spend long hours trying to help young people learn, only to be belittled by students and parents. Pastors and other church workers are more often criticized than encouraged and thanked.

How do we maintain our enthusiasm for serving others when we see so little return on our investment in the here and now? We keep in mind that we are not simply serving other people; we are serving the Lord Christ. The reward we should yearn for is His commendation, "Well done, good and faithful servant."

If we serve with enthusiasm, we have God's promise that we will receive a full return on all that we invest in others for Him.

GOD'S PROMISES IN THE THESSALONIAN EPISTLES

Paul's letters to the church at Thessalonica may have been the first epistles written by Paul. A major theme in these brief letters is the second coming of Christ and associated events. This theme is closely linked to the promises in these two letters.

A PROMISE OF REUNION

The promise: "For the Lord Himself will descend from heaven with a shout, with the voice of an archangel, and with the trumpet of God. And the dead in Christ will rise first. Then we who are alive and remain shall be caught up together with them in the clouds to meet the Lord in the air. And thus we shall always be with the Lord" (1 Thess. 4:16, 17).

The context of the promise. During the brief time that Paul was in Thessalonica, he taught many basic Christian doctrines. One doctrine was that of the parousia, the second coming of Jesus Christ. The prospect excited the Thessalonians, and they looked forward eagerly to Christ's return.

But as time went on, some in the church died. Their loved ones were troubled. What would happen to the dead when Jesus returned? Had those who died missed out on the blessings associated with Jesus' return?

In 1 Thessalonians 4:13–18, Paul dealt with this concern and conveyed one of Scripture's most wonderful promises.

Understanding the promise. Paul first reaffirmed his teaching about the Second Coming. "The Lord Himself will descend from heaven with a shout, with the voice of an archangel, and with the trumpet of God." Paul then went on to describe what Jesus' return would mean for believers who had died, and for those who were still alive at His coming.

"The dead in Christ will rise first" (4:16). Christians who have died will be raised and given resurrection bodies (cf. 1 Cor. 15:52).

"Then we who are alive and remain" (4:17). Living Christians will be transformed at the same moment and given their resurrection bodies (cf. 1 Cor. 15: 51).

"Shall be caught up together." Here is the answer to the real concern that troubled the Thessalonians. Loved ones who have died will be reunited with the living. We will all be caught up *together.* Christ's return will mean not only transformation but reunion as well.

"To meet the Lord in the air." Surely those who have died will miss out on nothing. They and the living will leap up to meet Jesus together. And, never to be separated from our loved ones again, "we shall always be with the Lord."

Responding to the promise. The apostle immediately added, "Therefore comfort one another with these words" (1 Thess. 4:18). We grieve when our loved ones in the Lord die. But we never despair. We have God's promise of reunion when Jesus returns.

A PROMISE OF RETRIBUTION

The promise: "These shall be punished with everlasting destruction from the presence of the Lord and from the glory of His power" (2 Thess. 1:9).

The context of the promise. In Paul's second letter to the Thessalonians, he returned to matters linked with the second coming of Jesus. In chapter 1, Paul praised the Thessalonian church for its patience and faith in spite of persecutions and tribulations (2 Thess. 1:4). Paul then went on to speak to those who were troubled by the unfairness of it all. When Jesus comes, there will be rest for believers and tribulation for those who have troubled the church.

Is this fair? Yes. Indeed, "it is a righteous thing" for God to repay sinners. When Jesus comes, He will "in flaming fire" take vengeance on those who neither know God nor obey the gospel. One of the most striking teachings in Scripture is that God displays His righteousness in two ways: in forgiving (Rom. 3:23, 24) and in punishing (1 Thess. 1:6).

Understanding the promise. Like many other promises in the Bible, this promise expressed clearly what God intended to do. The promise has three dimensions.

First, it assures believers who are suffering tribulation that God remains in charge of His universe. Those who "trouble" the believer with apparent immunity will suffer the consequences of their acts.

Second, the promise warns all who do not yet know God. The "hellfire and brimstone" sermon of old, which frightened sinners into turning to God, was not out of line. Punishment and "everlasting destruction" await those who fail to respond to God and His gospel.

Third, this promise affirms God's justice. God will hold court to judge sin and sinners. When He does, the evil of sin will be displayed in the punishment awaiting sinners.

Responding to the promise. While Christians may be subjected to injustice and tribulation, we can never doubt that we live in a moral universe. God will deal with sin and sinners when Jesus returns, and the moral balance of our universe will be displayed.

At the same time, we are to remember that God withholds punishment until the time of Jesus' return. In withholding punishment, God gives sinners an opportunity to repent and turn to Him. Thus, today is the day of grace—not retribution.

We are not to seek vengeance but to join with God in sharing the good news of forgiveness, reflecting His love to all.

A PROMISE OF PROTECTION

The promise: "But the Lord is faithful, who will establish you and guard you from the evil one" (2 Thess. 3:3).

The context of the promise. Some in Thessalonica had the peculiar notion that the Second Coming had already occurred and that they had missed it! In chapter 2 of his second letter to the Thessalonians, Paul reminded them of his earlier teaching. He had told them before that certain things would take place before Jesus returned. A world ruler—the "man of sin," the Antichrist—would appear and assume political power. Satan himself would support this evil ruler with signs (miracles) and "lying wonders."

Until then, Paul urged the Thessalonian Christians to stand firm and "hold the traditions which you were taught." As they waited for these events to take place, the Thessalonian Christians could be confident that the Lord was faithful, and that He would establish them and guard them from the evil one.

Understanding the promise. This promise is one of inner security [He will establish, or strengthen] and of outward protection. The Greek word translated protect, *phylaxei*, is a military term, used of defense against a violent onslaught. Satan may hurl his forces against the believer, but our faithful Lord will provide a defense against him.

Responding to the promise. This promise, rooted in God's own character as a faithful Person, is made to us as well as to the Thessalonians. The military imagery is suggestive. Some Christians seem to live in fear of real and imagined enemies, retreating to fortified enclaves where they associate only with other Christians with similar convictions. But our true defense is the Lord, and He is with us always.

As believers, we may feel secure in every situation. We need to remember Jesus' words to the Father, "I do not pray that You should take them out of the world, but that You should keep them from the evil one" (John 17:15). Jesus also prayed, "As You sent Me into the world, I also have sent them into the world" (John 17:18).

Jesus' prayer is being answered. God has promised to guard us from the evil one. Now it is our turn to trust Him and to step out into the world as representatives of our Lord.

GOD'S PROMISES IN THE PASTORAL EPISTLES

Three of Paul's letters are called "pastoral epistles." These letters were written to younger men whom Paul had trained for ministry, and they are filled with advice and counsel. The three letters are 1 and 2 Timothy and Titus. Of the three, the second letter to Timothy contains promises that we can claim today.

A PROMISE OF FAITHFULNESS

The promise:

For if we died with Him,
    We shall also live with Him.
If we endure,
    We shall also reign with Him.
If we deny Him,
    He also will deny us.
If we are faithless,
    He remains faithful;
He cannot deny Himself (2 Tim. 2:11–13).

The context of the promise. Most commentators view these verses as a hymn of the early church. Paul used it here as a bridge linking a reference about his own commitment to ministry to his exhortation to Timothy: "Be diligent to present yourself approved of God" (2 Tim. 2:15). The promise expressed in this early hymn reminds us that our choices have eternal consequences. But no choice we make can change God's commitment to us.

Understanding the promise. This early hymn affirmed certain realities and their consequences. In each case, the "if" is assumed to have happened. Thus there is no question of whether we died with Christ. Paul is saying:

- We died with Christ. The consequence is that we now live with Him.
- We are presently enduring. We will reign with Jesus.
- We do deny Christ. He will deny us.
- We are faithless. But he remains faithful, for he cannot deny himself.

The first two of these truth-and-consequences sayings are encouraging. The third is a serious warning which some have assumed threatens the loss of one's salvation. But this is a serious misunderstanding.

The Greek word translated deny is *arnesometha*. It is better understood in this context as "disown." "Deny" implies rejection of a truth, while "disown" implies refusal to acknowledge a person. The tense of the verb is aorist, indicating punctiliar action. The hymn looks upon disowning as a single, completed act. When an action of ours fails to acknowledge Jesus as Lord, Jesus does not acknowledge us in regards to that act.

The final affirmation makes it very clear that the third verse of this hymn could not imply a loss of salvation. The word translated "faithless" is a strong one, and it is in the present tense. It indicates a habitual refusal to trust Jesus and obey Him. Rather than threatening such faithless believers with rejection, the hymn concludes, "He remains faithful; He cannot deny Himself."

No wonder these words were sung or chanted in the early church's gatherings and celebrations. The first two verses celebrated the blessings we have in Christ as we walk with Him. And the next two celebrated Christ Himself, whose faithfulness to us does not depend on what we do but on His own eternal character.

Responding to the promise. Like first-century Christians, we can celebrate with joy and thanksgiving the goodness and greatness of our God. How humbling it is to recognize our own flaws and faithlessness. Yet how grand it is to see, against the background of our frailty, the steadfast grace and stable love of God.

A PROMISE OF USEFULNESS

The promise: "Therefore if anyone cleanses himself from the latter, he will be a vessel for honor, sanctified and useful for the Master, prepared for every good work" (2 Tim. 2:21).

The context of the promise. The apostle Paul had warned against false teachers and their message. Yet the church rests secure on the solid foundation of God's sovereign choice of those who are His, who display their allegiance as they "depart from iniquity" (2 Tim. 2:19). Having said this, Paul went on to develop an analogy. In any large household are found all sorts of dishes and utensils. Some, Paul said, were of gold and silver, others of wood and clay. All are useful, but the vessels of wood and clay are adapted to ordinary tasks, while those of gold and silver are for use on special occasions.

Understanding the promise. Paul applied his image. Those who cleanse themselves "from the latter" (the "iniquity" mentioned in 2 Tim. 2:19) become vessels for honor—persons whom God can use in special ways.

The promise is clearly conditional. Just as clearly, it is for all believers. If we cleanse ourselves from iniquity, we will be "sanctified and useful." We will be set apart to God and made usable by God, ready for every good work that He wants to accomplish through us.

Any vessel can be made useful for God's work.

Claiming the promise. We claim this promise by turning our backs on iniquity. Preparation for ministry is more than a matter of the schools at which we study; it also involves commitment to holy living.

THE PROMISE OF A CROWN

The promise: "Finally, there is laid up for me the crown of righteousness, which the Lord, the righteous Judge, will give to me on that Day, and not to me only but also to all who have loved His appearing" (2 Tim. 4:8).

The context of the promise. The "crown" in this verse is not a royal crown (a *diadema*) but the crown made of leaves (*stephanos*) awarded to the victor in an athletic contest. Such crowns are also mentioned in 1 Corinthians 9:25, James 1:12, 1 Peter 5:4, and Revelation 2:10. While the victor's crown of leaves had no monetary value, it was greatly prized. It

represented an achievement that brought honor to the athlete and to the city he represented.

When the apostle Paul looked back at his life as a race run for the Lord, he expressed confidence that Christ Himself would award Paul the victor's crown. This type of crown is available to every believer who loves Christ's appearing.

Understanding the promise. The crown is described as a "crown of righteousness." The phrase is somewhat ambiguous in Greek. It may mean "the crown appropriate for the righteous man," or "the crown won by righteousness," or even "the crown which consists of (eternal) righteousness." We can settle on the second of these possibilities when we see the implications of his promise that this same crown will be awarded "all those who have loved His appearing."

There are three Greek words used in speaking of Jesus' return. *Parousia* emphasizes Jesus' coming to be with us. *Apocolypsis* emphasizes Jesus' coming as the ultimate unveiling of reality. The word used here, *epiphaneia,* emphasizes the fact that Jesus' return will constitute a disrupting intervention in a world that remains blind to God's grace. Shattered by His appearing, the world system of today will be replaced by the long-awaited kingdom of righteousness, and evil will be judged (*Expository Dictionary of Bible Words,* 1985, p. 66).

Thus, to love Jesus' appearing as *epiphaneia* is to be fully dedicated to Him. We should love nothing in this world so much that it draws us away from our commitment to Christ and God's will.

Claiming the promise. The *Expository Dictionary* sums it up for us:

For the believer, *epiphaneia* contains a challenge. We are to look at the ways of the world in which we live and utter a decisive no! to human society's values. We are to commit ourselves simply to doing good while we long for Jesus to return to intervene and at last restore the tangled world to its intended beauty (67).

SCRIPTURE'S LAST WORDS:

PROMISES IN THE GENERAL EPISTLES AND REVELATION
Hebrews—Revelation

The General Epistles include all the New Testament letters not written by the apostle Paul. They are Hebrews, James, 1 and 2 Peter, 1, 2, and 3 John, and Jude. While in a special category all its own, Revelation is also surveyed in this chapter.

GOD'S PROMISES IN HEBREWS

Hebrews was written to Jewish believers whose lifelong commitment to an Old Testament lifestyle continued to tug at their hearts. The writer compared the old covenant instituted through Moses with the New Covenant inaugurated by Jesus Christ, showing how Jesus and the New Covenant are superior at every point.

The discussion of these two covenants in the first part of this book provides important background for understanding the epistle to the Hebrews. The wonderful promises in Hebrews are rooted in the unique nature of the New Covenant given us in Christ.

A PROMISE OF REST

The promise: "Therefore, since a promise remains of entering His rest, let us fear lest any of you seem to have come short of it. . . . There remains therefore a rest for the people of God" (Heb. 4:1, 9).

The context of the promise. The "rest" section of Hebrews extends from Hebrews 3:7 through 4:13. The writer of Hebrews warned his readers against hardening their hearts when God spoke to them. He pointed to the Exodus generation, which hardened its heart when God told Israel to go into Canaan. Their unbelief kept them from entering the "rest" of Canaan and doomed them to wander for 38 years in the wilderness.

To the writer of Hebrews, Canaan's "rest" was a symbol of a spiritual rest which God makes available to every generation of believers. Another analogy is found in the rest that God experienced on the seventh day, after finishing creation. The rabbis noted that while the first six days of Genesis reported a morning and an evening, only the morning of the seventh day was mentioned in the text.

The conclusion drawn from this was that God is still enjoying His Sabbath rest. Throughout history God has been active, but He has been at rest, for every contingency has been planned for. History unfolds in accordance with

His plan, and with no event unexpected or beyond His control.

Understanding the promise. When God declared that "there remains a rest for the people of God," He invited us to experience the same peace and certainty about the future which He Himself enjoys. How is this possible?

The writer of Hebrews reminded us that "the word of God is living and powerful, and sharper than any two-edged sword, piercing even to the division of soul and spirit, and of joints and marrow, and is a discerner of the thoughts and intents of the heart" (Heb. 4:12). That is, God knows us totally.

"All things are naked and open to the eyes of Him to whom we must give an account" (Heb. 4:13). There is no pain, no need of ours, that God does not understand completely. And the God who is master of history *is intimately involved in our lives!* Even as God has planned for every cosmic contingency from the time of creation, so God has planned how to meet every need of ours from the very beginning of time. The rest which we are offered is a rest found in trusting God to know what is best for us, and following His leading.

Claiming the promise. How do we claim this promise of rest? It is clear that this promise is contingent, for Hebrews urges "Let us therefore be diligent to enter that rest" (Heb. 4:11).

The answer is found in two words: "today" and "voice." Several times in this passage the writer repeated "today if you will hear His voice" (Heb. 3:7, 13, 15; 4:7). In each setting, the writer urged his readers to respond with faith and to obey when God's voice is heard. We enter God's rest by responding obediently each time we hear His voice.

Responding to the promise. When we grasp the teaching of this passage, we gain a wonderful new perspective on Christian living. God, who knows our every need and has already planned for every contingency in our lives, will guide us. He will speak to us every day. When we hear His voice, all we need do is obey. We find our rest in trusting and responding to God's voice as He guides.

A PROMISE OF MERCY AND GRACE

The promise: "Let us therefore come boldly to the throne of grace, that we may obtain mercy and find grace to help in time of need" (Heb. 4:16).

The context of the promise. The old covenant had its high priest, who represented the people before the Lord, and who conveyed God's blessing to the people. Under the New Covenant, Jesus is our High Priest. Unlike the Mosaic Covenant's high priests, who ministered on earth as God's representatives and then died, Jesus has "passed through the heavens" and now sits with the Father on heaven's throne.

Understanding the promise. We are invited to "come boldly" to the throne of grace, aware that Jesus sympathizes with the pressures to which we human beings are subject. There, on His throne, we have a High Priest willing and able to provide what we need.

Mercy. In the New Testament, "mercy" is a compassionate response to those who are suffering. In this specific passage, mercy is closely associated with Christ's awareness of our human limitations and our tendency to sin. Christ subjected Himself to the limitations under which we live, with the exception that He never sinned. When we sin, we are invited to approach the throne of God with confidence, certain that we will obtain mercy from Jesus (see Eph. 2:4–5).

Grace. Grace in Scripture is the compassionate response of a person to help someone who is unable to help himself. While both mercy and grace flow out of compassion, the first is closely related to forgiveness while the second is more closely related to enabling. We appeal for mercy after failing; we seek "grace to help" to enable us to meet the challenges in our lives. When we come to the throne of grace seeking grace to help, Jesus will give us the strength we need to live godly lives.

Claiming the promise. This is a promise which we can claim at any time. There is no need to wait for Sunday or to go to church. Our cry of "help" reaches God's throne in the moment of our need, whether for forgiveness or enabling. As soon as we sense failure, we can turn to Jesus for mercy; as soon as we feel overwhelmed or inadequate, we can appeal to Jesus for grace to help. And we can be sure that Jesus our High Priest will gladly supply what we need.

A PROMISE OF REMEMBRANCE

The promise: "For God is not unjust to forget your work and labor of love which you have shown toward His name, in that you have ministered to the saints, and do minister" (Heb. 6:10).

The context of the promise. The writer of Hebrews had just urged his readers to go on in their Christian lives and not to return to foundational salvation truths. The believer who is sure of his or her salvation is free to focus on producing fruit. Those who doubt their salvation become unproductive.

In this context, the writer of Hebrews let his readers know that he did not consider them unproductive. In fact, he was "confident of better things concerning you, yes, things that accompany salvation" (Heb. 6:9). In the following promise verse, the writer pointed to evidence that his readers' Christian lives had been productive, and assured them that God would not "forget" their service.

Understanding the promise. To understand this promise, we need to realize that "forget" and "remember" are not primarily mental terms in the Bible, especially when ascribed to God. "Forget" and "remember" are action words. To remember means *to act on what is remembered.* Thus, when God's Old Testament people turned back to Him after sinning, the Scripture often notes that "God remembered His covenant" and came to their aid or helped them (cf. Lev. 26:42, 45).

To remember the covenant means that God acted to keep the covenant promises He had made to Israel. In the same way, for God to forget or fail to remember our sins (cf. Ps. 25:7; Isa. 43:25) means that God will not punish us as our sins deserve. He chooses instead to forgive us.

Here, then, Scripture's word that God will not "forget your work and labor of love" is a promise of reward.

Claiming the promise. While this promise was made specifically to the recipients of this New Testament letter, it is clearly a promise for all of us. The promise is rooted in God's nature as a "rewarder of those who diligently seek Him" (Heb. 11:6). God will reward us graciously when we commit ourselves to labors of love in ministering to His saints.

FOUR NEW COVENANT PROMISES
(Hebrews 8:10–12)

(See the discussion of the New Covenant, pages 70–81.)

A PROMISE OF THE SECOND COMING

The promise: "So Christ was offered once to bear the sins of many. To those who eagerly wait for Him he will appear a second time, apart from sin, for salvation" (Heb. 9:28).

The context of the promise. First-century Judaism looked forward to the coming of a royal Messiah who would save the nation from foreign oppressors and establish a powerful earthly kingdom. But Jesus, although He was the Messiah, had not met these expectations. This must have concerned the Jewish Christians to whom the book of Hebrews was addressed.

Understanding the promise. The writer noted that "Christ was offered once" to bear the sins of many. The name *Christ* is the Greek translation of the Hebrew name for the promised Old Testament Messiah. The Messiah had come. And His first ministry was to be offered up as a sacrifice, that He might bear the sins of many.

But there was more to the Messiah's story. Christ was destined to appear "a second time." And when Jesus the Messiah returned, according to the writer of Hebrews, there would be a very different agenda.

Apart from sin. The mission of Jesus in His first coming was to deal with sin. He died on the Cross and paid the penalty of sin for all humankind. The sin question had thus been disposed of. But when Jesus returned, it would not be to deal with the sins of believers.

For salvation. The mission of Jesus in His second coming would be "for salvation." In the Old Testament, "salvation" referred primarily to deliverance from earthly enemies. God's Old Testament "plan of [earthly] salvation for Israel" was that the Messiah would deal with Israel's enemies and establish an earthly kingdom. In this phrase, the writer of Hebrews assured his Jewish readers that the prophets' hopes and expectations would still be fulfilled. God remained faithful to His ancient covenant promises, and every one would be kept.

Responding to the promise. Sometimes Christians see only the New Testament promises concerning personal salvation and overlook other aspects of God's plan. One day the Christ who has redeemed us by His blood will return, to establish His rule over all the earth. Contemplating this aspect of God's eternal plan, the apostle Paul cried out, "Oh, the depth of the riches both of the wisdom and the knowledge of God!" (Rom. 11:33). We should share Paul's wonder at the multifaceted plan of God.

A PROMISE OF FRUITFULNESS

The promise: "Now no chastening seems to be joyful for the present, but painful; nevertheless, afterward it yields the peaceable fruit of righteousness to those who have been trained by it" (Heb. 12:11).

The context of the promise. Hebrews 12 is Scripture's classic passage on divine discipline. It encourages us to understand when trials or suffering come that God is not punishing us, nor has He deserted us. Instead, God is treating us as a loving Father, who is intent on guiding us toward maturity. The pain we suffer through such discipline is "for our profit, that we may be partakers of His holiness" (Heb. 12:10).

Understanding the promise. God wants us to look beyond our painful experiences to the benefits they are intended to produce. God's discipline, although painful for the present, is training which produces righteousness.

Responding to the promise. The teaching of this passage on God's discipline is intended to shape our attitude toward the painful experiences of life. In Hebrews 12:12–17, the author gave some practical advice on our response to God's discipline.

"Strengthen the hands which hang down" (Hebrews 12:12). This image is one of hopelessness. We can easily envision this response to troubles. The person gives up. His head rests on his chest, his hands hang down at his side, and his knees almost give way. The word *strengthen* tells us that we should resolve to keep on rather than give up.

"Make straight paths" (Hebrews 12:13). We generally try to avoid the difficulties that God brings into our lives in order to mature us. Rather than run away from painful experiences, we need to move on through them. Healing comes through facing our problems rather than fleeing from them.

"Fall short of the grace of God" (Hebrews 12:15). One of the dangers of our times of trouble or suffering is that we might "fall short of the grace of God." This strange phrase is explained in the contrasting phrase that follows: "lest any root of bitterness springing up cause trouble."

More than one person undergoing divine discipline has become bitter, feeling that the treatment is unfair. But even our most painful experiences are gracious gifts of a loving Father, who intends to bless us rather than harm us. We "fall short of the grace of God" by failing to sense His grace in our experiences. When we lose the sense of God's grace in our lives, we become vulnerable to all sorts of sins.

What a wonderful thing it is to experience grace in times of suffering. How strengthening it is to realize that everything that happens to us is a gift from the God of love.

A PROMISE OF GOD'S PRESENCE
(Hebrews 13:5)

(See the commentary on Deut. 31:6, page 125.)

GOD'S PROMISES IN JAMES

The book of James may be the earliest of the New Testament epistles. It was written by James, the half-brother of Jesus, who emerged as a leader in the Jerusalem church.

The book of James is about faith. Some have seen a conflict between the writing of James and Paul's letters to the Romans and Galatians. However, the two writers dealt with different issues.

In Romans and Galatians, Paul presented Christ as the object of faith, promising salvation to all who trust in Him.

James wrote to those who had trusted Jesus, describing the lifestyle that faith produces. James made it clear that any "faith" which exists only as a set of beliefs about God cannot produce the kind of life that God requires. We must have faith *in* God rather than faith *about* God. And that kind of faith will be displayed in a changed life.

When we understand the issues that concerned James and Paul in their epistles, any apparent conflict is quickly resolved and we realize that the two are in complete harmony.

A PROMISE OF WISDOM

The promise: "If any of you lacks wisdom, let him ask of God, who gives to all liberally and without reproach, and it will be given to him" (James 1:5).

The context of the promise. James dealt with a variety of topics in his brief letter. Each topic had immediate, practical implications for daily life. In Scripture, wisdom is distinct from knowledge. Wisdom involves the application of spiritual truth to daily life, so that the individuals senses the godly thing to do in any given situation.

Understanding the promise. This promise of wisdom is a promise of divine guidance. If you don't know the godly thing to do in a situation—or if you don't know how to go about doing it—ask God. He doesn't get upset with us for asking—no matter how minor the thing that concerns us. Instead, God "gives to all liberally" and will surely give us wisdom when we ask for it.

Claiming the promise. This is one of those wonderful promises that we should claim each day. The more we desire to do those things that please the Lord, the more we will become aware of the "little" daily decisions that are essential elements in living godly lives. As we look to the Lord for guidance, He will show us what to do.

Responding to the promise. James gave us a warning with this promise (1:6–8). To receive guidance, we must "ask in faith" with no "doubting." What James means by "doubting" is explained by his image of a person tossed here and there by the waves and his description of that person as "double-minded." The person of faith is determined to do God's will when it is revealed to him. This person will be given the divine guidance he or she asks for.

On the other hand, the double-minded person who doubts is uncertain about his or her readiness to do God's will. Like the young person who prays, "God, should I propose to Mary?" and is willing to accept only God's "yes" answer, the double-minded individual wants to stand in judgment on God's directives.

What James tells us is that we are not to pray, "Lord, show me what to do, and if I like it, I'll do it." That kind of prayer for guidance will not be answered. What we must pray is,

"Lord, show me your will, and I'll obey, no matter what."

When we ask God for wisdom with this single-minded attitude, He will provide the guidance we need.

A PROMISE OF REWARD

The promise: "Blessed is the man who endures temptation; for when he has been approved, he will receive the crown of life which the Lord has promised to those who love Him" (James 1:12).

The context of the promise. One of the topics which James dealt with in chapter 1 was temptation. James identified the source of temptation as within the individual, not in his circumstances. Every circumstance is a good gift, intended by God to strengthen and bless us. We are tempted when we are drawn away from God's blessings by our own sinful desires.

Understanding the promise. God promises a "crown of life" to those who endure tempta-

❖

tions without giving in to them. (For a discussion of crowns, see the comment on 2 Tim. 4:8, page 243.)

Responding to the promise. What can keep us from giving in to temptations? Surely not the promise of a reward. The answer is found in the phrase, "Which the Lord has promised to those who love Him." Only love for the Lord is powerful enough to overcome the pull of temptation.

When we feel that pull, we are not to focus on the temptation or even to fight it. Instead, we are to focus on Jesus, to remember His love for us, and to let that love energize our love for Him. Love for Jesus will enable us to endure any temptation.

A PROMISE OF BLESSING

The promise: "But he who looks into the perfect law of liberty and continues in it, and is not a forgetful hearer but a doer of the word, this one will be blessed in what he does" (James 1:25).

Understanding the promise. God has given us His word to "do" rather than simply to "hear." The key to God's blessing is not to read or master the contents of the Bible. God's Word speaks to us in a living voice, calling us to respond. The blessing inherent in Scripture is found not in the knowing but in the doing.

Claiming the promise. This is another promise which is available to all, but it also requires action on our part. To claim the promise, we must become doers of the Word.

It is important to hold true doctrines. But as Paul wrote to Timothy, the end or goal of right doctrine is "love from a pure heart, from a good conscience, and from sincere faith" (1 Tim. 1:5). This is produced only in those who respond gladly to God's good word and put its teachings into practice. The blessing is found, always, in the doing.

A PROMISE OF POWER

The promise: "Resist the devil and he will flee from you" (James 4:7b).

The context of the promise. The Bible depicts Satan as a powerful fallen angel, who is hostile to humankind. He is particularly malicious toward those who trust in the Lord and is eager to harm them.

While he is powerful beyond our ability to imagine, Satan is a defeated enemy. Christ "disarmed" all demonic powers on the Cross, "triumphing over them in it" (Col. 2:15). As believers, we are in Christ and we share in His victory.

Understanding the promise. The promise that when we resist the devil he will flee from us is preceded by a call to "submit to God." (James 4:7a). We are not able to resist Satan in our own strength, nor should we try to do so. The secret of resisting Satan is to first submit to God, so that His power flows through us. When we are submitted to God, we are in the center of His will, relying completely on Him. When we enjoy this relationship with the Lord, Satan can do nothing but flee.

Responding to the promise. Christians are to have a healthy respect for Satan. This will keep us from rushing into spiritual conflicts for which we are not prepared. In the prayer that Jesus taught His disciples, one request was, "Deliver us *from* the evil one" (Luke 11:4).

On the other hand, some Christians credit Satan with too much power. Rather than resist Satan, they run from him and avoid spiritual warfare. Our fear of Satan can be just as harmful as overconfidence.

The balance is found in submitting daily to the Lord, making Him the focus of our faith. Then if Satan should trouble us, we can meet his challenge with confidence, resisting in the power of the Lord.

A PROMISE OF INTIMACY

The promise: "Draw near to God and He will draw near to you" (James 4:8).

The context of the promise. This promise flows from a statement James made about God. God is one who "gives grace" (James 4:6).

But how are we to receive the grace that God gives? The problem is not with God's willingness to give, but with our readiness to receive grace.

The answer to the question is one of attitude. We are to be humble rather than proud. James went on to spell out in a series of active verbs the characteristics of humble people. The humble:

- submit to God (4:7);
- draw near to God (4:8);
- cleanse their hands (4:8);
- purify their hearts (4:8);
- lament, mourn, and weep (4:9);
- [and thus] humble themselves (4:10).

It is important that we see these as progressive steps. We consciously submit to God. We then draw near to Him, seeking to know and love Him better. Our nearness to God makes us uncomfortable with sin, and we seek to cleanse our hands and to purify our hearts. But in the process we realize how truly sinful we are, and we lament, mourn, and weep. Only then are we truly humbled in God's sight. And then, amazingly, God lifts us up!

Understanding the promise. When we choose to draw near to God, we can be sure that He will draw near to us. God always responds to believers who want to know Him more intimately.

What may surprise us, however, is that in the process of drawing near to the Lord a purging process begins. God can only be near to those who are humble and who come to Him in complete honesty. If we draw near God, He *will* draw near us. And in the process we will be humbled, that He might lift us up to be nearer to Him.

Claiming the promise. This is a wonderful promise that any believer can claim. Yet when we claim this promise, we invite God into our lives to do a purifying work which may bring pain before it brings joy. We should take the risk involved in claiming this promise only if we wish to be close to the Lord and if we are convinced that this will lead to greater joy.

God will lift up the one who is humbled before Him.

A PROMISE OF EXALTATION

The promise: "Humble yourselves in the sight of the Lord, and He will lift you up" (James 4:10).

The context of the promise. (See the discussion of James 1:8, above.)

Understanding the promise. The *phrase lift up* means "to exalt," "to be raised up." This is one of the many paradoxes of the Christian faith. The way "up" is "down." The humble are exalted, and the proud are brought low. The weak are strong, and the strong are weak. When we humble ourselves before God, we make it possible for Him to exalt us.

The unsaved person can understand but never accept this kind of paradox. Too many Christians fail to accept such paradoxes as well. Yet each paradox reflects a spiritual reality by which we are called to live.

Claiming the promise. It may be hard for us to believe that the way up is down. But we can prove this promise of God for ourselves. We can take God at His word, humble ourselves, and wait to see how He will lift us up.

Actually, we also prove the promise by not taking God at His word. We can refuse to humble ourselves in the sight of the Lord. And if we do, we will discover that He does not lift us up but permits us to struggle unsuccessfully through life on our own.

In either case, God's promise will prove true.

A PROMISE OF HEALING

The promise: "The prayer of faith will save the sick, and the Lord will raise him up. And if he has committed sins, he will be forgiven" (James 5:15).

The context of the promise. The question of healing divides Christians. Some are convinced that every human ill can be cured with enough faith. Cancer? It will give way to prayer—if we have enough faith. This approach is sometimes carried to an extreme. Some children have died of curable diseases because their parents refused to seek medical treatment.

While it is clear that God sometimes heals persons miraculously, most Christians believe that prayer should be accompanied by medical treatment. Most also believe that healing is dependent on God—not on the faith of the person who prays or the individual who is sick. After all, the apostle Paul begged the Lord three times for healing from a chronic illness, and he was told "no" (2 Cor. 12:7–10).

James wrote that "the prayer of faith will save the sick, and the Lord will raise him up." Some would argue that the phrase *raise up* speaks of the resurrection and that our ultimate healing is meant here. But it is unlikely that this clear statement should be understood in this way.

James's topic was not sickness, but prayer and the power of prayer. What did James promise? Are all our diseases to give way to prayer? Is good health a Christian heritage, to be claimed by faith?

Understanding the promise. One approach to harmonizing this promise with the rest of Scripture's teaching on sickness and healing is to note the apparent connection of this sickness with sin. Thus, some have suggested that the promise of healing was limited to sicknesses which are punishment for sins. While this may be the case, the charge to pray for "anyone" who is sick (James 5:14) mitigates against it.

A comment by one authority sums up what we can say for sure about this passage:

Several things are clear from the text: (1) Prayer is needed when sickness comes. (2) One role of the elders of a church is to pray for the sick. (3) Prayer is primary, an active verb, and anointing with oil is secondary, expressed as a participle. (4) Oil was the most common ingredient in ancient medical treatments, and the verb describing its use (*aleipho*) means to "smear on" rather than the sacramental "to anoint" (*chrio*). Thus the passage teaches application of both prayer and normal medical treatments. (5) "Confession" is important if sin should happen to be the cause of the sickness, and thus the sickness is disciplinary. (6) Since confession and prayer are associated with good health, it is important for Christians to be sensitive to sin, confess their sins to each other, and pray for each other (*The Bible Reader's Companion*, 1991, p. 875).

We can add several observations to the above:

- The prayer James calls for is corporate rather than individual prayer.
- The phrase "prayer of faith" focuses our attention on God rather than on those praying. The efficacy of prayer does not depend on the amount of faith we have, but on the One in whom we place our trust.
- James precedes this call to prayer with an exhortation to have patience (James 5:10, 11). He refers us to Job, whose suffering included terrible ailments which were healed only after a long period of time. We should not assume that the healing promised will come quickly.
- James follows up the promise of healing with a reference to Elijah, whose prayers shut off and then restored rain. If the prayers of Elijah, a man like ourselves, affected the course of nature so drastically, we must believe in the efficacy of prayer.

Claiming the promise. How important it is to be part of a believing fellowship of Christians who have confidence in God and believe in the efficacy of prayer. When sickness comes, we can call on the leaders of our church to pray for us and ask our Christian brothers and sisters to join in as well.

PROMISES IN 1 AND 2 PETER

The two letters written by Peter have different themes. In his first letter, Peter wrote to those who were suffering persecution, encouraging them to remain faithful to Christ. In his second letter, Peter warned about dangers to the church from within, calling for purity in view of the coming judgment day of the Lord.

A PROMISE OF SECURITY

The promise: "But the word of the Lord endures forever" (1 Pet. 1:25).

The context of the promise. Peter wrote to those who had been "born again, not of corruptible seed but incorruptible, through the word of God which lives and abides forever"

(1 Pet. 1:23). He then quoted from Isaiah 40:6–8, which contrasts the impermanence of our biological life with the enduring Word of God. Peter's point is clear. We are no longer limited to our human nature. God's Word has entered our being, giving us eternal life.

Understanding the promise. It is fascinating how many ways the promise of security in Christ is conveyed to believers. Scripture tells us that Christ gives us *eternal* life (John 3:16; 3:36), not a life which can be turned on and off like a light switch.

The same truth is conveyed in this passage through a different image. The biological life God has given us is mortal and limited. But God's Word is enduring. We have been born again by the Word of God. Thus, God planted in us a life which will endure through time and eternity.

Responding to the promise. Every person who has been born again has been granted God's enduring life. This is not a promise to claim, but a promise whose wonder is to claim our hearts. As we grasp how amazing our salvation is, our appropriate response is to praise God and commit ourselves to love and serve Him all our lives.

A PROMISE TO LEADERS

The promise: "And when the Chief Shepherd appears, you will receive the crown of glory that does not fade away" (1 Pet. 5:4).

The context of the promise. Peter was writing as an elder to other elders of the church. In 1 Peter 5:1–4, he used the image of a shepherd to describe their ministry. As shepherds, spiritual leaders are to:

- serve willingly, not because they have to;
- serve eagerly, not for "dishonest gain"; elders are to be eager to *serve* rather than having hidden personal agendas in accepting the office;
- serve as examples rather than as church "bosses"; those whose motives and meth-

ods of leadership fit a shepherding pattern will be rewarded by the Lord when He returns.

Understanding the promise. The reward promised to elders who are dedicated to serve Jesus' people as shepherds is a "crown of glory." (For a discussion of crowns, see the comment on 2 Tim. 4:8, page 243.)

It is particularly fitting that these crowns are reserved for Jesus' second coming. Leaders especially are to value heaven's treasures rather than treasures on earth, for they are to set an example of Christian maturity for others.

Claiming the promise. There are special rewards for those who serve the church as leaders. But these rewards are for those whose desire is to *serve* God's flock. Any who wish to be elders should examine their motives carefully. Those who do serve as elders must be committed to servant leadership.

Fruitful, productive lives come from faith and disciplined commitment.

A PROMISE OF FRUITFULNESS

The promise: "For if these things are yours and abound, you will be neither barren nor unfruitful in the knowledge of our Lord Jesus Christ" (2 Pet. 1:8).

The context of the promise. Peter referred to the "exceeding great and precious promises" that believers have been given in the gospel. Specifically, Peter said that "His divine power has given to us all things that pertain to life and godliness." We have been granted in Christ all we need to live godly lives.

But these promises call us to make commitments of our own. We are to work diligently at adding to our basic faith in Christ such virtues as knowledge, self-control, perseverance, godliness, brotherly kindness, and love. These are the qualities that make a Christian's life fruitful.

Claiming the promise. The promise of fruitfulness is conditional. We are to work diligently at living the Christian life. At the same time, we must not assume that the call to diligence means we should live the Christian life on our own. Peter said that God's divine power has given us "all things that pertain to life and godliness." The diligent life is a life of faith, in which we draw on Christ's strength even as we commit ourselves to the disciplines of Christian living.

If we make the necessary commitments and these qualities become ours, our lives will be fruitful and productive. Life will have fresh meaning for us as well as others.

GOD'S PROMISES IN 1, 2, AND 3 JOHN

John's three brief epistles reflect the same themes as his Gospel. John wrote of light and darkness, life and death, love and hate, obedience and disobedience. Rather than being treated in sequence, these themes were woven together, occurring throughout John's writings. His first epistle especially included with these themes many special promises.

A PROMISE OF FELLOWSHIP

The promise: "If we walk in the light as He is in the light, we have fellowship with one another, and the blood of Jesus Christ His Son cleanses us from all sin" (1 John 1:7).

The context of the promise. John frequently contrasted light and darkness in his writings. In the preceding verse, John made this contrast explicit, writing "if we say we have fellowship with Him and walk in darkness, we lie and do not practice the truth." The question we must ask is, What did "darkness" and "light" mean to John?

Some have suggested that "walking in the light" means to live without sin. But John had written that if we walk in the light Christ's blood cleanses us from sin. If those walking in the light need cleansing, walking in the light cannot mean living a sinless life.

The keys to understanding John's imagery are found in the phrase, "And do not practice the truth," and in what Scripture says about sin. In Scripture something is *true* because it is in harmony with reality. God's Word is truth (John 7:17), not simply because God said it, but because what God says reveals reality as He alone knows it.

The person walking in darkness is someone who is dishonest, neither facing nor admitting reality. He says he has fellowship with God, but he is not being honest about his life.

What does God say about the believer and sin? John reminded us that the truth is, "If we say that we have no sin, we deceive ourselves and the truth is not in us" (1 John 1:8). A person who walks in the light is honest with himself and God about his sins. He looks at himself as God views him, he acknowledges his flaws and faults, and he relies on the blood of Christ to keep on cleansing him. A person like this has fellowship with God.

Understanding the promise. God's promise is that if we are honest with ourselves and with Him about our sins, we will stay in fellowship with Him. How can a sinner have fellowship with a holy God? Only on the basis of the

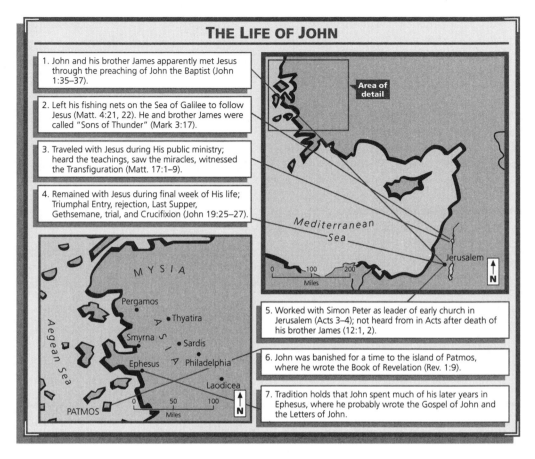

THE LIFE OF JOHN

1. John and his brother James apparently met Jesus through the preaching of John the Baptist (John 1:35–37).

2. Left his fishing nets on the Sea of Galilee to follow Jesus (Matt. 4:21, 22). He and brother James were called "Sons of Thunder" (Mark 3:17).

3. Traveled with Jesus during His public ministry; heard the teachings, saw the miracles, witnessed the Transfiguration (Matt. 17:1–9).

4. Remained with Jesus during final week of His life; Triumphal Entry, rejection, Last Supper, Gethsemane, trial, and Crucifixion (John 19:25–27).

5. Worked with Simon Peter as leader of early church in Jerusalem (Acts 3–4); not heard from in Acts after death of his brother James (12:1, 2).

6. John was banished for a time to the island of Patmos, where he wrote the Book of Revelation (Rev. 1:9).

7. Tradition holds that John spent much of his later years in Ephesus, where he probably wrote the Gospel of John and the Letters of John.

Area of detail

Mediterranean Sea

Jerusalem

MYSIA

Pergamos
Thyatira
Smyrna
Sardis
Ephesus
Philadelphia
Laodicea

Aegean Sea

PATMOS

---

blood of Christ, which keeps on cleansing us from our sins.

Claiming the promise. To claim this wonderful promise, all we have to do is agree with God that our sins are sins, trusting the blood of Jesus to keep on cleansing us.

Responding to the promise. Some Christian traditions hold that a person who is saved—or who has experienced a special infusion of God's grace after salvation—will never sin. Anger is dismissed as righteous indignation. Spiritual pride is ignored as lists of do's and don'ts replace love as the measure of one's spirituality. In spite of John's teaching that those who say "we have no sin" deceive themselves, believers in some traditions are pressured to present themselves as sinless.

How terrible it is to try to live a lie, to reinterpret sins as something less than sins.

When we take this approach, we shut ourselves off from the constant flow of God's forgiveness and miss the intimate fellowship with God which forgiveness maintains.

THE PROMISE OF FORGIVENESS

The promise: "If we confess our sins, He is faithful and just to forgive us our sins and to cleanse us from all unrighteousness" (1 John 1:9).

The context of the promise. John had just reminded his readers that they do sin. To maintain fellowship with God, believers must be honest with themselves and with God about their sins. If we treat our sins as sins, the blood of Christ will cleanse us and we will remain close to the Lord.

In introducing this promise, John continued this line of teaching, discussed more thoroughly in the explanation of 1 John 1:7, above. And John made even stronger statements about the believer and sins. In 1 John 1:8, he wrote that if we say we have no sin, we only deceive ourselves. In 1 John 1:10, he wrote, "If we say that we have not sinned, we make Him a liar, and His word is not in us."

Christian saints are also sinners. God knows it, and He declares it. Anyone who claims to live a sinless life in effect calls God a liar!

Understanding the promise. God responds to the fact that saints are still sinners by making us a wonderful promise. "If we confess our sins" God will forgive and keep on cleansing us. The Greek word for "confess" is *homologeo,* a word that means "to acknowledge." God promises that when we acknowledge our sins as sins, He is faithful and will step in to forgive us.

But the promise is even more wonderful, for John adds, "And to cleanse us from all unrighteousness." God not only forgives our sins, but He also continues to work within our personalities to change our hearts. God's cleansing work within us is part of a transformation process that He has begun and will continue. If this transformation is to proceed quickly, we need to walk in the light and to be honest with God about our sins.

A PROMISE OF ETERNITY

The promise: "He who does the will of God abides forever" (1 John 2:17).

The context of the promise. John had warned against loving the world. In John, the world, the *kosmos,* is a theological term depicting human culture and society as systems shaped by sin. Thus, John said, "All that is in the world" does not derive from God the Father, but is generated by the lust of the flesh (sinful cravings), the lust of the eyes (sinful values) and the pride of life (sinful attitudes).

God's judgment on the world is seen in the fact that it is "passing away." It has no permanence. Those who are caught up in its ways will end up with nothing.

Understanding the promise. God promised that "he who does the will of God abides forever." This was set against the fact that "the world is passing away" (1 John 2:17). Christians are called to live by desires, values, and attitudes which are in harmony with God's will. In contrast to the world which is passing away, the things of God "abide forever." They are eternal. In committing ourselves to live by God's will, we gain what can never be lost.

Claiming the promise. Christians, like others, can follow the ways of this world. But God has something far better in mind for us. It is wise to ignore the attractions of the world and commit ourselves fully to God's will.

A PROMISE OF LIKENESS

The promise: "Beloved, now we are the children of God; and it has not yet been revealed what we shall be, but we know that when He is revealed, we shall be like Him, for we shall see Him as He is" (1 John 3:2).

The context of the promise. One of the major themes of God's New Covenant is inner transformation. Sinful human beings come into a relationship with God through which He changes them from within, to become more and more like Jesus. This inner transformation is a process which goes on throughout our lives, but it never reaches perfection in this life.

Several biblical passages, such as 1 Thessalonians 4:12–16 and 1 Corinthians 15, speak of that final transformation which will take place at our resurrection. In sharing this promise, John was not adding anything new to the gospel but was reaffirming previous truths.

Understanding the promise. The gospel of Jesus is for both *now* and *then.* Now, John reminds his readers, "we are the children of God." In Christ, a family relationship with God the Father has been established, and our status has been changed from enemies (cf. Romans 5:10) to dearly loved children.

Knowing that we are children now does not tell us what we will become. We know that our destiny will be unveiled when Jesus comes. We know that we will be like Jesus. And we know that we will see Him as He is—in His full glory as God. All this is promised to us in the gospel in which we have believed! This wonderful future became ours when we first trusted in Jesus, and it can never be taken away from us.

Responding to the promise. We don't have to do anything to claim this promise which is already ours. But the prospect of seeing Jesus and of our ultimate transformation does suggest an appropriate response. John said, "Everyone who has this hope in Him purifies himself, just as He is pure."

In Scripture, "hope" is not a wish for the unlikely but a settled confidence that God will do what He has promised. John declared that everyone who has a settled confidence that Jesus will come and transform him or her "purifies himself, just as He is pure."

One of the findings of behavioral science is that people tend to act in harmony with their self-image. A child who sees herself as stupid tends not to study or do well in school, even if she has the ability. An adult who sees himself as competent will seize opportunities for advancement at work that a person who thinks of himself as less competent would never attempt.

How does God want us to see ourselves? As His children now—and as children who are destined to be like Jesus. This is our essential identity: we are little Christs. And how will we act if we have the hope, the settled confidence that we will be like Jesus one day? We will seek to purify ourselves even as Jesus is pure. We will seek to grow toward His perfect will for our lives.

What a glorious future God has in store for His children! And how wonderful that we can taste that future now as we seek to be more like our Lord each day.

A PROMISE OF ANSWERED PRAYER

The promise: "Now this is the confidence that we have in Him, that if we ask anything according to His will, He hears us. And if we know that He hears us, whatever we ask, we know that we have the petitions that we have asked of Him" (1 John 5:14, 15).

The context of the promise. In his Gospel, John quoted two sayings of Jesus about prayer. One promised that Christ would answer prayers offered in His name (John 14:14, see pages 198–199), and the other promised an answer to prayer for those in whom Jesus' words lived (John 15:7, see pages 201–202). The same promise is made in this passage to those who ask "anything according to His [God's] will."

Each of these promises described the same experience but in different ways. We Christians are called to love God and to stay close to our Lord. We do this by responding to His Word—both written and living—as God speaks to us. As we abide in Him, we learn to see life and life's issues as Jesus sees them. Thus when we pray in Christ's name, we will identify ourselves and our prayers with His goals and purposes. And when our prayers express Christ's own goals and purposes, we will surely stay in His will.

So these three prayer promises teach the same basic truth. To be sure our prayers are answered, we need to be in such harmony with God that our prayers will express what He wants us to pray for.

Understanding the promise. Prayer is an expression of our confidence in God. God is a person who loves us and who wants us to live close to Him. As we do so, the Lord will communicate His will to us—both objectively through the Scriptures and subjectively through the Holy Spirit. As we sense God's will, we are to turn to Him in prayer with the assurance that He will hear and respond.

Responding to the promise. As we draw closer to God, we will have a growing sensitivity to

Him and His will. Scripture tells us, "In everything by prayer and supplication with thanksgiving make your requests known to God" (Phil. 4:6). This promise implies that there will be times when the Holy Spirit guides our prayers so clearly that we will know ahead of time what God's answer will be.

GOD'S PROMISES IN REVELATION

The book of Revelation provides a stunning vision of history's end. It portrays devastating divine judgments on rebellious humanity. These culminate in the return of Jesus and the creation of a new and sinless heavens and earth. At history's end, sin will be judged and Satan and his fallen angels along with unbelieving humanity will be assigned to the lake of fire, while all the saved will be welcomed into eternity.

In one sense, the entire book is a promise—a promise that God will deal decisively with sin and that His people will share in the ultimate triumph of good over evil.

Yet as a narrative account of John's vision, the text contains no specific promises until we come to the book's last chapter. This promise is repeated three times.

THE PROMISE OF JESUS' COMING

The promise: "Behold, I am coming quickly!" (Rev. 22:7, 12, 20).

The context of the promise. John had given a vision of what we call heaven, which was in actuality a new and pure universe to be created by God. Following his description of the new heavens and earth and a great city from which God is to reign forever, John was told that the things he had been shown "must shortly take place."

John then heard Jesus repeating the promise, "Behold, I am coming quickly!"

Understanding the promise. If we look at this promise from the perspective of the two thousand years of the Christian era, it seems to make little sense. We cannot imagine "quickly" involving that span of time. Our problem is that God does not measure time as we do. He abides in eternity, and His life cannot be measured in centuries or periods of thousands of years.

But there is more to Jesus' promise. God wants each generation of believers to look forward eagerly to His coming and to realize that the day of His triumph really is near. The fact that Jesus is coming quickly is both a psychological and eternal reality.

As I write this material, I am 66 years old. Yet, 66 is a mere moment in the flow of history and less that a fraction of a millisecond when measured against eternity. And Jesus' return is quickly approaching this moment in which I live. Because He is coming quickly, I look forward to His return during my lifetime—even as my mother looked forward to Jesus' coming during her days on earth. Each new day that dawns brings Jesus' coming closer for me—and may in fact be *the* day of His appearing. The fact that He is coming *quickly* means that I look forward with expectation and excitement and that I want to be ready if His return should take place today.

It is in this sense that Christ's coming quickly is a psychological reality, which should shape each believer's view of tomorrow. Yes, we are to plan and prepare for the future. But always, echoing in our thoughts and keeping our lives focused on spiritual realities, is the repeated promise of Jesus: "Behold, I am coming quickly."

We need to be ready for that coming, today!

CHAPTER 21

EXPLORING PERSONAL RELATIONSHIP WITH GOD:

GUIDED BY WORDS TO COUNT ON
Selected Scriptures

Many of the Bible's words that we can count on deal with the believer's personal relationship with God. This chapter compiles God's wonderful words about our relationship with Him.

BLESSING

"I will cause showers to come down in their season; there shall be showers of blessing" (Ezek. 34:26).

"He who did not spare His own Son, but delivered Him up for us all, how shall He not with Him also freely give us all things?" (Rom. 8:32).

"Blessed be the God and Father of our Lord Jesus Christ, who has blessed us with every spiritual blessing in the heavenly places in Christ" (Eph. 1:3).

"Oh, how great is Your goodness, which You have laid up for those who fear You, which You have prepared for those who trust in You" (Ps. 31:19).

"God shall bless us, and all the ends of the earth shall fear Him" (Ps. 67:7).

"Blessed is the man whose strength is in You, whose heart is set on pilgrimage" (Ps. 84:5).

"Yes, the LORD will give what is good" (Ps. 85:12). "For He satisfies the longing soul, and fills the hungry soul with goodness" (Ps. 107:9).

"Say to the righteous that it shall be well with them, for they shall eat the fruit of their doings" (Isa. 3:10).

"Blessed is every one who fears the LORD, who walks in His ways" (Ps. 128:1).

"Blessed is the man who trusts in the LORD, and whose hope is the LORD" (Jer. 17:7).

"The LORD has been mindful of us;
He will bless us;
He will bless the house of Israel;
He will bless the house of Aaron;
He will bless those who fear the
    LORD,
Both small and great" (Ps. 115:
    12, 13).

"And I will make an everlasting covenant with them; that I will not turn away from doing them good (Jer. 32:40).

CARE

"And God is able to make all grace abound toward you, that you, always having all sufficiency in all things, may have an abundance for every good work" (2 Cor. 9:8).

"The LORD will guide you continually, and satisfy your soul in drought, and strengthen your bones; You shall be like a watered garden, and like a spring of water, whose waters do not fail" (Isa. 58:11).

"When you have eaten and are full, you shall bless the LORD your God for the good land which He has given you" (Deut. 8:10).

"The LORD is my shepherd; I shall not want" (Ps. 23:1).

"And you shall remember the LORD your God, for it is He who gives you power to get wealth, that He may establish His covenant which he swore to your fathers, as it is this day" (Deut. 8:18).

"For He is our God, and we are the people of His pasture, and the sheep of His hand" (Ps. 95:7).

"Behold, God is my helper; the LORD is with those who uphold my life" (Ps. 54:4).

"Yours, O LORD, is the greatness,
The power and the glory,
The victory and the majesty;
For all that is in heaven and in earth
 is Yours;
Yours is the kingdom, O LORD,
And You are exalted as head over all.
Both riches and honor come from
 You,
And You reign over all,   .
In Your hand is power and might;
In Your hand it is to make great
And to give strength to all" (1 Chron.
 29:11, 12).

"Therefore I say to you, do not worry about your life, what you will eat or what you will drink; nor about your body, what you will put on. Is not life more than food and the body more than clothing? Look at the birds of the air, for they neither sow nor reap nor gather into barns; yet your heavenly Father feeds them. Are you not of more value than they?" (Matt. 6:25–26).

"And my God shall supply all your need according to His riches in glory by Christ Jesus" (Phil. 4:19; see pages 237–238).

COMFORT

"The LORD of hosts is with us; the God of Jacob is our refuge" (Ps. 46:7).

"But the mercy of the LORD is from everlasting to everlasting on those who fear Him, and His righteousness to children's children" (Ps. 103:17).

"I am persuaded that neither death nor life, nor angels nor principalities nor powers, nor things present nor things to come, nor height nor depth, nor any other created thing, shall be able to separate us from the love of God which is in Christ Jesus our Lord (Rom. 8:38–39; see page 238).

"Be strong and of good courage, do not fear nor be afraid of them; for the LORD your God, He is the One who goes with you. He will not leave your nor forsake you (Deut. 31:6; see page 125).

"When my father and my mother forsake me, then the LORD will take care of me" (Ps. 27:10).

"Nevertheless I am continually with You; You hold me by my right hand. You will guide me with Your counsel, and afterward receive me to glory (Ps. 73:23, 24).

"Lo, I am with you always, even to the end of the age" (Matt. 28:20).

"All that the Father gives Me will come to Me, and the one who comes to Me I will by no means cast out" (John 6:37).

"I, the LORD, will hear them; I, the God of Israel, will not forsake them" (Isa. 41:17).

"For the LORD will not cast off His people, nor will He forsake His inheritance" (Ps. 94:14).

DISCIPLINE

"For I am with you,' says the LORD, 'to save you; though I make a full end of all nations where I have scattered you, yet I will not make a complete end of you. But I will correct you in justice, and will not let you go altogether unpunished' " (Jer. 30:11).

"You should know in your heart that as a man chastens his son, so the LORD your God chastens you" (Deut. 8:5).

"For they indeed for a few days chastened us as seemed best to them, but He for our profit, that we may be partakers of His holiness" (Heb. 12:10).

"Now no chastening seems to be joyful for the present, but painful; nevertheless, afterward it yields the peaceable fruit of righteousness to those who have been trained by it" (Heb. 12:11; see page 247).

Blessed is the man whom You
    instruct, O LORD,
And teach out of Your law,
That You may give him rest from the
    days of adversity,
Until the pit is dug for the wicked.
For the LORD will not cast off His
    people,
Nor will He forsake His inheritance"
    (Ps. 94:12–14).

"My son, do not despise the
    chastening of the LORD,

Nor detest His correction;
For whom the LORD loves He
    corrects,
Just as a father the son in whom He
    delights" (Prov. 3:11, 12).

"As many as I love, I rebuke and chasten" (Rev. 3:19).

"But when we are judged, we are chastened by the LORD, that we may not be condemned with the world" (1 Cor. 11:32).

"For the commandment is a lamp, and the law a light; reproofs of instruction are the way of life" (Prov. 6:23).

"He who spares the rod hates his son, but he who loves him disciplines him promptly" (Prov. 13:24).

ENCOURAGEMENT

"The LORD knows how to deliver the godly out of temptations and to reserve the unjust under punishment for the day of judgment" (2 Peter 2:9).

"The LORD will perfect that which concerns me; Your mercy, O LORD, endures forever" (Ps. 138:8).

"And now, Israel, what does the LORD your God require of you, but to fear the LORD your God, to walk in all His ways and to love Him, to serve the LORD your God with all your heart and with all your soul" (Deut. 10:12).

"For I know the thoughts that I think toward you, says the Lord, thoughts of peace and not of evil, to give you a future and a hope" (Jer. 29:11; see page 69).

"Now may our Lord Jesus Christ Himself, and our God and Father, who has loved us and given us everlasting consolation and good hope by grace, comfort your hearts and establish you in every good word and work" (2 Thess. 2:16, 17).

"For God is not unjust to forget your work and labor of love which you have shown toward His name, in that you have ministered to the saints, and do minister" (Heb. 6:10; see page 246).

"As each one has received a gift, minister it to one another, as good stewards of the manifold grace of God" (1 Peter 4:10).

EVERLASTING LIFE

"And this is the will of Him who sent Me, that everyone who sees the Son and believes in Him may have everlasting life; and I will raise him up at the last day" (John 6:40).

"Knowing that He who raised up our Lord Jesus will also raise us up with Jesus, and will present us with you" (2 Cor. 4:14).

"For our citizenship is in heaven, from which we also eagerly wait for the Savior, the Lord Jesus Christ, who will transform our lowly body that it may be conformed to His glorious body, according to the working by which He is able even to subdue all things to Himself" (Phil. 3:20, 21).

"For I know that my Redeemer lives,
And He shall stand at last on the
    earth;
And after my skin is destroyed, this I
    know,
That in my flesh I shall see God,
Whom I shall see for myself,
And my eyes shall behold, and not
    another" (Job 19:25–27).

"Your dead shall live;
Together with my dead body they
    shall arise.
Awake and sing, you who dwell in
    dust;
For your dew is like the dew of
    herbs,
And the earth shall cast out the
    dead" (Isa. 26:19; see page
    148).

"Behold, I tell you a mystery: We shall not all sleep, but we shall all be changed; in a moment, in the twinkling of an eye, at the last trumpet. For the trumpet will sound, and the dead will be raised incorruptible, and we shall be changed" (1 Cor. 15:51, 52; see pages 220–221).

"For if we have been united together in the likeness of His death, certainly we also shall be in the likeness of His resurrection" (Rom. 6:5).

"As for me, I will see Your face in righteousness; I shall be satisfied when I awake in your likeness" (Ps. 17:15).

"I will ransom them from the power
    of the grave;
I will redeem them from death.
O Death, I will be your plagues!
O Grave, I will be your destruction"
    (Hos. 13:14).

"Most assuredly, I say to you, the hour is coming, and now is, when the dead will hear the voice of the Son of God; and those who hear will live" (John 5:25).

EXCELLENCE

"For I have known him, in order that he may command his children and his household after him, that they keep the way of the LORD, to do righteousness and justice, that the LORD may bring to Abraham what He has spoken to him" (Gen. 18:19).

"And it shall come to pass
That just as you were a curse among
    the nations,
O house of Judah and house of
    Israel,
So I will save you, and you shall be a
    blessing.
Do not fear,
Let your hands be strong" (Zech.
    8:13).

"If you return, then I will bring you back" (Jer. 15:19).

"Most assuredly, I say to you, he who believes in Me, the works that I do he will do also; and greater works than these he will do, because I go to My Father" (John 14:12).

"And I thank Christ Jesus our Lord who has enabled me" (1 Tim. 1:12).

"My eyes shall be on the faithful of
    the land,
That they may dwell with me;
He who walks in a perfect way,
He shall serve me" (Ps. 101:6).

"And [he] has made us kings and priests to His God and Father, to Him be glory and dominion forever and ever" (Rev. 1:6).

"Yet it shall not be so among you; but whoever desires to become great among you, let him be your servant, and whoever desires to be first among you, let him be your slave; just as the Son of Man did not come to be served, but to serve, and to give His life a ransom for many" (Matt. 20:26–28).

"By this My Father is glorified, that you bear much fruit; so you will be My disciples" (John 15:8).

"There are diversities of gifts, but the same Spirit. There are differences of ministries, but the same Lord" (1 Cor. 12:4, 5).

FELLOWSHIP

"And the Lord God said, 'It is not good that man should be alone; I will make him a helper comparable to him" (Gen. 2:18).

"A new commandment I give to you, that you love one another; as I have loved you, that you also love one another. By this all will know that you are My disciples, if you have love for one another" (John 13:34, 35).

"Owe no one anything except to love one another, for he who loves another has fulfilled the law" (Rom. 13:8).

"Now may the God of patience and comfort grant you to be like-minded toward one another, according to Christ Jesus, that you may with one mind and one mouth glorify the God and Father of our Lord Jesus Christ" (Rom. 15:5, 6).

"For where two or three are gathered together in My name, I am there in the midst of them" (Matt. 18:20; see page 172).

"For you are all one in Christ Jesus" (Gal. 3:28).

"Since you have purified your souls in obeying the truth through the Spirit in sincere love of the brethren, love one another fervently with a pure heart" (1 Peter 1:22).

FORGIVENESS

"You have forgiven the iniquity of Your people; You have covered their sin" (Ps. 85:2).

"For You, Lord, are good, and ready to forgive, and abundant in mercy to all those who call upon You" (Ps. 86:5).

"Bless the Lord, O my soul;
And all that is within me, bless His
    holy name!
Bless the Lord, O my soul,
And forget not all His benefits;
Who forgives all your iniquities" (Ps.
    103:1–3).

"As far as the east is from the west,
So far has He removed our
    transgressions from us.
As a father pities his children,
So the Lord pities those who fear
    Him.
For He knows our frame;
He remembers that we are dust" (Ps.
    103:12–14).

"I acknowledged my sin to You,
And my iniquity I have not hidden.
I said, 'I will confess my
    transgressions to the LORD,'
And You forgave the iniquity of my
    sin" (Ps. 32:5, 6).

"For I will forgive their iniquity; and their sin I will remember no more" (Jer. 31:34).

"If we confess our sins, He is faithful and just to forgive us our sins and to cleanse us from all unrighteousness" (1 John 1:9; see pages 255–256).

"For You, LORD, are good, and ready to forgive, and abundant in mercy to all those who call upon You" (Ps. 86:5).

"Who is a God like You; Pardoning
    iniquity
And passing over the transgression
    of the remnant of His heritage?
He does not retain His anger forever,
Because He delights in mercy.
He will again have compassion on
    us,
And will subdue our iniquities" (Mic.
    7:18, 19).

"To Him all the prophets witness that, through His name, whoever believes in Him will receive remission of sins" (Acts 10:43).

FREEDOM

"Most assuredly, I say to you, whoever commits sin is a slave of sin. And a slave does not abide in the house forever, but a son abides forever. Therefore if the Son makes you free, you shall be free indeed" (John 8:34–36).

"For when you were slaves of sin, you were free in regard to righteousness. . . . But now having been set free from sin, and having become slaves of God, you have your fruit to holiness, and the end, everlasting life" (Rom. 6:20, 22).

"Knowing this, that our old man was crucified with Him, that the body of sin might be done away with, that we should no longer be slaves of sin" (Rom. 6:6).

"For sin shall not have dominion over you, for you are not under law but under grace" (Rom. 6:14; see pages 209–210).

"Whoever has been born of God does not sin, for His seed remains in him; and he cannot sin, because he has been born of God" (1 John 3:9).

"For I am not ashamed of the gospel of Christ, for it is the power of God to salvation for everyone who believes, for the Jew first and also for the Greek" (Rom. 1:16).

GROWTH

"But we all, with unveiled face, beholding as in a mirror the glory of the Lord, are being transformed into the same image from glory to glory, just as by the Spirit of the Lord" (2 Cor. 3:18; see also page 222).

"Being confident of this very thing, that He who has begun a good work in you will complete it until the day of Jesus Christ" (Phil. 1:6; see also pages 234–235).

"As newborn babes, desire the pure milk of the word, that you may grow thereby, if indeed you have tasted that the Lord is gracious. Coming to Him as to a living stone, rejected indeed by men, but chosen by God and precious, you also, as living stones, are being built up a spiritual house, a holy priesthood, to offer up spiritual sacrifices acceptable to God through Jesus Christ" (1 Pet. 2:2–5).

"But, speaking the truth in love, may grow up in all things into Him who is the head—Christ—from whom the whole body, joined and knit together by what every joint supplies, according to the effective working by which every part does its share, causes growth of the body for the edifying of itself in love" (Eph. 4:15, 16).

"By which have been given to us exceedingly great and precious promises, that through these you may be partakers of the divine nature, having escaped the corruption that is in the world through lust. But also for this very reason, giving all diligence, add to your faith virtue, to virtue knowledge, to knowledge self-control, to self-control perseverance, to perseverance godliness, to godliness, brotherly kindness, and to brotherly kindness love. For if these things are yours and abound, you will be neither barren nor unfruitful in the knowledge of our Lord Jesus Christ" (2 Pet. 1:4–8; see also page 254).

GUIDANCE

"You in Your mercy have led forth the people whom You have redeemed; You have guided them in Your strength to Your holy habitation" (Exod. 15:13).

"Now therefore, go, and I will be with your mouth and teach you what you shall say" (Exod. 4:12; see pages 111–112).

"Your ears shall hear a word behind you, saying, 'This is the way, walk in it,' Whenever you turn to the right hand or whenever you turn to the left" (Isa. 30:21).

"In all your ways acknowledge Him and He shall direct your paths" (Prov. 3:6).

"I will instruct you and teach you in the way you should go; I will guide you with my eye" (Ps. 32:8; see page 139).

"But the Helper, the Holy Spirit, whom the Father will send in My name, He will teach you all things, and bring to your remembrance all things that I said to you" (John 14:26; see page 200).

"But there is a spirit in man, and the breath of the Almighty gives him understanding. Great men are not always wise, nor do the aged always understand justice" (Job 32:8, 9).

"You will guide me with Your counsel, and afterward receive me to glory" (Ps. 73:24).

"The secret things belong to the LORD our God, but those things which are revealed belong to us and to our children forever, that we may do all the words of this law" (Deut. 29:29).

"For I will give you a mouth and wisdom which all your adversaries will not be able to contradict or resist" (Luke 21:15; see page 181).

"However, when He, the Spirit of truth, has come, He will guide you into all truth; for He will not speak on His own authority, but whatever He hears He will speak; and He will tell you things to come" (John 16:13; see page 202).

HEAVEN

" 'Sing and rejoice, O daughter of Zion! For behold, I am coming and I will dwell in your midst,' says the LORD" (Zech. 2:10).

"When Christ who is our life appears, then you also will appear with Him in glory" (Col. 3:4; see page 238).

"So Christ was offered once to bear the sins of many. To those who eagerly wait for Him He will appear a second time, apart from sin, for salvation" (Heb. 9:28; see pages 246–247).

"For yet a little while, and He who is coming will come and will not tarry" (Heb. 10:37).

"For the Lord Himself will descend from heaven with a shout, with the voice of an archangel, and with the trumpet of God. And the dead in Christ will rise first. Then we who are alive and remain shall be caught up together with them in the clouds to meet the Lord in the air. And thus we shall always be with the Lord" (1 Thess. 4:16, 17; see pages 239–240).

"In My Father's house are many mansions; if it were not so, I would have told you. I go to prepare a place for you. And if I go and prepare a place for you, I will come again and receive you to Myself; that where I am, there you may be also" (John 14:2, 3; see pages 197–198).

"Men of Galilee, why do you stand gazing up into heaven? This same Jesus, who was taken up from you into heaven, will so come in like manner as you saw Him go into heaven" (Acts 1:11).

"Beloved, now we are children of God; and it has not yet been revealed what we shall be, but we know that when He is revealed, we shall be like Him, for we shall see Him as He is" (1 John 3:2; see pages 256–257).

"Behold, He is coming with clouds, and every eye will see Him, even they who pierced Him" (Rev. 1:7).

"Therefore you also be ready, for the Son of Man is coming at an hour you do not expect" (Matt. 24:44).

HOLINESS

"For He made Him who knew no sin to be sin for us, that we might become the righteousness of God in Him" (2 Cor. 5:21).

"As His divine power has given to us all things that pertain to life and godliness, through the knowledge of Him who called us by glory and virtue" (2 Pet. 1:3).

"Consecrate yourselves therefore, and be holy, for I am the Lord your God" (Lev. 20:7).

"Just as He chose us in Him before the foundation of the world, that we should be holy and without blame before Him in love" (Eph. 1:4).

"Husbands, love your wives, just as Christ also loved the church and gave Himself for her, that He might sanctify and cleanse her with the washing of water by the word, that He might present her to Himself a glorious church, not having spot or wrinkle or any such thing, but that she should be holy and without blemish" (Eph. 5:25–27).

"So that He may establish your hearts blameless in holiness before our God and Father at the coming of our Lord Jesus Christ with all His saints" (1 Thess. 3:13).

"Now may the God of peace Himself sanctify you completely; and may your whole spirit, soul, and body be preserved blameless at the coming of our Lord Jesus Christ" (1 Thess. 5:23).

"Let them do good, that they may be rich in good works, ready to give, willing to share, storing up for themselves a good foundation for the time to come, that they may lay hold on eternal life" (1 Tim. 6:18, 19).

"We know that whoever is born of God does not sin; but he who has been born of God keeps himself, and the wicked one does not touch him" (1 John 5:18).

JOY

"Until now you have asked nothing in My name. Ask, and you will receive, that your joy may be full" (John 16:24).

"But let the righteous be glad; let them rejoice before God; Yes, let them rejoice exceedingly" (Ps. 8:3).

"Oh, satisfy us early with Your mercy, that we may rejoice and be glad all our days" (Ps. 90:14).

"You will show me the path of life; In Your presence is fullness of joy; At Your right hand are pleasures forevermore" (Ps. 16:11).

"If you keep My commandments, you will abide in My love, just as I have kept My Father's commandments and abide in His love. These things I have spoken to you, that My joy may remain in you, and that your joy may be full" (John 15:10, 11).

"So the ransomed of the LORD shall
    return,
And come to Zion with singing,
With everlasting joy on their heads.
They shall obtain joy and gladness;
Sorrow and sighing shall flee away"
    (Isa. 51:11).

"Looking unto Jesus, the author and finisher of our faith, who for the joy that was set before Him endured the cross, despising the shame, and has sat down at the right hand of the throne of God" (Heb. 12:2).

"Therefore you now have sorrow; but I will see you again and your heart will rejoice, and your joy no one will take from you" (John 16:22).

"Do not sorrow, for the joy of the LORD is your strength" (Neh. 8:10).

"Light is sown for the righteous, and gladness for the upright in heart" (Ps. 97:11).

"Now may the God of hope fill you with all joy and peace in believing, that you may abound in hope by the power of the Holy Spirit" (Rom. 15:13).

"Whom having not seen you love, though now you do not see Him, yet believing, you rejoice with joy inexpressible and full of glory" (1 Pet. 1:8).

LOVE

"But the very hairs of your head are all numbered. Do not fear therefore; you are of more value than many sparrows" (Matt. 10:30, 31).

"'You are My flock, the flock of My pasture; you are men, and I am your God,' says the LORD God" (Ezek. 34:31).

"But now, thus says the LORD, who created you, O Jacob, and He who formed you, O Israel: 'Fear not, for I have redeemed you; I have called you by your name; You are mine" (Isa. 43:1).

"'For the mountains shall depart and the hills be removed, but My kindness shall not depart from you, Nor shall My covenant of peace be removed,' says the LORD, who has mercy on you" (Isa. 54:10).

"Yes, I have loved you with an
    everlasting love;
Therefore with lovingkindness I have
    drawn you" (Jer. 31:3).

"But know that the LORD has set apart for Himself him who is godly; the LORD will hear when I call to Him" (Ps. 4:3).

"The LORD is good, a stronghold in the day of trouble; and He knows those who trust in Him" (Nah. 1:7).

"The LORD your God in your midst,
The Mighty One, will save;
He will rejoice over you with
    gladness,
He will quiet you with His love,
He will rejoice over you with
    singing" (Zeph. 3:17).

"He shall send from heaven and save me; He reproaches the one who would swallow me up. God shall send forth His mercy and His truth" (Ps. 57:3).

"Nevertheless My lovingkindness I will not utterly take from him, nor allow My faithfulness to fail" (Ps. 89:33).

"For God so loved the world that He gave His only begotten Son, that whoever believes in Him should not perish but have everlasting life" (John 3:16; see page 189).

" 'They shall be Mine,' says the LORD
    of hosts,
On the day that I make them My
    jewels,
And I will spare them
As a man spares his own son who
    serves him" (Mal. 3:17).

OBEDIENCE

"But this is the covenant that I will make with the house of Israel after those days, says the LORD: I will put My law in their minds, and write it on their hearts; and I will be their God, and they shall be My people" (Jer. 31:33).

"Clearly you are an epistle of Christ, ministered by us, written not with ink but by the Spirit of the living God, not on tablets of stone but on tablets of flesh, that is, of the heart" (2 Cor. 3:3).

"How much more shall the blood of Christ, who through the eternal Spirit offered Himself without spot to God, cleanse your conscience from dead works to serve the living God?" (Heb. 9:14).

"This is the thing which the LORD commanded you to do, and the glory of the LORD will appear to you" (Lev. 9:6).

"He who has my commandments and keeps them, it is he who loves Me. And he who loves Me will be loved by My Father, and I will love him and manifest Myself to him" (John 14:21).

"If anyone loves Me, he will keep My word; and My Father will love him, and We will come to him and make Our home with him. He who does not love Me does not keep My words" (John 14:23–24).

"For this is the love of God, that we keep His commandments. And His commandments are not burdensome. For whatever is born of God overcomes the world. And this is the victory that has overcome the world—our faith. Who is he who overcomes the world, but he who believes that Jesus is the Son of God" (1 John 5:3–5).

"I have chosen the way of truth;
    Your judgments I have laid before
        me.
I cling to Your testimonies;
    O LORD, do not put me to shame!
I will run the course of Your
    commandments,
For you shall enlarge my heart" (Ps.
    119:30–32).

PRAYER

"Ask, and it will be given to you; seek, and you will find; knock, and it will be opened to you" (Matt. 7:7; see page 168).

"For the eyes of the LORD are on the righteous, and His ears are open to their prayers" (1 Pet. 3:12).

"And whatever you ask in My name, that I will do, that the Father may be glorified in the Son" (John 14:13).

"If you ask anything in My name, I will do it" (John 14:14; see pages 198–199).

"Now this is the confidence that we have in Him, that if we ask anything according to His will, He hears us. And if we know that He hears us, whatever we ask, we know that we have the petitions that we have asked of Him" (1 John 5:14, 15; see pages 257–258).

"But know that the LORD has set apart for Himself him who is godly; the LORD will hear when I call to Him" (Ps. 4:3).

"Or what man is there among you who, if his son asks for bread, will give him a stone? Or if he asks for a fish, will he give him a serpent? If you then, being evil, know how to give good gifts to your children, how much more will your Father who is in heaven give good things to those who ask Him?" (Matt. 7:9–11).

"O You who hear prayer, to You all flesh will come. . . . By awesome deeds in righteousness You will answer us, O God of our salvation" (Ps. 65:2, 5). "Behold, the LORD's hand is not shortened, that it cannot save; nor His ear heavy, that it cannot hear" (Isa. 59:1).

PEACE

"Therefore, having been justified by faith, we have peace with God through our Lord Jesus Christ, through whom also we have access by faith into this grace in which we stand, and rejoice in hope of the glory of God" (Rom. 5:1, 2).

"And He said, 'My Presence will go with you, and I will give you rest' " (Exod. 33:14).

"Great peace have those who love Your law, and nothing causes them to stumble" (Ps. 119:165).

"You will keep him in perfect peace, whose mind is stayed on You, because he trusts in You. Trust in the LORD forever" (Isa. 26:3–4; see pages 148–149).

"He shall enter into peace;
They shall rest in their beds,
Each one walking in his uprightness"
(Isa. 57:2).

"The work of righteousness will be peace, and the effect of righteousness, quietness and assurance forever" (Isa. 32:17).

"Take My yoke upon you and learn from Me, for I am gentle and lowly in heart, and you will find rest for your souls" (Matt. 11:29).

"For He Himself is our peace, who has made both one, and has broken down the middle wall of separation, having abolished in His flesh the enmity, that is, the law of commandments contained in ordinances, so as to create in Himself one new man from the two, thus making peace" (Eph. 2:14, 15).

"And let the peace of God rule in your hearts, to which also you were called in one body, and be thankful" (Col. 3:15).

"Peace I leave with you, My peace I give to you; not as the world gives do I give to you. Let not your heart be troubled, neither let it be afraid" (John 14:27).

"The LORD bless you and keep you;
The LORD make His face shine upon
    you,
And be gracious to you;
The LORD lift up His countenance
    upon you,
And give you peace" (Num.
    6:24–26).

PROTECTION

"As for God, His way is perfect; the word of the LORD is proven; He is a shield to all who trust in Him?" (Ps. 18:30).

"And the LORD shall help them and deliver them; He shall deliver them from the wicked, and save them, because they trust in Him" (Ps. 37:40).

"Because he has set his love upon Me, therefore I will deliver him; I will set him on high, because he has known My name" (Ps. 91:14).

"The LORD preserves the simple; I was brought low, and He saved me" (Ps. 116:6).

"My help comes from the LORD, who made heaven and earth. He will not allow your foot to be moved; He who keeps you will not slumber" (Ps. 121:2, 3).

"And it shall come to pass, that as I have watched over them to pluck up, to break down, to throw down, to destroy, and to afflict, so I will watch over them to build and to plant, says the LORD" (Jer. 31:28).

"He shall cover you with His feathers, and under His wings you shall take refuge; His truth shall be your shield and buckler" (Ps. 91:4).

"Because you have made the LORD,
	who is my refuge,
Even the Most High, your dwelling
	place,
No evil shall befall you,
Nor shall any plague come near your
	dwelling" (Ps. 91:9, 10).

"I know whom I have believed and am persuaded that He is able to keep what I have committed to Him until that Day" (2 Tim. 1:12).

"For the LORD loves justice,
And does not forsake His saints;
They are preserved forever,
But the descendants of the wicked
	shall be cut off" (Ps. 37:28).

"You shall keep them, O LORD, You shall preserve them from this generation forever" (Ps. 12:7).

PROVISION

"For the LORD your God is He who goes with you, to fight for you against your enemies, to save you" (Deut. 20:4).

"Then all this assembly shall know that the LORD does not save with sword and spear; for the battle is the LORD's, and He will give you into our hands" (1 Sam. 17:47).

"He is your praise, and He is your God, who has done for you these great and awesome things which your eyes have seen" (Deut. 10:21).

"Our fathers trusted in You;
They trusted, and You delivered
	them.
They cried to You, and were
	delivered;
They trusted in You, and were not
	ashamed" (Ps. 22:4, 5).

"Have you not known?
Have you not heard?
The everlasting God, the LORD,
The Creator of the ends of the earth,
Neither faints nor is weary.
His understanding is unsearchable.
He gives power to the weak,
And to those who have no might He
	increases strength (Isa. 40:28,
	29; see page 150).

"You are the god who does wonders; You have declared Your strength among the peoples" (Ps. 77:14).

"For I, the LORD your God, will hold your right hand, saying to you, 'Fear not, I will help you'" (Isa. 41:13).

He raises the poor from the dust,
And lifts the beggar from the ash
	heap,
To set them among princes
And make them inherit the throne of
	glory.
For the pillars of the earth are the
	LORD's,
And He has set the world upon
	them.
He will guard the feet of His saints"
	(1 Sam. 2:8, 9).

"For the LORD is our Judge,
The LORD is our Lawgiver,

The LORD is our King;
He will save us" (Isa. 33:22).

REWARDS

"I, the LORD, search the heart,
I test the mind,
Even to give every man according to
  his ways,
According to the fruit of his doings"
  (Jer. 17:10).

"That your charitable deed may be in secret; and your Father who sees in secret will
Himself reward you openly" (Matt. 6:4).

"Assuredly I say to you, that in the regen-
eration, when the Son of Man sits on the
throne of His glory, you who have followed
Me will also sit on twelve thrones, judging the
twelve tribes of Israel. And everyone who has
left houses or brothers or sisters or father or
mother or wife or children or lands, for My
name's sake, shall receive a hundredfold, and
inherit eternal life" (Matt. 19:28, 29).

"If anyone serves Me, let him follow Me;
and where I am, there My servant will be also.
If anyone serves Me, him My Father will
honor" (John 12:26).

"Knowing that from the Lord you will receive the reward of the inheritance; for you
serve the Lord Christ" (Col. 3:24).

"For bodily exercise profits a little, but
godliness is profitable for all things, having
promise of life that now is and of that which is
to come" (1 Tim. 4:8).

"The LORD rewarded me according to my
righteousness; according to the cleanness of
my hands He has recompensed me" (2 Sam.
22:21).

"Blessed be the God and Father of our
Lord Jesus Christ, who according to His abundant mercy has begotten us again to a living
hope through the resurrection of Jesus Christ
from the dead, to an inheritance incorruptible
and undefiled and that does not fade away, reserved in heaven for you, who are kept by the
power of God through faith for salvation ready
to be revealed in this last time" (1 Peter 1:3–5).

"And when the Chief Shepherd appears,
you will receive the crown of glory that does
not fade away" (1 Pet. 5:4; see page 253).

SALVATION

"But as many as received Him, to them
He gave the right to become children of God,
to those who believe in His name" (John 1:
12).

"He who believes in the Son has everlasting life; and he who does not believe the Son
shall not see life, but the wrath of God abides
on him" (John 3:36; see pages 189–190).

"Most assuredly, I say to you, he who
hears My word and believes in Him who sent
Me has everlasting life, and shall not come
into judgment, but has passed from death into
life" (John 5:24).

"And I give them eternal life, and they
shall never perish; neither shall anyone snatch
them out of My hand" (John 10:28; see pages
195–196).

"Him God has exalted to His right hand
to Prince and Savior, to give repentance to Israel and forgiveness of sins" (Acts 5:31).

"And this is the testimony: that God has
given us eternal life, and this life is in His Son.
He who has the Son has life; he who does not
have the Son of God does not have life" (1
John 5:11, 12).

"Therefore He is also able to save to the
uttermost those who come to God through

Him, since He always lives to make intercession for them" (Heb. 7:25).

"Most assuredly, I say to you, he who believes in Me has everlasting life" (John 6:47).

"In Him we have redemption through His blood, the forgiveness of sins, according to the riches of His grace" (Eph. 1:7).

"For the Scripture says, 'Whoever believes on Him will not be put to shame.' For there is no distinction between Jew and Greek, for the same Lord over all is rich to all who call upon Him. For 'whoever calls on the name of the Lord shall be saved' " (Rom. 10:11–13).

SERVICE

"Blessed are the peacemakers, for they shall be called sons of God" (Matt. 5:9).

"And whoever gives one of these little ones only a cup of cold water in the name of a disciple, assuredly, I say to you, he shall by no means lose his reward" (Matt. 10:42).

"But the manifestation of the Spirit is given to each one for the profit of all" (1 Cor. 12:7).

"Moreover, as for me, far be it from me that I should sin against the LORD in ceasing to pray for you; but I will teach you the good and the right way" (1 Sam. 12:23).

"Blessed is he who considers the
        poor;
The LORD will deliver him in time of
        trouble" (Ps. 41:1).

"A good man deals graciously and lends" (Ps. 112:5).

"He who has pity on the poor lends to the LORD, and He will pay back what he has given" (Prov. 19:17).

"To him who is afflicted, kindness should be shown by his friend" (Job 6:14).

"Blessed by the God and Father of our Lord Jesus Christ, the Father of mercies and God of all comfort, who comforts us in all our tribulations, that we may be able to comfort those who are in any trouble, with the comfort with which we ourselves are comforted by God" (2 Cor. 1:3–4).

"Not that we are sufficient of ourselves to think of anything as being from ourselves, but our sufficiency is from God, who also made us sufficient as ministers of the new covenant, not of the letter but of the Spirit; for the letter kills, but the Spirit gives life" (2 Cor. 3:5, 6).

"As each one has received a gift, minister it to one another, as good stewards of the manifold grace of God" (1 Pet. 4:10).

STRENGTH

"And also on My menservants and on my maidservants I will pour out My Spirit in those days" (Joel 2:29).

" 'He who believes in Me, as the Scripture has said, out of his heart will flow rivers of living water.' " But this He spoke concerning the Spirit, whom those believing in Him would receive" (John 7:38–39; see pages 192–193).

"And I will pray the Father, and He will give you another Helper, that He may abide with you forever; the Spirit of truth, whom the world cannot receive, because it neither sees Him nor knows Him; but you know Him, for He dwells with you and will be in you" (John 14:16, 17; see page 199).

"But if the Spirit of Him who raised Jesus from the dead dwells in you, He who raised Christ from the dead will also give life to your mortal bodies through His Spirit who dwells in you" (Rom. 8:11; see pages 210–212).

"Or do you not know that your body is the temple of the Holy Spirit who is in you, whom you have from God, and you are not your own?" (1 Cor. 6:19).

"The LORD will give strength to His people; the LORD will bless His people with peace" (Ps. 29:11).

"My soul follows close behind You, Your right hand upholds me" (Ps. 63:8).

"Now to Him who is able to do exceedingly abundantly above all that we ask or think, according to the power that works in us" (Eph. 3:20).

"With whom My hand shall be established; also My arm shall strengthen him" (Ps. 89:21).

"Behold, God is my salvation, I will trust and not be afraid; for Yah, the LORD, is my strength and song; He also has become my salvation" (Isa. 12:2).

CHAPTER 22

ENCOURAGEMENT IN TIME OF NEED:

MORE BIBLE WORDS TO COUNT ON

Selected Scriptures

A ll of us are vulnerable to moments of uncertainty and times of doubt or discouragement. No matter how we feel or whatever emotions may dominate, God has good words in Scripture that speak to our hearts, bringing guidance and hope.

ANXIETY

"Come to Me, all you who labor and are heavy laden, and I will give you rest" (Matt. 11:28; see pages 169–170).

"These things I have spoken to you, that in Me you may have peace. In the world you will have tribulation; but be of good cheer. I have overcome the world" (John 16:33; see page 203).

"Behold, I am with you and will keep you wherever you go, and will bring you back to this land; for I will not leave you until I have done what I have spoken to you" (Gen. 28:15; see pages 103–104).

"Surely God will never do wickedly, nor will the Almighty pervert justice" (Job 34:12).

"Some trust in chariots, and some in horses; but we will remember the name of the LORD our God" (Ps. 20:7).

"Call upon Me in the day of trouble; I will deliver you, and you shall glorify Me" (Ps. 50:15).

"Cast your burden on the LORD,
And He shall sustain you;
He shall never permit
The righteous to be moved"
(Ps. 55:22).

"In the day of my trouble I will call upon You, for You will answer me" (Ps. 86:7).

"For I, the LORD your God, will hold your right hand, saying to you, 'Fear not, I will help you' " (Isa. 41:13).

"Trust in the LORD with all your
heart,
And lean not on your own
understanding;
In all your ways acknowledge Him,
And He shall direct your paths"
(Prov. 3:5, 6).

"He will gather the lambs with His arm, and carry them in His bosom, and gently lead those who are with young" (Isa. 40:11).

"Blessed be the LORD, who daily loads us with benefits, the God of our Salvation" (Ps. 68:19).

CONFUSION

"And this I pray, that your love may abound still more and more in knowledge and all discernment, that you may approve the things that are excellent, that you may be sincere and without offense till the day of Christ" (Phil. 1:9, 10).

"I am the light of the world. He who follows Me shall not walk in darkness, but have the light of life" (John 8:12; see page 193).

"If any of you lacks wisdom, let him ask of God, who gives to all liberally and without reproach, and it will be given to him" (James 1:5; see pages 248–249).

"Teach me Your way, O LORD; I will walk in Your truth" (Ps. 86:11).

"I will cause them to walk by the rivers of waters, in a straight way in which they shall not stumble" (Jer. 31:9).

"I will instruct you and teach you in the way you should go; I will guide you with My eye" (Ps. 32:8).

"But he who is spiritual judges all things, yet he himself is rightly judged by no one. For 'who has known the mind of the Lord that he may instruct Him?' But we have the mind of Christ" (1 Cor. 2:15, 16).

"For the Holy Spirit will teach you in that very hour what you ought to say" (Luke 12:12).

"I will bless the LORD who has given me counsel" (Ps. 16:7).

"The entrance of Your words gives light; it gives understanding to the simple" (Ps. 119:130).

DEJECTION

"For we do not have a High Priest who cannot sympathize with our weaknesses, but was in all points tempted as we are, yet without sin. Let us therefore come boldly to the throne of grace, that we may obtain mercy and find grace to help in time of need" (Heb. 4:15, 16; see page 245).

"And you will seek Me and find Me, when you search for Me with all your heart" (Jer. 29:13).

"Call to Me, and I will answer you, and show you great and mighty things, which you do not know" (Jer. 33:3).

"It shall come to pass that before they call, I will answer; and while they are still speaking, I will hear" (Isa. 65:24).

"Likewise the Spirit also helps in our weaknesses. For we do not know what we should pray for as we ought, but the Spirit Himself makes intercession for us with groanings which cannot be uttered. Now He who searches the hearts knows what the mind of the Spirit is, because He makes intercession for the saints according to the will of God" (Rom. 8:26, 27).

"O My God, incline Your ear and hear; open Your eyes and see our desolations, and the city which is called by Your name; for we do not present our supplications before You because of our righteous deeds, but because of Your great mercies" (Dan. 9:18).

"Draw near to God and He will draw near to you" (James 4:8; see page 250).

"For You, LORD, are good, and ready to forgive, and abundant in mercy to all those who call upon You" (Ps. 86:5).

"Then I will give them a heart to know Me, that I am the LORD; and they shall be My people, and I will be their God, for they shall return to Me with their whole heart" (Jer. 24:7).

"All Your works shall praise You, O LORD, and Your saints shall bless You" (Ps. 145:10).

DEPRESSION

"Blessed are those who mourn, for they shall be comforted" (Matt. 5:4).

"I will make all My goodness pass before you, and I will proclaim the name of the LORD before you" (Ex. 33:19; see pages 112–113).

"Now hope does not disappoint, because the love of God has been poured out in our hearts by the Holy Spirit who was given to us" (Rom. 5:5).

"Then shall the virgin rejoice in the
  dance,
And the young men and the old,
  together;
For I will turn their mourning to joy,
Will comfort them,
And make them rejoice rather than
  sorrow" (Jer. 31:13).

"Can a woman forget her nursing
  child,
And not have compassion on the son
  of her womb?
Surely they may forget,
Yet I will not forget you" (Isa. 49:15).

"Now may the God of hope fill you with all joy and peace in believing, that you may abound in hope by the power of the Holy Spirit" (Rom. 15:13).

"And the LORD, He is the One who goes before you. He will be with you, He will not leave you nor forsake you; do not fear nor be dismayed" (Deut. 31:8).

"For His anger is but for a moment, His favor is for life; weeping may endure for a night, but joy comes in the morning" (Ps. 30:5).

"'With a little wrath I hid My face from you for a moment; But with everlasting kindness I will have mercy on you,' says the LORD, your Redeemer" (Isa. 54:8).

"And the ransomed of the LORD shall
    return,
And come to Zion with singing,
With everlasting joy on their heads.
They shall obtain joy and gladness,
And sorrow and sighing shall flee
    away" (Isa. 35:10).

"And not only that, but we also glory in tribulations, knowing that tribulation produces perseverance" (Rom. 5:3).

"Let, I pray, Your merciful kindness be for my comfort" (Ps. 119:76).

"Why are you cast down, O my soul?
And why are you disquieted within
    me?
Hope in God;
For I shall yet praise Him,
The help of my countenance and my
    God" (Ps. 42:11).

DESPAIR

"Blessed is the man who endures temptation; for when he has been approved, he will receive the crown of life which the Lord has promised to those who love Him" (James 1:12; see page 249).

"I will seek what was lost and bring back what was driven away, bind up the broken and strengthen what was sick" (Ezek. 34:16).

"He gives power to the weak,
And to those who have no might
He increases strength" (Isa. 40:29;
    see page 150).

"But the Lord is faithful, who will establish you and guard you from the evil one" (2 Thess. 3:3; see page 241).

"Therefore do not cast away your confidence, which has great reward" (Heb. 10:35).

"Ah, LORD God! Behold, You have made the heavens and the earth by Your great power and outstretched arm. There is nothing too hard for You" (Jer. 32:17).

"The eyes of your understanding being enlightened; that you may know what is the hope of His calling, what are the riches of the glory of His inheritance in the saints" (Eph. 1:18).

"God is our refuge and strength,
A very present help in trouble.
Therefore we will not fear,
Even though the earth be removed,
And though the mountains be
    carried into the midst of the sea"
    (Ps. 46:1).

"Uphold me according to Your word, that I may live; and do not let me be ashamed of my hope" (Ps. 119:116).

"For the LORD is good; His mercy is everlasting" (Ps. 100:5).

DISAPPOINTMENT

"Trust in Him at all times, you people; pour out your heart before Him; God is a refuge for us" (Ps. 62:8).

"If you abide in Me, and My words abide in you, you will ask what you desire, and it shall be done for you" (John 15:7; see pages 201–202).

"You do not have because you do not ask. You ask and do not receive, because you ask amiss, that you may spend it on your pleasures" (James 4:2, 3).

"The LORD is near to all who call upon Him, to all who call upon Him in truth" (Ps. 145:18).

"And we know that all things work together for good to those who love God, to those who are the called according to His purpose" (Rom. 8:28; see pages 212–213).

"LORD, You have heard the desire of the humble; You will prepare their heart; You will cause Your ear to hear" (Ps. 10:17).

"If I regard iniquity in my heart, the LORD will not hear. But certainly God has heard me; He has attended to the voice of my prayer" (Ps. 66:18, 19).

"Behold, the eye of the LORD is on those who fear Him" (Ps. 33:18).

"Therefore I say to you, whatever things you ask when you pray, believe that you receive them, and you will have them" (Mark 11:24).

"Now to Him who is able to do exceedingly abundantly above all that we ask or think, according to the power that works in us" (Eph. 3:20).

"But as for me, I trust in You, O LORD; I say, 'You are my God' " (Ps. 31:14).

DISCOURAGEMENT

"Why are you cast down, O my soul?
And why are you disquieted within
    me?

Hope in God;
For I shall yet praise Him.
The help of my countenance and my
    God" (Ps. 42:11).

"I will be glad and rejoice in Your
    mercy,
For You have considered my trouble;
You have known my soul in
    adversities" (Ps. 31:7).

"The eyes of your understanding being enlightened; that you may know what is the hope of His calling, what are the riches of the glory of His inheritance in the saints, and what is the exceeding greatness of His power toward us who believe, according to the working of His mighty power" (Eph. 1:18, 19).

"But also for this very reason, giving all diligence, add to your faith virtue, to virtue knowledge, to knowledge self-control, to self-control perseverance, to perseverance godliness, to godliness brotherly kindness, and to brotherly kindness love. For if these things are yours and abound, you will be neither barren nor unfruitful in the knowledge of our Lord Jesus Christ" (2 Pet. 1:5–8; see page 254).

"Even the youths shall faint and be
    weary,
And the young men shall utterly fall,
But those who wait on the LORD
Shall renew their strength;
They shall mount up with wings like
    eagles,
They shall run and not be weary,
They shall walk and not faint" (Isa.
    40:30, 31).

DISOBEDIENCE

"More than that, blessed are those who hear the word of God and keep it" (Luke 11:28).

"If anyone wants to do His will, he shall know concerning the doctrine, whether it is from God or whether I speak on My own authority" (John 7:17; see page 192).

"If you keep My commandments, you will abide in My love, just as I have kept My Father's commandments and abide in His love" (John 15:10).

"But he who looks into the perfect law of liberty and continues in it, and is not a forgetful hearer but a doer of the work, this one will be blessed in what he does" (James 1:25; see page 249).

"But whoever keeps His word, truly the love of God is perfected in him" (1 John 2:5).

"Therefore whoever hears these sayings of Mine, and does them, I will liken him to a wise man who built his house on the rock" (Matt. 7:24).

"Make me walk in the path of Your commandments, for I delight in it" (Ps. 119:35).

"For the Son of Man will come in the glory of His Father with His angels, and then He will reward each according to his works" (Matt. 16:27).

"If anyone loves Me, he will keep My word; and My Father will love him, and We will come to him and make Our home with him" (John 14:23).

"Blessed is every one who fears the LORD, who walks in His ways" (Ps. 128:1).

"If you abide in My word, you are My disciples indeed. And you shall know the truth, and the truth shall make you free" (John 8:31, 32).

DOUBT

"Whoever confesses that Jesus is the Son of God, God abides in him, and he in God" (1 John 4:15).

"The LORD redeems the soul of His servants, and none of those who trust in Him shall be condemned" (Ps. 34:22).

"So then it is not of him who wills, nor of him who runs, but of God who shows mercy" (Rom. 9:16).

"O Israel, hope in the LORD;
For with the LORD there is mercy,
And with Him is abundant
   redemption" (Ps. 130:7).

"Jesus said to her, 'I am the resurrection and the life. He who believes in Me, though he may die, he shall live. And whoever lives and believes in Me shall never die' " (John 11:25, 26; see pages 196–197).

"For all have sinned and fall short of the glory of God, being justified freely by His grace through the redemption that is in Christ Jesus" (Rom. 3:23, 24).

"I did not come to call the righteous, but sinners, to repentance" (Matt. 9:13).

"But as many as received Him, to them He gave the right to become children of God, to those who believe in His name" (John 1:12).

"But to him who does not work but believes on Him who justifies the ungodly, his faith is accounted for righteousness" (Rom. 4:5).

"He who believes in Him is not condemned; but he who does not believe is condemned already, because he has not believed in the name of the only begotten Son of God" (John 3:18).

"But these are written that you may believe that Jesus is the Christ, the Son of God, and that believing you may have life in His name" (John 20:31).

FAILURE

"Do not be afraid. Stand still, and see the salvation of the LORD, which He will accomplish for you today" (Ex. 14:13).

"Fear not, for I am with you;
Be not dismayed, for I am your God.
I will strengthen you,
Yes, I will help you,
I will uphold you with My righteous
   right hand" (Isa. 41:10).

"But with me it is a very small thing that I should be judged by you or by a human court. In fact, I do not even judge myself. For I know nothing against myself, yet I am not justified by this, but He who judges me is the Lord. Therefore judge nothing before the time, until the Lord comes, who will both bring to light the hidden things of darkness and reveal the counsels of the hearts. Then each one's praise will come from the Lord" (1 Cor. 4:3–5).

"Therefore my beloved brethren, be steadfast, immovable, always abounding in the work of the Lord, knowing that your labor is not in vain in the Lord" (1 Cor. 15:58).

"For you have need of endurance, so that after you have done the will of God, you may receive the promise" (Heb. 10:36).

"Wisdom and knowledge will be the stability of your times, and the strength of salvation; the fear of the LORD is his treasure" (Isa. 33:6).

"Who are you to judge another's servant? To his own master he stands or falls. Indeed, he will be made to stand, for God is able to make him stand" (Rom. 14:4; see pages 214–215).

"Have I not commanded you? Be strong and of good courage; do not be afraid, nor be dismayed, for the LORD your God is with you wherever you go" (Josh. 1:9).

FEAR

"So we may boldly say, 'The Lord is my helper; I will not fear. What can man do to me?' " (Heb. 13:6).

"You shall not be terrified of them; for the LORD your God, the great and awesome God, is among you" (Deut. 7:21).

"For the LORD is great and greatly to
    be praised;
He is also to be feared above all gods.
For all the gods of the peoples are
    idols,
But the LORD made the heavens"
    (1 Chron. 16:25, 26).

" 'And I will make you to this people
    a fortified bronze wall;
And they will fight against you,
But they shall not prevail against
    you;
For I am with you to save you
And deliver you,' says the LORD" (Jer.
    15:20).

"Fear not, for I am with you;
Be not dismayed, for I am your God.
I will strengthen you,
Yes, I will help you,
I will uphold you with My righteous
    right hand" (Isa. 41:10).

"When a man's ways please the LORD, He makes even his enemies to be at peace with him" (Prov. 16:7).

"Say to those who are fearful-hearted, 'Be strong, do not fear! Behold, your God will come with vengeance, with the recompense of God; He will come and save you' " (Isa. 35:4).

"Who delivered us from so great a death, and does deliver us; in whom we trust that He will still deliver us" (2 Cor. 1:10).

"The things which you learned and received and heard and saw in me, these do, and the God of peace will be with you" (Phil. 4:9; see pages 236–237).

"And I looked, and arose and said to the nobles, to the leaders, and to the rest of the people, 'Do not be afraid of them. Remember the LORD, great and awesome, and fight for your brethren, your sons, your daughters, your wives, and your houses' " (Neh. 4:14).

"The LORD is my strength and my
    shield;
My heart trusted in Him, and I am
    helped;
Therefore my heart greatly rejoices,
And with my song I will praise Him"
    (Ps. 28:7).

"You shall not show partiality in judgment; you shall hear the small as well as the great; you shall not be afraid in any man's presence, for the judgment is God's" (Deut. 1:17).

"The LORD will be a shelter for His people, and the strength of the children of Israel" (Joel 3:16).

"I will both lie down in peace, and sleep; for You alone, O LORD, make me dwell in safety" (Ps. 4:8).

"Whenever I am afraid, I will trust in You" (Ps. 56:3).

FRUSTRATION

"Let each of you look out not only for his own interests, but also for the interests of others" (Phil. 2:4).

"Blessed is the man who endures temptation; for when he has been approved, he will receive the crown of life which the Lord has promised to those who love Him" (James 1:12; see page 249).

"And above all things have fervent love for one another, for 'love will cover a multitude of sins' " (1 Peter 4:8).

"Let all bitterness, wrath, anger, clamor, and evil speaking be put away from you, with all malice. And be kind to one another, tenderhearted, forgiving one another, just as God in Christ forgave you" (Eph. 4:31, 32).

"Set a guard, O LORD, over my mouth; keep watch over the door of my lips" (Ps. 141:3).

"Cease from anger and forsake wrath; Do not fret—it only causes harm. For evildoers shall be cut off; but those who wait on the LORD, they shall inherit the earth" (Ps. 37: 8, 9).

"Moreover if your brother sins against you, go and tell him his fault between you and him alone. If he hears you, you have gained your brother" (Matt. 18:15).

"Since it is a righteous thing with God to repay with tribulation those who trouble you, and to give you who are troubled rest with us when the Lord Jesus is revealed from heaven with His mighty angels" (2 Thess. 1:6, 7).

GRIEF

"When you pass through the waters,
    I will be with you;
And through the rivers,
    they shall not overflow you.
When you walk through the fire,
    you shall not be burned,
Nor shall the flame scorch you" (Isa. 43:2).

"Precious in the sight of the LORD is the death of His saints" (Ps. 116:15).

"But I do not want you to be ignorant, brethren, concerning those who have fallen asleep, lest you sorrow as others who have no hope. For if we believe that Jesus died and rose again, even so God will bring with Him those who sleep in Jesus" (1 Thess. 4:13, 14).

"But You have seen, for You
    observe trouble and grief,
To repay it by Your hand.
The helpless commits himself to You;
You are the helper of the Fatherless"
    (Ps. 10:14).

"And I heard a loud voice from heaven saying, 'Behold, the tabernacle of God is with men, and He will dwell with them, and they shall be His people. God Himself will be with them and be their God. And God will wipe away every tear from their eyes; there shall be no more death, nor sorrow, nor crying. There shall be no more pain, for the former things have passed away' " (Rev. 21:3, 4).

"You, who have shown me great and severe troubles, shall revive me again, and bring me up again from the depths of the earth" (Ps. 71:20, 21).

"And if I go and prepare a place for you, I will come again and receive you to Myself; that where I am, there you may be also" (John 14:3; see pages 197–198).

"My soul melts from heaviness; strengthen me according to Your word" (Ps. 119:28).

"This is my comfort in my affliction, for Your word has given me life" (Ps. 119:50).

GUILT

"But you were washed, but you were sanctified, but you were justified in the name of the Lord Jesus and by the Spirit of our God" (1 Cor. 6:11).

"In whom we have boldness and access with confidence through faith in Him" (Eph. 3:12).

"But You are God,
Ready to pardon,
Gracious and merciful,
Slow to anger,
Abundant in kindness,
And did not forsake them" (Neh.
     9:17).

"There is forgiveness with You,
That You may be feared.
I wait for the LORD, my soul waits,
And in His word I do hope" (Ps.
     130:4, 5).

"For we will surely die and become like water spilled on the ground, which cannot be gathered up again. Yet God does not take away a life; but He devises means, so that His banished ones are not expelled from Him" (2 Sam. 14:14).

"I, even I, am He who blots out your transgressions for My own sake; and I will not remember your sins" (Isa. 43:25).

"To the LORD our God belong mercy and forgiveness, though we have rebelled against Him" (Dan. 9:9).

"Let the wicked forsake his way,
And the unrighteous man his
     thoughts;
Let him return to the LORD,
And He will have mercy on him;
And to our God,
For He will abundantly pardon" (Isa.
     55:7).

"Blessed is the man to whom the LORD does not impute iniquity" (Ps. 32:2).

"I will cleanse them from all their iniquity by which they have sinned against Me, and I will pardon all their iniquities by which they have sinned and by which they have transgressed against Me" (Jer. 33:8).

" 'I will not cause My anger to fall on you. For I am merciful,' says the LORD. 'I will not remain angry forever' " (Jer. 3:12).

"He who believes in Him is not condemned; but he who does not believe is condemned already, because he has not believed in the name of the only begotten Son of God" (John 3:18).

INSECURITY

"Now I am no longer in the world, but these are in the world, and I come to You. Holy Father, keep through Your name those whom You have given Me" (John 17:11).

"For we are confident that we have a good conscience, in all things desiring to live honorably" (Heb. 13:18).

"The eyes of your understanding being enlightened; that you may know what is the hope of His calling, what are the riches of the glory of His inheritance in the saints, and what is the exceeding greatness of His power toward us who believe, according to the working of His mighty power" (Eph. 1:18, 19).

"May be able to comprehend with all the saints what is the width and length and depth and height; to know the love of Christ which passes knowledge; that you may be filled with all the fullness of God" (Eph. 3:18, 19).

"And this I pray, that your love may abound still more and more in knowledge and all discernment, that you may approve the things that are excellent, that you may be sincere and without offense till the day of Christ" (Phil. 1:9–11).

"Let the word of Christ dwell in you richly in all wisdom, teaching and admonishing one another in psalms and hymns and spiritual songs, singing with grace in your hearts to the Lord" (Col. 3:16).

LONELINESS

"Be hospitable to one another without grumbling" (1 Pet. 4:9).

"Rejoice with those who rejoice, and weep with those who weep" (Rom. 12:15).

"For you, brethren, have been called to liberty; only do not use liberty as an opportunity for the flesh, but through love serve one another" (Gal. 5:13).

"God sets the solitary in families" (Ps. 68:6).

"When you give a dinner or a supper, do not ask your friends, your brothers, your relatives, nor rich neighbors, lest they also invite you back, and you be repaid. But when you give a feast, invite the poor, the maimed, the lame, the blind. And you will be blessed, because they cannot repay you; for you shall be repaid at the resurrection of the just" (Luke 14:12–14).

"Do not be envious of evil men, nor desire to be with them" (Prov. 24:1).

"And let us consider one another in order to stir up love and good works, not forsaking the assembling of ourselves together, as is the manner of some, but exhorting one another, and so much the more as you see the Day approaching" (Heb. 10:24, 25).

"Receive one who is weak in the faith" (Rom. 14:1).

LONGING

"He will fulfill the desire of those who fear Him; He also will hear their cry and save them" (Ps. 145:19).

"Turn away my eyes from looking at worthless things, and revive me in your way" (Ps. 119:37).

"Commit your works to the LORD, and your thoughts will be established" (Prov. 16:3).

"I know how to be abased, and I know how to abound. Everywhere and in all things I have learned both to be full and to be hungry, both to abound and to suffer need. I can do all things through Christ who strengthens me" (Phil. 4:12, 13).

"For the LORD God is a sun and shield; the LORD will give grace and glory; no good thing will He withhold from those who walk uprightly" (Ps. 84:11).

"A man's heart plans his way, but the LORD directs his steps" (Prov. 16:9).

"All the ways of a man are pure in his own eyes, but the LORD weighs the spirits" (Prov. 16:2).

"He who tills his land will have plenty of bread, but he who follows frivolity will have poverty enough" (Prov. 28:19).

NEED

Yours, O LORD, is the greatness,
The power and the glory,
The victory and the majesty;
For all that is in heaven and in earth
   is Yours;
Yours is the kingdom, O LORD,
And you are exalted as head over all
   (1 Chron. 29:11).

"For He satisfies the longing soul, and fills the hungry soul with goodness" (Ps. 107:9).

"And my God shall supply all your need according to His riches in glory by Christ Jesus" (Phil. 4:19; see pages 237–238).

"He has given food to those who fear Him; He will ever be mindful of His covenant" (Ps. 111:5).

"Now may He who supplies seed to the sower, and bread for food, supply and multiply the seed you have sown and increase the fruits of your righteousness, while you are enriched in everything for all liberality, which causes thanksgiving through us to God" (2 Cor. 9:10, 11).

"Nor was there anyone among them who lacked; for all who were possessors of lands or houses sold them, and brought the proceeds of the things that were sold, and laid them at the apostles' feet; and they distributed to each as anyone had need" (Acts 4:34, 35).

"A little that a righteous man has is better than the riches of many wicked" (Ps. 37:16).

"But with righteousness He shall
    judge the poor,
And decide with equity for the meek
    of the earth" (Isa. 11:4).

"For the LORD hears the poor, and does not despise His prisoners" (Ps. 69:33).

PERSECUTION

"Blessed are those who are persecuted for righteousness' sake, for theirs is the kingdom of heaven" (Matt. 5:10).

"But as for you, you meant evil against me; but God meant it for good, in order to bring it about as it is this day, to save many people alive" (Gen. 50:20).

"I will call upon the LORD, who is worthy to be praised; so shall I be saved from my enemies" (2 Sam. 22:4).

"The lines have fallen to me in pleasant places; Yes, I have a good inheritance" (Ps. 16:6).

"Many sorrows shall be to the wicked; but he who trusts in the LORD, mercy shall surround him" (Ps. 32:10).

"Do not fret because of evildoers;
Nor be envious of the workers of
    iniquity.
For they shall soon be cut down like
    the grass,
And wither as the green herb" (Ps.
    37:1, 2).

"The LORD executes righteousness and justice for all who are oppressed" (Ps. 103:6).

"Sing to the LORD! Praise the LORD!
For He has delivered the life of the
    poor
From the hand of evildoers" (Jer.
    20:13).

'Let him turn away from evil and do
    good;
Let him seek peace and pursue it.
For the eyes of the LORD are on the
    righteous,
And His ears are open to their
    prayers;
But the face of the LORD is against
    those who do evil" (1 Peter
    3:11, 12).

"Even the captives of the mighty shall be taken away, and the prey of the terrible be delivered; for I will contend with him who contends with you, and I will save your children" (Isa. 49:25).

SELF-DOUBT

"He does not delight in the strength
    of the horse;
He takes no pleasure in the legs of a
    man.
The LORD takes pleasure in those
    who fear Him,
In those who hope in His mercy"
    (Ps. 147:10, 11).

"Wisdom and knowledge will be the stability of your times, and the strength of salvation (Isa. 33:6).

"And He said to me, 'My grace is sufficient for you, for My strength is made perfect in weakness.' Therefore most gladly I will rather boast in my infirmities, that the power of Christ may rest upon me" (2 Cor. 12:9).

"The LORD will guide you
        continually,
And satisfy your soul in drought,
And strengthen your bones;
You shall be like a watered
        garden,
And like a spring of water, whose
        waters do not
        fail" (Isa. 58:11).

"I would have lost heart, unless I had
        believed
That I would see the goodness of the
        LORD
In the land of the living.
Wait on the LORD;
Be of good courage,
And He shall strengthen your heart.
Wait, I say, on the LORD!" (Ps. 27:13,
        14).

"Consider the ravens, for they neither sow nor reap, which have neither storehouse nor barn; and God feeds them. Of how much more value are you than the birds?" (Luke 12:24).

"Now may our Lord Jesus Christ Himself, and our God and Father, who has loved us and given us everlasting consolation and good hope by grace, comfort your hearts and establish you in every good word and work" (2 Thess. 2:16, 17).

SHAME

"Also I say to you, whoever confesses Me before men, him the Son of Man also will confess before the angels of God" (Luke 12:8).

"Likewise, I say to you, there is joy in the presence of the angels of God over one sinner who repents" (Luke 15:10).

"I have not hidden Your
        righteousness within my heart;
I have declared Your faithfulness and
        Your salvation;
I have not concealed Your
        lovingkindness and Your truth
From the great assembly" (Ps.
        40:10).

" 'And I will sanctify My great name, which has been profaned among the nations, which you have profaned in their midst; and the nations shall know that I am the LORD,' says the LORD God, 'when I am hallowed in you before their eyes' " (Ezek. 36:23).

"By this all will know that you are My disciples, if you have love for one another" (John 13:35).

"But even if you should suffer for righteousness' sake, you are blessed. 'And do not be afraid of their threats, nor be troubled.' But sanctify the Lord God in your hearts, and always be ready to give a defense to everyone who asks you a reason for the hope that is in you, with meekness and fear, having a good conscience, that when they defame you as evildoers, those who revile your good conduct in Christ may be ashamed" (1 Pet. 3:14–16).

"For I am not ashamed of the gospel of Christ, for it is the power of God to salvation for everyone who believes, for the Jew first and also for the Greek" (Rom. 1:16).

"Therefore I testify to you this day that I am innocent of the blood of all men. For I have not shunned to declare to you the whole counsel of God" (Acts 20:26, 27).

"But when the Helper comes, whom I shall send to you from the Father, the Spirit of truth who proceeds from the Father, He will testify of Me" (John 15:26, 27).

SICKNESS

"My flesh and my heart fail; but God is the strength of my heart and my portion forever" (Ps. 73:26).

"Behold, I will bring . . . health and healing; I will heal them and reveal to them the abundance of peace and truth" (Jer. 33:6).

"Is anyone among you sick? Let him call for the elders of the church, and let them pray over him, anointing him with oil in the name of the Lord. And the prayer of faith will save the sick, and the Lord will raise him up. And if he has committed sins, he will be forgiven" (James 5:14, 15; see pages 251–252).

"Heal me, O LORD, and I shall be healed; save me, and I shall be saved, for You are my praise" (Jer. 17:14).

"Yea, though I walk through the
    valley of the shadow of death,
I will fear no evil;
For You are with me;
Your rod and Your staff, they comfort
    me" (Ps. 23:4).

"So you shall serve the LORD your God, and He will bless your bread and your water. And I will take sickness away from the midst of you" (Ex. 23:25).

"O LORD My God, I cried out to You, and You healed me" (Ps. 30:2).

"The LORD will strengthen him on his bed of illness; You will sustain him on his sickbed" (Ps. 41:3).

"Let, I pray, Your merciful kindness be for my comfort, according to Your word to Your servant" (Ps. 119:76).

"But You, O LORD, are a shield for
    me,

My glory and the One who lifts up
    my head" (Ps. 3:3).

"I have seen his ways, and will heal him; I will also lead him, and restore comforts to him and to his mourners" (Isa. 57:18).

SUFFERING

"And not only that, but we also glory in tribulations, knowing that tribulation produces perseverance; and perseverance character; and character, hope" (Rom. 5:3, 4).

"But even if you should suffer for righteousness' sake, you are blessed" (1 Pet. 3:14).

"But may the God of all grace, who called us to His eternal glory by Christ Jesus, after you have suffered a while, perfect, establish, strengthen, and settle you" (1 Pet. 5:10).

"You, who have shown me great and severe troubles, shall revive me again" (Ps. 71:20).

"But he said to her, 'You speak as one of the foolish women speaks. Shall we indeed accept good from God and shall we not accept adversity?' " (Job 2:10).

"Beloved, do not think it strange concerning the fiery trial which is to try you, as though some strange thing happened you; but rejoice to the extent that you partake of Christ's sufferings, that when His glory is revealed, you may also be glad with exceeding joy" (1 Pet. 4:12, 13).

He will swallow up death forever,
And the LORD God will wipe away
    tears from all faces" (Isa. 25:8).

"Many are the afflictions of the righteous, but the LORD delivers him out of them all" (Ps. 34:19).

"Who among you fears the LORD?
Who obeys the voice of His Servant?
Who walks in darkness
And has no light?
Let him trust in the name of the
    LORD
And rely upon his God" (Isa. 50:10).

"For what credit is it if, when you are beaten for your faults, you take it patiently? But when you do good and suffer, if you take it patiently, this is commendable before God. For to this you were called, because Christ also suffered for us, leaving us an example, that you should follow His steps" (1 Pet. 2:20, 21).

I will bring the blind by a way they
    did not know;
I will lead them in paths that they
    have
      not known.
I will make darkness light before
    them,
And crooked places straight.
These things I will do for them,
And not forsake them" (Isa. 42:16).

TEMPTATION

"No temptation has overtaken you except such as is common to man; but God is faithful, who will not allow you to be tempted beyond what you are able, but with the temptation will also make the way of escape, that you may be able to bear it" (1 Cor. 10:13).

"I say then, Walk in the Spirit, and you shall not fulfill the lust of the flesh" (Gal. 5:16; see pages 238–239).

"But He knows the way that I take; when He has tested me, I shall come forth as gold" (Job 23:10).

"Through Your precepts I get understanding; therefore I hate every false way" (Ps. 119: 104).

"Let no one say when he is tempted, 'I am tempted by God;' for God cannot be tempted by evil, nor does He Himself tempt anyone. But each one is tempted when he is drawn away by his own desires and enticed" (James 1:13, 14).

"Do not incline my heart to any evil thing, to practice wicked works" (Ps. 141:4).

"The labor of the righteous leads to life, the wages of the wicked to sin" (Prov. 10:16).

"Blessed are those who keep His testimonies, who seek Him with the whole heart" (Ps. 119:2).

UNCERTAINTY

"You also be patient. Establish your hearts, for the coming of the Lord is at hand" (James 5:8).

"I would have lost heart, unless I
    had believed
That I would see the goodness of the
    LORD
In the land of the living.
Wait on the LORD;
Be of good courage,
And He shall strengthen your heart;
Wait, I say, on the LORD" (Ps. 27:13,
    14).

"In returning and rest you shall be saved; in quietness and confidence shall be your strength" (Isa. 30:15).

"Wait on the LORD,
And keep His way,
And He shall exalt you to inherit the
    land;
When the wicked are cut off, you
    shall see it" (Ps. 37:34).

"Therefore be patient, brethren, until the coming of the Lord. See how the farmer waits for the precious fruit of the earth, waiting patiently for it until it receives the early and latter rain" (James 5:7).

"But those who wait on the LORD
Shall renew their strength;
They shall mount up with wings like
    eagles,
They shall run and not be weary,
They shall walk and not faint" (Isa.
    40:31).

"Eternal life to those who by patient continuance in doing good seek for glory, honor, and immortality" (Rom. 2:7).

"Rest in the LORD, and wait patiently for Him" (Ps. 37:7).

WEAKNESS

"When my spirit was overwhelmed within me, then You knew my path" (Ps. 142:3).

"The LORD lifts up the humble; He casts the wicked down to the ground" (Ps. 147:6).

"For thus says the High and Lofty
    One
Who inhabits eternity, whose name
    is Holy;
I dwell in the high and holy place

With him who has a contrite and
    humble spirit,
To revive the spirit of the humble,
And to revive the heart of the
    contrite ones" (Isa. 57:15).

"The LORD God is my strength" (Hab. 3:19).

"Seek the LORD and His strength; seek His face evermore!" (1 Chron. 16:11).

"For yet a little while and the wicked shall be no more; indeed, you will look carefully for his place, but it shall be no more. But the meek shall inherit the earth, and shall delight themselves in the abundance of peace" (Ps. 37:10, 11).

"He has redeemed my soul in peace from the battle that was against me" (Ps. 55:18).

"God has spoken once, twice I have heard this: That power belongs to God" (Ps. 62:11).

"My grace is sufficient for you, for My strength is made perfect in weakness" (2 Cor. 12:9).

"That He would grant you, according to the riches of His glory, to be strengthened with might through His Spirit in the inner man" (Eph. 3:16).

CHAPTER 23

GUIDELINES FOR HEALTHY RELATIONSHIPS:

MORE BIBLE WORDS TO COUNT ON

Selected Scriptures

Our relationships with other persons are important to us and to God. How we relate to our spouses, our children, our fellow believers, and the unsaved raises questions for which we need God's guidance. In this final chapter of *Every Covenant and Promise,* we look at words from God which we can count on in the important relationships of our lives.

I. RELATIONSHIP WITH A SPOUSE

GOD'S IDEAL FOR MARRIAGE

"And the LORD God said, 'It is not good that man should be alone; I will make him a helper comparable to him.' . . . Then the rib which the LORD God had taken from man He made into a woman, and He brought her to the man. And Adam said:

'This is now bone of my bones
And flesh of my flesh;
She shall be called Woman,
Because she was taken out of Man.'

Therefore a man shall leave his father and mother and be joined to his wife, and they shall become one flesh" (Gen. 2:18, 22–24).

"And he took Rebekah and she became his wife, and he loved her" (Gen. 24:67).

"Nevertheless, neither is man independent of woman, nor woman independent of man, in the Lord. For as woman came from man, even so man also comes through woman" (1 Cor. 11:11, 12).

"Therefore, as the elect of God, holy and beloved, put on tender mercies, kindness, humility, meekness, longsuffering; bearing with one another, and forgiving one another" (Col. 3:12–14).

HUSBAND/WIFE ROLES

"Husbands, likewise, dwell with them with understanding, giving honor to the wife, as to the weaker vessel, and as being heirs together of the grace of life, that your prayers may not be hindered" (1 Pet. 3:7).

"Submitting to one another in the fear of God" (Eph. 5:21).

"Husbands, love your wives, just as Christ also loved the church and gave Himself for her, that he might sanctify and cleanse her with the washing of water by the word, that He might present her to Himself a glorious church, not having spot or wrinkle or any such thing, but that she should be holy and without blemish. So husbands ought to love their own wives as their own bodies; he who loves his wife loves himself. . . . let each one of you in particular so love his own wife as himself, and let the wife see that she respects her husband" (Eph. 5:25–28, 33).

"Wives, submit to your own husbands, as is fitting in the Lord. Husbands, love your wives and do not be bitter toward them" (Col. 3:18, 19).

"Admonish the young women to love their husbands, to love their children to be discreet, chaste, homemakers, good, obedient to their own husbands, that the word of God may not be blasphemed" (Titus 2:4, 5).

SEX IN MARRIAGE

"So God created man in His own image; in the image of God He created him; male and female He created them" (Gen. 1:27).

"Therefore a man shall leave his father and mother and be joined to his wife, and they shall become one flesh" (Gen. 2:24).

"Marriage is honorable among all, and the bed undefiled; but fornicators and adulterers God will judge" (Heb. 13:4).

"Let the husband render to his wife the affection due her, and likewise also the wife to her husband. The wife does not have authority over her own body, but the husband does. And likewise the husband does not have authority over his own body, but the wife does.

Do not deprive one another except with consent for a time, that you may give yourselves to fasting and prayer; and come together again so that Satan does not tempt you because of your lack of self-control" (1 Cor. 7:3–5).

DEALING WITH CONFLICT

"In humility correcting those who are in opposition, if God perhaps will grant them repentance, so that they may know the truth" (2 Tim. 2:25).

"But the wisdom that is from above is first pure, then peaceable, gentle, willing to yield, full of mercy and good fruits, without partiality and without hypocrisy. Now the fruit of righteousness is sown in peace by those who make peace" (James 3:17, 18).

"Let the word of Christ dwell in you richly in all wisdom, teaching and admonishing one another in psalms and hymns and spiritual songs, singing with grace in your hearts to the Lord" (Col. 3:16).

"Poverty and shame will come to him who disdains correction, but he who regards a rebuke will be honored" (Prov. 13:18).

"For where there are envy, strife, and divisions among you, are you not carnal and behaving like mere men" (1 Cor. 3:3).

"Fulfill my job by being like-minded, having the same love, being of one accord, of one mind" (Phil. 2:2).

"Where do wars and fights come from among you? Do they not come from your desires for pleasure that war in your members?" (James 4:1).

DEALING WITH HURTS

"Not returning evil for evil or reviling for reviling, but on the contrary blessing, knowing that you were called to this, that you may inherit a blessing" (1 Pet. 3:9).

"And let us not grow weary while doing good, for in due season we shall reap if we do not lose heart" (Gal. 6:9; see pages 229–230).

"And just as you want men to do to you, you also do to them likewise" (Luke 6:31).

"Give, and it will be given to you: good measure, pressed down, shaken together, and running over will be put into your bosom. For with the same measure that you use, it will be measured back to you" (Luke 6:38; see pages 179–180).

"And may the Lord make you increase and abound in love to one another and to all, just as we do to you" (1 Thess. 3:12).

"Therefore if you bring your gift to the altar, and there remember that your brother has something against you, leave your gift there before the altar, and go your way. First be reconciled to your brother, and then come and offer your gift" (Matt. 5:23, 24).

"Commit your way to the LORD,
Trust also in Him,
And He shall bring it to pass.
He shall bring forth your
    righteousness as the light,
And your justice as the noonday"
(Ps. 37:5, 6).

DEALING WITH ANGER

"There is one who speaks like the
    piercings of a sword,
But the tongue of the wise
    promotes health" (Prov. 12:18).

"Cease from anger, and forsake wrath; do not fret; it only causes harm" (Ps. 37:8).

"With a little wrath I hid My face from you for a moment; But with everlasting kindness I will have mercy on you" (Isa. 54:8).

"The work of righteousness will be peace, and the effect of righteousness, quietness and assurance forever" (Isa. 32:17).

"Who is a God like You,
Pardoning iniquity
And passing over the
    transgression of the remnant
    of His heritage?
He does not retain His anger forever,
Because He delights in mercy.
He will again have compassion on
    us,
And will subdue our iniquities" (Mic.
    7:18, 19).

"Judge not, and you shall not be judged. Condemn not, and you shall not be condemned. Forgive, and you will be forgiven" (Luke 6:37; see pages 179–180).

THE IMPORTANCE OF FORGIVENESS

"Take heed to yourselves. If your brother sins against you, rebuke him; and if he repents, forgive him. And if he sins against you seven times in a day, and seven times in a day returns to you, saying, 'I repent,' you shall forgive him" (Luke 17:3, 4).

"If you, LORD, should mark
    iniquities,
O LORD, who could stand?
But there is forgiveness with You,
That You may be feared" (Ps.
    130:3, 4).

"For if you forgive men their trespasses, your heavenly Father will also forgive you. But if you do not forgive men their trespasses, neither will your Father forgive your trespasses" (Matt. 6:14, 15; see page 167).

"Therefore I say to you, her sins, which are many, are forgiven, for she loved much" (Luke 7:47).

"In returning and rest you shall be saved; in quietness and confidence shall be your strength" (Isa. 30:15).

"Bearing with one another, and forgiving one another, if anyone has a complaint against another; even as Christ forgave you, so you also must do" (Col. 3:13).

II. ON RELATIONSHIPS WITH CHILDREN

HOW TO PARENT

"You shall therefore keep His statutes and His commandments which I command you today, that it may go well with you and with your children after you" (Deut. 4:40).

"Only take heed to yourself, and diligently keep yourself, lest you forget the things your eyes have seen, and lest they depart from your heart all the days of your life. And teach them to your children and your grandchildren" (Deut. 4:9).

"I call heaven and earth as witnesses today against you, that I have set before you life and death, blessing and cursing; therefore choose life, that both you and your descendants may live. That you may love the LORD your God, that you may obey His voice, and that you may cling to Him, for He is your life and the length of your days" (Deut. 30: 19, 20).

"In all things showing yourself to be a pattern of good works" (Titus 2:7).

"Therefore do not cast away your confidence, which has great reward. For you have need of endurance, so that after you have done the will of God, you may receive the promise" (Heb. 10:35, 36).

"For I have known him, in order that he may command his children and his household after him, that they keep the way of the LORD, to do righteousness and justice" (Gen. 18:19).

"And you, fathers, do not provoke your children to wrath, but bring them up in the training and admonition of the Lord" (Eph. 6:4).

GOALS IN CHILD REARING

"As you know how we exhorted, and comforted, and charged every one of you, as a father does his own children, that you would walk worthy of God who calls you into His own kingdom and glory" (1 Thess. 2:11, 12).

"To know wisdom and instruction, to perceive the words of understanding, to receive the instruction of wisdom, justice, judgment, and equity" (Prov. 1:2, 3).

"'Teacher, which is the great commandment in the law?' Jesus said to him, 'You shall love the Lord your God with all your heart, with all your soul, and with all your mind.' This is the first and great commandment. And the second is like it: 'You shall love your neighbor as yourself.' On these two commandments hang all the Law and the Prophets' " (Matt. 22:36–40).

"Let no one despise your youth, but be an example to the believers in word, in conduct, in love, in spirit, in faith, in purity" (1 Tim. 4:12).

"And that from childhood you have known the Holy Scriptures, which are able to make you wise for salvation through faith which is in Christ Jesus" (2 Tim. 3:15).

PURPOSES IN DISCIPLINE

"For they indeed for a few days chastened us as seemed best to them, but He for our profit, that we may be partakes of His holiness. Now no chastening seems to be joyful for the present, but painful; nevertheless, afterward it yields the peaceable fruit of righteousness to those who have been trained by it" (Heb. 12:10, 11).

"My son, do not despise the chastening of the LORD, nor detest His correction. For whom the LORD loves He corrects, just as a father the son in whom he delights" (Prov. 3:11, 12).

"He shall die for lack of instruction, and in the greatness of his folly he shall go astray" (Prov. 5:23).

"But when we are judged, we are chastened by the Lord, that we may not be condemned with the world" (1 Cor. 11:32).

"Do not withhold correction from a child, for if you beat him with a rod, he will not die" (Prov. 23:13).

"Rebuke a wise man, and he will love you" (Prov. 9:8).

"All Scripture is given by inspiration of God, and is profitable for doctrine, for reproof, for correction, for instruction in righteousness" (2 Tim. 3:16).

RESOURCES FOR DISCIPLINE

"Preach the word! Be ready in season and out of season. Convince, rebuke, exhort, with all longsuffering and teaching" (2 Tim. 4:2).

"Anxiety in the heart of man causes depression, but a good word makes it glad" (Prov. 12:25).

"You shall surely rebuke your neighbor, and not bear sin because of him" (Lev. 19:17).

"The rod and rebuke give wisdom, but a child left to himself brings shame to his mother" (Prov. 29:15).

"Foolishness is bound up in the heart of a child; the rod of correction will drive it far from him" (Prov. 22:15).

"If we confess our sins, He is faithful and just to forgive us our sins and to cleanse us from all unrighteousness" (1 John 1:9).

"God was in Christ reconciling the world to Himself, not imputing their trespasses to them, and has committed to us the word of reconciliation" (2 Cor. 5:19).

"Train up a child in the way he should go, and when he is old he will not depart from it" (Prov. 22:6; see page 142).

"For though you might have ten thousand instructors in Christ, yet you do not have many fathers; for in Christ Jesus I have begotten you through the gospel. Therefore I urge you, imitate me" (1 Cor. 4:15, 16).

ENCOURAGING SPIRITUAL GROWTH

"He who earnestly seeks good finds favor" (Prov. 11:27).

"Therefore let us not judge one another anymore, but rather resolve this, not to put a stumbling block or a cause to fall in our brother's way" (Rom. 14:13).

"Let not mercy and truth forsake
    you;
Bind them around your neck,
Write them on the tablet of your
    heart,
And so find favor and high esteem
In the sight of God and man" (Prov.
    3:3, 4).

"The secret things belong to the LORD our God, but those things which are revealed belong to us and to our children forever, that we may do all the words of this law" (Deut. 29:29).

"Let us consider one another in order to stir up love and good works, not forsaking the assembling of ourselves together, as is the manner of some, but exhorting one another, and so much the more as you see the Day approaching" (Heb. 10:24, 25).

"You shall love the LORD your God with all your heart, with all your soul, and with all your strength. And these words which I command you today shall be in your heart. You shall teach them diligently to your children, and shall talk of them when you sit in your house, when you walk by the way, when you lie down, and when you rise up" (Deut. 6:5–7).

PRAYING FOR CHILDREN

"[I] do not cease to give thanks for you, making mention of you in my prayers; that the God of our Lord Jesus Christ, the Father of glory, may give to you the spirit of wisdom and revelation in the knowledge of Him" (Eph. 1:16, 17).

"That He would grant you, according to the riches of His glory, to be strengthened with might through His Spirit in the inner man, that Christ may dwell in your hearts through faith" (Eph. 3:16, 17).

"And this I pray, that your love may abound still more and more in knowledge and all discernment, that you may approve the things that are excellent, that you may be sincere and without offense till the day of Christ" (Phil. 1:9, 10).

COMMUNICATING LOVE TO CHILDREN

"In this the love of God was manifested toward us, that God has sent His only begotten Son into the world, that we might live through Him. In this is love, not that we loved God, but that He loved us and sent His Son to be the propitiation for our sins" (1 John 4:9, 10).

"There is no fear in love; but perfect love casts out fear, because fear involved torment" (1 John 4:18).

"Moreover, as for me, far be it from me that I should sin against the LORD in ceasing to pray for you; but I will teach you the good and the right way" (1 Sam. 12:23).

"Nevertheless My lovingkindness I will not utterly take from him, nor allow My faithfulness to fail" (Ps. 89:33).

"And Solomon loved the LORD, walking in the statutes of his father David" (1 Kin. 3:3).

"For whom the LORD love He chastens, and scourges every son whom He receives" (Heb. 12:6).

"Love suffers long and is kind; love does not envy; love does not parade itself, is not puffed up; does not behave rudely, does not seek its own, is not provoked, thinks no evil; does not rejoice in iniquity, but rejoices in the truth; bears all things, believes all things, hopes all things, endures all things" (1 Cor. 13:4–7).

TEACHING CHILDREN ABOUT GOD

"And that you may tell in the hearing of your son and your son's son the mighty things I have done in Egypt, and My signs which I have done among them, that you may know that I am the LORD" (Ex. 10:2).

"You shall love the LORD your God with all your heart, with all your soul, and with all your strength. And these words which I command you today shall be in your heart. You shall teach them diligently to your children, and shall talk of them when you sit in your house, when you walk by the way, when you lie down, and when you rise up. . . . You shall write them on the doorposts of your house and on your gates" (Deut. 6:5–7, 9).

"Let the word of Christ dwell in you richly in all wisdom, teaching and admonishing one another in psalms and hymns and spiritual songs, singing with grace in your hearts to the Lord" (Col. 3:16).

III. RELATIONSHIPS WITH OTHER BELIEVERS

FINDING A GOOD CHURCH

"And they continued steadfastly in the apostles' doctrine and fellowship, in the breaking of bread, and in prayers" (Acts 2:42).

"Sing to Him, sing psalms to Him;
Talk of all His wondrous works!
Glory in His holy name;
Let the hearts of those rejoice who
    seek the LORD" (Ps. 105:2, 3).

"So continuing daily with one accord in the temple, and breaking bread from house to house, they ate their food with gladness and simplicity of heart, praising God and having favor with all the people. And the Lord added to the church daily those who were being saved" (Acts 2:46, 47).

"Do not be carried about with various and strange doctrines. For it is good that the heart be established by grace" (Heb. 13:9).

"But be doers of the word, and not hearers only, deceiving yourselves" (James 1:22).

"Whom having not seen you love. Though now you do not see Him, yet believing, you rejoice with joy inexpressible and full of glory, receiving the end of your faith; the salvation of your souls" (1 Pet. 1:8, 9).

"Pure and undefiled religion before God and the Father is this: to visit orphans and widows in their trouble, and to keep oneself unspotted from the world" (James 1:27).

SPIRITUAL GIFTS

"But the manifestation of the Spirit is given to each one for the profit of all. . . . But one and the same Spirit works all these things, distributing to each one individually as He wills" (1 Cor. 12:7, 11).

"For I long to see you, that I may impart to you some spiritual gift, so that you may be established; that is, that I may be encouraged together with you by the mutual faith both of you and me" (Rom. 1:11, 12).

"And on My menservants and on My maidservants I will pour out My Spirit in those days, and they shall prophesy" (Acts 2:18).

"As each one has received a gift, minister it to one another, as good stewards of the manifold grace of God" (1 Pet. 4:10).

"This is a faithful saying, and these things I want you to affirm constantly, that those who have believed in God should be careful to maintain good works. These things are good and profitable to men" (Titus 3:8).

"With goodwill doing service, as to the Lord, and not to men, knowing that whatever good anyone does, he will receive the same from the Lord, whether he is a slave or free" (Eph. 6:7, 8).

FELLOWSHIP

"Be of the same mind toward one another. Do not set your mind on high things, but associate with the humble. Do not be wise in your own eyes" (Rom. 12:16).

"Again I say to you that if two of you agree on earth concerning anything that they ask, it will be done for them by My Father in heaven. For where two or three are gathered together in My name, I am there in the midst of them" (Matt. 18:19–20; see page 172).

"But if we walk in the light as He is in the light, we have fellowship with one another, and the blood of Jesus Christ His Son cleanses us from all sin" (1 John 1:7).

"If it is possible, as much as depends on you, live peaceably with all men" (Rom. 12:18).

"Now may the God of patience and comfort grant you to be like-minded toward one another, according to Christ Jesus, that you may with one mind and one mouth glorify the God and Father of our Lord Jesus Christ" (Rom. 15:5, 6).

"Now I urge you, brethren, note those who cause divisions and offenses, contrary to the doctrine which you learned, and avoid them" (Rom. 16:17).

"Finally, all of you be of one mind, having compassion for one another; love as brothers, be tenderhearted, be courteous" (1 Pet. 3:8).

GIVING

"Distributing to the needs of the saints, given to hospitality" (Rom. 12:13).

"But whoever has this world's goods, and sees his brother in need, and shuts up his heart from him, how does the love of God abide in him? My little children, let us not love in word or in tongue, but in deed and in truth" (1 John 3:17, 18).

"For I do not mean that others should be eased and you burdened; but by an equality, that now at this time your abundance may supply their lack, that their abundance also may supply your lack; that there may be equality" (2 Cor. 8:13, 14).

"But this I say: He who sows sparingly will also reap sparingly, and he who sows bountifully will also reap bountifully" (2 Cor. 9:6).

"So let each one give as he purposes in his heart, not grudgingly or of necessity; for God loves a cheerful giver" (2 Cor. 9:7).

"Now may He who supplies seed to the sower, and bread for food, supply and multiply the seed you have sown and increase the fruits of your righteousness, while you are enriched in everything for all liberality, which causes thanksgiving through us to God" (2 Cor. 9:10, 11).

LEADERSHIP

"He will feed His flock like a
   shepherd;

He will gather the lambs with His
   arm,
And carry them in His bosom,
And gently lead those who are with
   young" (Isa. 40:11).

"You know that the rulers of the Gentiles lord it over them, and those who are great exercise authority over them. Yet it shall not be so among you; but whoever desires to become great among you, let him be your servant; and whoever desires to be first among you, let him be your slave; just as the Son of Man did not come to be served, but to serve, and to give His life a ransom for many" (Matt. 20:25–28).

"Likewise deacons must be reverent, not double-tongued, not given to much wine, not greedy for money, holding the mystery of the faith with a pure conscience" (1 Tim. 3:8–9).

"'I will feed My flock, and I will make them lie down,' says the LORD God. 'I will seek what was lost and bring back what was driven away, bind up the broken and strengthen what was sick'" (Ezek. 34:15, 16).

"And we urge you, brethren, to recognize those who labor among you, and are over you in the Lord and admonish you, and to esteem them very highly in love for their work's sake" (1 Thess. 5:12, 13).

"Do not receive an accusation against an elder except from two or three witnesses. Those who are sinning rebuke in the presence of all, that the rest also may fear" (1 Tim. 5:19, 20).

"Remember those who rule over you, who have spoken the word of God to you, whose faith follow, considering the outcome of their conduct" (Heb. 13:7).

"Likewise you younger people, submit yourselves to your elders. Yes, all of you be submissive to one another, and be clothed with humility, for 'God resists the proud, but gives grace to the humble' " (1 Peter 5:5, 6).

"Obey those who rule over you, and be submissive, for they watch out for your souls, as those who must give account. Let them do so with joy and not with grief, for that would be unprofitable for you" (Heb. 13:17).

BUILDING RELATIONSHIPS

"Reject a divisive man after the first and second admonition" (Titus 3:10).

"Repay no one evil for evil" (Rom. 12:17).

"Praying always with all prayer and supplication in the Spirit, being watchful to this end with all perseverance and supplication for all the saints" (Eph. 6:18).

"If you lend money to any of My people who are poor among you, you shall not be like a moneylender to him; you shall not charge him interest" (Ex. 22:25).

"Open rebuke is better than love carefully concealed" (Prov. 27:5).

"Do not lie to one another, since you have put off the old man with his deeds, and have put on the new man who is renewed in knowledge according to the image of Him who created him" (Col. 3:9, 10).

"Therefore receive one another, just as Christ also received us, to the glory of God" (Rom. 15:7).

"Mark the blameless man, and observe the upright" (Ps. 37:37).

"Finally, all of you be of one mind, having compassion for one another; love as brothers, be tenderhearted, be courteous" (1 Pet. 3:8).

"He who covers a transgression seeks love, but he who repeats a matter separates friends" (Prov. 17:9).

IV. RELATIONSHIPS WITH THE WORLD

HOW CHRISTIAN VALUES DIFFER

"Therefore know this day, and consider it in your heart, that the LORD Himself is God in heaven above and on the earth beneath; there is no other" (Deut. 4:39).

"But you, O man of God, flee these things and pursue righteousness, godliness, faith, love, patience, gentleness" (1 Tim. 6:11).

"For what is highly esteemed among men is an abomination in the sight of God" (Luke 16:15).

"And now, Israel, what does the LORD your God require of you, but to fear the LORD your God, to walk in all His ways and to love Him, to serve the LORD your God with all your heart and with all your soul" (Deut. 10:12).

"That I may know Him and the power of His resurrection, and the fellowship of His sufferings, being conformed to His death" (Phil. 3:10).

RELATING TO THE WORLD

"Do not love the world or the things in the world. If anyone loves the world, the love of the Father is not in him. For all that is in the world; the lust of the flesh, the lust of the eyes, and the pride of life, is not of the Father but is of the world" (1 John 2:15, 16).

"And do not be conformed to this world but be transformed by the renewing of your mind, that you may prove what is that good and acceptable and perfect will of God" (Rom. 12:2).

"Do not lay up for yourselves treasures on earth, where moth and rust destroy and where thieves break in and steal; but lay up for yourselves treasures in heaven, where neither moth nor rust destroys and where thieves do not break in and steal" (Matt. 6:19–21).

"And the world is passing away, and the lust of it; but he who does the will of God abides forever" (1 John 2:17; see page 256).

"And the base things of the world and the things which are despised God has chosen, and the things which are not, to bring to nothing the things that are" (1 Cor. 1:28).

RESPONDING TO UNSAVED INDIVIDUALS

"Owe no one anything except to love one another, for he who loves another has fulfilled the law" (Rom. 13:8).

"Do not be unequally yoked together with unbelievers. For what fellowship has righteousness with lawlessness? And what communion has light with darkness?" (2 Cor. 6:14).

"Listen to Me, you who know
     righteousness,
You people in whose heart is My law;
Do not fear the reproach of men,
Nor be afraid of their insults" (Isa.
     51:7).

"I wrote to you in my epistle not to keep company with sexually immoral people. Yet I certainly did not mean with the sexually immoral people of this world, or with the covetous, or extortioners, or idolators, since then you would need to go out of the world" (1 Cor. 5:9, 10).

"Do not be afraid when one becomes
     rich,
When the glory of his house is
     increased;
For when he dies he shall carry
     nothing away;

His glory shall not descend after
     him" (Ps. 49:16, 17).

"Render therefore to all their due: taxes to whom taxes are due, customs to whom customs, fear to whom fear, honor to whom honor" (Rom. 13:7).

"I did not come to call the righteous, but sinners, to repentance" (Matt. 9:13).

"Let your light so shine before men, that they may see your good works and glorify your Father in heaven" (Matt. 5:16).

"But even if you should suffer for righteousness' sake, you are blessed. 'And do not be afraid of their threats, nor be troubled.' But sanctify the Lord God in your hearts, and always be ready to give a defense to everyone who asks you a reason for the hope that is in you, with meekness and fear" (1 Pet. 3:14, 15).

"But love your enemies, do good, and lend, hoping for nothing in return; and your reward will be great, and you will be sons of the Most High. For He is kind to the unthankful and evil. Therefore be merciful, just as your Father also is merciful" (Luke 6:35–36; see page 178).

"But avoid foolish and ignorant disputes, knowing that they generate strife. And a servant of the Lord must not quarrel but be gentle to all, able to teach, patient, in humility correcting those who are in opposition" (2 Tim. 2:23, 24).

"Having your conduct honorable among the Gentiles, that when they speak against you as evildoers, they may, by your good works which they observe, glorify God in the day of visitation" (1 Pet. 2:12).

EXPOSITORY INDEX

An expository index organizes information by topic and guides the reader to Bible verses and book pages which are critical to understanding the subject. It does not list every verse referred to in the book, but seeks to identify key verses. It does not list every mention of a topic in the book, but directs the reader to pages where a topic is discussed in some depth. Thus an expository index helps the reader avoid the frustration of looking up verses in the Bible or the book, only to discover that they contribute in only a small way to one's understanding of the subject.

This expository index organizes references to covenants and promises by topic. Topics and sub-topics are identified in the left-hand column. Key Bible verses and passages are listed in the center column under "Scriptures." The far right column identifies pages in this book where the topic is covered.

In most instances, several of the key verses in the "Scriptures" column will be discussed on the book pages referred to. Very often additional verses will be referred to on the pages where the topic is covered. Our goal is to help you keep in focus the critical Bible verses and passages. Similarly, the book pages referred to are only those which make a significant contribution to understanding a topic, not every page on which a topic may be mentioned.

Please note that material under sub-topics is sometimes organized chronologically by the sequence of appearance in Scripture, and sometimes alphabetically, depending upon which organization will be most helpful in understanding and locating information.

TOPIC	SCRIPTURES	PAGE(S)
ABRAHAMIC COVENANT		
Principles underlying		
Grace, not works	Ps. 14:1–3; Rom. 3:10	21–23
Faith response	Gen. 15:6; Rom. 4:16	23
Content of	Gen. 12:1–3, 7	23–25
*make a great nation	Gen. 12:2	24
fulfilled		29–30
*bless you	Gen. 12:2	24–25
fulfilled		30–31
*make name great	Gen. 12:2	24–25
fulfilled		31–32
*be a blessing	Gen. 12:2	24–25
fulfilled		31–32
*bless those who bless	Gen. 12:3	25
fulfilled		32–33
*all blessed in you	Gen. 12:3	25–26
fulfilled		32–33
*give the land	Gen. 12:7	25–26
fulfilled		33–34

TOPIC	SCRIPTURES	PAGE(S)
About peace		269
About God's protection		269–270
About God's provision		270–271
About rewards		271
About salvation		271–272
About serving God		272
About strength from God		272–273

PROMISES TO GOD'S PEOPLE IN THE NEW TESTAMENT
Promises in the Gospels

Of salvation	Matt. 1:21	162–165
Of a better baptism	Matt. 3:11	165
Of future reward	Matt. 5:11	165–166
Of public reward	Matt. 6:3–4, 6	166–167
Of forgiveness	Matt. 6:14, 15; Mark 11:25–26	167
Of divine provision	Matt. 6:33	167–168
Of answered prayer	Luke 11:9–13; Matt. 7:7	168, 180
Of acknowledgment	Matt. 10:32	168–169
Of a new self	Matt. 10:39; 16:25–27; Mark 8:35–36; Luke 9:34, 35	169
Of rest	Matt. 11:28	169–170
Of divine participation	Matt. 18:18	171–172
Of divine participation	Matt. 18:19–20	171–172
Of treasure in heaven	Matt. 19:21; Mark 10:21, 30; Luke 18:29–30	172–173
Of answered prayer	Matt. 21:22; Mark 11:23–24	173–174
Of significance	Mark 1:17	174–175
Of guidance	Mark 13:11; see Ex. 4:12, 15; Luke 21:14, 15	176
Of reward	Luke 6:35	177–178
Of initiative rewarded	Luke 6:37–38	179–180
Of power	Luke 17:6	180–181
Of personal attention	Luke 21:17, 18	181
Of perseverance	Luke 21:32	181–182
Of salvation	John 3:16	189
Of wrath	John 3:36	189–190
Of endless refreshment	John 4:14	190–191
Of resurrection	John 5:25	191
Of eternal life	John 6:51	191–192
Of discernment	John 7:17	192
Of the Holy Spirit	John 7:38	192–193
Of light	John 8:12	193
Of knowing the truth	John 8:31, 32	193–194
Of salvation	John 10:9	194–195

❖ SCRIPTURE INDEX

(Bible references are in boldface type, followed by the pages on which they appear in this book.)